Spreadsheets for Management Accounting

Tutorial

Wendy Yates

Published by Osborne Books Limited
Tel 01905 748071
Email books@osbornebooks.co.uk
Website www.osbornebooks.co.uk

Design by Laura Ingham

Printed by CPI Group (UK) Limited, Croydon, CR0 4YY, on environmentally friendly, acid-free paper from managed forests.

British Library Cataloguing in Publication Data
A catalogue record for this book is available from the British Library

ISBN 978-1-911198-65-9

Contents

Introduction

Qualifications covered

This book has been written to support the Osborne Books Management Accounting Techniques Tutorial, which specifically covers the unit 'Management Accounting Techniques'. This unit is mandatory for the following qualifications:

AAT Level 3 Diploma in Accounting

AAT Diploma in Accounting – SCQF Level 7

The book contains a clear text with many examples and illustrations. Each chapter concludes with exercises to practise the techniques covered.

To speed up the learning process in the exercises, Osborne Books has provided a number of spreadsheet files for free download from its website www.osbornebooks.co.uk. Access to these can be gained via the Spreadsheets for Management Accounting Tutorial book page.

Spreadsheet software

The illustrations in this text are based on Excel, part of the Microsoft Office 365 suite, but we appreciate that a variety of spreadsheet software will be in use at any one time. Wherever possible, the text aims to be as generic as possible.

Osborne Study and Revision Materials

Our materials are tailored to the needs of students studying the Management Accounting Techniques unit and revising for the assessment. They include:

- **Tutorials**: paperback books with practice activities
- **Workbooks**: paperback books with practice activities and exams
- **Student Zone**: access to Osborne Books online resources
- **Osborne Books App**: Osborne Books ebooks for mobiles and tablets

Visit www.osbornebooks.co.uk for details of study and revision resources and access to online material.

Contents – a quick guide

This section explains, at a glance, the main contents of each of the eight chapters in this book.

1 Spreadsheet basics

This chapter covers the following basic principles and techniques:

- Some preliminaries
- Basic spreadsheet structure
- Dealing with worksheets
- Dealing with workbooks
- Entering data into cells
- Copying the data in cells
- Rows and columns
- Changing the height of a row or width of a column
- Using basic formulas

2 Formatting the spreadsheet data

This chapter covers the formatting of a spreadsheet:

- Formatting – style
- Formatting – fonts and size
- Number formats
- Cell alignment
- Date format
- Printing and page setup

3 Advanced formatting

This chapter covers more advanced formatting and improving spreadsheet presentation:

- Cell display – borders, fill colours
- Moving rows and columns
- Hiding rows and columns
- Specifying row height and column width
- Cell and sheet protection
- Conditional formatting
- Data validation

4 Spreadsheet functions

This chapter explains the use of built-in functions which are found in most common spreadsheet software packages:

- Formulas
- Mathematical operators
- Functions
- Ranges

- Mathematical functions
- Cell addressing
- Date functions
- Logical functions and operators
- Lookup functions
- Circular references in formulas

5 Sorting, checking and importing data

This chapter explains some of the built-in tools found in normal spreadsheet packages:

- Formula validation
- Spell check
- Remove duplicates
- Find and replace
- Sorting and filtering data
- Introducing subtotals
- Embedding, linking and screenshots
- Import/Export

6 Statistical functions

This chapter explains and illustrates some of the statistical functions and data analysis tools which you can use. It covers:

- Simple statistical functions
- Analysis tools
- Comments

7 Charts

This chapter provides guidance on working with charts:

- Types of charts
- Parts of a chart
- Chart creation
- Modification of charts
- Pie charts
- 3D or exploded charts

8 Pivot tables and workbook management

This chapter deals with Pivot Tables and other techniques for manipulating data:

- Managing windows – freeze panes
- Using Paste Special
- Working with multiple worksheets and workbooks
- Creating and formatting pivot tables
- Using subsets of data
- Goal seeking
- What-if scenarios
- Forecasting
- Hyperlinks

Practice exercises

Learning about spreadsheet software is an essentially practical process and this book contains a wide range of practical exercises which will enable students to gain the spreadsheet skills needed to tackle the AAT assessment. These exercises and details of their contents are set out below.

Some exercises require the download of spreadsheet files from www.osbornebooks.co.uk Visit the Spreadsheets for Management Accounting Tutorial page in 'AAT books'. These files are in Excel .xlsx format.

1 Spreadsheet basics

Exercise 1	Create a workbook, name a worksheet, move around a worksheet, enter data, save a workbook
Exercise 2	Open an existing workbook, copy and paste
Exercise 3	Adjust column width, insert a column
Exercise 4	Adjust row height, insert a row
Exercise 5	Insert columns, adjust column width, copy columns
Exercise 6	Insert rows, copy rows, delete rows
Exercise 7	Create a formula for addition, copy a formula
Exercise 8	Use the SUM function, copy a formula
Exercise 9	Create a multiplication formula, use the SUM function, copy a formula
Exercise 10	Create simple formulas, with subtraction and addition, copy a formula

2 Formatting the spreadsheet data

Exercise 1	Set currency to £, include comma for thousands
Exercise 2	Merge cells and centre, align right, make bold
Exercise 3	Apply underline, double underline, and italics
Exercise 4	Enter dates, format numbers
Exercise 5	Change date format, time format, format a number as a percentage
Exercise 6	Change font face and font size
Exercise 7	Align centre, left and right
Exercise 8	Format currency £ and Euro, format a number as a percentage
Exercise 9	Work with Page setup to create headers and footers
Exercise 10	Use print orientation settings Portrait and Landscape
Exercise 11	Print settings scaling
Exercise 12	Set a print area, insert a page break

3 Advanced formatting

Exercise 1	Apply borders
Exercise 2	Apply fill colour and shading
Exercise 3	Lock and unlock cells, protect your worksheet
Exercise 4	Move rows and columns
Exercise 5	Hide and unhide rows and columns
Exercise 6	Wrap text
Exercise 7	Use cell orientation

1 Spreadsheet basics

this chapter covers...

This chapter is an introduction for those new to spreadsheets. It explains and takes you through some of the basic concepts and techniques for working with spreadsheets. By the time you have finished this chapter and carried out the exercises which follow, you should be competent in setting up and manipulating a basic spreadsheet. The concepts and techniques covered are:

- *some preliminaries*
- *basic spreadsheet structure*
- *dealing with worksheets*
- *dealing with workbooks*
- *entering data into cells*
- *copying the data in cells*
- *dealing with rows and columns*
- *changing the height of a row or the width of a column*
- *using basic formulas*

Note that the step by step instructions given in this chapter are based on the Microsoft® Excel model, but the concepts and techniques described relate to all spreadsheet packages.

SOME PRELIMINARIES

numbers

Within a spreadsheet, a series of digits (0 - 9) will be treated as a NUMBER provided there are no spaces. A number can also have a decimal point (.) eg 12.99 would be twelve point nine-nine.

To ease interpretation of a number, it can include commas (,) to represent thousands eg 34,567 would represent thirty four thousand, five hundred and sixty seven. It is advisable to always enter numbers in their most basic form and use the formatting facilities in the spreadsheet to display the number in the way you want eg number of decimal places, currency, percentage etc.

dates

Dates are normally entered in the form 31/10/21, day, month, year separated by / (slash). Dates and times are stored as numbers, allowing for calculations using dates. Dates can be formatted in a number of ways.

text

Any series of characters which cannot be recognised as a number or a date is known as TEXT.

mouseclick

Whenever a CLICK of the mouse is mentioned, this is referring to a click of the LEFT mouse button. Any RIGHT mouse clicks will be specifically preceded by RIGHT. DOUBLE CLICK refers to two clicks in quick succession of the LEFT mouse key.

undo

If at any stage you wish to Undo the changes which you have just made, click on the Undo icon (left pointing curved arrow) to remove the last edit to a cell. To remove the edit before that, click the Undo icon again and so on. You can also hold down the CTRL key and tap Z (CTRL and Z) to Undo.

redo

Following an Undo of some changes which you have just made, if you change your mind and want to reinstate those edits, click on the Redo icon (right pointing curved arrow) to put the last changes back. To redo the edit before that, click the Redo icon again and so on.

keyboard

Keys on the keyboard which you will need to be familiar with are:

RETURN (or ENTER) ESC

TAB CTRL (CONTROL)

It is worth spending a minute or two identifying where these keys are located.

menus

As with all computer programs, there is a main menu bar, with tabs identifying different options available. These are usually grouped by relevance; the common tabs which we will make use of are:

- FILE, HOME, INSERT, PAGE LAYOUT, FORMULAS, DATA, REVIEW and VIEW

An example menu ribbon is shown here.

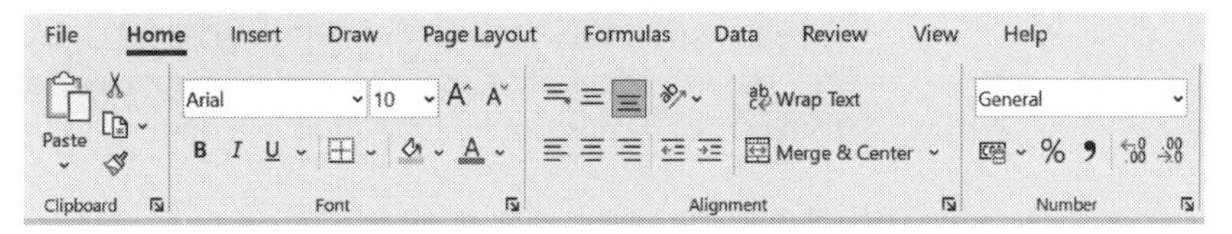

The options below the menu (the Ribbon) will vary depending on which menu option you have chosen. For simplicity, the menu and ribbon are not included in explanatory images.

It is possible that your menu may differ, depending on the setup of your software, since menus can be customised to suit individual needs.

help

If you require additional information or clarification on any action, formula or general query, Help is available within your spreadsheet program by clicking the help icon (usually a ? in a blue circle situated to the far right of the main menu bar). Alternatively, press the F1 function key.

Below is a table of the common CTRL key combinations which you may find useful.

CTRL and							
A	B	C	I	P	V	X	Z
Select all cells	Bold	Copy	Italics	Print	Paste	Cut	Undo

SPREADSHEET STRUCTURE

definition

A spreadsheet is a grid or table of rows and columns which is used to manipulate numbers and perform calculations.

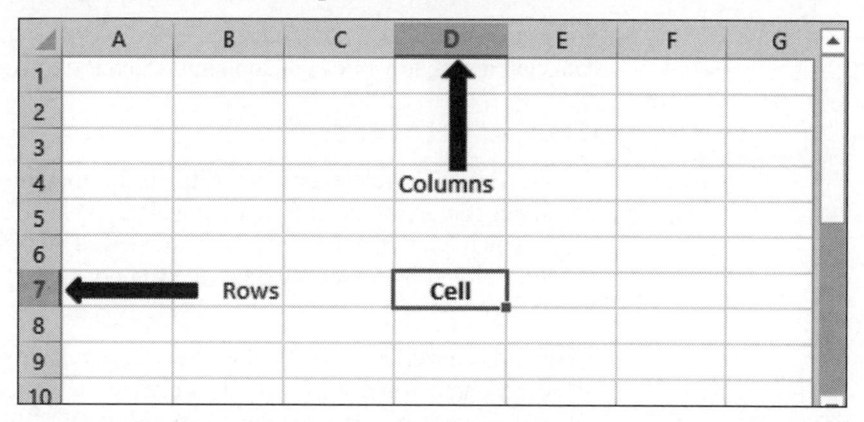

rows, columns and cells

Rows are in a horizontal direction, and are identified by numbers: 1, 2, 3, and so on.

Columns are vertical, and are identified by letters: A, B, C, and so on through the alphabet. Columns beyond Z (26) continue in the format AA, AB, AC and so on, changing to BA, BB etc. for columns 53 and onwards.

The maximum number of rows and columns allowed in a spreadsheet is determined by the software package you are using and the memory within your computer. For Excel you can have more than one million rows and more than 16 thousand columns if your computer has the capacity.

Where a row and column cross or intersect, it is called a **cell**.

The cell is referred to by a combination of a letter (the column identifier) and a number (the row reference) to identify its location. This is known as a **cell reference**.

Cell reference D7 would refer to the cell at the intersection of column D (the fourth column) and row 7. See the cell highlighted on the screen image on the previous page.

The lines marking the edges of the rows and columns are called **gridlines**. **Scroll bars** are provided to cater for larger spreadsheets and allow scrolling both vertically and horizontally, changing the rows and columns displayed as you move up, down and across the spreadsheet.

WORKBOOKS AND WORKSHEETS

A **workbook** is the computer file created when you start a new spreadsheet.

A workbook contains a set of **worksheets**.

Each worksheet is an individual **spreadsheet**.

For example, a workbook could have two worksheets, one worksheet with data, and a second worksheet containing a chart representing the data.

files and folders

Each workbook is held as one file. A file is the computer equivalent of a paper document containing the information which you have entered. Each file has a name which you specify when it is created. This should be chosen to be meaningful and help identify what the file contains, for example Timesheet March 2021.

To organise our files in a logical way we store related files in a **folder**, which we again name when we create it to clarify the sort of files/documents the folder will contain. For example: Timesheets 2021-2022.

Within Excel the File and Folder tools mentioned below are available whenever you select one of the menu options such as **Open**, **Save As** or **Share**, all of which are located under the **File** menu.

create a folder

Creating a folder can be achieved by using the **New Folder** option, and naming the folder appropriately.

finding a file

If you are unable to locate a file, you can use the **Search tool** provided when you select OPEN within the FILE menu.

renaming a file

To rename a file, click the filename once, then once more, and type in the new name. Press **RETURN** to complete the edit. **ESC** will cancel the edit.

sharing a file

This can be done in two ways, either using the **Share** option within Excel, or by allowing direct access to the file either on the network, or your computer.

The **Share** option, found under the **File** menu, allows you to save the file online, and invite people to share it, or you can email the file to one or more people directly, in a variety of formats, such as PDF.

To allow the sharing of a file on the network, or on your computer, the file needs to be in a folder which is accessible to other people. By right mouse clicking on the folder name, and setting the **share with** options as required, you can specify who can access the file.

worksheets

Each **worksheet** has a name, which is usually displayed as a tab at the bottom of the spreadsheet work area.

When you create a new **workbook** it will contain at least one worksheet – named Sheet1; more may be included, depending on how your Excel is set up. Excel allows up to 255 worksheets in one workbook and potentially more if memory allows but it is highly unlikely you would ever need this many.

Worksheet **names** can be changed (renamed), by double clicking on the name tab or right-clicking and selecting **Rename**, and entering the required text of the new name.

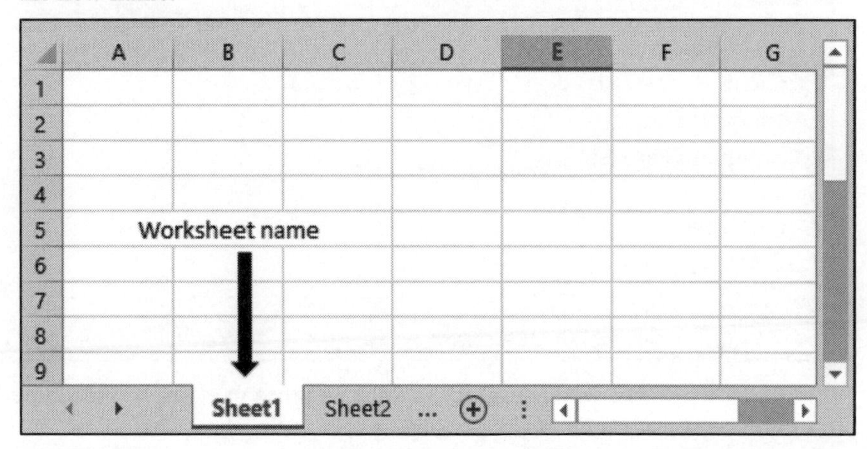

It is possible to add one or more additional worksheets should you require them.

New worksheets are added one at a time, either by clicking on the plus (+) symbol in the circle next to the sheet name tabs, or by using **Insert**, and selecting **Worksheet**.

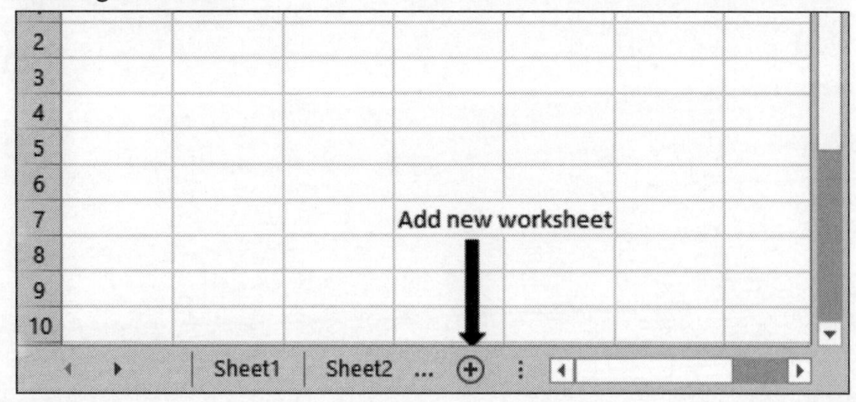

Worksheets which are not required can be deleted, by using **Delete** from the **Home** menu by selecting the worksheet, or right-clicking on the sheet to be deleted and selecting **Delete**.

You can easily **change the relative order of the worksheets within the workbook**, just by selecting the name tab, holding the mouse down, and dragging the worksheet to its new position in the order.

Each worksheet can represent one spreadsheet, or data from different worksheets may be linked together to form one more complex spreadsheet.

Switching between worksheets is achieved by clicking on the name tab of the worksheet which you want to see on the screen.

If there are a lot of worksheets in the workbook, not all name tabs can be displayed, as shown in the example below:

	A	B	C	D	E	F	G	H
1	Work bookings							
2	Client	Week1	Week2	Week3				
3	Smiths Ltd							
4	Jones and Partner							
5	Redwoods							
6	Underhills							
7								
8								

... Exercise2 | Exercise3 | Exercise4 | Exercise5 ...

In this example, to access those worksheets preceding Exercise2, either click the left arrow button next to the sheet name tabs, or the three dots preceding the Exercise2 name tab.

Similarly, to access those worksheets beyond Exercise5, either click the right arrow button next to the sheet name tabs, or the three dots following the Exercise5 name tab.

workbooks

As noted earlier, a workbook is a collection of worksheets ranging from one worksheet upwards to a maximum number which will be dependent on the software package and available computer memory.

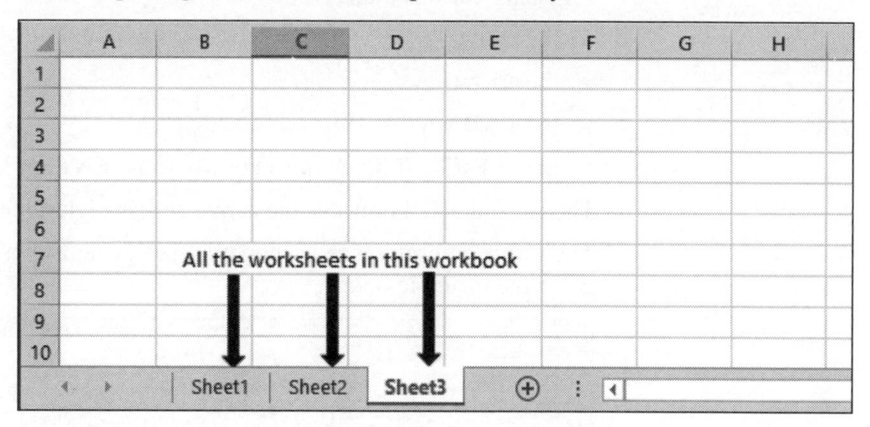

For example, a workbook could have two worksheets, one worksheet with data, and a second worksheet containing a chart representing the data.

When you want to start your first spreadsheet, you will select **New** from the **File** menu, select **Blank Workbook** from the available templates, and a new workbook will open, usually containing one or more blank worksheets ready for you to enter data.

The information which you have entered should be regularly saved using the standard disk icon or **Save** under the **File** menu.

To open a previously saved workbook, you would either select **Open** from the **File** menu, navigate to the required folder and select the required workbook from the appropriate folder or, if it is listed, select the workbook from the list of recently used documents.

To save a copy of the workbook with a different name, either as a backup or as a fresh starting point, you would use **Save as** usually found under the **File** menu and supply a new name for the copy of the workbook. You would also use **Save as** if you wanted to save the workbook as a different type of file, eg PDF to send to other people. For security purposes, a copy of an important workbook should be saved to removable media such as a memory stick and stored off-site.

It is also good practice to add a version number or part of a date to the filename so that different versions can be saved as the spreadsheet evolves.

This also allows a previous version to be identified and opened, if required, or just kept as an archive copy of the original workbook.

ENTER DATA INTO CELLS

Within the grid of cells on your worksheet, you can move around from cell to cell using various methods:

- the mouse
- the arrow keys
- the **TAB** key
- or the **RETURN** key (also known as the **ENTER** key)

The current cell, known as the active cell, is highlighted.

The active cell reference is shown in the **Name Box** above column A; this is B5 in the example below.

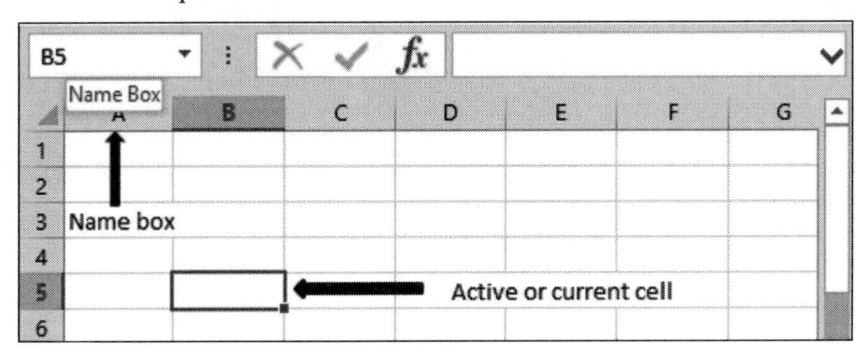

To enter data into a cell:

- click on the cell where you want the data to go
- type your data into the cell
- either press the **RETURN** key, or click on another cell with the mouse

Other useful keys when entering data are the **TAB** key which moves the active cell to the next cell in the current row, and the **ESC** key which cancels the current data entry.

If you just wish to edit the current data, you will see the data held in the current cell displayed in the **Formula Bar**, (in this example Income forecast).

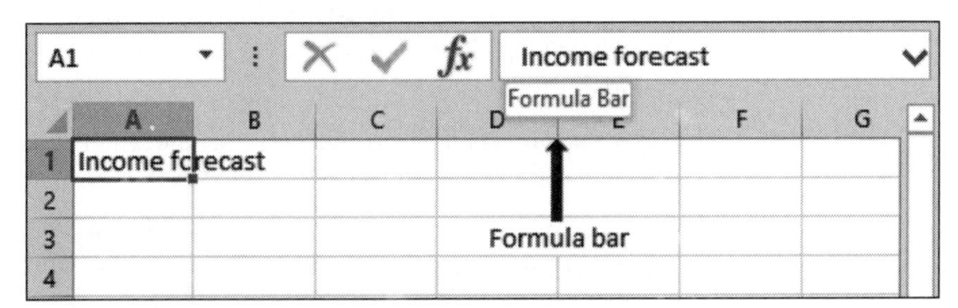

To modify the contents of a cell:

- click on the required cell
- either enter the new data directly
- or click into the Formula Bar
- make any changes
- press **RETURN**

If at any time you wish to cancel the changes, press the **ESC** key before pressing **RETURN**, or if you have pressed RETURN, click on the **Undo** icon as described in the preliminaries.

To remove data:

- select the cell to be changed
- press the **Delete** key
- or select **Clear Contents** from the drop-down menu displayed when you right-click on the cell

selecting multiple cells

If at any time you wish to select more than one cell:

- select the first cell by clicking on the cell
- keep the left mouse button pressed and drag the mouse over the other cells you wish to select

A series of selected cells is shown below:

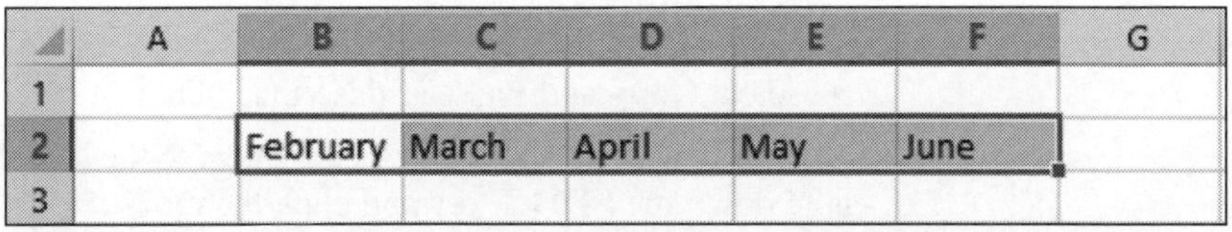

	A	B	C	D	E	F	G
1							
2		February	March	April	May	June	
3							

If the cells you wish to select are not consecutive (ie not next to each other):

- select the first cell by clicking on the cell
- hold down the **CONTROL** key while clicking on the other cells you want to select (as shown below)

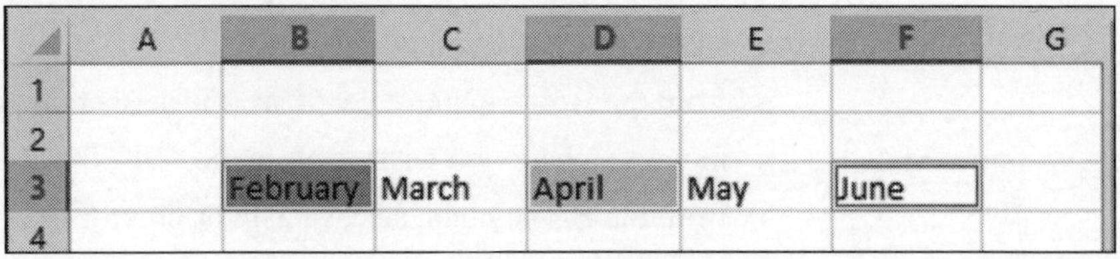

	A	B	C	D	E	F	G
1							
2							
3		February	March	April	May	June	
4							

COPYING CELLS

The simplest method of copying data in a cell is to:

- move to the cell you wish to copy
- from the **Home** menu, select the **Copy** icon, a small icon of two pages
- move to the cell where you wish to place the copy
- from the **Home** menu select **Paste**

If you wish to paste the data into more than one cell, select all the cells where the data is to go, then select **Paste**.

Alternatively, to copy the selected cell, right-click on the selected cell and select **Copy** from the drop down menu if there is one or press **CTRL** and **C** together; then to paste, move to the required location, right-click on the selected cell and select **Paste**, or press **CTRL** and **V** together.

It is also possible to move the contents of one cell to a new cell reference:

- click on the data cell to move
- move the cursor over the edge of the cell until you see a four headed arrow, press down on the left mouse key
- drag to the cell where the data is to go
- release the mouse

You will see the data move to the new location.

If at any time you wish to copy more than one cell at a time:

- select the cells to copy by clicking on the first cell
- keeping the left mouse key pressed drag the mouse in the appropriate direction until all the required cells are selected
- select **Copy** and **Paste** as described above

Alternatively, click on the first cell, move to the last of the cells to be selected, hold down the **SHIFT** key and click the mouse.

If the cells which you wish to copy are not consecutive, for each of the cells to be copied, hold down the **CTRL** key and click the cell, as described in the section on selecting multiple cells.

It is also possible to **Cut** - remove data from a cell or group of cells and place it somewhere else using **Paste.**

To use Cut and Paste:

- select the cell(s) you wish to cut
- from the Home menu, select **Cut** (the scissors icon) or press CTRL and X
- move to where you wish to place the cells(s)
- from the Home menu select **Paste** or press CTRL and V.

DEALING WITH ROWS AND COLUMNS

On a worksheet, each column is identified by a letter or combination of letters; this is called the **Column header**.

Similarly, each row is identified by a number called the **Row header**.

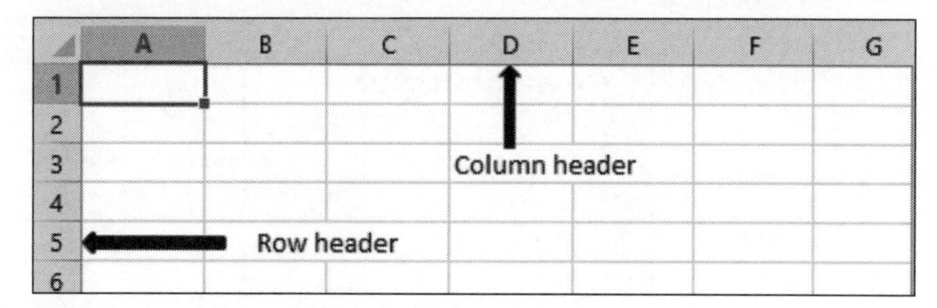

One click on a column header will select the entire column. Similarly with a row header, one click on the row header will select the whole row.

If you realise that you have missed out a row or a column once you have entered data, it is straightforward to insert extra rows or columns.

inserting a column

- select the column to the right of where you want to insert another column, by right-clicking on the column header
- select **Insert** from the menu displayed

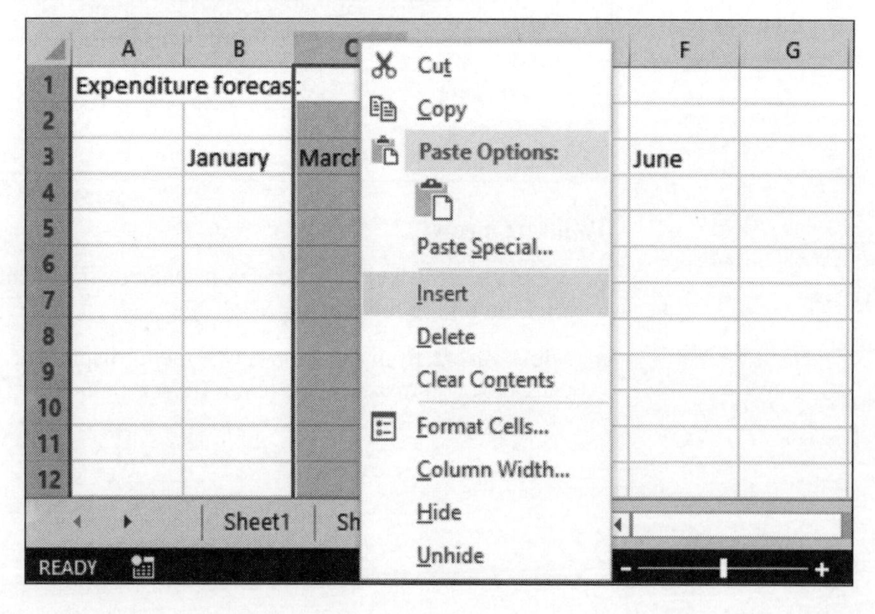

The new column will be inserted at the position of the selected column, and all existing columns will move right, as shown in the example below. You can then enter data in the new column. If you want to insert several columns eg 3, you select the 3 columns to the right and select **Insert** as before.

Note that for some spreadsheet packages you may need to select **Insert**, then **Column** from the menus.

	A	B	C	D	E	F	G
1	Expenditure forecas						
2							
3		January		March	April	May	June
4							
5							
6							

inserting a row

If we take an example expenditure worksheet as shown in the image below.

	A	B	C	D	E	F	G
1	Expenditure forecast						
2							
3		January	February	March	April	May	June
4							
5	Salaries						
6	Rent						
7	Accountancy						
8	Advertising						
9	Postage						
10	Stationery						

To insert a row:

- select the row below where you want to insert another row, by right-clicking on the row header
- select **Insert** from the drop-down menu displayed; for some spreadsheet packages you may need to select **Insert**, then **Row** from the menu

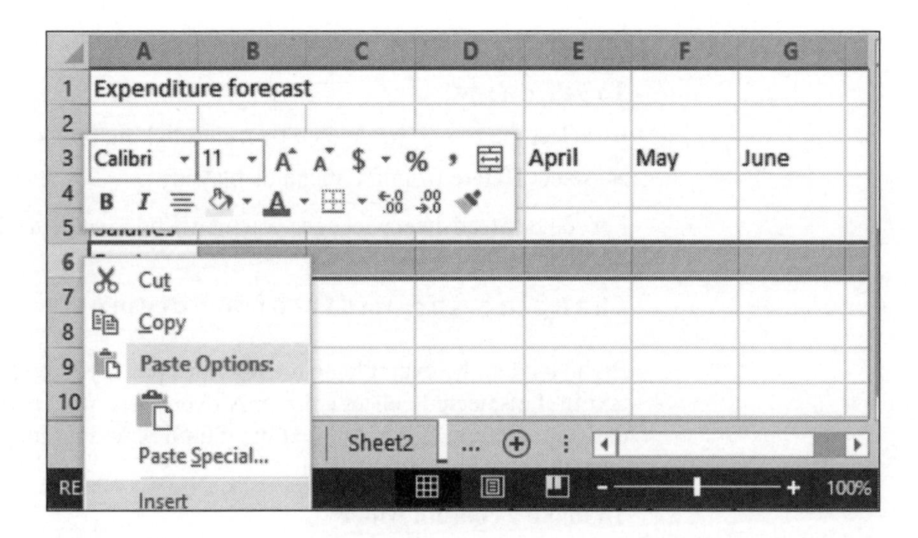

In the screen below a new row has been inserted between the rows for Salaries and Rent (rows 5 and 6), and the text 'Insurance' has been entered in cell A6. Note that the new row will be inserted at the selected row (row 6), and all the existing rows will then move down. You can then enter data in the new row. You could also enter several rows by selecting the appropriate number of rows below and pressing Insert.

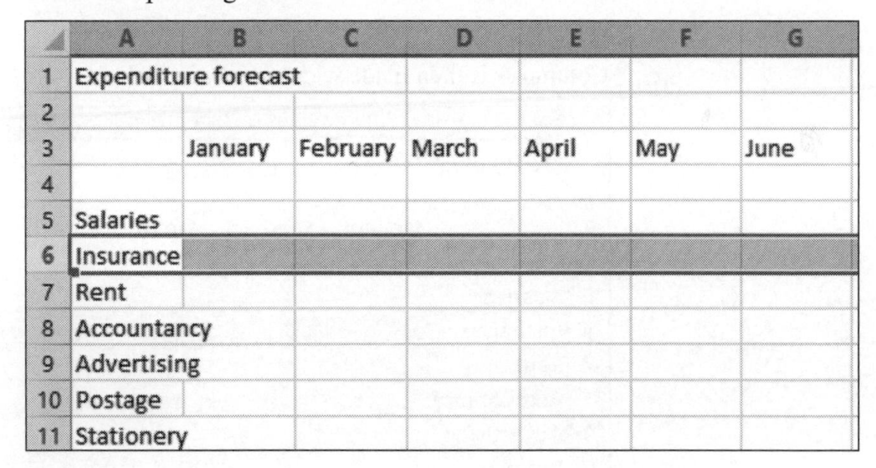

deleting a column

To delete a column:

- select the column to be deleted, by right-clicking on the column header
- select **Delete** from the menu displayed.

For some spreadsheet packages you may need to select **Delete**, then **Column** from the menus.

deleting a row

To delete a row:

- select the row to be deleted by right-clicking on the row header
- select **Delete** from the menu displayed

For some spreadsheet packages you may need to select **Delete**, then **Row** from the menus.

changing the width of a column

If you look at the example on the previous page, you will see that some of the text in the selected cell in column A overflows into column B. Once we put data into column B, the full text in column A will no longer be visible, so we need to make column A wider.

To make a column wider:

- click on the column header
- move the cursor to the line at the right edge of the column header box, the cursor changes shape to a black cross with arrow heads
- press the mouse down
- drag to the **right** as far as is required to display all information correctly
- release the mouse

Column A is then made wider, as shown below:

	A	B	C	D	E	F	G
1	Expenditure forecast						
2							
3		January	February	March	April	May	June
4							
5	Salaries						
6	Insurance						
7	Rent						
8	Accountancy						
9	Advertising						
10	Postage						

There are several alternative ways to make a column wider. If you double click on the right edge of the column header box, the column will automatically widen to contain the longest data within the column.

Also, if you right-click on the column header, you can select Column Width from the drop-down menu and specify a width as a number from 0 to 255, which represents the number of characters that can be displayed in a cell that is formatted with the standard font.

If a cell contains a date, number or result of a formula, and the column is not wide enough to display the whole of the value, you will see ###### displayed in the cell instead. To resolve this, just make the column wider until all is displayed.

To make a column narrower:

- click on the column header
- move the cursor to the line at the right edge of the column header box, the cursor changes shape to a black cross with arrow heads
- press the mouse down
- drag to the **left** as far as is required to display all information correctly
- release the mouse

If you right-click on the column header, you can select **Column Width** and specify the width as a number of characters (in the default character font used in the workbook).

changing the height of a row

The method used **to modify the height of a row** is very similar:

- click on the row header
- move the cursor to the bottom edge of the row header box, the cursor changes shape to a black cross with arrow heads
- press the mouse down
- drag down or up until you are satisfied with the row height
- release the mouse

You can see in the image below how we have made the height of row 1 containing 'Expenditure forecast' larger to make it stand out as a heading.

	A	B	C	D	E	F	G
1	Expenditure forecast						
2							
3		January	February	March	April	May	June
4							
5	Salaries						
6	Insurance						
7	Rent						
8	Accountancy						
9	Advertising						
10	Postage						
11	Stationery						

Also, if you right-click on the row header, you can select **Row Height** and specify the height as a number from 0 to 409, which represents the height measurement in points (1 point equals approximately 1/72 inch or 0.35mm).

If the row height is set to zero, the row is hidden.

copying a column

To copy a column:

- select the column to be copied, by **RIGHT-clicking** on the column header
- select **Copy** from the menu displayed
- **Right-click** on the column header of the column to the right of the column where you want to insert the copy
- select **Insert copied cells**

copying a row

To copy a row:

- select the row to be copied, by **RIGHT-clicking** on the row header
- select **Copy** from the menu displayed
- **Right-click** on the row header of the row below where you want to insert the copy
- select **Insert copied cells**

USING BASIC FORMULAS

The most powerful feature of a spreadsheet is its ability to perform calculations. To **create a formula**, click on the cell where you wish to place the formula. Enter the "=" sign to indicate that this cell is going to contain a formula. The formula can contain numbers, cell references and arithmetic symbols, eg '+' as shown below:

A simple formula for **addition** might be something like:

=B4+B5+B6+42

This would add up the values in the cells B4, B5, B6 and the number 42.

A simple formula for **subtraction** is: =B4–B5

For **multiplication**: =B4*B5

And **division**: =B4/B5

To include a cell in a formula once you have entered the "=" sign just click on the cell, or enter the cell reference, then either press the mathematical operator, or ENTER if the formula is complete.

To make one cell always hold the same value as another, eg B2 having the same value as A1, enter the formula =A1 in cell B2.

In the example on the next page, we want to enter formulas to calculate the totals for each month.

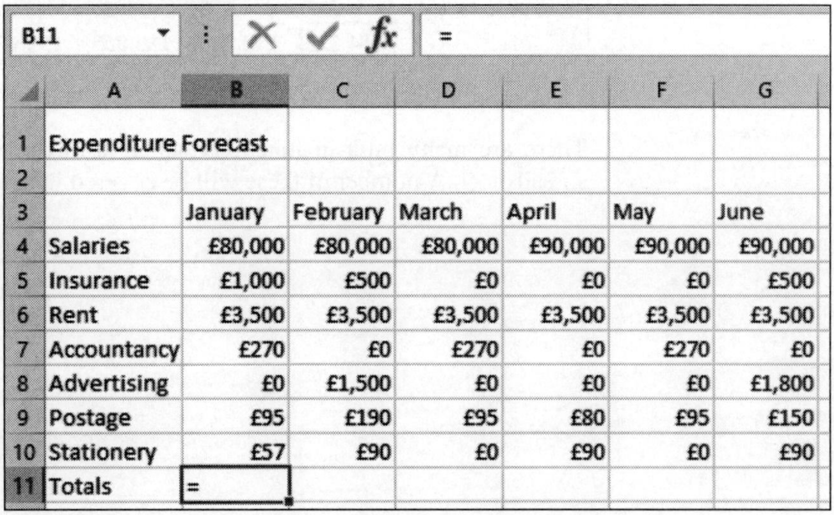

B11 | fx | =

	A	B	C	D	E	F	G
1	Expenditure Forecast						
2							
3		January	February	March	April	May	June
4	Salaries	£80,000	£80,000	£80,000	£90,000	£90,000	£90,000
5	Insurance	£1,000	£500	£0	£0	£0	£500
6	Rent	£3,500	£3,500	£3,500	£3,500	£3,500	£3,500
7	Accountancy	£270	£0	£270	£0	£270	£0
8	Advertising	£0	£1,500	£0	£0	£0	£1,800
9	Postage	£95	£190	£95	£80	£95	£150
10	Stationery	£57	£90	£0	£90	£0	£90
11	Totals	=					

The formula we could enter in cell B11 to add up column B, would be =B4+B5+B6+B7+B8+B9+B10

There is a better way of adding these numbers, using the built-in function **SUM( )**.

The equivalent formula would be =SUM(B4:B10) which will add up all the cells from B4 to B10 inclusive. If any new rows or columns are inserted, the formula will automatically update to reflect this.

This formula could then be copied to each of the cells in the Totals row in each column to produce a monthly total for the expenditure forecast, using **Copy** and **Paste** as described previously.

Note that as the formula is copied to the new cells it will **automatically change** to reflect the new row/column references.

B11 =SUM(B4:B10)

	A	B	C	D	E	F	G
1	Expenditure Forecast						
2							
3		January	February	March	April	May	June
4	Salaries	£80,000	£80,000	£80,000	£90,000	£90,000	£90,000
5	Insurance	£1,000	£500	£0	£0	£0	£500
6	Rent	£3,500	£3,500	£3,500	£3,500	£3,500	£3,500
7	Accountancy	£270	£0	£270	£0	£270	£0
8	Advertising	£0	£1,500	£0	£0	£0	£1,800
9	Postage	£95	£190	£95	£80	£95	£150
10	Stationery	£57	£90	£0	£90	£0	£90
11	Totals	£84,922	£85,780	£83,865	£93,670	£93,865	£96,040

There are many built-in functions which are available to use within your spreadsheet. A number of these will be covered in subsequent chapters.

Chapter Summary

In this chapter we have covered the following spreadsheet concepts and techniques:

- some preliminaries
- basic spreadsheet structure
- worksheets
- workbooks
- entering data into cells
- copying the data in cells
- rows and columns
- changing the height of a row or the width of a column
- using basic formulas

Exercises are available on the next few pages in order to practise and reinforce your learning.

Activities

Here are a group of exercises to allow you to practise the topics covered in this chapter. They can be done individually, or as a sequence, working your way through them.

If you choose to work your way through them, you may not need to open the exercise workbook as suggested at the start of each exercise, as it may already be open.

The saving at the end of each exercise is also optional, although it serves as a reminder to regularly save your work. You can also save to different file names and may choose to keep using the same name to avoid having lots of files.

Exercise 1

Spreadsheet skills:

- Create a workbook
- Name a worksheet
- Move around a worksheet
- Enter data manually
- Save a workbook

1. Open a new blank workbook
2. Select Sheet1
3. Change the name of the sheet to Time data
4. Move to cell A1, enter Work bookings
5. Move to cell A2, enter Client
6. Move to cell B2, enter Week1
7. Save the workbook with the name Chapter1_Exercise1

Your spreadsheet should appear as shown in the screen below:

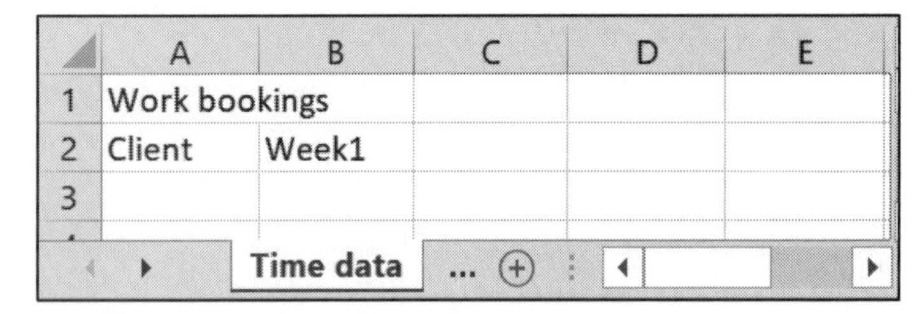

Exercise 2

Spreadsheet skills:

- Open an existing workbook
- Copy and paste values
- Enter data manually

1. Open workbook T1Exercises,
2. Select worksheet Exercise 2
3. For Smiths Ltd, enter the value 15 for Week1 (cell B3), copy this value into Week2 (cell C3), and Week3 (cell D3)
4. The values for Underhills are the same as those for Redwoods. Use Copy and Paste to put these values in cells B6, C6, D6
5. Save your spreadsheet with the name: Chapter1_Exercise2

Your spreadsheet should appear as shown in the screen below:

	A	B	C	D	E
1	Work bookings				
2	Client	Week1	Week2	Week3	
3	Smiths Ltd	15	15	15	
4	Jones and	12	8	10	
5	Redwoods	13	20	11	
6	Underhills	13	20	11	

Exercise 3

Spreadsheet skills:

- Adjust column width
- Insert a column

1. Open workbook T1Exercises,
2. Select worksheet Exercise 3
3. Widen column A to allow for the longest entry in column A
4. Insert a new column before Week1

5. Enter Totals in cell B2
6. Adjust column B width to be the same width as columns C and D
7. Save your spreadsheet with the name: Chapter1_Exercise3

Your spreadsheet should appear as shown in the screen below:

	A	B	C	D	E
1	Work bookings				
2	Client	Totals	Week1	Week2	Week3
3	Smiths Ltd		15	15	15
4	Jones and Partner		12	8	10
5	Redwoods		13	20	11
6	Underhills		13	20	11

Exercise 4

Spreadsheet skills:

- Adjust row height
- Insert a row

1. Open workbook T1Exercises
2. Select worksheet Exercise 4
3. Insert a row below Work bookings to improve the presentation
4. Insert a row Between Client and Smiths Ltd
5. Adjust the height of row 1 to be 20 units
6. Save your spreadsheet with the name: Chapter1_Exercise4

Your spreadsheet should appear as shown in the screen below:

	A	B	C	D	E
1	Work bookings				
2					
3	Client	Totals	Week1	Week2	Week3
4					
5	Smiths Ltd		15	15	15
6	Jones and Partner		12	8	10
7	Redwoods		13	20	11
8	Underhills		13	20	11

Exercise 5

Spreadsheet skills:

- Insert columns
- Adjust column width
- Copy and paste in columns

1. Open workbook T1Exercises
2. Select worksheet Exercise 5

We are going to insert blank columns to make a clear split between Received, Issued and Balances

3. Insert a column before Column B, set the width to 1
4. Copy column B and insert before column F
5. Copy column F and insert before column J
6. Widen column L so that Cost per unit is fully displayed
6. Save your spreadsheet with the name: Chapter1_Exercise5

Your spreadsheet should appear as shown in the screen below:

	A	B	C	D	E	F	G	H	I	J	K	L	M
1	Inventory Record			Average cost valuation									
2	Item RT12548												
3	Date			Receipts				Issues				Balance	
4			Quantity	Cost per unit	Total cost		Quantity	Cost per unit	Total cost		Quantity	Cost per unit	Total cost
5	02/04/2021		100	3									
6	03/04/2021						50						
7	05/04/2021		100	4.5									
8	06/04/2021						100						
9													
10													
11	Total												

Exercise 6

Spreadsheet skills:

- Insert rows
- Copy and paste rows
- Delete rows

1. Open workbook T1Exercises
2. Select worksheet Exercise 6
3. Insert a row cell between rows 2 and 3
4. Delete row 11

There has been another delivery:

5. Copy row 8 and insert below row 9
6. In the new row (row 10), change the date to 08/04/21, and quantity to 150
7. Save your spreadsheet with the name: Chapter1_Exercise6

Your spreadsheet should appear as shown in the screen below:

	A	B	C	D	E	F	G	H	I	J	K	L	M
1	Inventory Record			Average cost valuation									
2	Item RT12548												
3													
4	Date			Receipts				Issues				Balance	
5			Quantity	Cost per unit	Total cost		Quantity	Cost per unit	Total cost		Quantity	Cost per unit	Total cost
6	02/04/2021		100	3									
7	03/04/2021						50						
8	05/04/2021		100	4.5									
9	06/04/2021						100						
10	08/04/2021		150	4.5									
11													
12	Total												

Exercise 7

Spreadsheet skills:

- Create a formula for addition
- Copy a formula

1. Open workbook T1Exercises
2. Select worksheet Exercise 7
3. Enter in cell B5 the formula to total cells C5 through to E5, selecting individual cells to create the formula
4. Copy the formula from cell B5 into B6, B7 and B8 to calculate the other totals
5. Save your spreadsheet with the name: Chapter1_Exercise7

Your spreadsheet should appear as shown in the screen below:

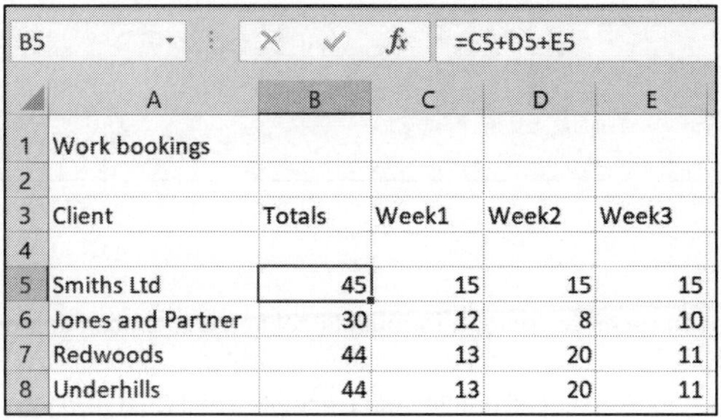

B5 =C5+D5+E5

	A	B	C	D	E
1	Work bookings				
2					
3	Client	Totals	Week1	Week2	Week3
4					
5	Smiths Ltd	45	15	15	15
6	Jones and Partner	30	12	8	10
7	Redwoods	44	13	20	11
8	Underhills	44	13	20	11

Exercise 8

Spreadsheet skills:

- Function - SUM
- Copy and paste a formula

1. Open workbook T1Exercises
2. Select worksheet Exercise 8
3. In cell A10 enter Totals
4. Enter the formula in cell B10 to total cells B5 through to B8 (using the SUM function)
5. Copy the formula from cell B10 into C10, D10 and E10 to calculate the other totals
6. Save your spreadsheet with the name: Chapter1_Exercise8

Your spreadsheet should appear as shown in the screen below:

B10 =SUM(B5:B8)

	A	B	C	D	E
1	Work bookings				
2					
3	Client	Totals	Week1	Week2	Week3
4					
5	Smiths Ltd	45	15	15	15
6	Jones and Partner	30	12	8	10
7	Redwoods	44	13	20	11
8	Underhills	44	13	20	11
9					
10	Totals	163	53	63	47

Exercise 9

Spreadsheet skills:

- Create a multiplication formula
- Function - SUM
- Copy and paste - formula

1. Open workbook T1Exercises
2. Select worksheet Exercise 9
3. In those rows where a quantity has been received, enter a formula in column E to calculate the Total cost (Quantity x Cost per unit)
4. Enter formulas in the Total row (row 12) for Receipts Quantity and Receipts Total Cost using the SUM function with range (C6:C11). Note: it doesn't matter that blank cells are included but it does allow for new rows or data to be inserted in the future
5. Save your spreadsheet with the name: Chapter1_Exercise9

Your spreadsheet should appear as shown in the screen below:

E6 =C6*D6

	A	B	C	D	E	F	G	H	I	J	K	L	M
1	Inventory Record			Average cost valuation									
2	Item RT12548												
3													
4	Date			Receipts				Issues				Balance	
5			Quantity	Cost per unit	Total cost		Quantity	Cost per unit	Total cost		Quantity	Cost per unit	Total cost
6	02/04/2021		100	3	300								
7	03/04/2021						50						
8	05/04/2021		100	4.5	450								
9	06/04/2021						100						
10	08/04/2021		150	4.5	675								
11													
12	Total		350		1425								

Exercise 10

Spreadsheet skills:

- Create simple formulas - subtraction and addition
- Copy and paste - formula

1. Open workbook T1Exercises
2. Select worksheet Exercise 10

To calculate the Balance Quantity, the value for the first Balance Quantity cell K6, will be the quantity first received, cell C6

3. Enter a formula in cell K6, such that the value is equal to the value in C6

In cell K7, the formula will be the Balance Quantity (from the cell above) + Receipt Quantity – Issues Quantity, even if one of the quantities is blank - 0

4. Copy the formula from K6 into cells K7 to K10
5. Save your spreadsheet with the name: Chapter1_Exercise10

Your spreadsheet should appear as shown in the screen below:

K7 =K6+C7-G7

	A	B	C	D	E	F	G	H	I	J	K	L	M
1	Inventory Record			Average cost valuation									
2	Item RT12548												
3													
4	Date			Receipts				Issues				Balance	
5			Quantity	Cost per unit	Total cost		Quantity	Cost per unit	Total cost		Quantity	Cost per unit	Total cost
6	02/04/2021		100	3	300						100		
7	03/04/2021						50				50		
8	05/04/2021		100	4.5	450						150		
9	06/04/2021						100				50		
10	08/04/2021		150	4.5	675						200		
11													
12	Total		350		1425								

2 Formatting the spreadsheet data

this chapter covers...

In this chapter we describe ways of formatting data within a spreadsheet using different text fonts and styles. We also explain different ways of representing numeric data, including currencies and dates. Page layouts will also be explained.

When you have finished this chapter and carried out the exercises which follow, you should be competent in formatting and also printing a spreadsheet.

The concepts and techniques covered are:

- *formatting – style*
- *formatting – fonts and size*
- *number formats*
- *cell alignments*
- *date formats*
- *printing and page setup*

Note that the step-by-step instructions given in this chapter are based on the Microsoft® Excel model, but the concepts and techniques described relate to all spreadsheet packages.

FORMATTING – STYLE

Text formatting within a spreadsheet, as with other types of document, is often used to make an item stand out or to emphasise specific data.

Some of the options described in this and subsequent chapters are identified in the image below.

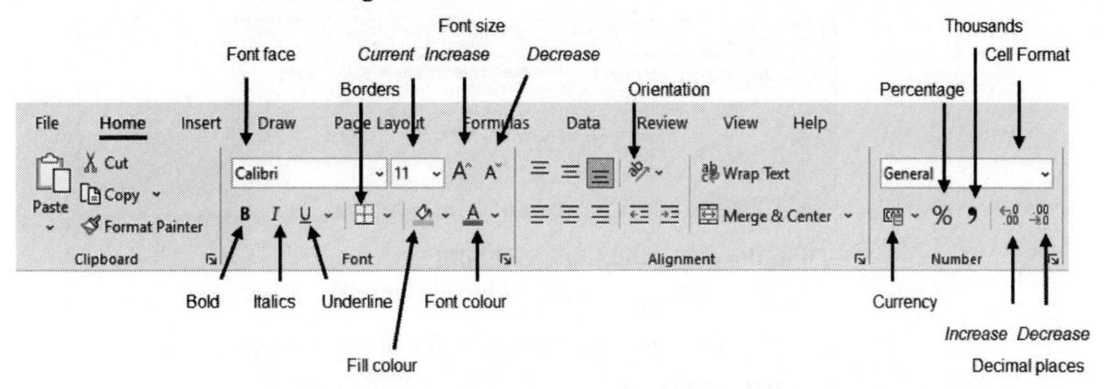

We will use the expenditure worksheet shown below as an example.

making data bold

To make data bold:

- click on the required cell

then

- click on the **Bold** icon on the menu bar if visible

or

- right-click on the selected cell
- select **Format cells**

- select **Font**
- make the font style **Bold**

or

- press **CTRL** and **B** together (hold down the **CONTROL** key and tap the **B** key and release)

Now look at the next page to see the result.

	A	B	C	D	E	F	G
1	**Expenditure forecast**		←		**Now bold**		
2							
3		January	February	March	April	May	June
4							
5	Salaries						

To make more than one cell bold:

- select all the required cells
- and follow the steps set out on the previous page

using italics

To use italics in one cell:

- click on the required cell

then

- click on the **Italics** icon on the menu bar if visible

or

- right-click on the selected cell
- select **Format cells**
- select **Font**
- make the font style **Italics**

or

- press **CTRL** and **I** together (hold down the **CONTROL** key and tap the **I** key and release)

See the spreadsheet screen below.

To make more than one cell italicised:

- select all the required cells
- and follow one of the formatting choices explained above

4						
5	*Salaries*					
6	*Insurance*					
7	*Rent*					
8	*Accountancy*	←	*Now Italics*			
9	*Advertising*					
10	*Postage*					
11	*Stationery*					

underlining data

To underline data:

- click on the required cell

then

- click on the **Underline** icon on the menu bar if visible

or

- right-click on the selected cell, select **Format cells**, select **Font** and make the underline style **Single**

or

- press **CTRL** and **U** together (hold down the **CONTROL** key and tap the **U** key and release)

	A	B	C	D	E	F	G
1	Expenditure forecast		⟵		Now Underlined		
2							
3		January	February	March	April	May	June
4							
5	*Salaries*						

To underline data in more than one cell, select all the required cells and follow the steps set out above.

To double underline data:

- click on the required cell

then

- click on the drop-down arrow by the **Underline** icon
- select **Double** underline

or

- right-click on the selected cell, select **Format cells**, select **Font** and make the underline style **double**

	A	B	C	D	E	F	G
1	Expenditure forecast		⟵		Now Double Underlined		
2							
3		January	February	March	April	May	June
4							
5	*Salaries*						

note – changing back to normal text

To turn off the style, such as bold, underline, italics, you follow exactly the same steps described above and the style will change back to normal.

FORMATTING TEXT – FONT AND SIZE

font face

The **font face** (often known as the '**font**') of text is the style of the lettering:

This is Times This is Helvetica

To change the font face:

- click on the required cell

then

- click on the **Font** list drop-down on the menu bar if visible
- select the required font

or

- right-click on the selected cell
- select **Format cells**
- select **Font**
- choose the required **Font** from the list

To change the font in more than one cell, select all the required cells and follow the steps above.

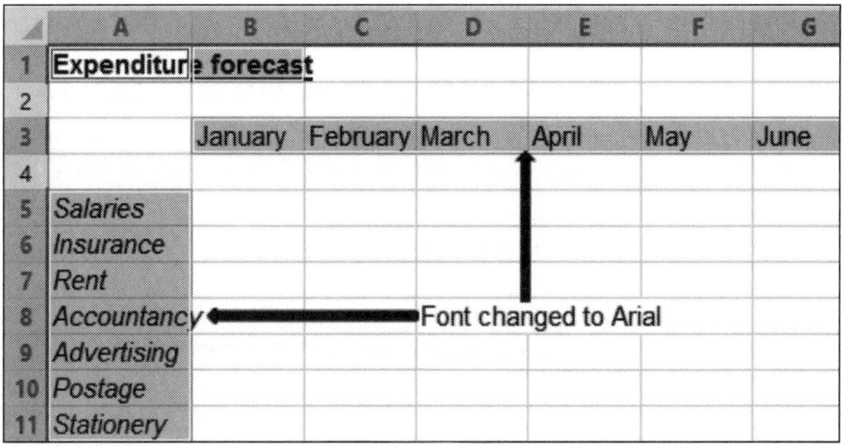

	A	B	C	D	E	F	G
1	**Expenditure forecast**						
2							
3		January	February	March	April	May	June
4							
5	*Salaries*						
6	*Insurance*						
7	*Rent*						
8	*Accountancy*			Font changed to Arial			
9	*Advertising*						
10	*Postage*						
11	*Stationery*						

font size

To change the font size:

- click on the required cell

then

- click on the **Font size** drop-down on the menu bar if visible
- select the required font face size

or

- right-click on the selected cell, select **Format cells**, select **Font** and choose the required font size by selecting from the current font size drop down list, or using the increase or decrease size options

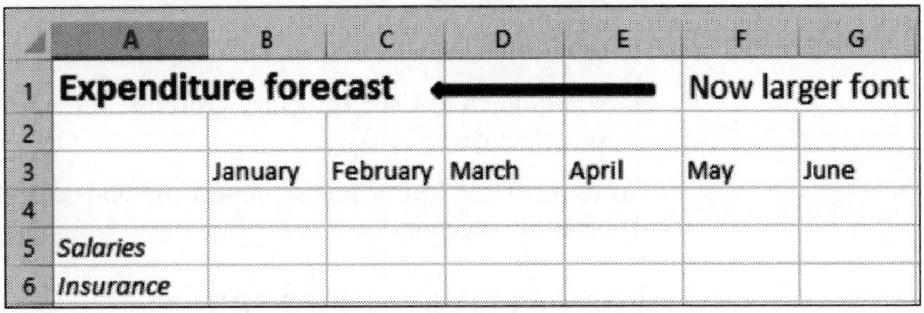

	A	B	C	D	E	F	G
1	**Expenditure forecast**			⟵		Now larger font	
2							
3		January	February	March	April	May	June
4							
5	*Salaries*						
6	*Insurance*						

To change the font size in more than one cell, select all the required cells and follow the steps above.

font colour

To change the font colour:

- click on the required cell

then

- click on the **Font colour** dropdown on the menu bar if visible (usually displayed as a capital A, with the current colour displayed as a bar underneath)
- select the required font colour

or

- right-click on the selected cell, select **Format cells**, select **Font** and choose the required colour from the list

To change the font colour in more than one cell, select all the required cells and follow the steps above.

mini toolbar

Depending on the set up of your spreadsheet program, when you select text to modify, you may see the mini toolbar appear, as shown below:

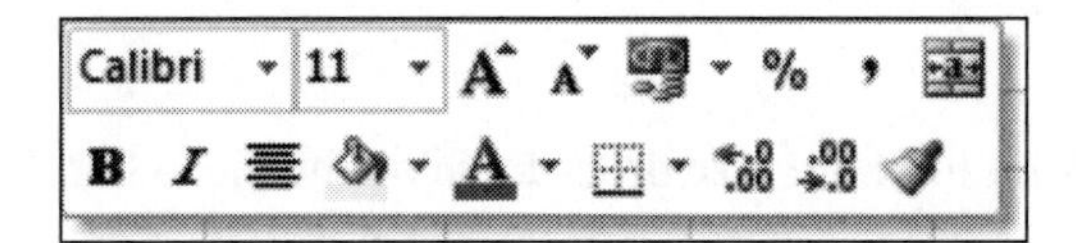

This toolbar provides a quick way of getting to formatting options which you might require when working on your spreadsheet. If you are using Excel, and it does not appear, you can change this as described below.

- select the **File** menu
- select Options
- select General
- scroll down to **User Interface Options**, and **check Show Mini Toolbar** on selection

To turn off the Mini Toolbar, repeat the above, and **uncheck Show Mini** Toolbar on selection.

FORMATTING – NUMBERS

The word 'format' is used in this context to describe the way in which a number will be displayed.

dealing with decimal places

When you enter a number into a cell it is displayed exactly as you type it, except that any trailing zeros (zeros after the last non-zero digit on the right of the decimal point), and leading zeros (zeros before the first non-zero digit at the front of the number) will be ignored.

For example, if you type 0000125.76000 into a cell and press RETURN (Enter) you will see 125.76 displayed.

If you want to see trailing zeros after a decimal point, you will need to change the number of decimal places which are displayed.

For example, if you are dealing with money amounts, you will want to see £34.10 rather than £34.1, which looks very odd. It is quite common that you would want all values in a particular column or row to display to a certain number of decimal places, to give a consistent view to the spreadsheet.

You can see in the example on the next page that several of the data entries are displayed with only one digit after the decimal point.

	A	B	C	D	E	G	H
1	**Unit cost of Grande Pizza Oven**						
2	**Currency exchange rate**		**Euro**	**1.2**	**:£**		
3				**Supplier**	**Cost (local currency)**		
4	Aluminium			UK	60.5		*One decimal place*
5	Insulation			UK	30.99		
6	Consumables (screws, etc)			UK	15.75		
7	Chimney			UK	25		
8	Door handle			UK	5.2		
9	Burner door			UK	10.99		
10	Burner handle			UK	5		

To change the number of decimal places:

- select the required cells, row or column

either

- click on the **Increase** or **Decrease** decimal places icon to adjust the number of decimal places as required

or

- right-click on the selection
- select **Format cells**
- select the **Number** tab
- select category **Number**
- adjust the number of decimal places as required

You can see the effect below where the number formats for column E have been changed to display two decimal places.

	A	B	C	D	E
1	**Unit cost of Grande Pizza Oven**				
2	**Currency exchange rate**		**Euro**	**1.2**	**:£**
3				**Supplier**	**Cost (local currency)**
4	Aluminium			UK	60.50
5	Insulation			UK	30.99
6	Consumables (screws, etc)			UK	15.75
7	Chimney			UK	25.00
8	Door handle			UK	5.20
9	Burner door			UK	10.99
10	Burner handle			UK	5.00

dealing with currencies

Often when we are dealing with money it is simpler to use the built-in format of currency for our data. A format of currency does not affect the values but merely the way the data is displayed.

One of the most used currencies is the UK pound sterling.

To display data as Currency sterling with a £ symbol:

- select the required cells, row or column

either

- select the **Currency** icon from the menu bar
- select £ (English)

or

- right-click on the selection
- select **Format cells**
- select the **Number** tab
- select category **Currency**
- adjust the decimal places as required
- or Symbol select the £ (pound sterling) from the list displayed

The effect of formatting some of the values in column E as currency sterling is shown below:

	A	B	C	D	E
1	**Unit cost of Grande Pizza Oven**				
2	**Currency exchange rate**		**Euro**	**1.2**	**:£**
3				**Supplier**	**Cost (local currency)**
4	Aluminium			UK	£60.50
5	Insulation			UK	£30.99
6	Consumables (screws, etc)			UK	£15.75
7	Chimney			UK	£25.00
8	Door handle			UK	£5.20
9	Burner door			UK	£10.99
10	Burner handle			UK	£5.00

Some of the parts are sourced from Italy and cost is specified in euros. For these items we could use the same procedure as for the pound sterling (see above) and select the € or EUR as the symbol from the list displayed. The image on the next page illustrates the use of both symbols for the Euro, generally one or other would be used.

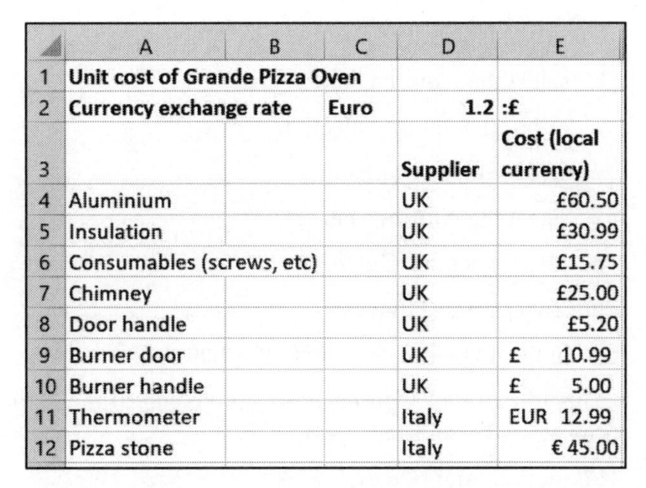

	A	B	C	D	E
1	**Unit cost of Grande Pizza Oven**				
2	**Currency exchange rate**		**Euro**	**1.2**	**:£**
3				**Supplier**	**Cost (local currency)**
4	Aluminium			UK	£60.50
5	Insulation			UK	£30.99
6	Consumables (screws, etc)			UK	£15.75
7	Chimney			UK	£25.00
8	Door handle			UK	£5.20
9	Burner door			UK	£ 10.99
10	Burner handle			UK	£ 5.00
11	Thermometer			Italy	EUR 12.99
12	Pizza stone			Italy	€ 45.00

Once we have chosen the currency, we can also choose **accounting** format from the list of available formats. Accounting format lines up the currency symbols and the decimal points, as illustrated in cells E9, E10 and E11 in the image above.

negative numbers

We can choose how negative numbers are displayed.

To display negative numbers in red:

- select the required cells, row or column
- right-click on the selection
- select **Format cells**
- select the **Number** tab
- in the negative numbers box select the appropriate red format

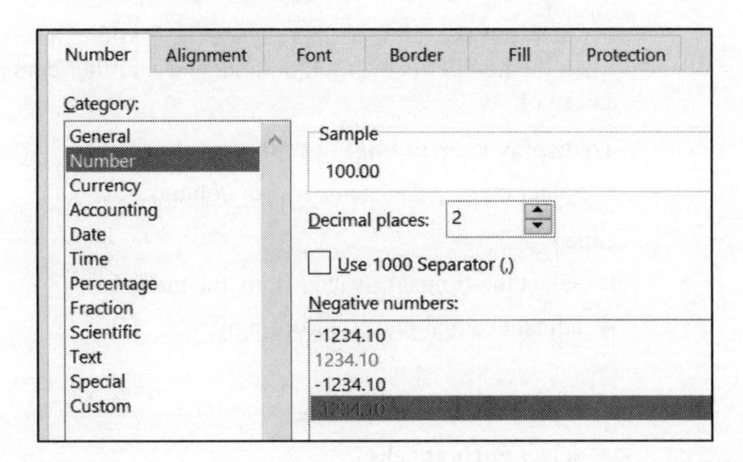

To display negative numbers with brackets:

- select the required cell
- right-click on the selection
- select **Format cells**
- select the **Number** tab
- select category **Custom**

For **two decimal places**:

- in the **Type** box enter **##0.00;(0.00)**

This format will then be added to the end of the list of custom formats and can easily be selected again.

For **no decimal places**:

- in the **Type** box enter **##0;(0)**

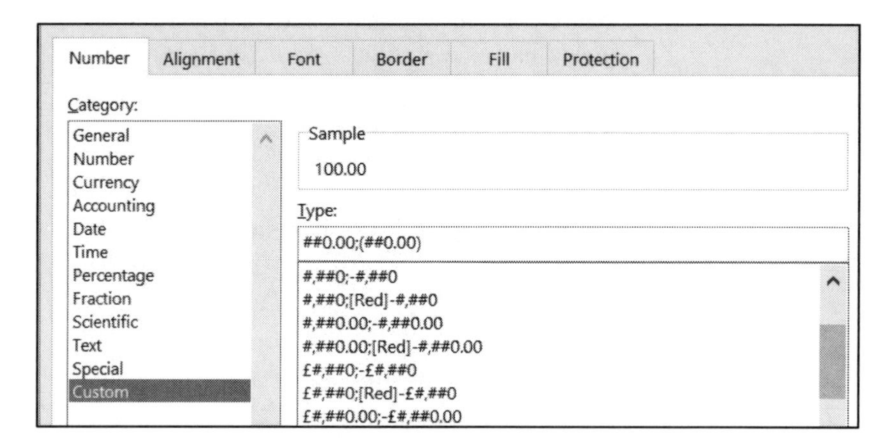

displaying commas in figures

In order to make numbers more readable, we often insert a comma to identify when the number is over a thousand, and a further comma for over a million and so on.

To display a , (comma) to represent thousands:

- select the required cells, row or column

either

- select the **thousands** icon from the menu bar
- adjust decimal places accordingly

or

- right-click on the selection
- select **Format cells**

- select the **Number** tab
- select category **Number**
- **tick** the **Use 1000 Separator box**

In the picture below, both Sales Volume and Projected Revenue include commas.

	A	B	C	D	E	F
1	**Unit cost of Grande Pizza Oven**					
2	**Currency exchange rate**		**Euro**	**1.2**	**:£**	
3				**Supplier**	**Cost (local currency)**	**Cost GBP**
4	Aluminium			UK	£60.50	£60.50
5	Insulation			UK	£30.99	£30.99
6	Consumables (screws, etc)			UK	£15.75	£15.75
7	Chimney			UK	£25.00	£25.00
8	Door handle			UK	£5.20	£5.20
9	Burner door			UK	£10.99	£10.99
10	Burner handle			UK	£5.00	£5.00
11	Thermometer			Italy	EUR 12.99	£10.83
12	Pizza stone			Italy	EUR 45.00	£37.50
16	Selling price					£350.00
17						
22	Sales Volume			2,000		
23						
24	Projected Revenue					£700,000

dealing with percentages

It is also possible to display a number as a **percentage** (%).

If you enter numbers followed by a % sign, the data will be recognised as a percentage and the % sign will be displayed.

If you have a calculation, and you want the result to display as a percentage rather than decimals, you would use the format options to change the way the result is displayed.

In our pizza oven example, we want to calculate a Gross profit %. To do this, we enter the appropriate formula in cell F17.

To make cell F17 display as a percentage:

- select the required cell

either

- click on the percentage icon on the menu bar

or

- right-click on the selection
- select **Format cells**
- select the **Number** tab
- select category **Percentage**
- adjust the decimal places as required

The spreadsheet will then appear as shown below:

	A	B	C	D	E	F
1	**Unit cost of Grande Pizza Oven**					
2	**Currency exchange rate**		**Euro**	**1.2**	**:£**	
3				**Supplier**	**Cost (local currency)**	**Cost GBP**
4	Aluminium			UK	£60.50	£60.50
5	Insulation			UK	£30.99	£30.99
6	Consumables (screws, etc)			UK	£15.75	£15.75
7	Chimney			UK	£25.00	£25.00
8	Door handle			UK	£5.20	£5.20
9	Burner door			UK	£10.99	£10.99
10	Burner handle			UK	£5.00	£5.00
11	Thermometer			Italy	EUR 12.99	£10.83
12	Pizza stone			Italy	EUR 45.00	£37.50
13	Total cost					£201.76
14	Selling price					£350.00
15	Gross profit					£148.25
16						
17	Gross profit %					42.36%

Note: applying a format of percentage will automatically multiply the selected cell (or cells) by 100 to create a percentage.

CELL ALIGNMENT

Alignment is used to describe the relative position of data within a cell.

With **left alignment** the data is shown up against the left edge of the cell.

Right alignment means that the data is shown up against the right edge of the cell.

For **centre alignment** the data is positioned in the centre of the cell.

Examples of all of these are shown in the screen below. By default, any text entered is aligned to the left. Data which is recognised as a number will be automatically aligned to the right.

	A	B	C	D	E	F	G	H
1	**Unit cost of Grande Pizza Oven**							
2	**Currency exchange rate**		**Euro**	**1.2**	**:£**			
3				**Supplier**	**Cost (local currency)**	**Cost GBP**		
4	Aluminium			UK	£60.50	£60.50	←	Right
5	Insulation			UK	£30.99	£30.99		
6	Consumables (screws, etc)			UK	£15.75	£15.75	←	Centre
7	Chimney			UK	£25.00	£25.00		
8	Door handle			UK	£5.20	£5.20	←	Left
9	Burner door			UK	£10.99	£10.99		

To change the way data is aligned in a cell or cells:

- select the required cells, row or column
- right-click on the selection
- select **Format cells**
- select the **Alignment** tab
- on the Horizontal drop-down select **Left**, **Right** or **Centre** as required

or with the cells selected

- click on the appropriate **Alignment** icon on the menu bar if visible

merged cells

Sometimes we have some text which we specifically want to spread across several cells, perhaps as a heading, and we may wish it to be centred across these cells.

To achieve this, we effectively merge the cells together to make one big cell and then apply standard alignment options within this merged cell. Merged cells are only useful for cells containing text.

	A	B	C	D	E	F	N	O	P
1	Inventory Record			Average cost valuation					
2	Item RT12548								
3									
4	Date		Receipts				←	Merged and centred	
5			Quantity	Cost per unit	Total cost				
6	02/04/2021		100	3	£300.00				
7	03/04/2021								
8	05/04/2021		100	4.5	£450.00				

You can see in the example above that the merged cells (C4, D4, E4) are now treated as just one cell, when selected, and this allows us to centre the text over the three columns C, D and E.

To merge cells:

- select the required cells
- right-click on the selection
- select **Format cells**
- select the **Alignment** tab
- on the text control section click the **Merge cells** checkbox

or with the cells selected

- click on the **Merge cells** option from the Merge & Center drop-down menu available on the **Home** menu ribbon

To unmerge cells:

- select the required cells
- right-click on the selection
- select **Format cells**
- select the **Alignment** tab
- on the text control section click the **Merge cells** checkbox so that it is unchecked

or with the cells selected

- click on the **Unmerge cells** option from the Merge & Center drop-down menu available on the **Home** menu ribbon

DATE FORMATS

There are a variety of different ways in which dates can be displayed.

The common way of describing dates is to use 'd' for day, 'm' for month and 'y' for year.

If we take the date of 10th February 2021, it can be displayed in several formats (for UK dates) eg:

- dd/mm/yyyy would display as 10/02/2021
- dd/mm/yy would display as 10/02/21

To change the way a date is displayed:

- select the required cells
- right-click on the selection
- select **Format cells**
- select the **Number** tab
- select category **Date**
- choose the format you require from the drop-down list

The spreadsheet below shows the year date amended from 2021 to 21.

	A	B	C	D	E
1	Inventory Record			Average cost valuation	
2	Item RT12548				
3					
4	Date			Receipts	
5			Quantity	Cost per unit	Total cost
6	02/04/21		100	3	£300.00
7	03/04/21				
8	05/04/21		100	4.5	£450.00
9	06/04/21				
10	08/04/21		150	4.5	£675.00

You can also use other date formats which are available under category Custom.

dates and time

Occasionally it is useful to include the time within a date, or even just to show the time on its own. There are specific formats to allow for this, within the format options. The common way of describing times is to use 'h' for hour, 'm' for minutes and 's' for seconds. The default time format is hh:mm:ss.

For example, 40 seconds after half past one in the afternoon could be displayed as:

13:30:40

Or

01:30:40 PM

Additional date and time formats are available under the category **Custom**.

PAGE SETUP AND PRINTING

Once we have created and formatted our spreadsheet it is quite possible that we will want to print it.

Spreadsheets are not like word-processed documents – they do not automatically fit within one horizontal page width and flow on downwards.

The first step is to see what the spreadsheet would look like when printed, without actually printing. From the **File** menu, select **Print**. You will then see all the print settings which you can change, together with a **Print Preview** of the worksheet on the right hand side of the screen. Alternatively, you can select **Page Setup** from the **Page Layout** menu, then **Print Preview**.

If you need to make adjustments to the layout for printing, this can be done through **Settings** within the **Print** option, or **Page Setup** within the **Page Layout** menu.

Print Settings allows you to:

- change the **orientation**, so if the spreadsheet is slightly too wide to fit on one page width, you might change the orientation to **Landscape**
- adjust the **Margins** – you might want to reduce these to a minimum to give as much space as possible
- select **Fit to page** – you can specify how many pages wide, by how many pages tall you want to fit the spreadsheet into; it is important to make sure that the text of the spreadsheet remains legible

The two images that follow show print previews where the page orientations are:

- portrait – the page is taller than it is wider – like a portrait picture
- landscape – the page is wider than it is taller – like a landscape painting

The image on the next page shows a print preview where the page orientation is **Portrait**.

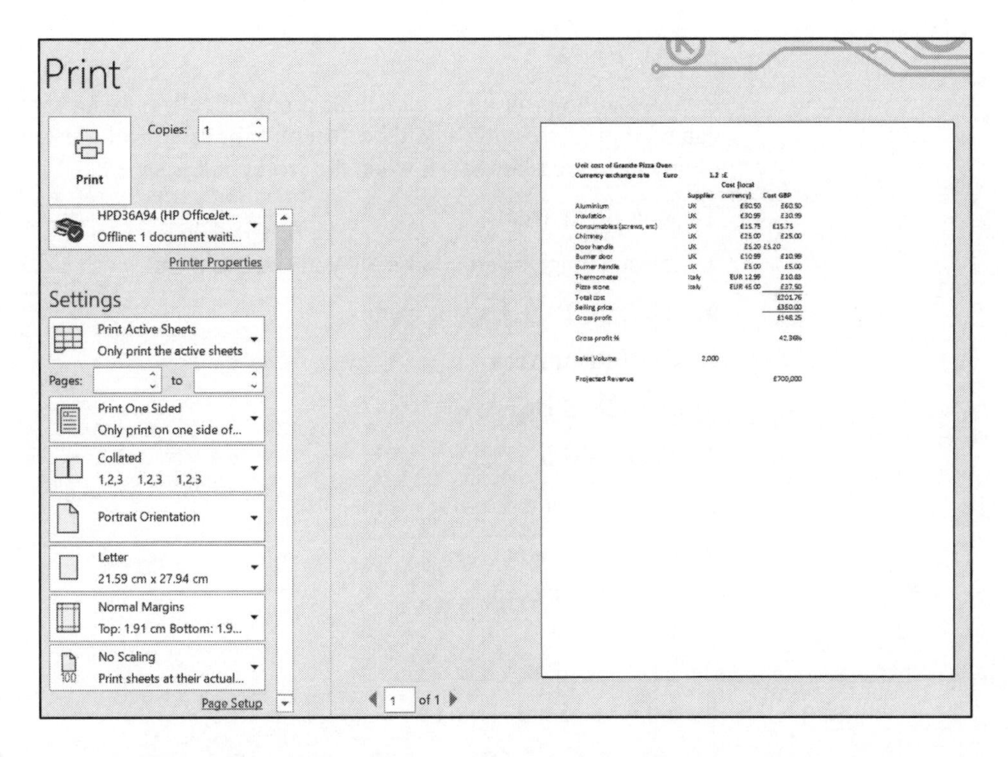

The image below shows a print preview where the page orientation is **Landscape**.

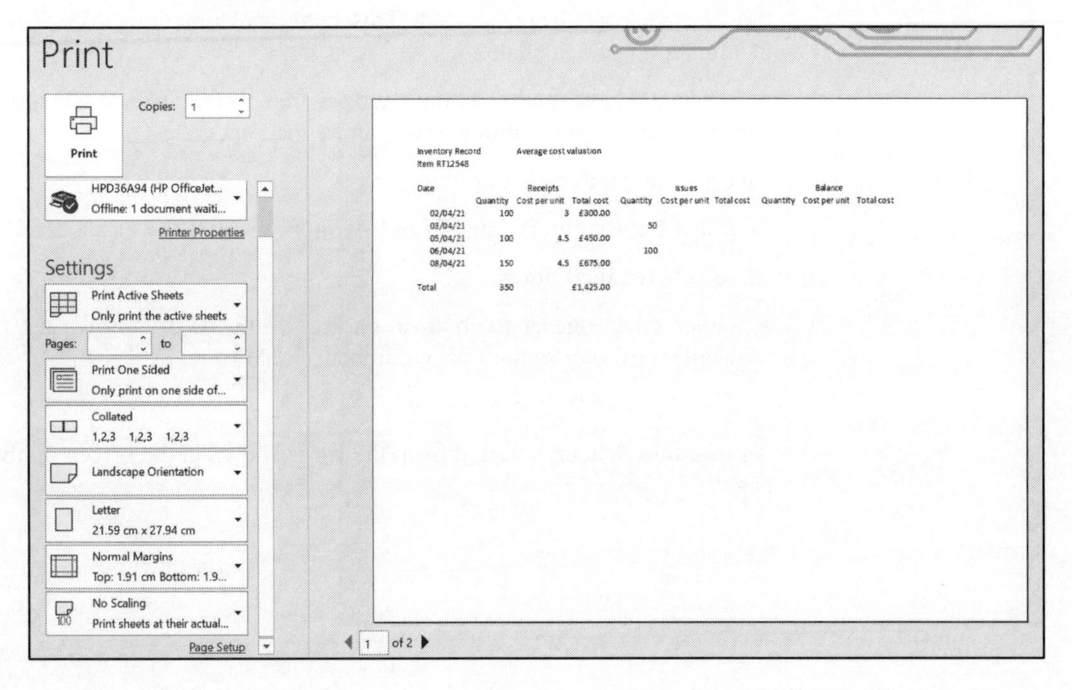

print area

If you want to print just a particular group of cells on your spreadsheet, you can set a print area, this could be different for each worksheet and the details of any print areas are saved when the workbook is saved.

To set a print area:

- select a range or group of cells you want to print
- select the **Page Layout** menu
- select **Print Area**
- select **Set Print Area**

To clear a print area:

- select the **Page Layout** menu
- select **Print** Area
- select **Clear Print Area**

headers and footers

It is sometimes useful to add a **header** or a **footer** to your spreadsheet.

As you would expect a **header** is something which will usually appear at the top of each page when printed. This could be something like "Company Confidential" and the date.

A **footer** will appear at the bottom and is often used to include the author and a page number if the printing covers more than one page.

To create a header or a footer:

- select **Page setup** (within **Page Layout)**
- select **Header/Footer**
- either select one of the built-in choices from the drop-down list for the header or footer such as page number or date
- or create your own custom piece of text

An example Header, selected from the list is shown in the screen on the next page:

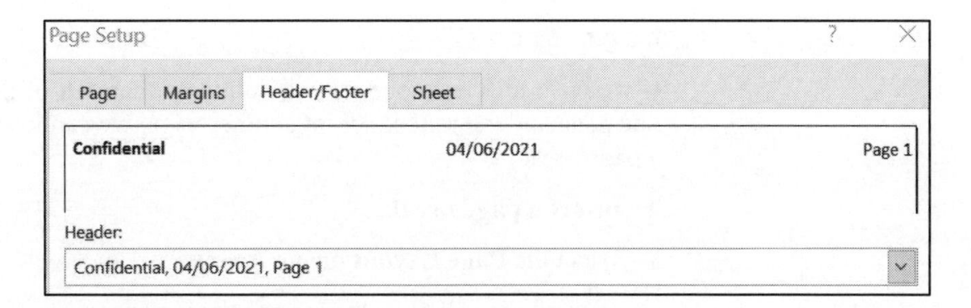

An example Footer, selected from the list, is shown in the screen below:

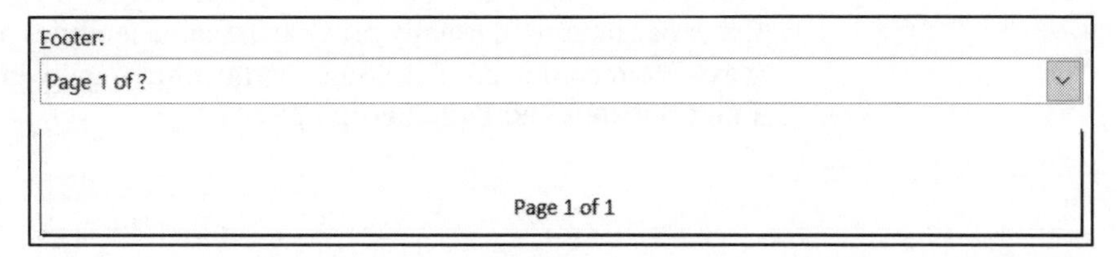

There are a number of additional items which can be inserted into either a header or a footer. These are available if you select Custom for your header or footer, and then pick the items you want and where you want to position them, for example:

- text
- time
- filename
- picture

This can be seen in the image below:

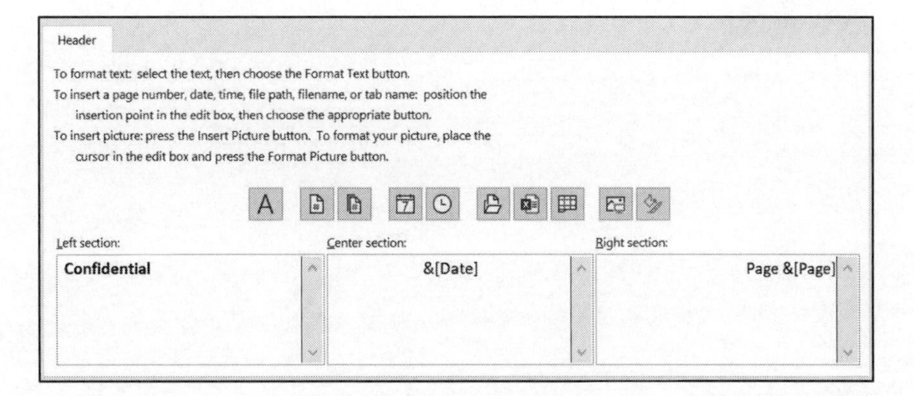

page break

If we wish to format our printed output so that part of the information is on one page and the remainder on another page, we can insert what is known as a page break.

To insert a page break:

- select the **Page Layout** menu
- click on the cell to be the start of the new page
- select **Breaks**

Other packages will usually provide the same facilities presented in a different way. We recommend that you experiment and gain an understanding of the **Print Settings** and **Page Setup** options.

This chapter has covered in detail the following topics:

- formatting – style
- formatting – fonts and size
- number formats
- cell alignments
- date formats
- page setup

Exercises are available on the next few pages in order to practise and reinforce your learning.

Activities

Here are a group of exercises to allow you to practise the topics covered in this chapter. They can be done individually, or as a sequence, working your way through them.

If you choose to work your way through them, you may not need to open the exercise workbook as suggested at the start of each exercise, as it may already be open.

The saving at the end of each exercise is also optional, although it serves as a reminder to regularly save your work. You can also save to different file names and may choose to keep using the same name to avoid having lots of files.

Exercise 1

Spreadsheet skills:

- Format cells - currency (£)
- Format cells - thousands separator

1. Open workbook T2Exercises
2. Select worksheet Exercise 1
3. Format cells B6 to B9 as currency, no decimal places with currency symbol £
4. Format cells C6 to C9 as currency, no decimal places with currency symbol £ and comma for thousands
5. Save your spreadsheet with the name: Chapter2_Exercise1

Your spreadsheet should appear as shown in the screen below:

	A	B	C	D
1	Production costs			
2				
3	No of units	12000		
4				
5		Unit cost	Total cost	
6	Materials	£5	£60,000	
7	Labour	£2	£24,000	
8	Fixed costs	£3	£36,000	
9	Total	£10	£120,000	

Exercise 2

Spreadsheet skills:

- Format cells - merge and centre
- Format cells - align right
- Format cells - bold

1. Open workbook T2Exercises
2. Select worksheet Exercise 2
3. Merge and centre the heading Production Costs in row 1 across columns A to C, and make it bold.
4. Align the column headings in row 5 – Right
5. Make the column headings in row 5 Bold
6. Save your spreadsheet with the name: Chapter2_Exercise2

Your spreadsheet should appear as shown in the screen below:

	A	B	C	D
1	**Production costs**			
2				
3	No of units	12000		
4				
5		**Unit cost**	**Total cost**	
6	Materials	£5	£60,000	
7	Labour	£2	£24,000	
8	Fixed costs	£3	£36,000	
9	Total	£10	£120,000	

Exercise 3

Spreadsheet skills:

- Format font (text) - underline, double underline, and italics

1. Open workbook T2Exercises
2. Select worksheet Exercise 3
3. Add underline to the Total cost for Fixed costs (cell C8)
4. Add double underline to the Total of the Total costs (cell C9)
5. Change No of units text and value to Italics
6. Save your spreadsheet with the name: Chapter2_Exercise3

Your spreadsheet should appear as shown in the screen below:

	A	B	C	D
1	Production costs			
2				
3	*No of units*	*12000*		
4				
5		**Unit cost**	**Total cost**	
6	Materials	£5	£60,000	
7	Labour	£2	£24,000	
8	Fixed costs	£3	£36,000	
9	Total	£10	£120,000	

Exercise 4

Spreadsheet skills:

- Format cells - dates
- Format cells - numbers

1. Open workbook T2Exercises
2. Select worksheet Exercise 4
3. Enter 1st February 2021 for the Invoice date (cell B1) in format dd/mm/yy
4. Format the Price column as number with two decimal places
5. Save your spreadsheet with the name: Chapter2_Exercise4

Your spreadsheet should appear as shown in the screen below:

	A	B	C	D	E	F	G	H	I
1	Invoice date:	01/02/21							
2									
3	Customer no.:	1498							
4									
5	**Product**	**Description**	**Qty**	**Price**	**Unit**	**Total**	**Discount**	**Discount**	**Net**
6	**code**			**£**		**£**	**%**	**£**	**£**
7	PAPER-R	Paper -Ream	4	2.15	each				
8	PEN-50	Pens box - 50	2	9.99	each				
9	A4FOLD-3	A4 Ring Folder - 3	3	2.50	each				
10	PAD-1	Lined pads - 1	6	1.70	each				
11	ENVA4-100	Envelopes A4 -100	3	10.99	each				

Exercise 5

Spreadsheet skills:

- Format cells - date, time
- Format cells - percentage

1. Open workbook T2Exercises
2. Select worksheet Exercise 5
3. Change the format of the Invoice date to display four digits for year, dd/mm/yyyy

Note: both 4 and 5 below require you to use custom formats.

4. Change the format of the Delivery date to display three characters for month, dd-mmm-yy
5. The delivery time will be 12.35 pm, enter this value and display with the appropriate format
6. Save your spreadsheet with the name: Chapter2_Exercise5

Your spreadsheet should appear as shown in the screen below:

	A	B	C	D	E	F	G	H	I
1	Invoice date:	01/02/2021							
2									
3	Customer no.:	1498							
4									
5	**Product**	**Description**	**Qty**	**Price**	**Unit**	**Total**	**Discount**	**Discount**	**Net**
6	**code**			**£**		**£**	**%**	**£**	**£**
7	PAPER-R	Paper -Ream	4	2.15	each	8.60			
8	PEN-50	Pens box - 50	2	9.99	each	19.98			
9	A4FOLD-3	A4 Ring Folder - 3	3	2.50	each	7.50			
10	PAD-1	Lined pads - 1	6	1.70	each	10.20			
11	ENVA4-100	Envelopes A4 -100	3	10.99	each	32.97			
12									
13	**Delivery date:**	19-Feb-21							
14									
15	**Delivery time:**	12:35 PM							

Exercise 6

Spreadsheet skills:

- Format font (text) - font type, font size and colour

1. Open workbook T2Exercises
2. Select worksheet Exercise 6

Some of the invoice is Arial Font, some is Calibri.

3. Change the font face for all cells to Arial Narrow, size 12
4. Change text My Company Ltd to font size 14, colour Grey
5. Save your spreadsheet with the name: Chapter2_Exercise6

Your spreadsheet should appear as shown in the screen below:

	A	B	C	D	E	F	G	H	I
1	Invoice date:	01/02/2021							
2						My Company Ltd			
3	Customer no.:	1498							
4									
5	**Product**	**Description**	**Qty**	**Price**	**Unit**	**Total**	**Discount**	**Discount**	**Net**
6	**code**			**£**		**£**	**%**	**£**	**£**
7	PAPER-R	Paper -Ream	4	2.15	each	8.60	5%		
8	PEN-50	Pens box - 50	2	9.99	each	19.98	10%		
9	A4FOLD-3	A4 Ring Folder - 3	3	2.50	each	7.50	5%		
10	PAD-1	Lined pads - 1	6	1.70	each	10.20	2%		
11	ENVA4-100	Envelopes A4 -100	3	10.99	each	32.97	4%		
12									
13	Delivery date:	19-Feb-21							
14									
15	Delivery time:	12:35 PM							

Exercise 7

Spreadsheet skills:

- Format cells - align centre, left and right

1. Open workbook T2Exercises
2. Select worksheet Exercise 7
3. Align all the column headings (rows 5 and 6) in the centre of the column
4. Align Invoice date and Customer no values (cells B1 and B3) left
5. Values for Unit (E7 to E11) should be aligned right
6. Save your spreadsheet with the name: Chapter2_Exercise7

Your spreadsheet should appear as shown in the screen below:

	A	B	C	D	E	F	G	H	I
1	Invoice date:	01/02/2021							
2						My Company Ltd			
3	Customer no.:	1498							
4									
5	Product	Description	Qty	Price	Unit	Total	Discount	Discount	Net
6	code			£		£	%	£	£
7	PAPER-R	Paper -Ream	4	2.15	each	8.60	5%		
8	PEN-50	Pens box - 50	2	9.99	each	19.98	10%		
9	A4FOLD-3	A4 Ring Folder - 3	3	2.50	each	7.50	5%		
10	PAD-1	Lined pads - 1	6	1.70	each	10.20	2%		
11	ENVA4-100	Envelopes A4 -100	3	10.99	each	32.97	4%		
12									
13	Delivery date:	19-Feb-21							
14									
15	Delivery time:	12:35 PM							

Exercise 8

Spreadsheet skills:

- Format cells - Currency £ and Euro
- Format cells - percentage

1. Open workbook T2Exercises
2. Select worksheet Exercise 8
3. Format Cost (local currency) to either £ or EUR as appropriate with two decimal places
4. Format Cost GBP to £ with two decimal places
5. Format Selling price and Gross profit £ with no decimal places
6. Change Gross profit % value to a percentage with one decimal place
7. Save your spreadsheet with the name: Chapter2_Exercise8

Your spreadsheet should appear as shown in the screen below:

	A	B	C	D	E	F
1	**Unit cost of Grande Pizza Oven**					
2	**Currency exchange rate**		**Euro**	**1.2**	**:£**	
3				**Supplier**	**Cost (local currency)**	**Cost GBP**
4	Aluminium			UK	£60.50	£60.50
5	Insulation			UK	£30.99	£30.99
6	Consumables (screws, etc)			UK	£15.75	£15.75
7	Chimney			UK	£25.00	£25.00
8	Door handle			UK	£5.20	£5.20
9	Burner door			UK	£10.99	£10.99
10	Burner handle			UK	£5.00	£5.00
11	Thermometer			Italy	EUR 12.99	£10.83
12	Pizza stone			Italy	EUR 45.00	£37.50
13	Total cost					£201.76
14						
15	Selling price					£350
16						
17	Gross profit					£148
18						
19	Gross profit %					42.4%

Exercise 9

Spreadsheet skills:

- Page setup - insert header and footer

1. Open workbook T2Exercises
2. Select worksheet Exercise 9
3. In Page Setup, create a custom header with the date in the left section, and the time in the right section
4. Select the footer that shows 'Page 1 of ?' from the dropdown list to display in the centre
5. Do a Print preview

The preview should appear as shown below:

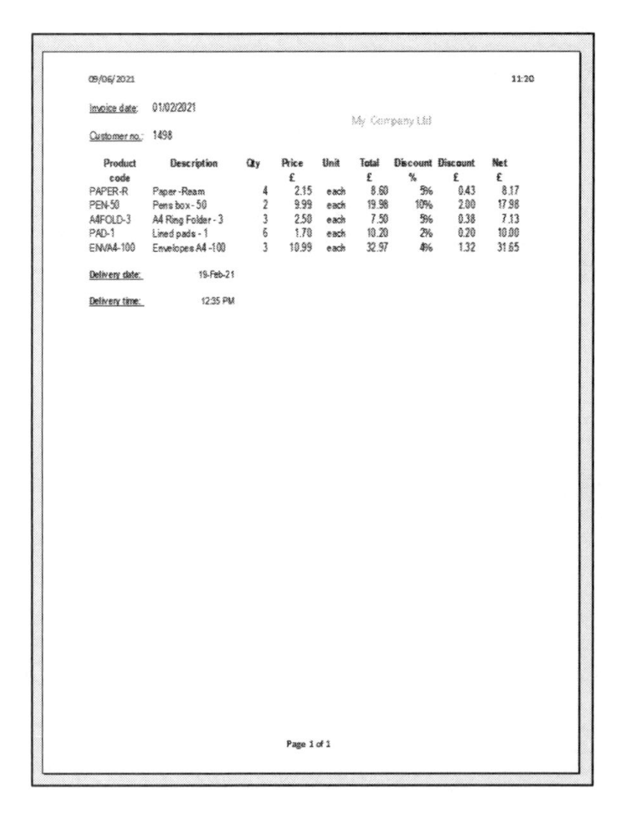

09/06/2021 11:20

Invoice date: 01/02/2021

My Company Ltd

Customer no.: 1498

Product code	Description	Qty	Price £	Unit	Total £	Discount %	Discount £	Net £
PAPER-R	Paper -Ream	4	2.15	each	8.60	5%	0.43	8.17
PEN-50	Pens box - 50	2	9.99	each	19.98	10%	2.00	17.98
A4FOLD-3	A4 Ring Folder - 3	3	2.50	each	7.50	5%	0.38	7.13
PAD-1	Lined pads - 1	6	1.70	each	10.20	2%	0.20	10.00
ENVA4-100	Envelopes A4 -100	3	10.99	each	32.97	4%	1.32	31.65

Delivery date: 19-Feb-21

Delivery time: 12:35 PM

Page 1 of 1

Exercise 10

Spreadsheet skills:

- Page setup - print orientation, portrait and landscape

1. Open workbook T2Exercises
2. Select worksheet Exercise 10
3. Within Print settings, set the orientation so that the page will print Portrait
4. Do a Print preview

The preview should appear as shown below:

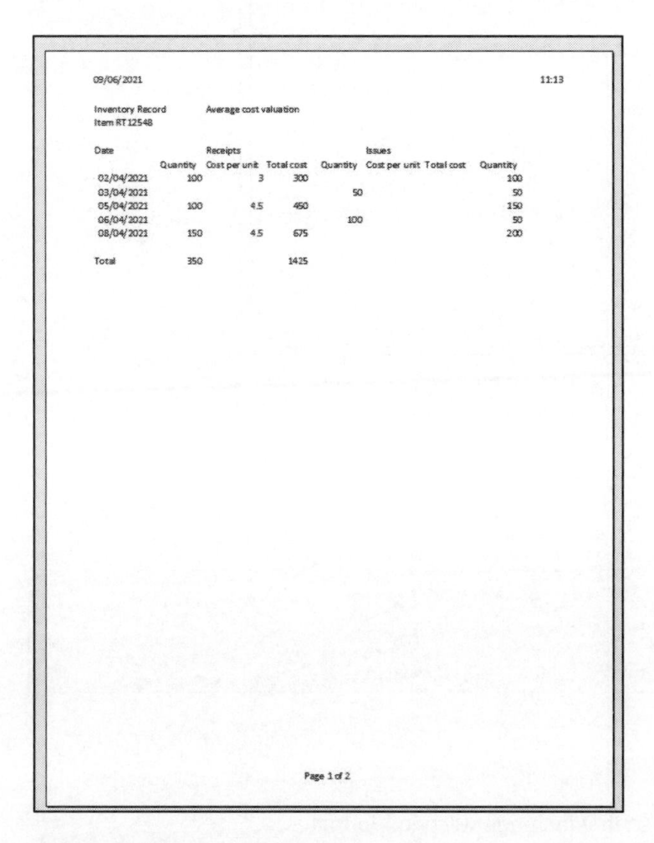

09/06/2021 11:13

Inventory Record Average cost valuation
Item RT 12548

Date		Receipts			Issues		
	Quantity	Cost per unit	Total cost	Quantity	Cost per unit	Total cost	Quantity
02/04/2021	100	3	300				100
03/04/2021				50			50
05/04/2021	100	4.5	450				150
06/04/2021				100			50
08/04/2021	150	4.5	675				200
Total	350		1425				

Page 1 of 2

Showing that the print output would be on two pages:

5. Within Print settings, set the orientation so that the page will print Landscape
6. Do a Print preview

The preview should appear as shown below:

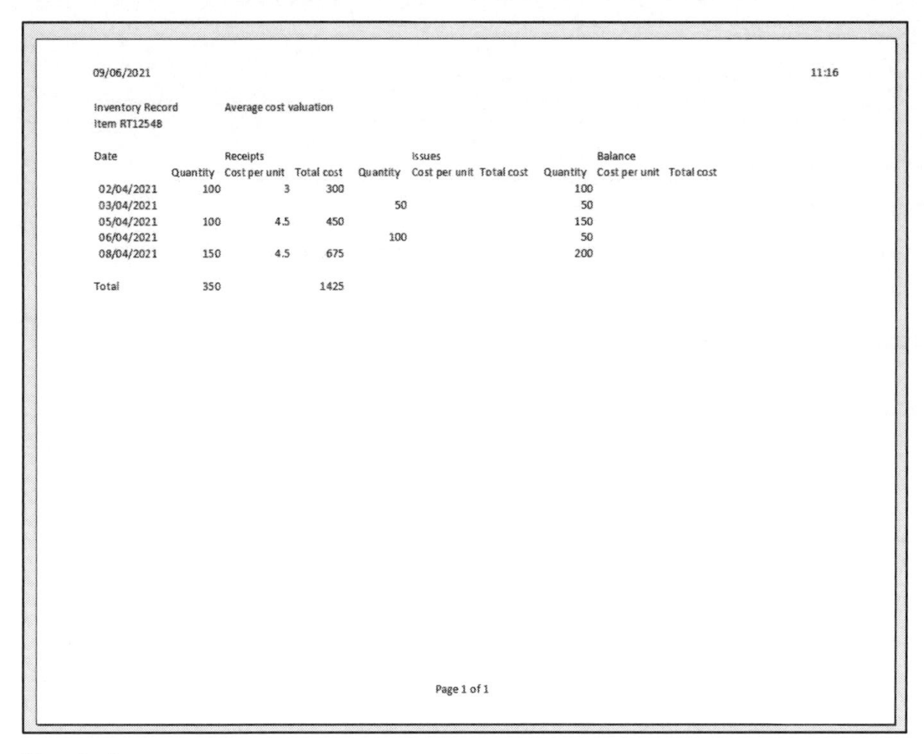

09/06/2021 11:16

Inventory Record Average cost valuation
Item RT12548

Date	Receipts			Issues			Balance		
	Quantity	Cost per unit	Total cost	Quantity	Cost per unit	Total cost	Quantity	Cost per unit	Total cost
02/04/2021	100	3	300				100		
03/04/2021				50			50		
05/04/2021	100	4.5	450				150		
06/04/2021				100			50		
08/04/2021	150	4.5	675				200		
Total	350		1425						

Page 1 of 1

Now, just one page.

Exercise 11

Spreadsheet skills:

- Page setup - scaling

1. Open workbook T2Exercises
2. Select worksheet Exercise 11
3. Within Print settings set the orientation so that the page will print Portrait
4. Within Print settings set the scaling to Fit Sheet on One page
5. Do a Print preview

09/06/2021 11:32

Inventory Record Average cost valuation
Item RT12548

Date		Receipts			Issues			Balance	
	Quantity	Cost per unit	Total cost	Quantity	Cost per unit	Total cost	Quantity	Cost per unit	Total cost
02/04/2021	100	3	300				100		
03/04/2021				50			50		
05/04/2021	100	4.5	450				150		
06/04/2021				100			50		
08/04/2021	150	4.5	675				200		
Total	350		1425						

Page 1 of 1

Exercise 12

Spreadsheet skills:

- Page setup - Print Area
- Page setup - insert Page Break

1. Open workbook T2Exercises
2. Select worksheet Exercise 12
3. Set the Print Area to cells A4 to I11 inclusive
4. Do a Print preview

The preview should appear as shown below:

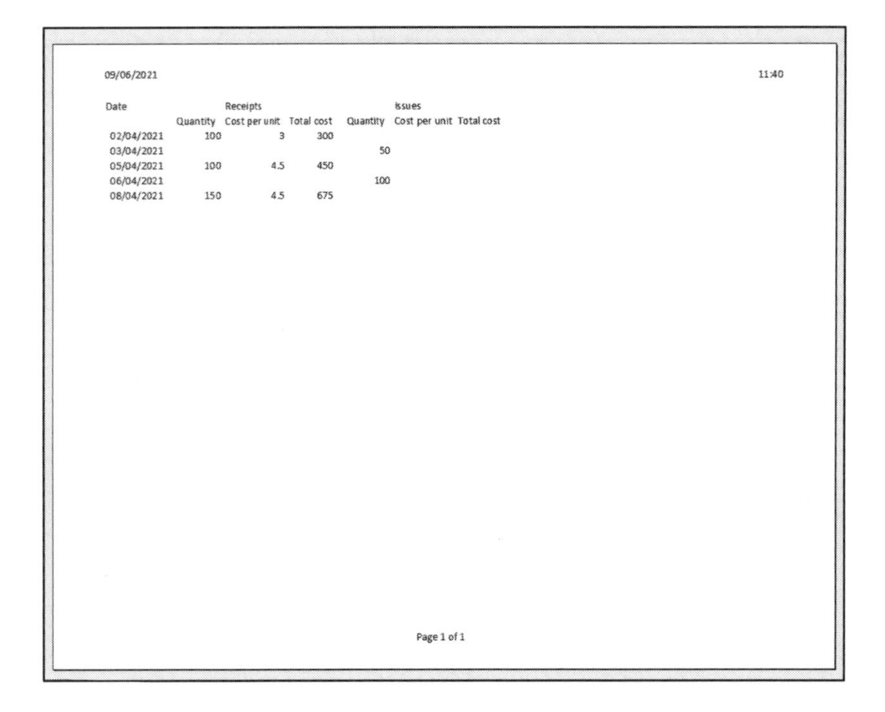

09/06/2021 11:40

Date	Receipts			Issues		
	Quantity	Cost per unit	Total cost	Quantity	Cost per unit	Total cost
02/04/2021	100	3	300			
03/04/2021				50		
05/04/2021	100	4.5	450			
06/04/2021				100		
08/04/2021	150	4.5	675			

Page 1 of 1

5. Clear the Print Area
6. Insert a Page Break in cell A11
7. Do a Print preview

The page 1 preview should appear as shown on the next page:

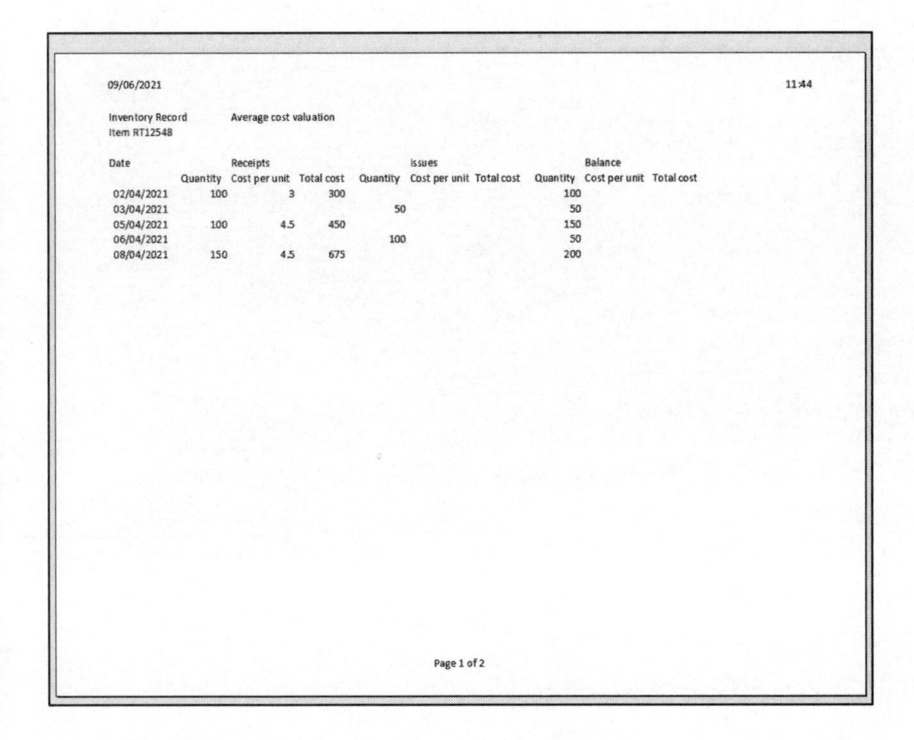

09/06/2021 11:44

Inventory Record Average cost valuation
Item RT12548

Date	Receipts			Issues			Balance		
	Quantity	Cost per unit	Total cost	Quantity	Cost per unit	Total cost	Quantity	Cost per unit	Total cost
02/04/2021	100	3	300				100		
03/04/2021				50			50		
05/04/2021	100	4.5	450				150		
06/04/2021				100			50		
08/04/2021	150	4.5	675				200		

Page 1 of 2

The page 2 preview should appear as shown below:

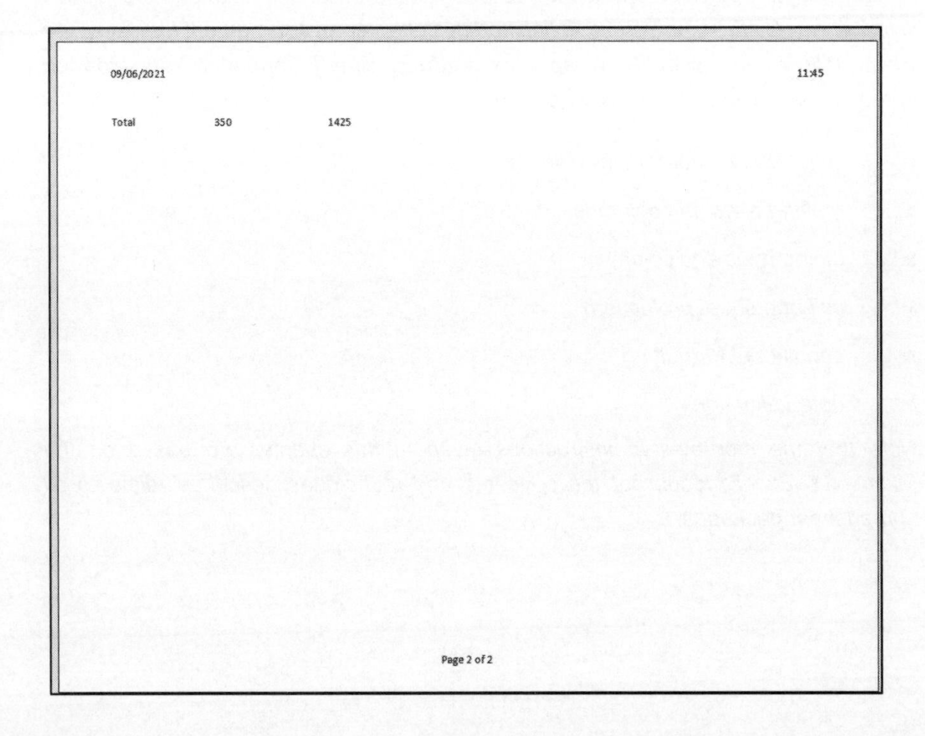

09/06/2021 11:45

Total	350		1425

Page 2 of 2

3 Advanced formatting

this chapter covers...

This chapter provides an introduction to advanced formatting for those new to spreadsheets. It explains and takes you through the basic concepts and techniques listed below. By the time you have finished this chapter and carried out the exercises which follow, you should be able to produce clearly formatted, easy-to-read spreadsheets. The concepts covered are:

- *cell display – borders, fill colours*
- *moving rows and columns*
- *hiding rows and columns*
- *cell and sheet protection*
- *conditional formatting*
- *data validation*

Note that the step-by-step instructions given in this chapter are based on the Microsoft® Excel model, but the concepts and techniques described relate to all spreadsheet packages.

CELL DISPLAY

using borders

We sometimes want to make a cell or group of cells stand out within the spreadsheet.

One of the ways we can do this is to use **Borders**, which are just lines which we add around the edges of a cell or group of cells.

Borders can vary in colour and thickness; they can also be dotted or broken.

They can also be used to split groups of numbers to improve legibility by applying the border to just one edge of a cell.

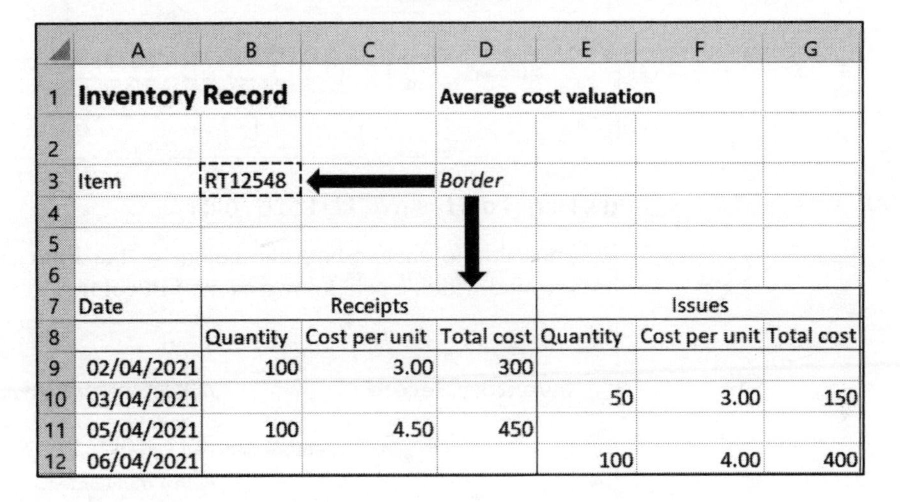

	A	B	C	D	E	F	G
1	**Inventory Record**			**Average cost valuation**			
2							
3	Item	RT12548		*Border*			
4							
5							
6							
7	Date	Receipts			Issues		
8		Quantity	Cost per unit	Total cost	Quantity	Cost per unit	Total cost
9	02/04/2021	100	3.00	300			
10	03/04/2021				50	3.00	150
11	05/04/2021	100	4.50	450			
12	06/04/2021				100	4.00	400

To apply borders:

- select all the required cells

either

- select the **Border** icon from the menu bar
- select the required Border
- choose the **Line style** and **Colour**

or

- right-click on the selected cell or cells
- select **Format cells**
- select **Border**
- choose the **Line style** and **Colour**

- apply to the required edges using either preset borders
- or by clicking within the Border box to select edges (as shown in the screen illustration below)

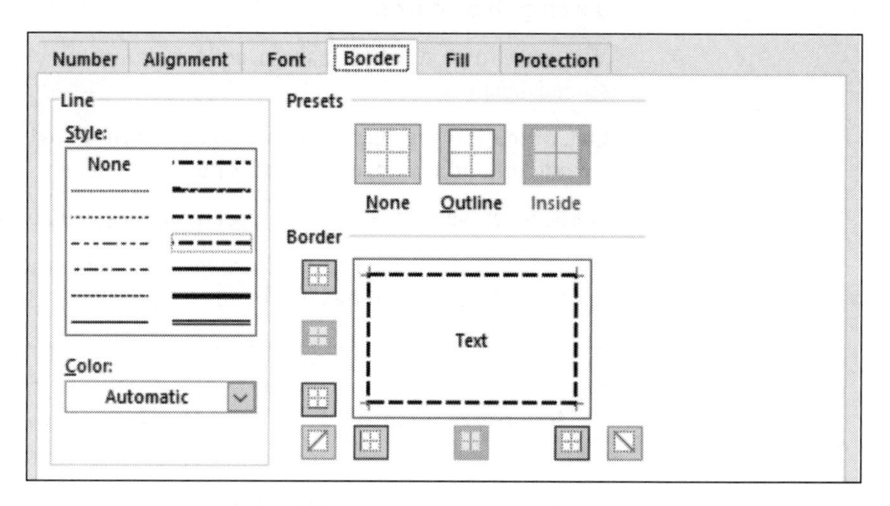

using font and fill colour

It is possible to change both the colour of the **Font** and the colour of the background within a cell, known as the **Fill colour**.

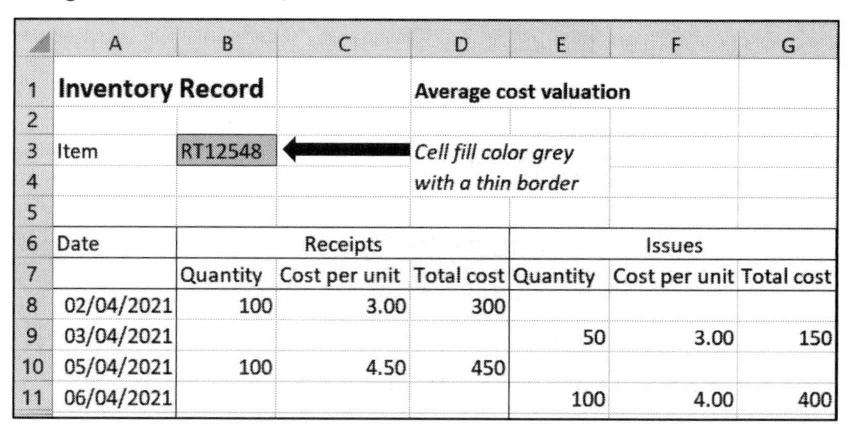

	A	B	C	D	E	F	G
1	**Inventory Record**			**Average cost valuation**			
2							
3	Item	RT12548		*Cell fill color grey*			
4				*with a thin border*			
5							
6	Date		Receipts			Issues	
7		Quantity	Cost per unit	Total cost	Quantity	Cost per unit	Total cost
8	02/04/2021	100	3.00	300			
9	03/04/2021				50	3.00	150
10	05/04/2021	100	4.50	450			
11	06/04/2021				100	4.00	400

To change the Font colour:

- select all the required cells

either

- select the **Font Colour** icon from the **Home** menu ribbon
- select the required colour

or

- right-click on the selected cell or cells
- select **Format cells**
- select **Font**
- choose the **Colour** you require

To set the cell Fill colour:

- select all the required cells

either

- select the **Fill Colour** icon from the **Home** menu ribbon
- select the required colour

or

- right-click on the selected cell or cells
- select **Format cells**
- select **Fill**
- choose the **Background Colour** you require

In addition to the Fill colour, you can also apply shading to make a particular row, column, or group of cells stand out. A variety of different patterns are available.

In the example below we have applied shading to the Total row.

	A	B	C	D	E	F	G
1	**Inventory Record**			**Average cost valuation**			
2							
3	Item	RT12548		*Grey fill with*			
4				*shading*			
5							
6	Date		Receipts			Issues	
7		Quantity	Cost per unit	Total cost	Quantity	Cost per unit	Total cost
8	02/04/2021	100	3.00	300			
9	03/04/2021				50	3.00	150
10	05/04/2021	100	4.50	450			
11	06/04/2021				100	4.00	400
13							
14	Total	350		1425	150		550

To set the shading:

- select all the required cells
- right-click on the selected cell or cells
- select **Format cells**
- select **Fill**
- choose the **Pattern colour**, and **Pattern style** you require

ADVANCED CELL ALIGNMENT

wrap text

If the text which you enter into a cell is longer than the width of the cell, the text entered will appear as a single line of text across adjacent cells, as shown in the example below:

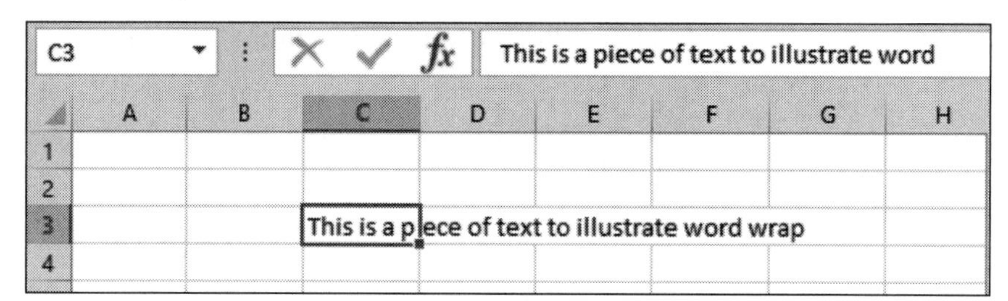

If we want to force the text to fit in just column C, we can use wrap text, and the row height will automatically adjust to fit the text, without changing the column width, wrapping it into one cell. This can be seen in the image below:

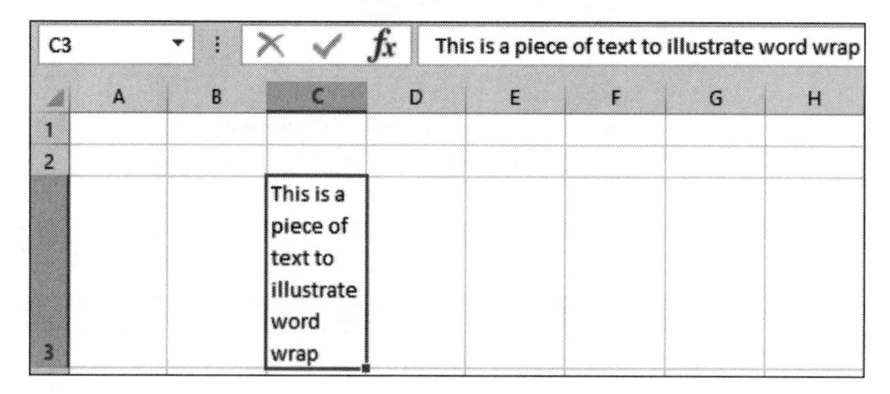

To apply Wrap text to a cell:

- select the required cells

either

- select **Wrap text** from the **Home** menu ribbon

or

- right-click on the selection
- select **Format cells**
- select the **Alignment** tab
- on the text control section click the **Wrap text** checkbox

justify

If we have some text which has been word wrapped and occupies multiple lines within a cell, it is possible to justify the text, either horizontally or vertically. The example below shows some text in a cell:

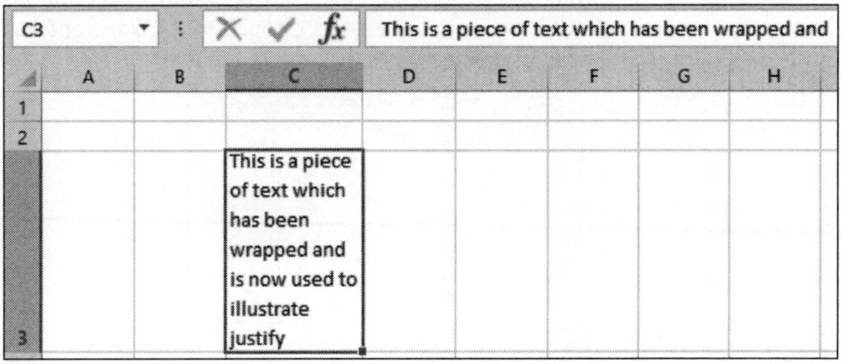

If we now format the cell to justify horizontally, the text reformats as shown:

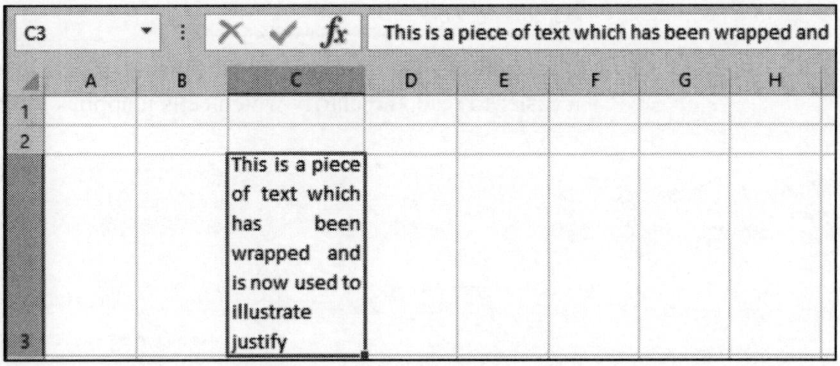

The text has been spread horizontally, to fill the cell to the edges as much as possible.

To justify the contents of a cell:

- select the required cells
- right-click on the selection
- select **Format cells**
- select the **Alignment** tab
- on the text alignment section for **Horizontal**, select **Justify** from the **Horizontal** drop-down list, or for **Vertical**, select **Justify** from the **Vertical** drop-down list.

Note: justification can be applied as a format to any cell, not just those containing text.

orientation

Orientation is the direction in which the text reads when it is displayed in a cell, the default which we use most of the time is horizontal and left to right, this can be changed using the **Format Cells** options. In the example below we have merged cells A2 through to A13, and entered the text 2021-2022 into the merged cells:

	A	B	C	D
1	Year	Month		
2		Jan		
3		Feb		
4		Mar		
5		Apr		
6		May		
7		Jun		
8		Jul		
9		Aug		
10		Sep		
11		Oct		
12		Nov		
13	2021-2022	Dec		

If we now change the orientation of the text in the merged cells, we can make it easier to read and clarify which cells it applies to, as shown below:

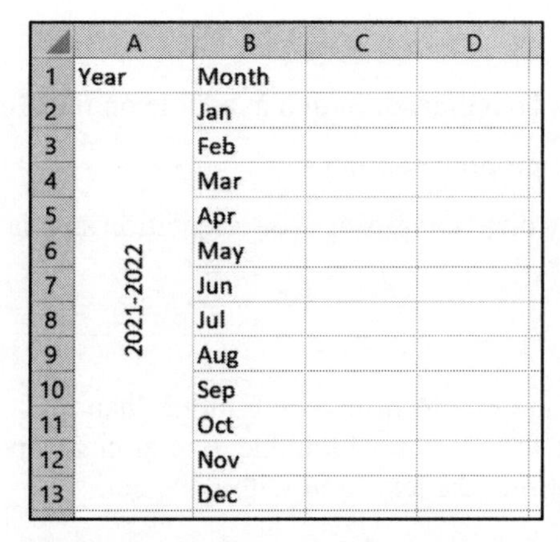

Here we have changed the orientation to 90 degrees, still with the text centered vertically.

To change the orientation of the contents of a cell:

- select the required cells

and

- right-click on the selection
- select **Format cells**
- select the **Alignment** tab

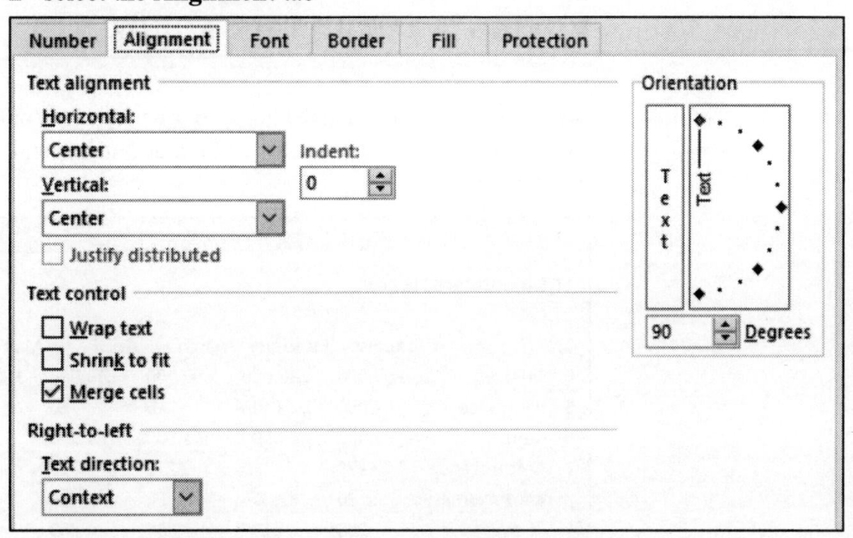

- on the orientation section for **Vertical**, click on **Text** in the vertical box or for greater flexibility click on the **red diamond**, and drag up or down to specify the orientation of the text or enter a specific value (between 90 and –90) in the **degrees** box. You will also normally make the Vertical text alignment center to centre the text in the merged cells.

or

- click on the **Orientation** option available on the **Home** menu ribbon
- select the appropriate option

There are many different settings for orientation so it is worth trying a variety to see their effect.

shrink to fit

When text is too large to fit in a cell, rather than resize the cell, if you don't want to change the column width, due to retaining a specific layout format, it is possible to shrink the text to fit within the cell.

To shrink text:

- select the required cells

and

- right-click on the selection
- select **Format cells**
- select the **Alignment** tab
- click on **Shrink to fit**

MOVING A COLUMN OR A ROW

Sometimes we may wish to change our basic layout and move either a **column or a row** within the layout. If we look at our Expenditure forecast worksheet as shown below:

	A	B	C	D	E	F	G	H
1	Expenditure Forecast							
2								
3		January	February	March	April	May	June	**Totals**
4	Salaries	£80,000	£80,000	£80,000	£90,000	£90,000	£90,000	**£510,000**
5	Insurance	£1,000	£500	£0	£0	£0	£500	**£2,000**
6	Rent	£3,500	£3,500	£3,500	£3,500	£3,500	£3,500	**£21,000**
7	Accountancy	£270	£0	£270	£0	£270	£0	**£810**
8	Advertising	£0	£1,500	£0	£0	£0	£1,800	**£3,300**
9	Postage	£95	£190	£95	£80	£95	£150	**£705**
10	Stationery	£57	£90	£0	£90	£0	£90	**£327**
11	**Totals**	**£84,922**	**£85,780**	**£83,865**	**£93,670**	**£93,865**	**£96,040**	**£538,142**

We might wish to move the Totals column to display before the months, as you can see in the image on the next page:

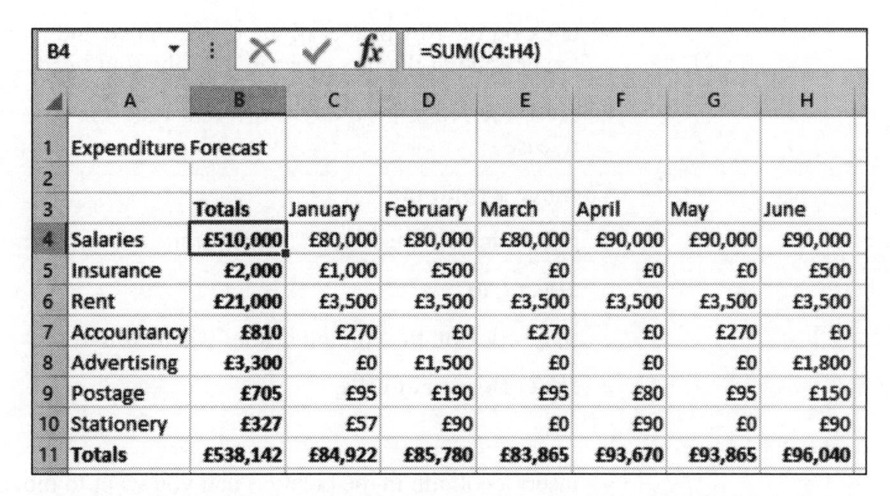

B4 =SUM(C4:H4)

	A	B	C	D	E	F	G	H
1	Expenditure Forecast							
2								
3		**Totals**	January	February	March	April	May	June
4	Salaries	**£510,000**	£80,000	£80,000	£80,000	£90,000	£90,000	£90,000
5	Insurance	**£2,000**	£1,000	£500	£0	£0	£0	£500
6	Rent	**£21,000**	£3,500	£3,500	£3,500	£3,500	£3,500	£3,500
7	Accountancy	**£810**	£270	£0	£270	£0	£270	£0
8	Advertising	**£3,300**	£0	£1,500	£0	£0	£0	£1,800
9	Postage	**£705**	£95	£190	£95	£80	£95	£150
10	Stationery	**£327**	£57	£90	£0	£90	£0	£90
11	**Totals**	**£538,142**	**£84,922**	**£85,780**	**£83,865**	**£93,670**	**£93,865**	**£96,040**

Notice how the formulas in the Totals column have automatically changed so that they are still adding each of the monthly columns.

Alternatively, we might want to move the rows around so that the Salaries row comes before the Stationery row, as shown on the next page.

C11 =SUM(C4:C10)

	A	B	C	D	E	F	G	H
1	Expenditure Forecast							
2								
3		**Totals**	January	February	March	April	May	June
4	Insurance	**£2,000**	£1,000	£500	£0	£0	£0	£500
5	Rent	**£21,000**	£3,500	£3,500	£3,500	£3,500	£3,500	£3,500
6	Accountancy	**£810**	£270	£0	£270	£0	£270	£0
7	Advertising	**£3,300**	£0	£1,500	£0	£0	£0	£1,800
8	Postage	**£705**	£95	£190	£95	£80	£95	£150
9	Salaries	**£510,000**	£80,000	£80,000	£80,000	£90,000	£90,000	£90,000
10	Stationery	**£327**	£57	£90	£0	£90	£0	£90
11	**Totals**	**£538,142**	**£84,922**	**£85,780**	**£83,865**	**£93,670**	**£93,865**	**£96,040**

To move a row:

- right-click on the row header of the row to move
- select **Cut**
- right-click on the row header to where you want to move the row
- select **Insert cut cells**

or

- insert a row in the position that you want to move the row to

- click on the row header of the row to move and move the cursor over the lower edge of the row selected until the four headed arrow appears
- press the left mouse key down and drag the row to the blank row and release

To move a column:

- right-click on the column header of the column to move
- select **Cut**
- right-click on the column header where you to move the column to
- select **Insert cut cells**

or

- insert a column in the position that you want to move the column to
- click on the column header of the column to move and move the cursor over the lower edge of the column header until the four headed arrow appears
- press the left mouse key down and drag the column to the blank column and release

HIDE A ROW OR A COLUMN

Sometimes we may wish to hide certain data or calculations used in a spreadsheet from public view, for example salary data. The Hide row or column option allows us to do this and still make use of the data within our spreadsheet. In the spreadsheet below, Column B the Totals column has been hidden.

	A	C	D	E	F	G	H
1	Expenditure Forecast						
2							
3		January	February	March	April	May	June
4	Insurance	£1,000	£500	£0	£0	£0	£500
5	Rent	£3,500	£3,500	£3,500	£3,500	£3,500	£3,500
6	Accountancy	£270	£0	£270	£0	£270	£0
7	Advertising	£0	£1,500	£0	£0	£0	£1,800
8	Postage	£95	£190	£95	£80	£95	£150
9	Salaries	£80,000	£80,000	£80,000	£90,000	£90,000	£90,000
10	Stationery	£57	£90	£0	£90	£0	£90
11	**Totals**	**£84,922**	**£85,780**	**£83,865**	**£93,670**	**£93,865**	**£96,040**

To hide a row:

- right-click on the row header
- select **Hide**

To hide a column:

- right-click on the column header
- select **Hide**

It is also possible to unhide a row or column to make modifications:

To unhide a row:

- select the row headers of the rows either side of the hidden row
- right-click on the selected row headers
- select **Unhide Rows**

To unhide a column:

- select the column headers of the columns either side of the hidden column
- right-click on the selected column headers
- select **Unhide Columns**

CELL AND WORKSHEET PROTECTION

It can be important that the values within certain cells do not get changed by a user, for example a formula.

To prevent a cell being changed we can lock it. The default setting for a cell is usually locked. Locking a cell has no effect until the worksheet (also known as a 'sheet') containing the cell is protected. If a user tries to change a locked cell on a protected worksheet he/she will get a message to the effect that the cell is protected and therefore read-only.

To lock a cell or cells:

- select all the required cells
- right-click on the selected cell or cells
- select **Format cells**
- click the **Protection** tab
- check the **Locked** box (see the screen on the next page)

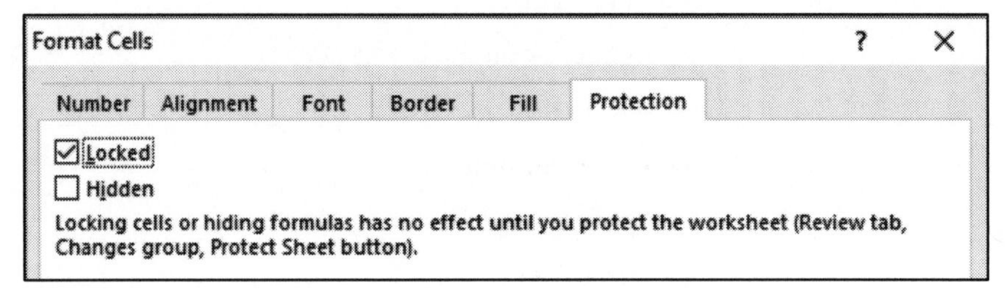

Alternatively,

- select **Format** from the **Home** menu ribbon, then **Lock Cell**

The Lock Cell menu option acts as an on /off switch.

If the cell(s) are already locked, you will see the square around the padlock, next to the Lock Cell menu item, as shown in the image on the right.

If the cell(s) are NOT already locked, you will just see the the padlock, as shown in this image.

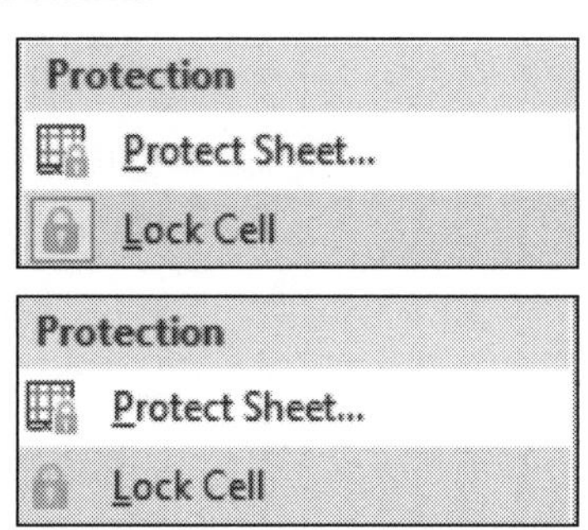

To unlock a cell or range of cells:

- select all the required cells

either

- right-click on the selected cell or cells
- select **Format cells**
- click the **Protection** tab
- uncheck the **Locked** box

or

- select **Format** from the **Home** menu ribbon, **Lock Cell**

If locking a cell is to have any effect the worksheet containing the locked cells **must be protected**.

To protect a worksheet:

- select the sheetname tab of the required worksheet
- select **Protect sheet** from the **Review** menu bar
- there is an option to enter a password but it's not compulsory

It is very important to keep a note of the password, because if you lose a password, **you cannot recover it**. Without the necessary password all changes to protected cells would not be permitted, even by the creator of the worksheet.

If you do have the password and wish to change cells you first need to **unprotect the sheet:**

- select the sheetname tab of the required worksheet
- select **Unprotect sheet** from the **Review** menu bar
- enter the password if required

CONDITIONAL FORMATTING

We have covered the concepts of displaying cells with different fill colours and text colours, by selecting and changing.

Sometimes we may want a cell to change colour or display a different font face automatically depending on the value it may hold; this is known as **conditional formatting**. This is especially useful if we have a large amount of data, where it would be easy to miss seeing certain values.

Conditional formatting allows you to define a rule or rules, and if the data meets the rules (conditions), it will display in the format that you have specified, in a different font or fill colour. For example, we may want all values less than £1,000 on a financial worksheet to be displayed in red text, so that they stand out. Another example would be to display all negative (less than zero) values within a row or column in red.

logical operators

We can apply comparison 'operators' to create rules where **conditional formatting** can be used. These include:

- equal to
- not equal to
- greater than, greater than or equal to
- between
- less than, less than or equal to
- text that contains
- a date occurring

Alternatively, we can create a **top/bottom** rule, these include:

- top 10 items, or top any number of items
- top 10%
- bottom 10 items
- bottom 10%
- above average
- below average

You can define more than one rule, and each rule can have several conditions within it. Once you have created a conditional formatting rule, you can edit the rule, to change the criteria, change cells you want to apply it to, or change the way the cells meeting the criteria are displayed.

In the example below we have created a conditional formatting rule to apply to the Postage costs in Cells C8 through to H8. If the value is greater than 100, we want to fill the cell with a grey background.

The rule is displayed below:

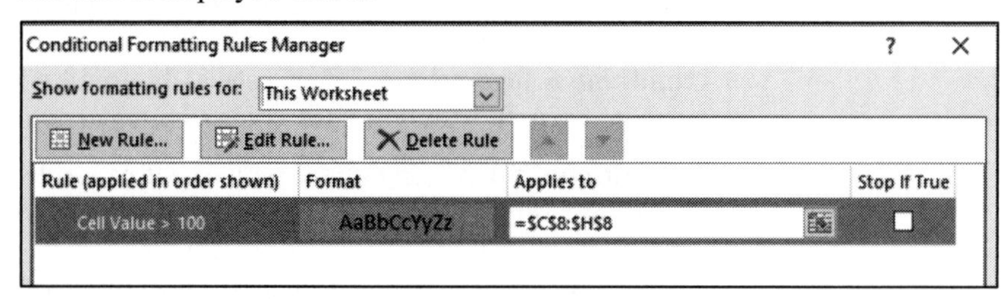

Note: $ symbols are automatically inserted within the cell range; the meaning of these $ symbols is described later in the book. As you can see in the image below, all cells where Postage costs are greater than £100 are shown filled with a grey background.

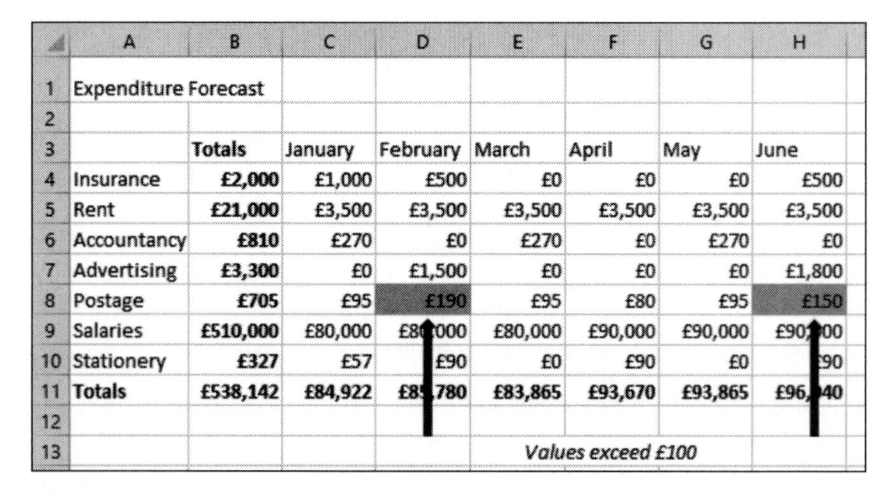

	A	B	C	D	E	F	G	H
1	Expenditure Forecast							
2								
3		**Totals**	January	February	March	April	May	June
4	Insurance	**£2,000**	£1,000	£500	£0	£0	£0	£500
5	Rent	**£21,000**	£3,500	£3,500	£3,500	£3,500	£3,500	£3,500
6	Accountancy	**£810**	£270	£0	£270	£0	£270	£0
7	Advertising	**£3,300**	£0	£1,500	£0	£0	£0	£1,800
8	Postage	**£705**	£95	£190	£95	£80	£95	£150
9	Salaries	**£510,000**	£80,000	£8[illegible]000	£80,000	£90,000	£90,000	£90[illegible]00
10	Stationery	**£327**	£57	£90	£0	£90	£0	[illegible]90
11	**Totals**	**£538,142**	**£84,922**	**£8[illegible]780**	**£83,865**	**£93,670**	**£93,865**	**£96,[illegible]40**
12								
13					*Values exceed £100*			

To set conditional formatting for a group of cells:

- select the required cells
- select **Conditional formatting** from the **Home** menu ribbon
- enter the rule which you want to apply using the drop-down list of 'greater than, less than, equal to' etc, and the required value
- select the **Font style** and **Colour**, together with the fill colour and any other effects

  either from the choices in the drop-down list,

  or by selecting **Custom format** from the bottom of the list, and choosing from the standard format cells options.

To clear conditional formatting for a group of cells:

- select the required cells
- select **Conditional formatting**
- select **Clear Rules**, then **Clear rules from selected cells**

To clear all conditional formatting for a worksheet:

- select **Conditional formatting**
- select **Clear Rules**, then **Clear rules from entire sheet**

DATA VALIDATION

When a spreadsheet is being used, it is possible we may only want to allow certain values in a particular cell; this might be to prevent data entry errors such as misspelling or to ensure consistency across the data.

It is possible to restrict the type of data which may be entered, such as a date, a whole number, or to provide a list of acceptable values, which will then be displayed as a drop-down list when the user moves to the cell. This restriction of values is called **data validation**.

In the image on the next page we have restricted the values allowed in cells in the month column (column A) to three character month names. When you move to one of these cells, a drop-down list appears showing the acceptable choices. You are only allowed to select from this list.

A6

	A	B	C	D	E	F
1	Sales					
2						
3	Month	Product	Value			
4	Feb	Clothing	£1,500.00			
5	Feb	Jewellery	£220.00			
6						

Jan
Feb
Mar
Apr
May
Jun
Jul
Aug

In the image below you can see that the choice of Product has also been restricted to allow only four specific values and Other. When you select any of the cells in the product column the drop-down list of products is displayed and you can choose from this list.

B6

	A	B	C	D	E	F
1	Sales					
2						
3	Month	Product	Value			
4	Feb	Clothing	£1,500.00			
5	Feb	Jewellery	£220.00			
6	Mar					

Accessories
Clothing
Footwear
Jewellery
Other

To define the data validation for a group of cells:

- select the required cells
- select **Data validation** from the **Data** menu ribbon
- select the validation criteria from the drop-down list (as seen in the screen below)
- if you select **List**, enter the values you want to allow, separated by commas. Alternatively, if you enter an "=" sign in the Source box, you can then select cells from the worksheet to make up the valid entries for the list.

The data validation for our restricted months in column A looks like:

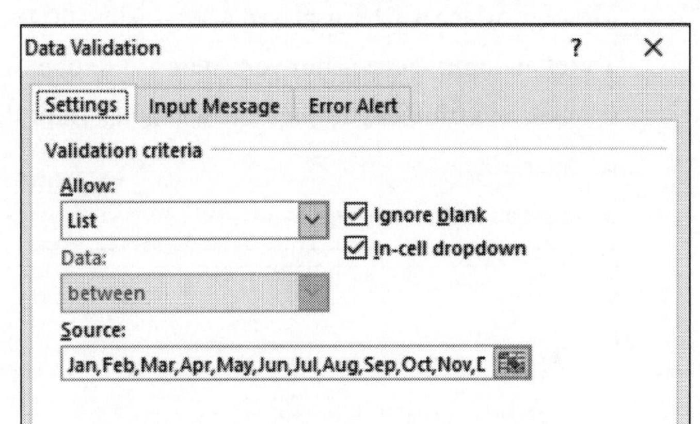

And for the Product column:

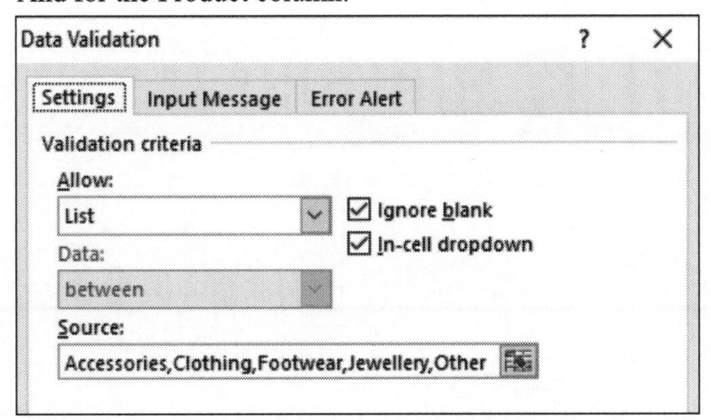

If we wanted to restrict a cell or group of cells to contain just dates between April and September, example settings are shown below:

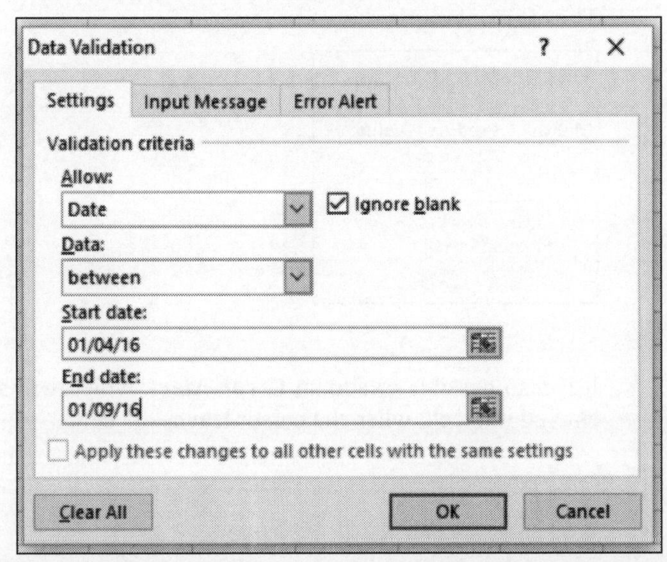

To complete the setup of the Data Validation, it is possible to add an **Input Message**, which will be displayed when a cell with Data validation is selected.

To set an input message for your data validation

- click on the **Input Message** tab, within the **Data Validation** screen
- enter a Title
- enter an input message

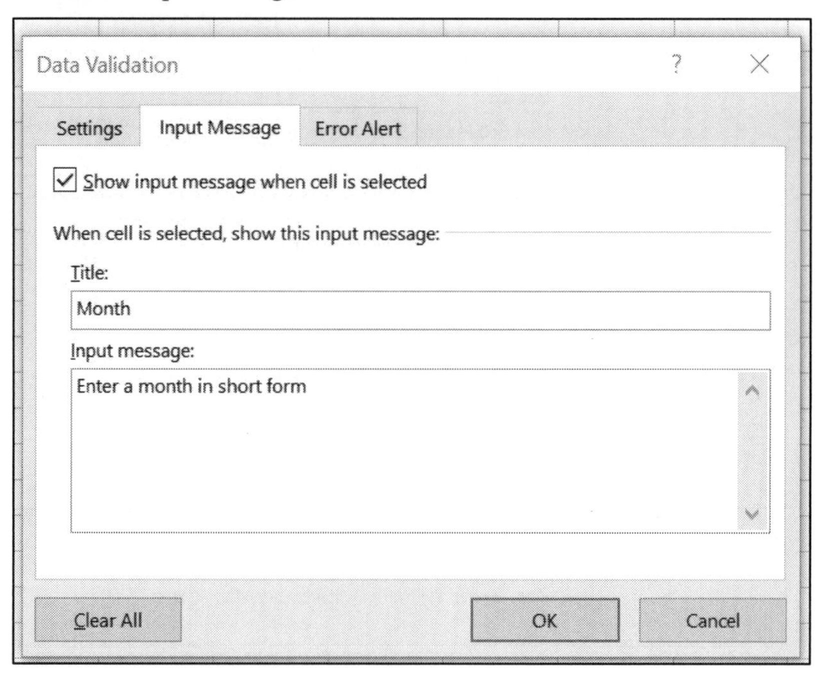

The effect of this is shown below:

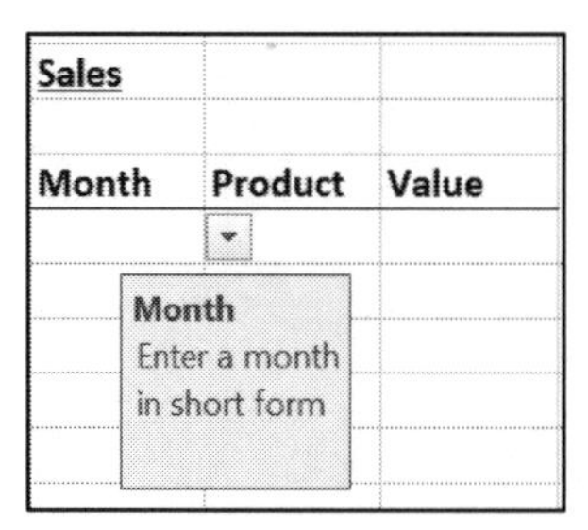

It is also possible to add an **Error Alert,** which will show if invalid data is entered into cell, when the cursor leaves the cell.

To add an Error Alert for your data validation:

- click on the **Error Alert** tab, within the **Data Validation** screen
- complete as required

An example is shown below:

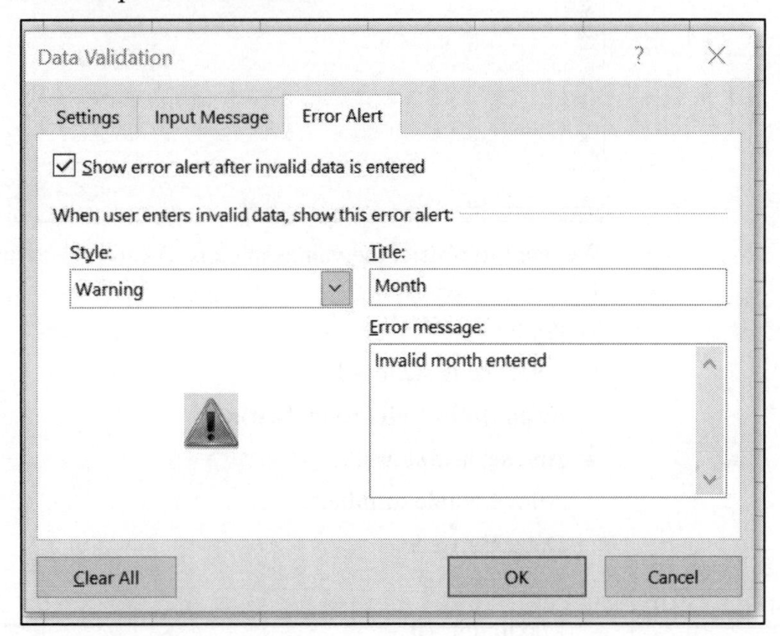

With the effect shown here:

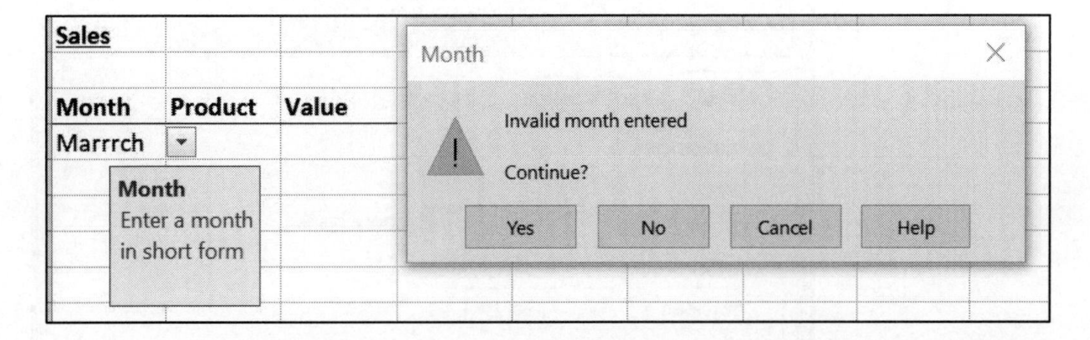

It is also possible to apply **data validation** to cells that already contain data. For example, suppose we had values in column A as shown on the next page.

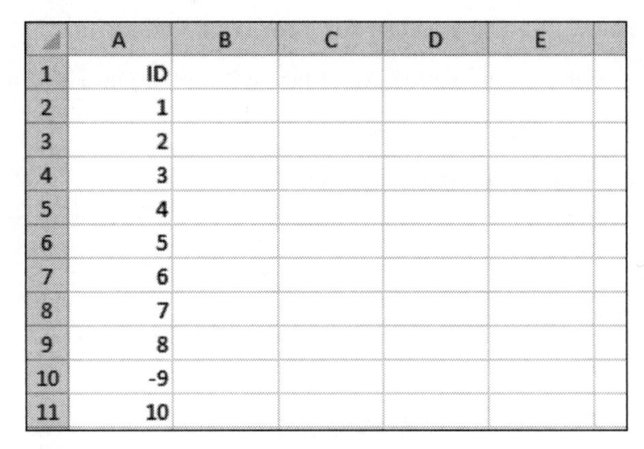

	A	B	C	D	E
1	ID				
2	1				
3	2				
4	3				
5	4				
6	5				
7	6				
8	7				
9	8				
10	-9				
11	10				

We want to restrict the values in cells A2 to A11 to numbers between 1 and 10.

To do this:

- Select cells A2 to A11,
- Select **Data Validation**, **Settings**
- And set as follows:

  Allow: **whole number**

  Data: **Between**

  Minimum: **0**

  Maximum: **10**

  As shown in the image below.

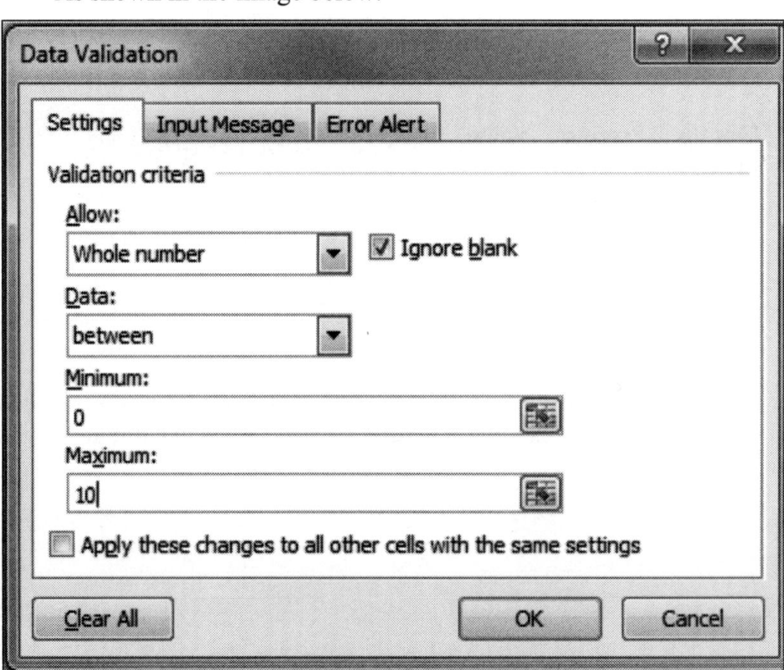

Note: although we now have data validation on these cells, invalid values are not automatically highlighted.

To identify any invalid values:

Select **Data Validation, Circle Invalid Values**

And as shown below, the -9 value is highlighted.

	A	B	C	D	E
1	ID				
2	1				
3	2				
4	3				
5	4				
6	5				
7	6				
8	7				
9	8				
10	-9				
11	10				

To remove the red validation circles:

Select **Data Validation, Clear Validation Circles**

a note on copying data validation

Once you have formatted a cell with data validation, if you want to apply that same validation to another cell or cells, you can use normal Copy and Paste facilities and the data validation will apply to the cells where you paste.

Chapter Summary

In this chapter we have covered the following spreadsheet concepts and techniques:

- cell display – using borders, fill colours
- moving rows and columns
- hiding rows and columns
- cell and sheet protection
- conditional formatting
- data validation

You should now carry out some or all of the exercises on the next few pages in order to practise and reinforce your learning.

Here are a group of exercises to allow you to practise the topics covered in this chapter. They can be done individually, or as a sequence, working your way through them.

If you choose to work your way through them, you may not need to open the exercise workbook as suggested at the start of each exercise, as it may already be open.

The saving at the end of each exercise is also optional, although it serves as a reminder to regularly save your work. You can also save to different file names and may choose to keep using the same name to avoid having lots of files.

Exercise 1

Spreadsheet skills:

- Format cells - borders

All borders should be a thin solid black border unless otherwise specified.

1. Open workbook T3Exercises
2. Select worksheet Exercise 1
3. Format cells C2 to C4 with a border all the way round each cell
4. Apply borders to cells B7 to D20 to create the layout shown below
5. Apply a double line border to the bottom of cells C5 and D5
6. Save your spreadsheet with the name: Chapter3_ Exercise1

Your spreadsheet should appear as shown in the screen below:

	A	B	C	D
1		**Client work log**		
2		Name		
3		Department		
4		Month		
5			Total	
6				
7		Date	Client	Hours
8				
9				
10				
11				
12				
13				
14				
15				
16				
17				
18				
19				
20				

Exercise 2

Spreadsheet skills:

- Format cells - cell fill with colour and shading

1. Open workbook T3Exercises
2. Select worksheet Exercise 2
3. Fill cells C3 to C5 with a light grey
4. Fill cells B8 to D20 with pattern colour grey, and pattern style dots.
5. Save your spreadsheet with the name: Chapter3_Exercise2

Your spreadsheet should appear as shown in the screen below:

	A	B	C	D
1		**Client work log**		
2		Name		
3		Department		
4		Month		
5			Total	
6				
7		Date	Client	Hours
8				
9				
10				
11				
12				
13				
14				
15				
16				
17				
18				
19				
20				

Exercise 3

Spreadsheet skills:

- Format cells – protection (lock and unlock cells)
- Protect your worksheet

1. Open workbook T3Exercises
2. Select worksheet Exercise 3
3. Lock all cells A1 to D20
4. Unlock cells C2, C3, C4, all cells B8 to D20 inclusive
5. Protect the sheet with password ex3
6. Enter My Name for Name (C2)

You should not receive a warning message.

7. Try and change cell C5, Total to Total hours

If you have locked cells as decribed above, you should see the warning message shown below:

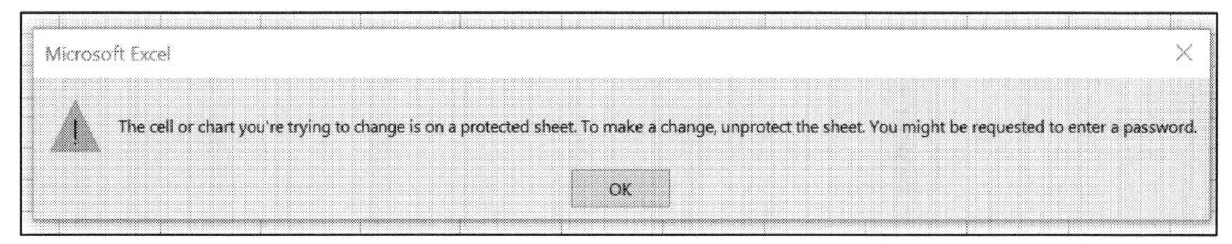

8. Unprotect the sheet, and change cell C5, Total to Total Hours
9. Protect the sheet with password ex3
10. Save your spreadsheet with the name: Chapter3_Exercise3

Exercise 4

Spreadsheet skills:

- Move rows and columns

1. Open workbook T3Exercises
2. Select worksheet Exercise 4
3. Move the Totals column to the column after June
4. Move the Totals row to between the month headings (row 3) and the Insurance row (row 4)
5. Save your spreadsheet with the name: Chapter3_Exercise4

	A	B	C	D	E	F	G	H
1	Expenditure Forecast							
2								
3		January	February	March	April	May	June	**Totals**
4	**Totals**	**£84,922**	**£85,780**	**£83,865**	**£93,670**	**£93,865**	**£96,040**	**£538,142**
5	Insurance	£1,000	£500	£0	£0	£0	£500	**£2,000**
6	Rent	£3,500	£3,500	£3,500	£3,500	£3,500	£3,500	**£21,000**
7	Accountancy	£270	£0	£270	£0	£270	£0	**£810**
8	Advertising	£0	£1,500	£0	£0	£0	£1,800	**£3,300**
9	Postage	£95	£190	£95	£80	£95	£150	**£705**
10	Salaries	£80,000	£80,000	£80,000	£90,000	£90,000	£90,000	**£510,000**
11	Stationery	£57	£90	£0	£90	£0	£90	**£327**

Exercise 5

Spreadsheet skills:

- Hide and unhide rows and columns

1. Open workbook T3Exercises
2. Select worksheet Exercise 5
3. Unhide column G
4. Hide the Totals row (row 4)
5. Save your spreadsheet with the name: Chapter3_Exercise5

	A	B	C	D	E	F	G	H
1	Expenditure Forecast							
2								
3		January	February	March	April	May	June	**Totals**
5	Insurance	£1,000	£500	£0	£0	£0	£500	**£2,000**
6	Rent	£3,500	£3,500	£3,500	£3,500	£3,500	£3,500	**£21,000**
7	Accountancy	£270	£0	£270	£0	£270	£0	**£810**
8	Advertising	£0	£1,500	£0	£0	£0	£1,800	**£3,300**
9	Postage	£95	£190	£95	£80	£95	£150	**£705**
10	Salaries	£80,000	£80,000	£80,000	£90,000	£90,000	£90,000	**£510,000**
11	Stationery	£57	£90	£0	£90	£0	£90	**£327**

Exercise 6

Spreadsheet skills:

- Format cells - wrap text

1. Open workbook T3Exercises
2. Select worksheet Exercise 6
3. Wrap all text on row 3
4. Save your spreadsheet with the name: Chapter3_Exercise6

	A	B	C	D	E	F
1	Inventory report					
2						
3	Product code	Inventory quantity	Cost	Total cost	Re-order level	Inventory v Re-order
4	ab1	967	£2.50	£2,416	174	793
5	ab2	946	£3.25	£3,074	286	660
6	ab3	458	£0.99	£453	677	-219
7	ab4	149	£0.45	£67	32	117
8	ab8	73	£3.29	£241	454	-381
9	ab10	663	£2.25	£1,492	177	486
10	ab11	890	£1.35	£1,201	790	100
11	bb4	7	£0.45	£3	961	-954
12	bb8	825	£3.29	£2,715	650	176
13	bb10	236	£2.25	£530	31	204
14	bb11	562	£1.35	£758	782	-221

Exercise 7

Spreadsheet skills:

- Format cells - cell orientation

1. Open workbook T3Exercises
2. Select worksheet Exercise 7
3. Change the orientation of cells A2 to A13 to 90 degrees, center text vertically
4. Save your spreadsheet with the name: Chapter3_Exercise7

	A	B	C
1	Year	Month	
2	2021-2022	Jan	
3		Feb	
4		Mar	
5		Apr	
6		May	
7		Jun	
8		Jul	
9		Aug	
10		Sep	
11		Oct	
12		Nov	
13		Dec	

Exercise 8

Spreadsheet skills:

- Format cells - justify text

1. Open workbook T3Exercises
2. Select worksheet Exercise 8
3. Change the text alignment of cell B3 to justify
4. Save your spreadsheet with the name: Chapter3_Exercise8

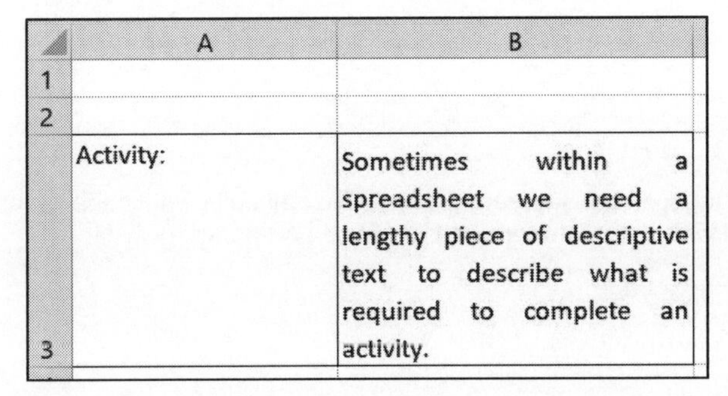

	A	B
1		
2		
3	Activity:	Sometimes within a spreadsheet we need a lengthy piece of descriptive text to describe what is required to complete an activity.

Exercise 9

Spreadsheet skills:

- Format cells - shrink to fit

1. Open workbook T3Exercises
2. Select worksheet Exercise 9
3. Change the text alignment of cell B3 to shrink to fit
4. Save your spreadsheet with the name: Chapter3_Exercise9

	A	B
1		
2		
3	Activity:	Sometimes within a spreadsheet we need a lengthy piece of descriptive text to describe what is required to complete an activity.
4		

Exercise 10

Spreadsheet skills:

- Format cells - conditional (advanced) formatting

1. Open workbook T3Exercises
2. Select worksheet Exercise 10
3. Apply conditional formatting (Highlight cell rules) to column F, so that all cells where the number is negative (less than 0) are displayed with a custom format, black text and a dark grey fill

   The first few rows are shown on the next page:

	A	B	C	D	E	F
1	Inventory report					
2						
3	Product code	Inventory quantity	Cost	Total cost	Re-order level	Inventory v Re-order
4	ab1	967	£2.50	£2,416	174	793
5	ab2	946	£3.25	£3,074	286	660
6	ab3	458	£0.99	£453	677	-219
7	ab4	149	£0.45	£67	32	117
8	ab8	73	£3.29	£241	454	-381
9	ab10	663	£2.25	£1,492	177	486
10	ab11	890	£1.35	£1,201	790	100
11	bb4	7	£0.45	£3	961	-954
12	bb8	825	£3.29	£2,715	650	176
13	bb10	236	£2.25	£530	31	204
14	bb11	562	£1.35	£758	782	-221

4. In the Total cost column (column D), using conditional formatting, highlight the top 10 Total cost values, display with a custom format, black border, fill with background colour light grey and pattern style dots

	A	B	C	D	E	F
1	Inventory report					
2						
3	Product code	Inventory quantity	Cost	Total cost	Re-order level	Inventory v Re-order
4	ab1	967	£2.50	£2,416	174	793
5	ab2	946	£3.25	£3,074	286	660
6	ab3	458	£0.99	£453	677	-219
7	ab4	149	£0.45	£67	32	117
8	ab8	73	£3.29	£241	454	-381
9	ab10	663	£2.25	£1,492	177	486
10	ab11	890	£1.35	£1,201	790	100
11	bb4	7	£0.45	£3	961	-954
12	bb8	825	£3.29	£2,715	650	176
13	bb10	236	£2.25	£530	31	204
14	bb11	562	£1.35	£758	782	-221

5. In the Cost column (column C), identify our five lowest cost items using conditional formatting, highlight the lowest 10 priced item values, display with a custom format, italic font, and a light grey fill

6. Save your spreadsheet with the name: Chapter3_Exercise10

	A	B	C	D	E	F
1	Inventory report					
2						
3	Product code	Inventory quantity	Cost	Total cost	Re-order level	Inventory v Re-order
4	ab1	967	£2.50	£2,416	174	793
5	ab2	946	£3.25	£3,074	286	660
6	ab3	458	£0.99	£453	677	-219
7	ab4	149	£0.45	£67	32	117
8	ab8	73	£3.29	£241	454	-381
9	ab10	663	£2.25	£1,492	177	486
10	ab11	890	£1.35	£1,201	790	100
11	bb4	7	£0.45	£3	961	-954
12	bb8	825	£3.29	£2,715	650	176
13	bb10	236	£2.25	£530	31	204
14	bb11	562	£1.35	£758	782	-221
15	cb4	456	£0.45	£205	289	166

The conditional formatting rules are shown below:

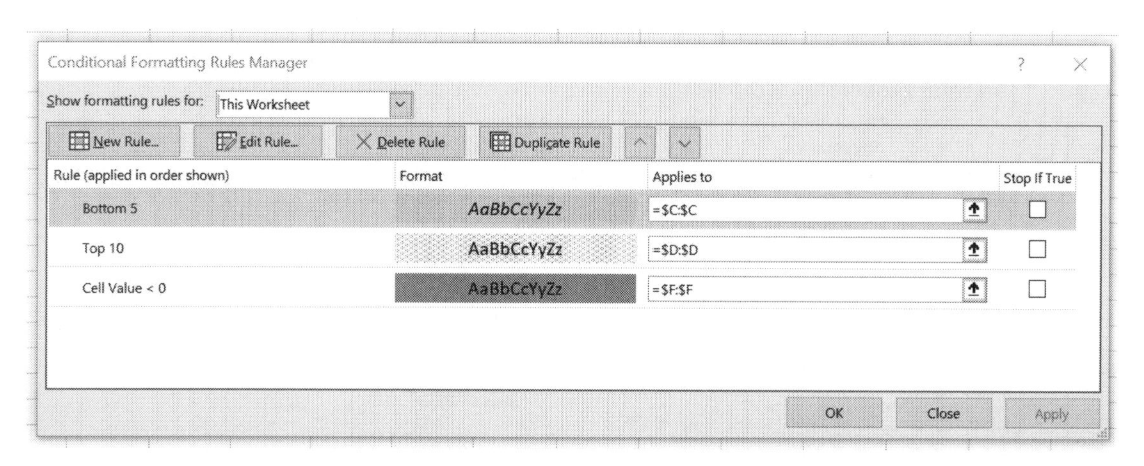

Exercise 11

> Spreadsheet skills:
> - Data validation

1. Open workbook T3Exercises
2. Select worksheet Exercise 11
3. In cell C4, to allow the user to pick the name of the month from a list of three character month names, ie Jan, Feb, Mar, and so on for the whole year, displayed in calendar order

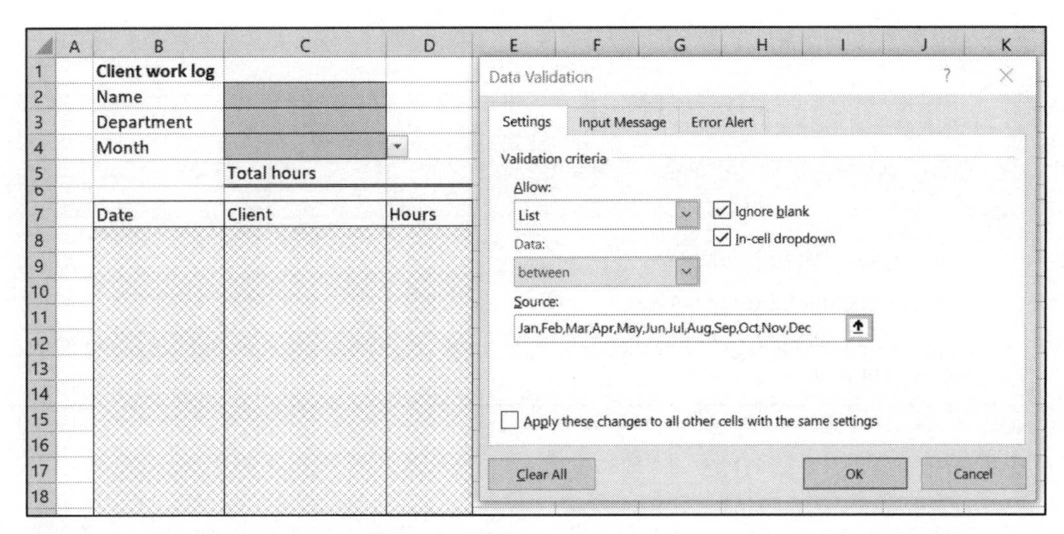

4. Check what happens when you click on cell C4

   Cell C3 should allow the user to choose the Department, either Support or Consultancy and not be left blank

5. Enter the text Support in cell E3 and Consultancy in F3
6. For cell C3, set the Data validation to List, and for the source, highlight cells E3 and F3

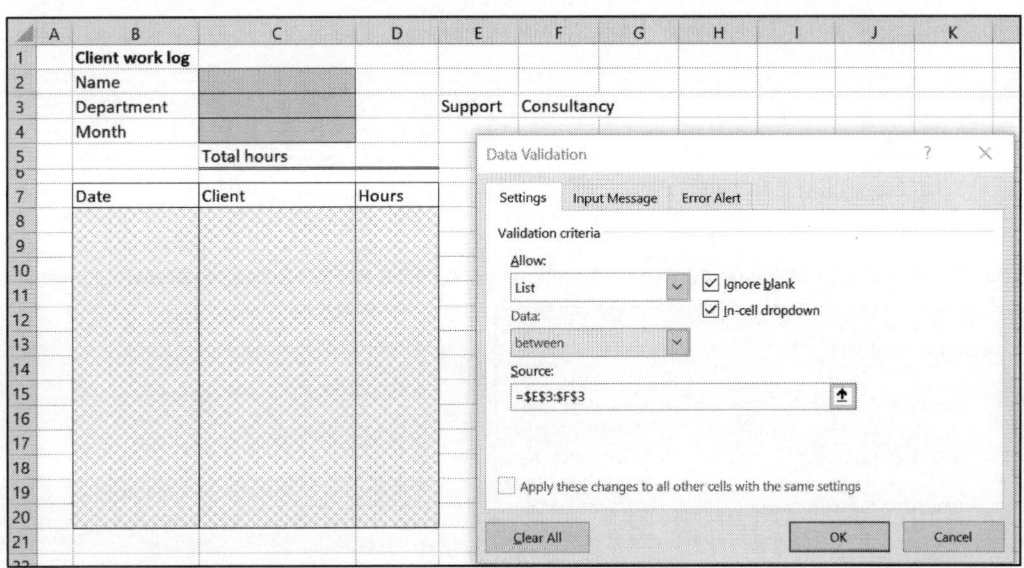

7. Check what happens when you click on cell C3
8. Save your spreadsheet with the name: Chapter3_Exercise11

Exercise 12

Spreadsheet skills:

- Data validation for values already entered

1. Open workbook T3Exercises
2. Select worksheet Exercise 12
3. Apply Data Validation to the Invoice Dates, to allow only Dates between 1st April, and 30th April of the current year

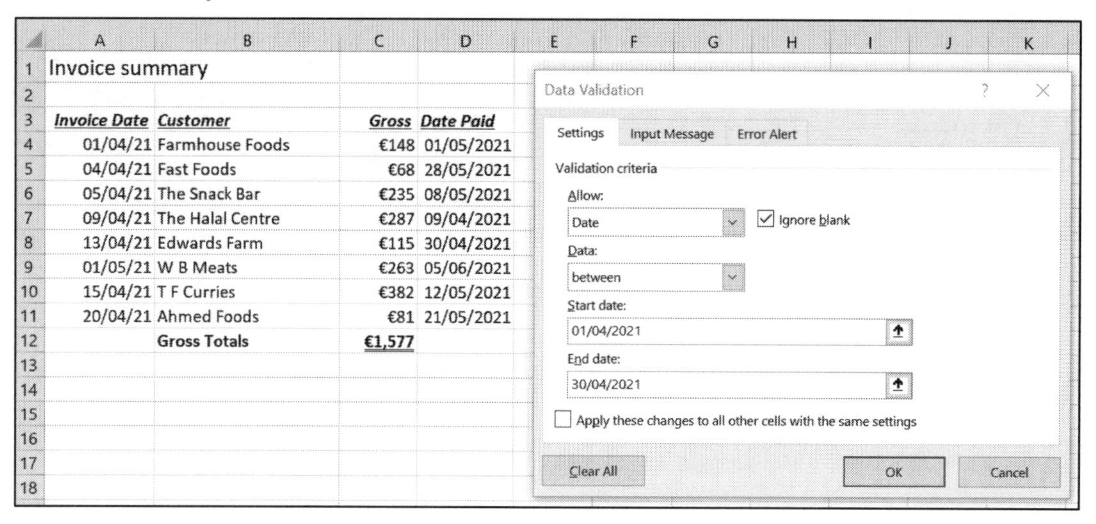

	A	B	C	D
1	Invoice summary			
2				
3	***Invoice Date***	***Customer***	***Gross***	***Date Paid***
4	01/04/21	Farmhouse Foods	€148	01/05/2021
5	04/04/21	Fast Foods	€68	28/05/2021
6	05/04/21	The Snack Bar	€235	08/05/2021
7	09/04/21	The Halal Centre	€287	09/04/2021
8	13/04/21	Edwards Farm	€115	30/04/2021
9	01/05/21	W B Meats	€263	05/06/2021
10	15/04/21	T F Curries	€382	12/05/2021
11	20/04/21	Ahmed Foods	€81	21/05/2021
12		**Gross Totals**	**€1,577**	

4. Now select Circle Invalid Data

You should see the invoice dated 01/05/21 circled, since this is a May invoice, as shown below:

	A	B	C	D
1	Invoice summary			
2				
3	***Invoice Date***	***Customer***	***Gross***	***Date Paid***
4	01/04/21	Farmhouse Foods	€148	01/05/2021
5	04/04/21	Fast Foods	€68	28/05/2021
6	05/04/21	The Snack Bar	€235	08/05/2021
7	09/04/21	The Halal Centre	€287	09/04/2021
8	13/04/21	Edwards Farm	€115	30/04/2021
9	01/05/21	W B Meats	€263	05/06/2021
10	15/04/21	T F Curries	€382	12/05/2021
11	20/04/21	Ahmed Foods	€81	21/05/2021
12		**Gross Totals**	**€1,577**	

4 Spreadsheet functions

this chapter covers...

This chapter covers the creation of formulas, and shows how you can make use of some of the built-in calculation facilities provided by spreadsheet software. It explains and takes you through the concepts and techniques listed below. By the time you have finished this chapter and carried out the exercises which follow, you should be able to produce spreadsheets which perform a variety of calculations. The concepts and techniques covered are:

- *formulas*
- *mathematical operators*
- *functions*
- *ranges*
- *mathematical functions*
- *cell addressing*
- *date functions*
- *logical functions and operators*
- *lookup functions*
- *circular references in formulas*

Note that the step-by-step instructions given in this chapter are based on the Microsoft® Excel model, but the concepts and techniques described relate to all spreadsheet packages.

FORMULAS

As we have seen in previous chapters, whenever we wish to carry out a calculation or enter a formula into a cell within our spreadsheet, we move to the cell where we want the formula to appear and start by entering an equals sign =.

The formula can take a simple form, containing just numbers, or a mixture of numbers and cell references, or as we have seen earlier, a function and cell references.

Examples of formulas include:

=3+2

=D6–1.15

=D6*D7

=D32

Note that as we create the formula, any spaces we insert within the formula are automatically ignored.

One of the most significant points about formulas, which has already been mentioned, is that when we copy a formula from one cell to another cell or group of cells, the row and column numbers automatically change as appropriate. they will automatically relate to the row or column references of the new cell to which the formula has been copied.

MATHEMATICAL OPERATORS

The common mathematical operators which we will use in our formulas are as follows:

- Addition: +
- Subtraction: –
- Multiplication: *
- Division: /

We also make use of brackets: ( )

As with our normal mathematics there is an **order** that will be followed when a formula is interpreted, known as the **operator precedence**.

The order of calculations within any formula is as follows:

- any calculation contained in brackets is done first
- division and multiplication come next and are ranked the same
- addition and subtraction come last and are ranked the same

So, if we want to group parts of our calculation to ensure that certain parts are calculated before a subsequent part, then we would use brackets.

For example:

= (B3 + 5)/100

Here 5 is added to B3 and the result is divided by 100.

This gives a different result to:

= B3+5/100

Here 5 is divided by 100 and the result is added to B3

As you can see brackets play a very important part in our construction of formulas.

FUNCTIONS – AN EXPLANATION

Spreadsheet packages contain built-in formulas called **Functions** that make it easy to perform common calculations on data. For example, **=SUM( )** is a function which can be used to add up values, as we have seen in the earlier chapters of this book.

Most functions are designed to accept data which is then used in the calculations. This data is entered within the round brackets which follow the function's name.

For example, **=SUM(A1,A2,A3)** is a formula which uses the SUM function to add up the values of the three cells.

These values are also known as **arguments**.

As you can see, each argument (or value) is usually separated from the previous argument (value) by a comma.

The **type** of argument will vary from function to function: it could be a number, or a cell reference, or group of cells.

The **number** of arguments may also vary from function to function.

The most common forms of argument are a cell reference, or group of cell references, as we shall see in the examples which follow. Look at cell A1 in the screen at the top of the next page.

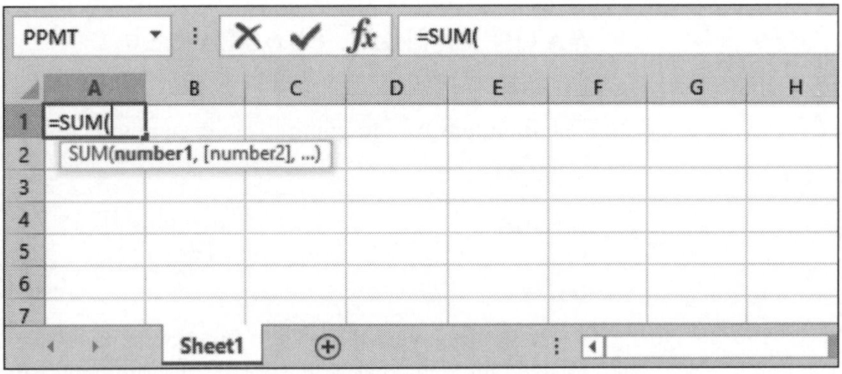

As you can see in this screen, the SUM function is prompting the user to enter the first argument or number to be added. This could be a cell reference or an actual number.

If an argument is **optional** (ie you don't have to enter it) you will see the argument in square brackets, for example [number2], as shown above.

The result which a function creates is said to be the value **returned** by the function, and is known as the **return value**.

RANGES

A range is a **group or block of cells in a worksheet**. It is essentially a shorthand way of specifying the first and last cell and automatically including all the cells in-between.

A range is identified by the cell reference of the first cell (upper left cell), followed by a colon, then the cell reference of the last cell (bottom right).

Examples of a range of cells include:

D4:D11 – all the cells are in the same column

C4:F4 – all the cells are in the same row

D4:F10 – a block of cells across several rows and columns

A range of cells as described above can be used as an argument within a function, for example =SUM(D4:D11).

MATHEMATICAL FUNCTIONS

The functions we are going to cover in this section are as follows:

- SUM
- ABS

SUM

We have already used the SUM function in this book. The SUM function adds all the numbers that you specify as arguments. Each argument can be a number, a cell reference, a range of cells, or the result of another function:

=SUM(number1, [number2], [number3],...)

The SUM function has these arguments:

- **number1 is required**
- **number2, number3, etc. are optional**

You can specify up to a total of 255 arguments (values) to be added together. For example:

=SUM(C2,C16,C20)

This would return the sum of the numbers in the cells C2, C16, and C20.

The screen illustrated on the next page adds the values for the 'odd' numbered weeks for Smiths Ltd, using =SUM(B4, D4, F4), producing a total value of 45.

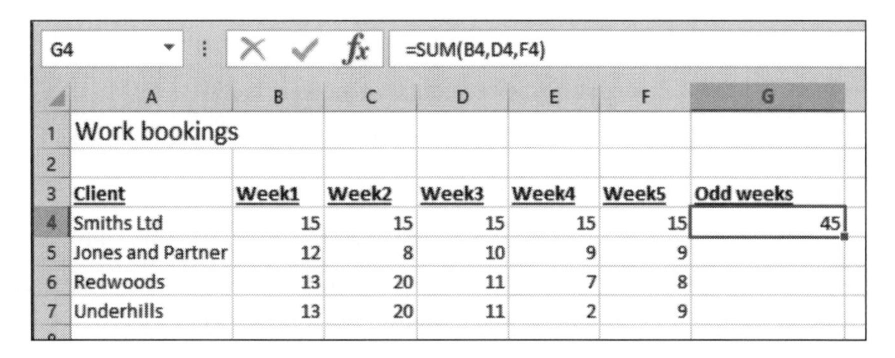

G4 =SUM(B4,D4,F4)

	A	B	C	D	E	F	G
1	Work bookings						
2							
3	Client	Week1	Week2	Week3	Week4	Week5	Odd weeks
4	Smiths Ltd	15	15	15	15	15	45
5	Jones and Partner	12	8	10	9	9	
6	Redwoods	13	20	11	7	8	
7	Underhills	13	20	11	2	9	

When we are positioned on a cell containing a formula, if we click on the formula in the formula bar, all cells used in that formula are highlighted, as can be seen on the next page.

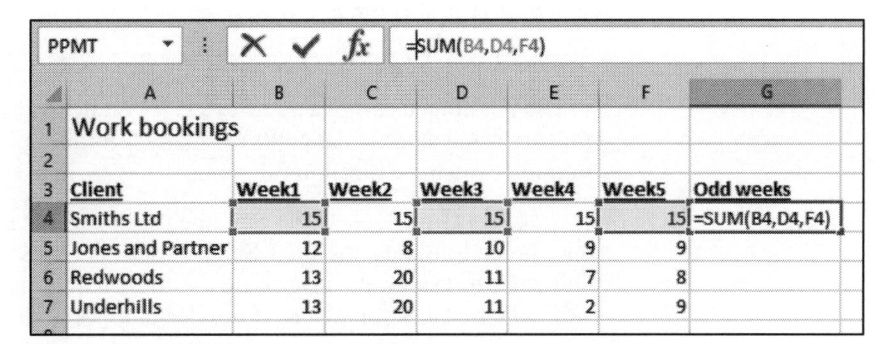

PPMT | =SUM(B4,D4,F4)

	A	B	C	D	E	F	G
1	Work bookings						
2							
3	Client	Week1	Week2	Week3	Week4	Week5	Odd weeks
4	Smiths Ltd	15	15	15	15	15	=SUM(B4,D4,F4)
5	Jones and Partner	12	8	10	9	9	
6	Redwoods	13	20	11	7	8	
7	Underhills	13	20	11	2	9	

SUM is most often used for a **range of cells**, for example:

=SUM(C2:C16)

This would return the sum of all the numbers in the range C2 to C16, ie cells C2,C3,C4,C5, etc. all the way to C16.

The screen illustrated below uses the formula =SUM(B4:F4,50) to total all five weeks for Smiths Ltd and add a value of 50. This produces a total of 125.

G4 | =SUM(B4:F4,50)

	A	B	C	D	E	F	G
1	Work bookings						
2							
3	Client	Week1	Week2	Week3	Week4	Week5	Forecast
4	Smiths Ltd	15	15	15	15	15	125
5	Jones and Partner	12	8	10	9	9	
6	Redwoods	13	20	11	7	8	
7	Underhills	13	20	11	2	9	

ABS

The ABS function 'returns' the **absolute value** of a number, which is the value of a number without its sign:

=ABS(number)

The ABS function has just one argument:

- **a number is required**

  For example:

  =ABS(-2) means that the number's sign will be removed and will return the value 2

  =ABS(2) will also return the value 2

There are many other mathematical functions available including AVERAGE, MIN, MAX, some of which are covered later in the book.

MORE ON RANGES

It is also possible to assign a name to a cell or range of cells, this can be useful if you are using a particular cell(s) in many formulas, or to give clarity within a formula by using a meaningful name.

For example, if we look at the Statement of Profit or Loss below, we could name the cell holding the total Sales values as **Sales** and the Cost of sales value as **CostofSales**, then we could use these names in the formula for Gross profit, which makes for an easy-to-understand formula.

Sales | fx =SUM(D8:D10)

	A	B	C	D	E	F
2						
3			**Statement of profit or loss**			
4			for the year ended 31 March 2021			
5						
6			£	£		
7	**Sales revenue**					
8	Software			251,783		
9	Hardware			161,723		
10	Consultancy			55,276		
11				468,782		
12						
13	Cost of Sales			120,156		
14						
15	**Gross Profit**			348,626		

We have named cell D11 Sales, and now whenever we select it, the name sales is displayed in the name box.

Similarly in the image on the next page, we have named cell D13, as CostofSales.

CostofSales | fx 120156

	A	B	C	D	E	F
2						
3			**Statement of profit or loss**			
4			for the year ended 31 March 2021			
5						
6			£	£		
7	**Sales revenue**					
8	Software			251,783		
9	Hardware			161,723		
10	Consultancy			55,276		
11				468,782		
12						
13	Cost of Sales			120,156		
14						
15	**Gross Profit**			348,626		

We can now enter a formula in D15 just using these names, as shown below:

D15 | fx =Sales-CostofSales

	A	B	C	D	E	F
2						
3			**Statement of profit or loss**			
4			for the year ended 31 March 2021			
5						
6			£	£		
7	**Sales revenue**					
8	Software			251,783		
9	Hardware			161,723		
10	Consultancy			55,276		
11				468,782		
12						
13	Cost of Sales			120,156		
14						
15	**Gross Profit**			348,626		

Alternatively, as mentioned we could name a group of cells, as illustrated on the next page, where we have named D8 through to D10 as SalesValues.

SalesValues		fx	251783		
A	**B**	**C**	**D**	**E**	**F**
2					
3		Statement of profit or loss			
4		for the year ended 31 March 2021			
5					
6		£	£		
7 Sales revenue					
8 Software			251,783		
9 Hardware			161,723		
10 Consultancy			55,276		
11			468,782		
12					
13 Cost of Sales			120,156		
14					
15 Gross Profit			348,626		

We could then make use of this name in the formula in cell D11 for the total sales, as shown below:

Sales		fx	=SUM(SalesValues)		
A	**B**	**C**	**D**	**E**	**F**
5					
6		£	£		
7 Sales revenue					
8 Software			251,783		
9 Hardware			161,723		
10 Consultancy			55,276		
11			468,782		
12					
13 Cost of Sales			120,156		
14					
15 Gross Profit			348,626		

To assign a name to a range of cell(s):

- select the required cells

either

- click in the name box
- enter the required name

or

- select the **Formulas** menu
- select **Define Name**
- enter the name we want to use to refer to this range of cells

Note: names should not contain spaces

As shown in the image on the next page, we are about to define a name for cell D8. To make any changes to Names which we have defined, use the **Name Manager** option, found within the **Formulas** menu.

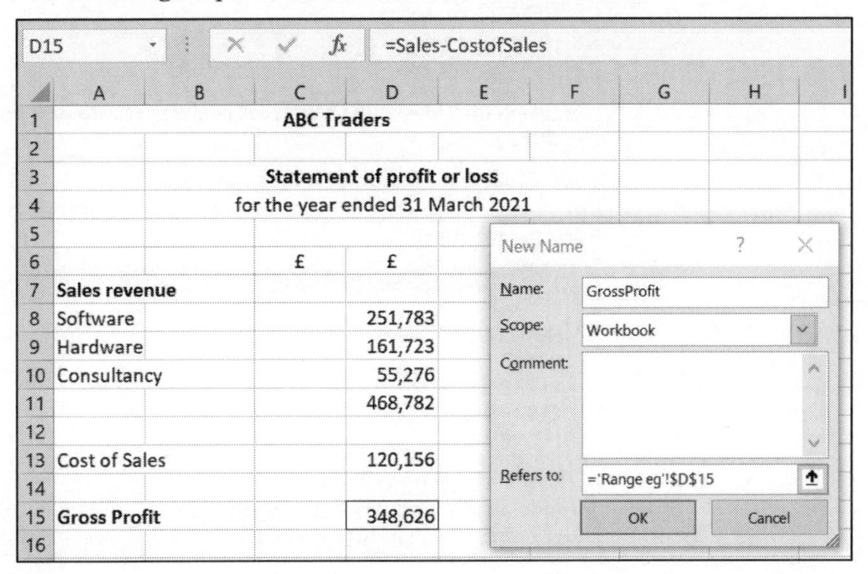

	A	B	C	D
1			ABC Traders	
2				
3			Statement of profit or loss	
4			for the year ended 31 March 2021	
5				
6			£	£
7	**Sales revenue**			
8	Software			251,783
9	Hardware			161,723
10	Consultancy			55,276
11				468,782
12				
13	Cost of Sales			120,156
14				
15	**Gross Profit**			348,626
16				

FUNCTION WIZARD

Within Excel®, there is a function wizard which helps us to use any functions. It is found in the **Formulas** menu, Insert function, and also the fx symbol displayed just above the spreadsheet columns.

	A	B	C	D	E	F	G
1		**Monthly Sales Value**					
2							
3	**Customer Name**	**Month1**	**Month2**	**Month3**	**Month4**	**Month5**	**Month6**
4	*Farmhouse Foods*		£112				£26
5	*Engineering Services*					£67	
6	*Another Food Service*				£58	£116	
7	*Top Quality Supplies*		£56				
8	*Halal Foods*						
9	*Edwards Farm*					£40	
10	*Allen and co*	£45	£68	£231	£0	£331	£37
11	*Ahmed and son*						
12	*Green & Sons Wholesalers*	£700		£104			
13	*Higginbottom and son*						
14	*W B Meats*		£45				
15	*The Halal Centre*			£50			£0
16							

If in our spreadsheet, we select a cell, say cell C16, and then select **Insert function** we get the following:

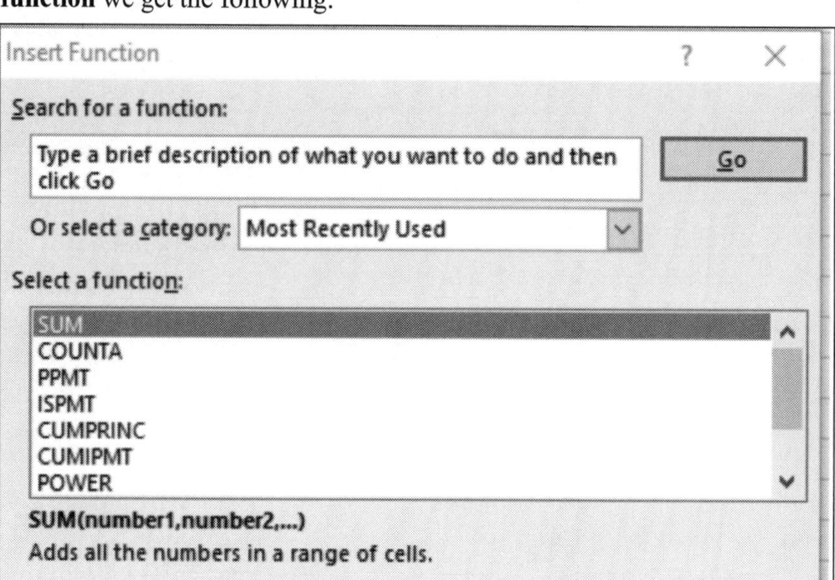

Let's assume we want to total some values, we will select the SUM function from the list offered. (If the function we want to use is not listed, we can just type the name or a description in the SEARCH for box.)

We can now enter the function arguments, (it is possible that some cell references are automatically inserted as the tool tries to guess which cells we want to add up), as shown below:

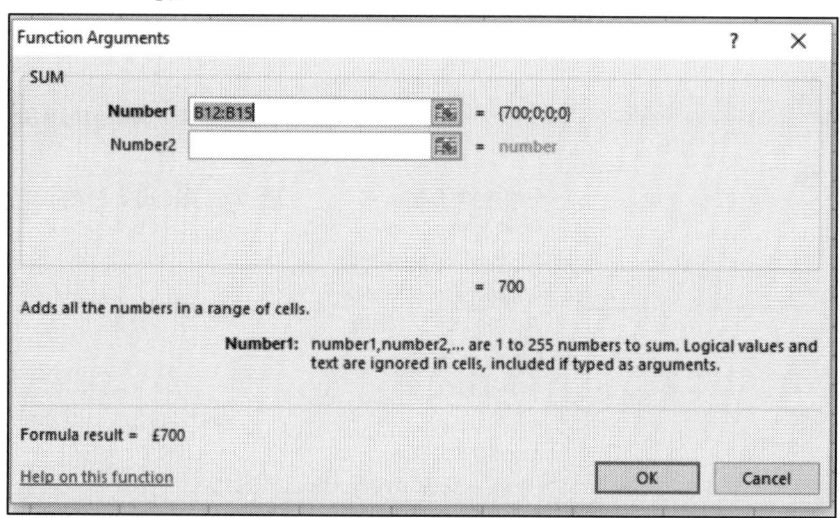

This isn't what we want, so make sure the entry in box Number1 is highlighted and then drag the cursor to select the cells we want to sum, eg B4 to B15.

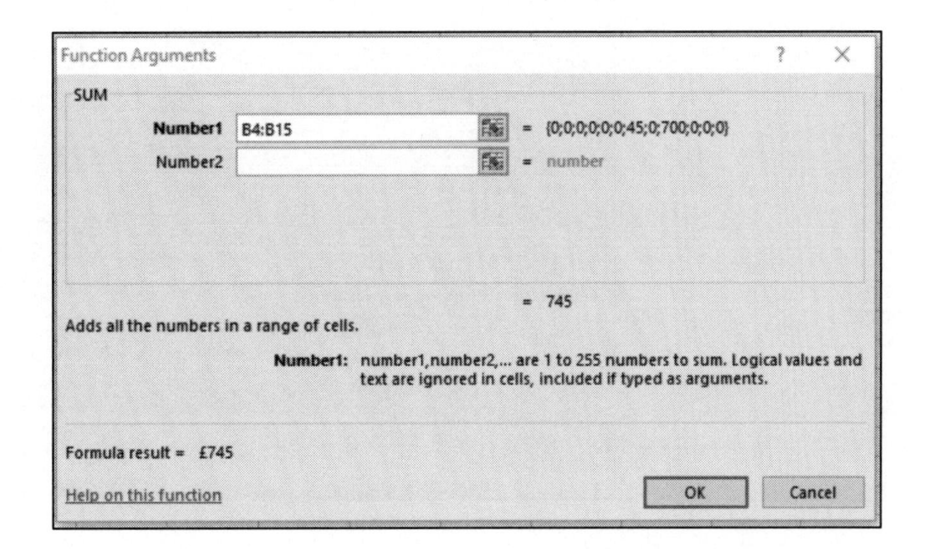

This is what we want, so click OK and the formula will be inserted.

If we already have a formula which we wish to edit, select the cell containing the formula, click **Insert Function** and make your changes.

To add the contents of an entire column:

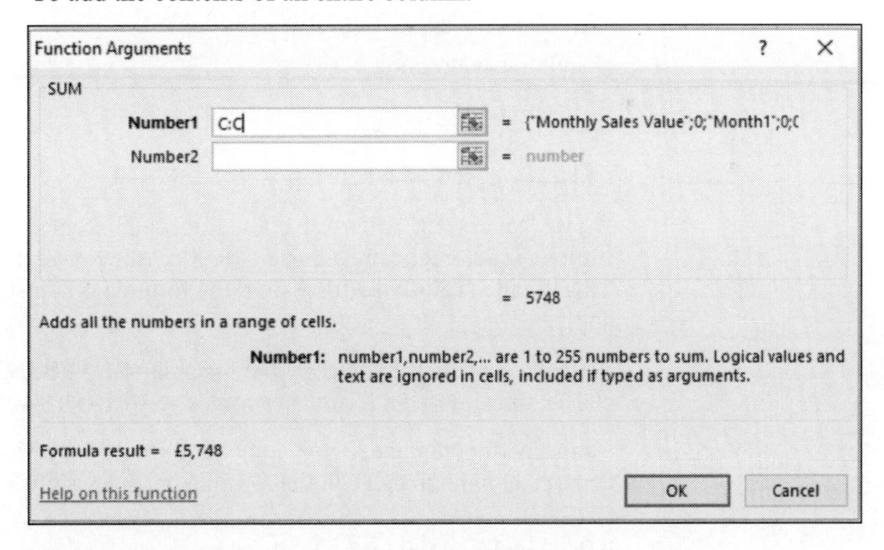

To include all the values in row 4, would be 4:4.

If we had named cells B4 to B15 as a range **Month1**, we could easily insert this into the formula by selecting **Use in Formula** from the **Formulas** menu and selecting Month1 from the list of defined ranges.

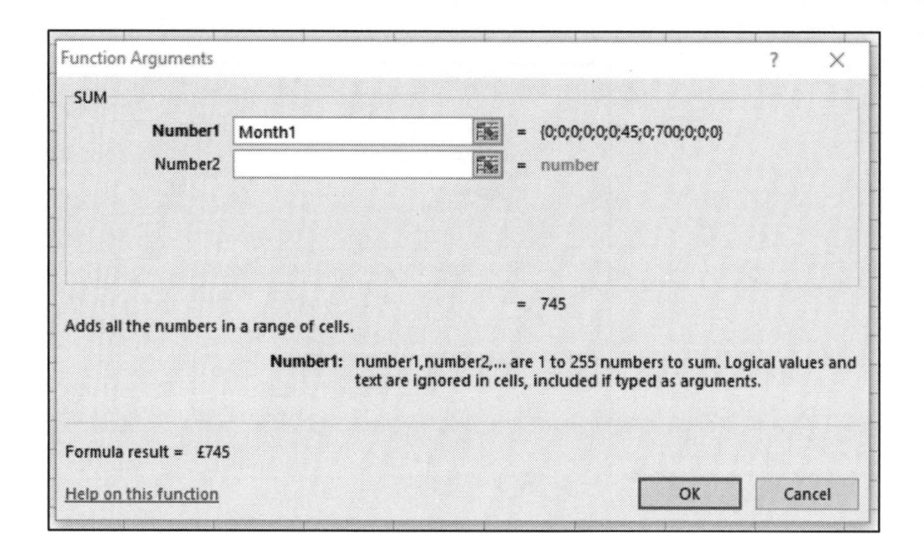

CELL ADDRESSING

The way in which a cell is referenced is known as its address, for example A12, B49. This becomes important when we are using formulas. We have two ways of referencing cells within formulas:

- relative addressing
- absolute addressing

relative addressing

As we have seen, when we copy a formula from one cell to another, the formula is automatically adjusted to reflect the row or column of the new cell. This is called **relative addressing**: the formula is adjusted relative to the new cell.

We have seen that if you copy the formula **=SUM(B3:E3)** down a row from cell F3 to cell F4, the formula becomes **=SUM(B4:E4)**.

Similarly, for columns, if you copy the formula **=SUM(B4:B8)** from cell B9 across a column to cell C9, the formula becomes = **SUM(C4:C8)**.

absolute addressing

Sometimes we do not want the cell reference to change as we copy a formula – we want to keep a reference to an original cell or cells. To do this we use the **dollar sign: $.**

For example, $B$3 would refer to cell B3, and, when placed in a formula and copied, the copies would all also refer to B3.

In the example below we have entered an hourly rate in cell B3, which we wish to apply to all the totals. We have created a formula in cell G6 to give us a monetary value for the work carried out for the client using the formula:

=F6*B3

MINUTE | fx =F6*B3

	A	B	C	D	E	F	G
1	Work bookings						
2							
3	Hourly rate	£30					
4							
5	Client	Week1	Week2	Week3	Week4	Total	Value
6	Smiths Ltd	15	15	15	15	60	=F6*B3
7	Jones and Partner	12	8	10	9	39	
8	Redwoods	13	20	11	7	51	
9	Underhills	13	20	11	2	46	

We will now change the formula to =F6*$B$3 so that we can copy it and still keep the reference to B3, the cell where the hourly rate of £30 is entered.

MINUTE | fx =F6*$B$3

	A	B	C	D	E	F	G
1	Work bookings						
2							
3	Hourly rate	£30					
4							
5	Client	Week1	Week2	Week3	Week4	Total	Value
6	Smiths Ltd	15	15	15	15	60	=F6*$B$3
7	Jones and Partner	12	8	10	9	39	
8	Redwoods	13	20	11	7	51	
9	Underhills	13	20	11	2	46	

When the formula =F6*$B$3 is then copied to cell G7, you can see on the screen image on the next page that the cell reference has not changed, but remains B3. If the hourly rate changes from £30 to £35, then all you need to do is amend the amount entered in cell B3.

G7 =F7*$B$3

	A	B	C	D	E	F	G
1	Work bookings						
2							
3	Hourly rate	£30					
4							
5	Client	Week1	Week2	Week3	Week4	Total	Value
6	Smiths Ltd	15	15	15	15	60	£1,800
7	Jones and Partner	12	8	10	9	39	£1,170
8	Redwoods	13	20	11	7	51	
9	Underhills	13	20	11	2	46	

Absolute cell addressing is a very important part of creating formulas within spreadsheets, and is covered further in chapter 6.

As an alternative, you could name the cell B3 which holds the rate, for example **HrlyRate**, and use this name in your formulas.

To insert an absolute cell reference into a formula, using the same multiplication example, but with an absolute cell reference for B4:

= $B$4 *B5

- in the formula bar enter "="
- click on cell B4
- press the function key F4, and you see B4 becomes $B$4 in the formula bar
- enter "*" for multiply
- click on cell B5
- press enter

If you keep pressing F4, it toggles through the different options ie $B$4, B$4, $B4, B4

DATE FUNCTIONS

We often want to include date information in a spreadsheet, and we may want to perform a calculation on the information. For example, in a purchasing department, we might want a spreadsheet to display the expected interval of time between an order being placed with a supplier and the delivery date of the goods.

To enable date-based calculations, a spreadsheet stores all dates as numbers, based on the number of days from 1/1/1900. This is referred to as a **serial number** representation.

The time element of the date/time is also stored numerically as the decimal part of the serial number, for example the serial number 0.5 represents 12:00 noon.

You can see dates displayed as serial numbers, if you enter a date in a cell and the cell is not formatted as a date.

The functions we are going to cover in this section are as follows: **TODAY**, **NOW** and **DAYS**.

TODAY

The **TODAY** function returns the serial number of today's date based on your computer system clock, it does not include the time. The function is:

=TODAY( )

The TODAY function has no arguments (values).

For example, the formula:

= TODAY( ) +14

This would return the current date plus 14 days.

The =TODAY( ) function is useful if you want to have the current date displayed on a worksheet.

Another use would be if you wished to calculate a person's age as of today and you only had their date of birth.

In the example below, we have placed today's date in cell G1. This will change every time we reopen this workbook.

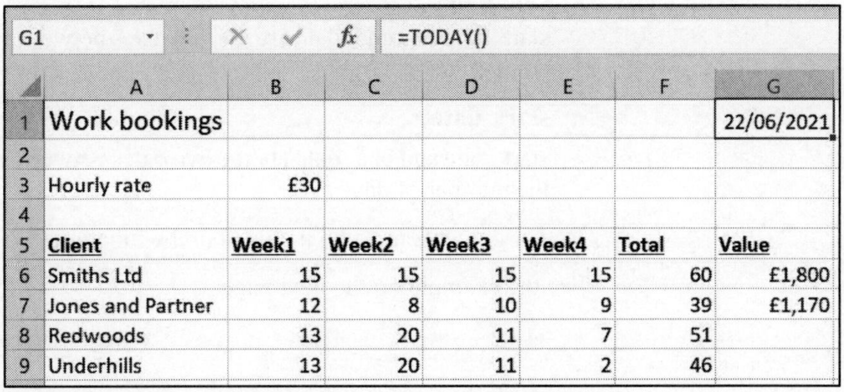

G1 =TODAY()

	A	B	C	D	E	F	G
1	Work bookings						22/06/2021
2							
3	Hourly rate	£30					
4							
5	Client	Week1	Week2	Week3	Week4	Total	Value
6	Smiths Ltd	15	15	15	15	60	£1,800
7	Jones and Partner	12	8	10	9	39	£1,170
8	Redwoods	13	20	11	7	51	
9	Underhills	13	20	11	2	46	

In some instances the result may appear as the serial number. If this happens, change the cell format to be date, as described previously, and it will display correctly.

NOW

The **NOW** function returns the serial number of today's date and the current time based on your computer system clock:

=NOW ( )

The NOW function has no arguments (values).

In the example below, we have used the =NOW( ) function in cell G1, and set the cell format to Custom, with format type dd/mm/yyyy hh:mm.

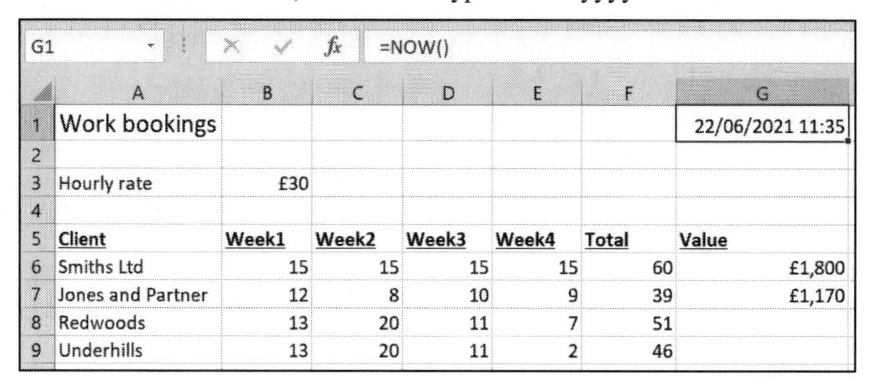

G1 =NOW()

	A	B	C	D	E	F	G
1	Work bookings						22/06/2021 11:35
2							
3	Hourly rate	£30					
4							
5	Client	Week1	Week2	Week3	Week4	Total	Value
6	Smiths Ltd	15	15	15	15	60	£1,800
7	Jones and Partner	12	8	10	9	39	£1,170
8	Redwoods	13	20	11	7	51	
9	Underhills	13	20	11	2	46	

The time will change every time the worksheet recalculates or is reopened.

DAYS

The **DAYS** function returns the number of days between a specified end date and a specified start date

=DAYS(end_date, start_date)

The **DAYS** function has two arguments:

- **end_date**

  start_date and end_date are the two dates between which you want to know the number of days

- **start_date**

  start_date and end_date are the two dates between which you want to know the number of days

Both arguments must be included in the function.

See the example on the next page:

E6 =DAYS(B3,C6)

	A	B	C	D	E
1	Outstanding invoices				
2					
3	Date:	30/06/2021			
4					
5	**Client**	**Invoice date**	**Due date**	**Paid (Y/N)**	**Days overdue**
6	Smiths Ltd	15/04/2021	15/05/2021	N	46
7	Jones and Partner				
8	Redwoods				
9	Underhills				

The Days overdue will update every time the worksheet recalculates or is reopened.

LOGICAL FUNCTIONS AND OPERATORS

A concept used regularly in spreadsheets is **conditional logic**.

This is a concept where if something is true, then something else happens.

For example:

__if__ I do no work __then__ I will not get paid

Within the spreadsheet environment, we often want to test a cell for a certain value, and:

- if it is this value we make one thing happen
- if it is not this value, we want something different to happen

logical operators

We can apply the standard comparison 'operators' to create situations where **conditional logic** can be used. These include:

- equal to (=)
- greater than (>)
- greater than or equal to (>=)
- less than (<)
- less than or equal to(<=)
- not equal to (<>)

For example, a condition could be that cell B10 is greater than 100 which we would express as:

B10>100

The main logical function which is used in spreadsheets is the IF( ) function.

IF

The **IF** function returns one value if the condition you specify evaluates to **TRUE**, and another value if that condition evaluates to **FALSE**.

Looking at the Inventory record example on the next page, if the Balance Quantity is less than 100, we want to reorder, otherwise we don't need to reorder yet.

	A	B	C	D	E	F	G	H	I	J	K
1	Inventory Record		Average cost valuation								
2											
3	Item RT12548										
4											
5	Date		Receipts			Issues			Balance		
6		Quantity	Cost per unit	Total cost	Quantity	Cost per unit	Total cost	Quantity	Cost per unit	Total cost	Low Balance <100
7	02/04/2021	100	3	300				100	3	300	
8	03/04/2021				50	3	150	50	3	150	
9	05/04/2021	100	4.5	450				150	4	600	
10	06/04/2021				100	4	400	50	4	200	
11	21/04/2021	150	4	600				200	4	800	
12											
13	Total	350		750	150		550				

Using the IF function you can use a spreadsheet to work out whether a value is a 'favourable' result, or an 'adverse' result based on your criteria, as we will see in a later example.

The IF function is made up of three parts:

=IF(logical test, value if true, value if false)

These three parts can be explained as follows:

- **logical test**

  This can be any value or expression which can be evaluated to TRUE or FALSE. In the case of the Direct materials:

  =IF(Balance Quantity < 100...

- **value if true**

  This is the value which will be returned by the function if the condition evaluates to TRUE ie if Balance Quantity <100 the answer is "YES"

- **value if false**

  This is the value which will be returned by the function if the condition evaluates to FALSE ie if Balance Quantity >=100 the answer is "NO"

Note that:

- any text which is to appear in the spreadsheet should be shown in quotes: **"YES"**

In the example screen below, we have entered formulas in column K, for each row.

The formula in cell K7 for 02/04/21 is shown below:

MINUTE | fx =IF(H7<100,"YES","NO")

	A	B	C	D	E	F	G	H	I	J	K
1	Inventory Record		Average cost valuation								
2											
3	Item RT12548										
4											
5	Date		Receipts			Issues			Balance		
6		Quantity	Cost per unit	Total cost	Quantity	Cost per unit	Total cost	Quantity	Cost per unit	Total cost	Low Balance <100
7	02/04/2021	100	3	300				100	3	300	=IF(H7<100,"YES","NO")
8	03/04/2021				50	3	150	50	3	150	
9	05/04/2021	100	4.5	450				150	4	600	
10	06/04/2021				100	4	400	50	4	200	
11	21/04/2021	150	4	600				200	4	800	
12											
13	Total	350		750	150		550				

=IF(H7<100,"YES","NO")

This formula looks at the value in cell H7, and since it is 100, this returns a value of YES in cell K7.

Copying this formula into cells K8 to K11, we see the occurrences of low Balances.

	A	B	C	D	E	F	G	H	I	J	K
1	Inventory Record		Average cost valuation								
2											
3	Item RT12548										
4											
5	Date		Receipts			Issues			Balance		
6		Quantity	Cost per unit	Total cost	Quantity	Cost per unit	Total cost	Quantity	Cost per unit	Total cost	Low Balance <100
7	02/04/2021	100	3	300				100	3	300	NO
8	03/04/2021				50	3	150	50	3	150	YES
9	05/04/2021	100	4.5	450				150	4	600	NO
10	06/04/2021				100	4	400	50	4	200	YES
11	21/04/2021	150	4	600				200	4	800	NO
12											
13	Total	350		750	150		550				

If we wanted to either specify YES or leave it blank, rather than NO, a blank is “” (empty quote marks), so our formula would be:

=IF(H7<100,“YES”,“”)

This change is shown below:

K7 | fx =IF(H7<100,"YES","")

	A	B	C	D	E	F	G	H	I	J	K
1	Inventory Record		Average cost valuation								
2											
3	Item RT12548										
4											
5	Date		Receipts			Issues			Balance		
6		Quantity	Cost per unit	Total cost	Quantity	Cost per unit	Total cost	Quantity	Cost per unit	Total cost	Low Balance <100
7	02/04/2021	100	3	300				100	3	300	
8	03/04/2021				50	3	150	50	3	150	YES
9	05/04/2021	100	4.5	450				150	4	600	
10	06/04/2021				100	4	400	50	4	200	YES
11	21/04/2021	150	4	600				200	4	800	
12											
13	Total	350		750	150		550				

Here is another example.

Suppose we had a costing sheet containing Budget figures for our expected costs (column B) and Actual figures for each of these costs (column C). In column D we have calculated the Variance (Budget – Actual), as shown in the image below:

	A	B	C	D	E
1	Costing comparison				
2					
3	Cost type	Budget	Actual	Variance	Adverse or Favourable
4	Direct Materials	£12,000	£18,500	-£6,500	
5	Direct Labour	£25,000	£24,500	£500	
6	Production Overheads	£15,000	£18,900	-£3,900	
7	Administration Overheads	£6,500	£5,050	£1,450	
8	Selling & Distribution Overheads	£11,000	£12,000	-£1,000	

We could manually identify whether the Actual figure compared to the Budget figure is **Adverse** (greater than Budget) or **Favourable** (less than or equal to Budget), but we are going to use the IF function to do it for us.

In cell E4, we are going to put the formula:

=IF(D4<0, “Adverse”, “Favourable”)

This formula equates to:

if the value in D4 is less than zero, ie the variance is negative, put ***Adverse*** *in cell E4, otherwise, put* ***Favourable*** *in E4.*

The results of this can be seen below:

E4 | =IF(D4<0,"Adverse","Favourable")

	A	B	C	D	E
1	Costing comparison				
2					
3	Cost type	Budget	Actual	Variance	Adverse or Favourable
4	Direct Materials	£12,000	£18,500	-£6,500	Adverse
5	Direct Labour	£25,000	£24,500	£500	Favourable
6	Production Overheads	£15,000	£18,900	-£3,900	Adverse
7	Administration Overheads	£6,500	£5,050	£1,450	Favourable
8	Selling & Distribution Overheads	£11,000	£12,000	-£1,000	Adverse

NESTED IF

Within an IF formula, it is possible to include another IF, this is known as **nested IF** statements.

Looking at our Inventory record worksheet:

	A	B	C	D	E	F	G	H	I	J	K
1	Inventory Record		Average cost valuation								
2											
3	Item RT12548										
4											
5	Date		Receipts			Issues			Balance		
6		Quantity	Cost per unit	Total cost	Quantity	Cost per unit	Total cost	Quantity	Cost per unit	Total cost	Low Balance
7	02/04/2021	100	3	300				100	3	300	
8	03/04/2021				50	3	150	50	3	150	
9	05/04/2021	100	4.5	450				150	4	600	
10	06/04/2021				100	4	400	50	4	200	
11	21/04/2021	150	4	600				200	4	800	
12											
13	Total	350		750	150		550				

Deciding whether or not the Balance quantity is low, very low or not, we want to apply the following logic:

If the Balance is greater than or equal to 150 return NO

If the Balance is less than 150 but more than 60, return LOW

IF the Balance is less than 60, return VERY LOW

This formula is shown below:

=IF(H7 >=150,"NO", IF(H7>=60," LOW"," VERY LOW"))

With the results shown below:

K7 | =IF(H7 >=150,"NO", IF(H7>=60,"LOW","VERY LOW"))

	A	B	C	D	E	F	G	H	I	J	K
1	Inventory Record		Average cost valuation								
2											
3	Item RT12548										
4											
5	Date		Receipts			Issues			Balance		
6		Quantity	Cost per unit	Total cost	Quantity	Cost per unit	Total cost	Quantity	Cost per unit	Total cost	Low Balance
7	02/04/2021	100	3	300				100	3	300	LOW
8	03/04/2021				50	3	150	50	3	150	VERY LOW
9	05/04/2021	100	4.5	450				150	4	600	NO
10	06/04/2021				100	4	400	50	4	200	VERY LOW
11	21/04/2021	150	4	600				200	4	800	NO
12											
13	Total	350		750	150		550				

Note: for each occurrence of IF within a formula, it must be followed by an opening bracket and at some point a closing bracket.

NESTED IF statements are useful when there are multiple outcomes, but should be used with caution as they can become complex, however it is a good idea to spend time to familiarise yourself with the IF function. It is used a great deal within spreadsheets and is very powerful.

LOOKUP FUNCTIONS

We can often have large amounts of data within a spreadsheet, and it may not be very easy to find a particular value, so we may wish to use an automated function to do it for us.

There are two built-in functions which are regularly used: **HLOOKUP** and **VLOOKUP**.

VLOOKUP

The v in VLOOKUP is to identify that the function searches in a vertical direction, ie down columns.

The function searches for a value in a particular column. If the value is found, it returns the matching value in the same row, from a specified column to the right of the column being searched.

=VLOOKUP(lookup_value, table_array, col_index_num, range_lookup)

The VLOOKUP function syntax has these arguments:

- **lookup_value**

  This is the value which you want to look for.

- **table array (range)**

  This is the horizontal group of cells where you want to look for the value, and should include at least two columns: the column containing the value, and the column holding the values to return, usually referred to as a table of values.

- **col_index_num**

  This is the value counting columns from the search column as 1, to the column holding the values to return, or the column number within the table.

- **range_lookup optional**

  This is either TRUE or FALSE, and specifies whether or not you want VLOOKUP to find an exact match to the lookup_value, or if there is no exact match, then a close match, which would be the next largest value less than the lookup_value.

  If TRUE or omitted, an approximate match is returned if an exact match is not found; this requires the lookup cells to be sorted in ascending order. The approximate match will return the next largest value that is less than your lookup value.

Look at the example on the next page and read the explanatory text that follows.

PPMT =VLOOKUP(B3,A6:B17,2,FALSE)

	A	B	C	D	E
1	Products				
2					
3	Lookup inventory code	P133		Quantity	=VLOOKU
4					
5	Inventory Code	Quantity			
6	A1	12			
7	A3	34			
8	B4	22			
9	A5	1			
10	D6	89			
11	H8	900			
12	K5	31			
13	S9	451			
14	C3	67			
15	P133	76			
16	A112	32			
17	W34	90			

We have entered data in columns A and B, giving the inventory code and quantity for a group of products.

In cell B3 we have entered an inventory code and we want to look up the quantity held for this inventory code.

In cell E3 where we want to display the quantity for this inventory code, we have created the VLOOKUP formula as follows:

=VLOOKUP(B3, A6:B17,2,FALSE)

Here B3 is the value we want to find.

Cells A6:B17 contain all the information we are wanting to look up, effectively a table (only two columns), the headings should not be included.

The column we want to return is the second column (Quantity) in the block of cells containing the data.

We want to return only an exact match for the inventory code we specify, so the final parameter is FALSE.

If you look at the image below, you can see that the formula returns 76, the quantity for inventory code P133.

E3		=VLOOKUP(B3,A6:B17,2,FALSE)			
	A	B	C	D	E
1	Products				
2					
3	Lookup inventory code	P133		Quantity	76
4					
5	Inventory Code	Quantity			
6	A1	12			
7	A3	34			
8	B4	22			
9	A5	1			
10	D6	89			
11	H8	900			
12	K5	31			
13	S9	451			
14	C3	67			
15	P133	76			
16	A112	32			
17	W34	90			

HLOOKUP

The H in HLOOKUP is to identify that the function searches in a horizontal direction, ie along rows.

The function searches for a value (the lookup_value) within a table of data, in a particular row (row_index_num), and if found, it returns the value in the same column, from the specified row.

=HLOOKUP(lookup_value, table_array, row_index_num, range_lookup)

The **HLOOKUP** function has these four arguments:

- **lookup_value**

  This is the value which you want to look for.

- **table array (range)**

  This is the horizontal group of cells where you want to look for the value, and should include at least two rows, the row containing the value, and the row holding the values to return, usually referred to as a table of values.

- **row_index_num**

  This is the value counting rows from the search row as 1, to the row holding the values to return, or the row number within the table.

- **range_lookup optional**

  This is either TRUE or FALSE, and specifies whether or not you want HLOOKUP to find an exact match to the lookup_value, or if there is no exact match, then a close match, which would be the next largest value less than the lookup_value.

If TRUE or omitted, an approximate match is returned if an exach match is not found; this requires the lookup cells to be sorted in ascending order.

In our example below, we have a table in rows 6 to 9 which allows us to look up the wages rate and wages band for a small selection of people.

	A	B	C	D	E	F	G
1	**Wages rates**		22/06/2021				
2							
3			**Person**	**Wages rate**	**Wages band**		
4			HB	16	5		
5							
6	Person	JP	HB	PS	JW	LP	NF
7	Wages rate	18.30	16.00	19.00	18.30	19.10	16.00
8	Wage band	4	5	6	4	7	5
9	Full name	Jo Powell	Hal Boden	Priya Samal	Jacob Webb	Lila Petrusco	Nina Faye

The data in rows 6 to 9 gives the initials, the wages rate, the wage band and each person's full name.

In cell C4, we will select the person for whom we will **lookup** wages rate and wages band.

To make this easier, we have applied data validation to cell C4, so that we can pick from the list of people in cells B6 to G6, as shown below:

	A	B	C	D	E	F	G
1	**Wages rates**		22/06/2021				
2							
3			**Person**	**Wages rate**	**Wages band**		
4			HB ▾	16	5		
5			JP				
6	Person	JP	HB PS		JW	LP	NF
7	Wages rate	18.30	JW	19.00	18.30	19.10	16.00
8	Wage band	4	LP NF	6	4	7	5
9	Full name	Jo Powell	Hal Boden	Priya Samal	Jacob Webb	Lila Petrusco	Nina Faye

In cell D4, we want to display the wages rate for the person selected in C4. We have created the HLOOKUP formula as follows:

=HLOOKUP(C4,B6:G9,2,FALSE)

Cell C4 is the value we want to find.

Cells B6:G9 contain all the information we are wanting to look up; this is effectively a table.

The row containing the value we want to return is the second row (wages rate) in the block of cells containing the data.

We want to return only an exact match for the person we specify, so the final parameter is FALSE.

D4 =HLOOKUP(C4,B6:G9,2,FALSE)

	A	B	C	D	E	F	G
1	**Wages rates**		22/06/2021				
2							
3			**Person**	**Wages rate**	**Wages band**		
4			NF	16	5		
5							
6	Person	JP	HB	PS	JW	LP	NF
7	Wages rate	18.30	16.00	19.00	18.30	19.10	16.00
8	Wage band	4	5	6	4	7	5
9	Full name	Jo Powell	Hal Boden	Priya Samal	Jacob Webb	Lila Petrusco	Nina Faye

Similarly, if we now want to look up the wages band, into cell E4, we create the formula:

=HLOOKUP(C4,B6:G9,3,FALSE)

E4 =HLOOKUP(C4,B6:G9,3,FALSE)

	A	B	C	D	E	F	G
1	**Wages rates**		22/06/2021				
2							
3			**Person**	**Wages rate**	**Wages band**		
4			HB	16	5		
5							
6	Person	JP	HB	PS	JW	LP	NF
7	Wages rate	18.30	16.00	19.00	18.30	19.10	16.00
8	Wage band	4	5	6	4	7	5
9	Full name	Jo Powell	Hal Boden	Priya Samal	Jacob Webb	Lila Petrusco	Nina Faye

If we now change the person in cell C4, the wages rate and wages band will automatically change too, as you can see below.

	A	B	C	D	E	F	G
1	**Wages rates**		22/06/2021				
2							
3			**Person**	**Wages rate**	**Wages band**		
4			LP	19.1	7		
5							
6	Person	JP	HB	PS	JW	LP	NF
7	Wages rate	18.30	16.00	19.00	18.30	19.10	16.00
8	Wage band	4	5	6	4	7	5
9	Full name	Jo Powell	Hal Boden	Priya Samal	Jacob Webb	Lila Petrusco	Nina Faye

notes on lookups

- When doing a lookup for a text value, the search does not distinguish between upper and lower case text. They are both regarded as the same.
- If there is a space in the text string, it must be in the search string.

circular references

A Circular Reference occurs when a cell containing a formula includes its own cell reference in the formula. A simple example would be if cell B7 held the formula =SUM(B2:B7).

When this occurs you will be given a warning, as shown in the image below.

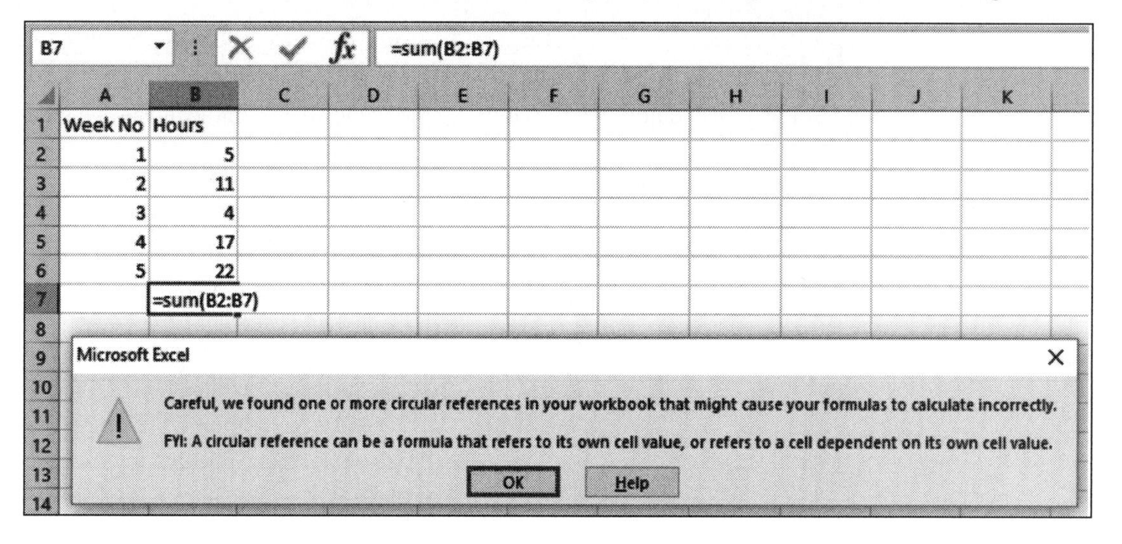

To remove the error, select OK and correct the formula in the cell.

SOME USEFUL SHORTCUTS

To insert a cell reference into a formula

When creating a formula you can click on the cell to include its reference in the formula.

For example, if we were creating a formula to multiply two cells

= B4*B5

- in the formula bar enter "="
- click on cell B4
- enter "*" for multiply
- click on cell B5
- press enter

To copy a formula

An easy way to copy a formula to adjacent cells in the row or column:

- select the cell containing a formula
- move the cursor to the bottom right corner of the cell, until a plus sign (+) appears. This is called the **Fill Handle**
- press down the left mouse key and drag across the adjacent cells

When you release the mouse the new formulas will be inserted.

Chapter Summary

In this chapter we have covered the following spreadsheet concepts and techniques:

- formulas
- mathematical operators
- functions
- ranges
- mathematical functions
- cell addressing
- date functions
- logical functions and operators
- lookup functions
- circular references in formulas

You should now carry out some or all of the exercises on the next few pages in order to practise and reinforce your learning.

Activities

Here are a group of exercises to allow you to practise the topics covered in this chapter. They can be done individually, or as a sequence, working your way through them.

If you choose to work your way through them, you may not need to open the exercise workbook as suggested at the start of each exercise, as it may already be open.

The saving at the end of each exercise is also optional, although it serves as a reminder to regularly save your work. You can also save to different file names and may choose to keep using the same name to avoid having lots of files.

Exercise 1

Spreadsheet skills:

- Formulas - addition, subtraction, multiplication, division

1. Open workbook T4Exercises
2. Select worksheet Exercise 1
3. In column D, enter a formula to calculate the Productivity bonus (Gross pay – Bonus pay)
4. Enter a formula in column E to calculate the percentage of Basic pay represented by the Productivity bonus, display as a percentage to three decimal places (Productivity bonus / Basic pay)
5. In column F, calculate the weekly Productivity bonus (Productivity bonus / 52)
6. In cell C3 calculate the average Productivity bonus for Begum and Sheppard, display as currency £ with no decimal places (add up the productivity bonus values for Begum and Sheppard and divide by two, you will need to use brackets to ensure the correct calculation)
7. Save your spreadsheet with the name: Chapter4_Exercise1

C3 =(D13+D15)/2

	A	B	C	D	E	F
1	Employees wages information					
2						
3	Average productivity value £		£2,526			
4	(Begum and Sheppard)					
5	Surname	Basic pay	Gross pay	Productivity bonus	Productivity bonus %	Weekly productivity bonus
6		£	£	£	%	£
7	Patel	£31,200.00	£32,620.50	£1,420.50	4.553%	£27.32
8	Johnson	£28,900.00	£31,425.33	£2,525.33	8.738%	£48.56
9	Singh	£31,200.00	£31,500.00	£300.00	0.962%	£5.77
10	Gregory	£24,900.00	£28,950.31	£4,050.31	16.266%	£77.89
11	Williams	£24,900.00	£26,750.50	£1,850.50	7.432%	£35.59
12	Reed	£28,900.00	£31,850.67	£2,950.67	10.210%	£56.74
13	Khan	£28,900.00	£31,450.72	£2,550.72	8.826%	£49.05
14	Begum	£24,900.00	£28,650.00	£3,750.00	15.060%	£72.12
15	Sheppard	£28,900.00	£31,400.50	£2,500.50	8.652%	£48.09
16	Total					

Exercise 2

Spreadsheet skills:

- Function - SUM

1. Open workbook T4Exercises
2. Select worksheet Exercise 2
3. In cell B16, use the SUM function to total the Basic pay values
4. In cell C16, use the SUM function to total the Gross pay values
5. Enter a new formula in cell C3 to calculate the average productivity bonus value £ (column D) for all employees, using the SUM function and the number of employees, format as currency with two decimal places
6. Save your spreadsheet with the name: Chapter4_Exercise2

C3	=SUM(D7:D15)/9				
	A	B	C	D	E
1	Employees wages information				
2					
3	Average productivity bonus value £		£2,433.17		
4					
5	Surname	Basic pay	Gross pay	Productivity bonus	Productivity bonus %
6		£	£	£	%
7	Patel	£31,200.00	£32,620.50	£1,420.50	4.553%
8	Johnson	£28,900.00	£31,425.33	£2,525.33	8.738%
9	Singh	£31,200.00	£31,500.00	£300.00	0.962%
10	Gregory	£24,900.00	£28,950.31	£4,050.31	16.266%
11	Williams	£24,900.00	£26,750.50	£1,850.50	7.432%
12	Reed	£28,900.00	£31,850.67	£2,950.67	10.210%
13	Khan	£28,900.00	£31,450.72	£2,550.72	8.826%
14	Begum	£24,900.00	£28,650.00	£3,750.00	15.060%
15	Sheppard	£28,900.00	£31,400.50	£2,500.50	8.652%
16	Total	£252,700.00	£274,598.53		

Exercise 3

Spreadsheet skills:

- Function - ABS (Absolute value)
- Naming a cell

1. Open workbook T4Exercises
2. Select worksheet Exercise 3
3. Assign a name to cell C3 “Average_Bonus”
4. Create a formula for the Variance from average in column F using the named cell Average_Bonus
5. In column G, use the ABS function to calculate the absolute value of the variance
6. Save the workbook with the name Chapter4_Exercise3

Your spreadsheet should appear as follows:

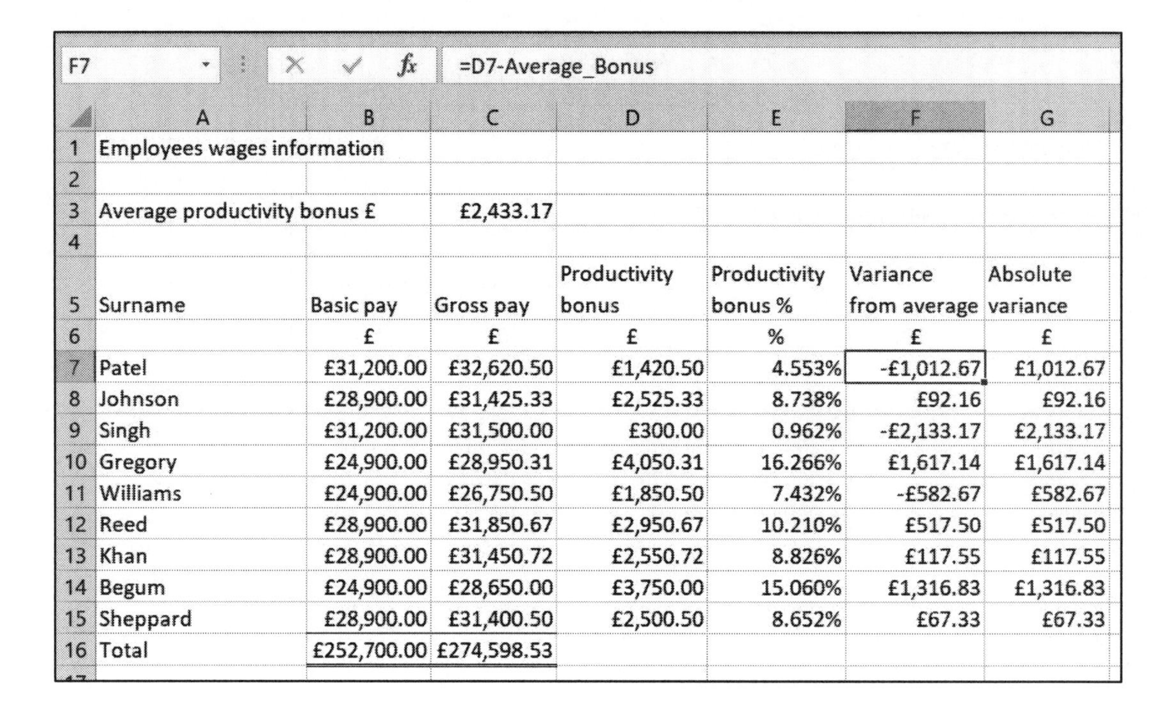

F7 =D7-Average_Bonus

	A	B	C	D	E	F	G
1	Employees wages information						
2							
3	Average productivity bonus £		£2,433.17				
4							
5	Surname	Basic pay	Gross pay	Productivity bonus	Productivity bonus %	Variance from average	Absolute variance
6		£	£	£	%	£	£
7	Patel	£31,200.00	£32,620.50	£1,420.50	4.553%	-£1,012.67	£1,012.67
8	Johnson	£28,900.00	£31,425.33	£2,525.33	8.738%	£92.16	£92.16
9	Singh	£31,200.00	£31,500.00	£300.00	0.962%	-£2,133.17	£2,133.17
10	Gregory	£24,900.00	£28,950.31	£4,050.31	16.266%	£1,617.14	£1,617.14
11	Williams	£24,900.00	£26,750.50	£1,850.50	7.432%	-£582.67	£582.67
12	Reed	£28,900.00	£31,850.67	£2,950.67	10.210%	£517.50	£517.50
13	Khan	£28,900.00	£31,450.72	£2,550.72	8.826%	£117.55	£117.55
14	Begum	£24,900.00	£28,650.00	£3,750.00	15.060%	£1,316.83	£1,316.83
15	Sheppard	£28,900.00	£31,400.50	£2,500.50	8.652%	£67.33	£67.33
16	Total	£252,700.00	£274,598.53				

And for the Absolute variance column:

G7 =ABS(F7)

	A	B	C	D	E	F	G
1	Employees wages information						
2							
3	Average productivity bonus £		£2,433.17				
4							
5	Surname	Basic pay	Gross pay	Productivity bonus	Productivity bonus %	Variance from average	Absolute variance
6		£	£	£	%	£	£
7	Patel	£31,200.00	£32,620.50	£1,420.50	4.553%	-£1,012.67	£1,012.67
8	Johnson	£28,900.00	£31,425.33	£2,525.33	8.738%	£92.16	£92.16
9	Singh	£31,200.00	£31,500.00	£300.00	0.962%	-£2,133.17	£2,133.17
10	Gregory	£24,900.00	£28,950.31	£4,050.31	16.266%	£1,617.14	£1,617.14
11	Williams	£24,900.00	£26,750.50	£1,850.50	7.432%	-£582.67	£582.67
12	Reed	£28,900.00	£31,850.67	£2,950.67	10.210%	£517.50	£517.50
13	Khan	£28,900.00	£31,450.72	£2,550.72	8.826%	£117.55	£117.55
14	Begum	£24,900.00	£28,650.00	£3,750.00	15.060%	£1,316.83	£1,316.83
15	Sheppard	£28,900.00	£31,400.50	£2,500.50	8.652%	£67.33	£67.33
16	Total	£252,700.00	£274,598.53				

Exercise 4

Spreadsheet skills:

- Function - TODAY
- Function - DAYS
- Formulas - absolute cell references (addresses)

1. Open workbook T4Exercises
2. Select worksheet Exercise 4
3. In cell E1, enter a formula to display today's date, in the format dd/mm/yyyy
4. In cell F5, create a formula to display the person's age, using the DAYS function, today's date (cell E1), and the birth date (cell B5), and convert into years, by dividing by 365.25
5. Edit the formula to make the reference to cell E1 (today's date) an absolute address
6. Copy the formula into cells F6 to F11
7. Save the workbook with the name Chapter4_Exercise4

Your spreadsheet should appear as follows:

F5 =DAYS($E$1,B5)/365

	A	B	C	D	E	F
1	**Employee records**			Date	29/06/2021	
2						
3						**Calculated**
4	**Surname**	**Birth Date**	**Start Date**	**Department**	**Salary**	**Age**
5	Johal	02/03/1985	01/06/2010	Sales	30000	36.35
6	Jones	14/10/1973	01/07/2011	HR	26000	47.74
7	Wakula	03/09/1988	01/07/2012	Sales	30000	32.84
8	White	30/06/1977	03/01/2019	Accounts	25000	44.03
9	Hacek	24/05/1980	01/07/2020	Accounts	28000	41.13
10	Bhopal	12/02/1998	01/07/2020	Sales	30500	23.39
11	Plant	19/03/1996	01/09/2020	Sales	31500	25.30

Exercise 5

Spreadsheet skills:

- Function - IF

1. Open workbook T4Exercises
2. Select worksheet Exercise 5
3. In cell B3, enter 01/01/2011. Ensure it is formatted as a date
4. We are going to use a formula in column F to calculate whether or not an employee was employed before 1st January 2011, and should receive a service award.

   Use the IF( ) function to do the calculation, and cell B3 (where the date to compare against has been entered).

   For example: to calculate F7, IF the value in C7 is before (less than) B3 THEN "yes", OTHERWISE "no".
5. Edit the formula to make the reference to cell E1 (today's date) an absolute address
6. Copy the formula into cells F8 to F13
7. Save the workbook with the name Chapter4_Exercise5

Your spreadsheet should appear as follows:

F7 =IF(C7<$B$3,"yes","no")

	A	B	C	D	E	F
1	**Employee records**			Date	28/06/2021	
2						
3	Award date	01/01/2011				
4						
5						**Service**
6	**Surname**	**Birth Date**	**Start Date**	**Department**	**Salary**	**award**
7	Johal	02/03/1985	01/06/2010	Sales	30000	yes
8	Jones	14/10/1973	01/07/2011	HR	26000	no
9	Wakula	03/09/1988	01/07/2012	Sales	30000	no
10	White	30/06/1977	03/01/2009	Accounts	35000	yes
11	Hacek	24/05/1980	01/07/2020	Accounts	28000	no
12	Bhopal	12/02/1998	01/07/2020	Sales	30500	no
13	Plant	19/03/1996	01/09/2020	Sales	31500	no

Exercise 6

Spreadsheet skills:

- Function - IF(nested)

1. Open workbook T4Exercises
2. Select worksheet Exercise 6
3. There is a salary increase, all those in Sales are getting a pay rise of £1000, Accounts receive £750 and HR receive £500. Use a NESTED IF( ) function to do the calculation.

For example to calculate F7:

IF the value in D7 is "Sales", return Salary + £1000

IF "Accounts", return Salary + £750

otherwise, return Salary + £500

4. Copy the formula into cells F8 to F13
5. Format all salary data (columns E and F), so that each value displays with the 1000 separator (,) and no decimal places
6. Save the workbook with the name Chapter4_Exercise6

Your spreadsheet should appear as follows:

F7 =IF(D7="Sales",E7+1000,IF(D7="Accounts",E7+750,E7+500))

	A	B	C	D	E	F	G	H
1	**Employee records**			Date	01/07/2021			
2								
3	Award date	01/01/2011						
4								
5						**New**		
6	**Surname**	**Birth Date**	**Start Date**	**Department**	**Salary**	**Salary**		
7	Johal	02/03/1985	01/06/2010	Sales	30,000	31,000		
8	Jones	14/10/1973	01/07/2011	HR	26,000	26,500		
9	Wakula	03/09/1988	01/07/2012	Sales	30,000	31,000		
10	White	30/06/1977	03/01/2009	Accounts	35,000	35,750		
11	Hacek	24/05/1980	01/07/2020	Accounts	28,000	28,750		
12	Bhopal	12/02/1998	01/07/2020	Sales	30,500	31,500		
13	Plant	19/03/1996	01/09/2020	Sales	31,500	32,500		

7. Change the department for Bhopal (row 12) to Purchasing, this department will receive no salary increase
8. Modify your formula to allow for the fact there are other departments

For example to calculate F7:

IF the value in D7 is "Sales", return Salary + £1000

IF "Accounts", return Salary + £750

IF "HR", return Salary + £500

Otherwise return Salary

9. Copy the formula into cells F8 to F13
10. Save the workbook with the name Chapter4_Exercise6

Your spreadsheet should appear as follows:

F7 =IF(D7="Sales",E7+1000,IF(D7="Accounts",E7+750,IF(D7="HR",E7+500,E7)))

	A	B	C	D	E	F	G	H	I
1	**Employee records**			Date	01/07/2021				
2									
3	Award date	01/01/2011							
4									
5						**New**			
6	**Surname**	**Birth Date**	**Start Date**	**Department**	**Salary**	**Salary**			
7	Johal	02/03/1985	01/06/2010	Sales	30,000	31,000			
8	Jones	14/10/1973	01/07/2011	HR	26,000	26,500			
9	Wakula	03/09/1988	01/07/2012	Sales	30,000	31,000			
10	White	30/06/1977	03/01/2009	Accounts	35,000	35,750			
11	Hacek	24/05/1980	01/07/2020	Accounts	28,000	28,750			
12	Bhopal	12/02/1998	01/07/2020	Purchasing	30,500	30,500			
13	Plant	19/03/1996	01/09/2020	Sales	31,500	32,500			

Exercise 7

Spreadsheet skills:

- Data Validation
- Function - NOW
- Naming a range of cells
- Function - HLOOKUP

1. Open workbook T4Exercises
2. Select worksheet Exercise 7
3. Merge and centre cells D1 and E1, then use the NOW function to display today's date and time
4. Select cells B6 to G6 and name this range People
5. In cell C4 set Data Validation using a list with acceptable values range People

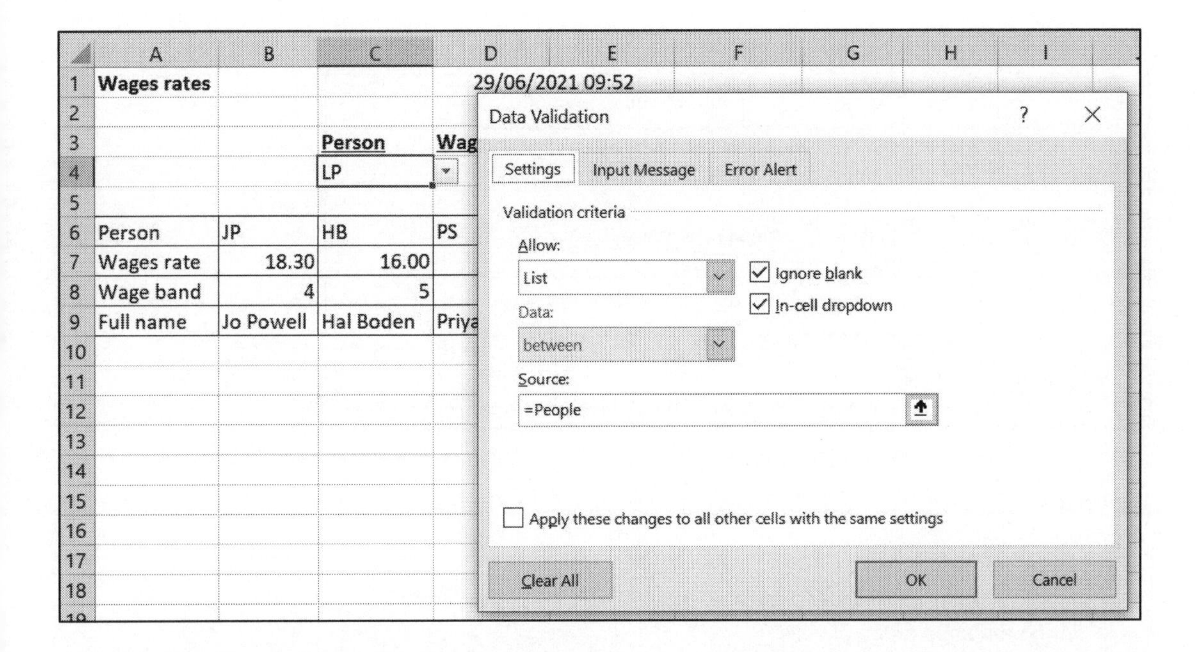

6. In cell D4, enter the HLOOKUP formula to lookup the Wages rate for the Person in cell C4, using the data in cells B6 to G9, named Wagedata
7. In cell E4, enter the HLOOKUP formula to lookup the Wage band for the Person in cell C4, using the data in cells B6 to G9, named Wagedata
8. In cell C4, select Person PS from the list
9. Save the workbook with the name Chapter4_Exercise7

For Wages rate:

D4 =HLOOKUP(C4,B6:G9,2,FALSE)

	A	B	C	D	E	F	G
1	**Wages rates**			29/06/2021 10:01			
2							
3			**Person**	**Wages rate**	**Wages band**		
4			PS	19	6		
5							
6	Person	JP	HB	PS	JW	LP	NF
7	Wages rate	18.30	16.00	19.00	18.30	19.10	16.00
8	Wage band	4	5	6	4	7	5
9	Full name	Jo Powell	Hal Boden	Priya Samal	Jacob Webb	Lila Petrusco	Nina Faye

For Wage band:

E4 =HLOOKUP(C4,B6:G9,3,FALSE)

	A	B	C	D	E	F	G
1	**Wages rates**			29/06/2021 10:01			
2							
3			**Person**	**Wages rate**	**Wages band**		
4			PS	19	6		
5							
6	Person	JP	HB	PS	JW	LP	NF
7	Wages rate	18.30	16.00	19.00	18.30	19.10	16.00
8	Wage band	4	5	6	4	7	5
9	Full name	Jo Powell	Hal Boden	Priya Samal	Jacob Webb	Lila Petrusco	Nina Faye

Exercise 8

Spreadsheet skills:

- Using a named range of cells
- Function - HLOOKUP

1. Open workbook T4Exercises
2. Select worksheet Exercise8
3. In cell B4, enter the HLOOKUP formula to lookup the Full name for the Person in cell A4, using the data in rows 6 to 9
4. Name cell C4 Hours, and D4 Wages_rate
5. Enter a formula in cell E4 to calculate the Wages to pay using Hours and Wages_rate
6. Enter 200 for the Hours in cell B4, see how the Wages to pay is calculated

	A	B	C	D	E	F	G
1	**Wages rates**			29/06/2021 10:36			
2							
3	**Person**	**Full name**	**Hours**	**Wages rate**	**Wages to pay**		
4	PS	Priya Samal	200	19	3800		
5							
6	Person	JP	HB	PS	JW	LP	NF
7	Wages rate	18.30	16.00	19.00	18.30	19.10	16.00
8	Wage band	4	5	6	4	7	5
9	Full name	Jo Powell	Hal Boden	Priya Samal	Jacob Webb	Lila Petrusco	Nina Faye

7. Select person NF in cell A4, enter 150 for Hours, see how everything updates

	A	B	C	D	E	F	G
1	**Wages rates**			29/06/2021 10:37			
2							
3	**Person**	**Full name**	**Hours**	**Wages rate**	**Wages to pay**		
4	NF	Nina Faye	150	16	2400		
5							
6	Person	JP	HB	PS	JW	LP	NF
7	Wages rate	18.30	16.00	19.00	18.30	19.10	16.00
8	Wage band	4	5	6	4	7	5
9	Full name	Jo Powell	Hal Boden	Priya Samal	Jacob Webb	Lila Petrusco	Nina Faye

8. Save your workbook with the name Chapter4_Exercise8

Full name lookup:

B4 =HLOOKUP(A4,B6:G9,4,FALSE)

	A	B	C	D	E	F	G
1	**Wages rates**			29/06/2021 10:27			
2							
3	**Person**	**Full name**	**Hours**	**Wages rate**	**Wages to pay**		
4	PS	Priya Samal		19	0		
5							
6	Person	JP	HB	PS	JW	LP	NF
7	Wages rate	18.30	16.00	19.00	18.30	19.10	16.00
8	Wage band	4	5	6	4	7	5
9	Full name	Jo Powell	Hal Boden	Priya Samal	Jacob Webb	Lila Petrusco	Nina Faye

Wages to pay formula:

E4 =Hours*Wages_rate

	A	B	C	D	E	F	G
1	**Wages rates**			29/06/2021 10:27			
2							
3	**Person**	**Full name**	**Hours**	**Wages rate**	**Wages to pay**		
4	PS	Priya Samal		19	0		
5							
6	Person	JP	HB	PS	JW	LP	NF
7	Wages rate	18.30	16.00	19.00	18.30	19.10	16.00
8	Wage band	4	5	6	4	7	5
9	Full name	Jo Powell	Hal Boden	Priya Samal	Jacob Webb	Lila Petrusco	Nina Faye

Exercise 9

Spreadsheet skills:

- Function - VLOOKUP

1. Open workbook T4Exercises
2. Select worksheet Exercise9
3. In cell B3 enter fr4
4. In cell D3 enter the formula to lookup the Warehouse location number from the data below, for the product code specified in cell B3

   (Use VLOOKUP on cell B3, specifying the lookup range to include codes and Warehouse location data only)
5. In cell F3 enter the formula to lookup the cost from the data below, for the product code in cell B3

   (Use VLOOKUP on cell B3, specifying the lookup range to include codes, Warehouse location and cost data)
6. Save the workbook with the name Chapter4_Exercise9

The workbook should appear as shown below:

	A	B	C	D	E	F	G
1	Warehouse information						
2							
3	**Product:**	fr4	**Location:**	4	**Cost:**	£7.00	
4							
5	**Code**	**Warehouse Location**	**Cost**				
6	ab1	1	£2.00				
7	ab2	2	£30.00				

Warehouse location lookup:

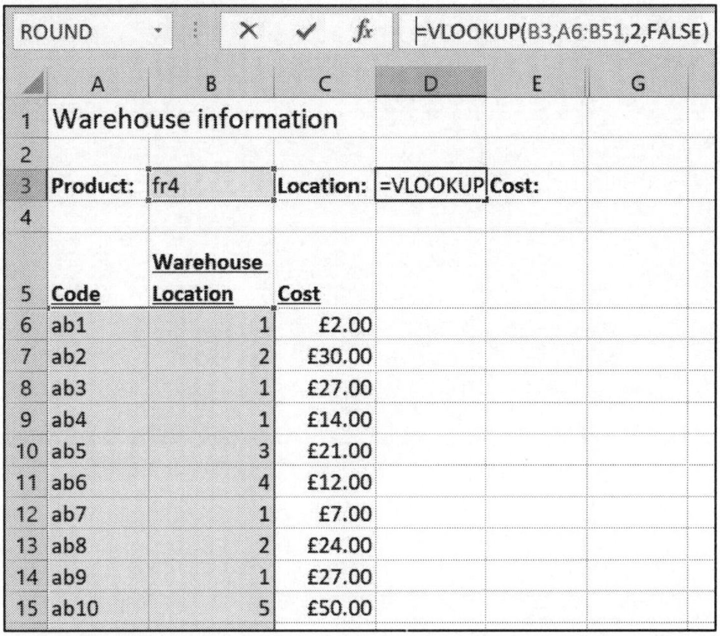

ROUND | =VLOOKUP(B3,A6:B51,2,FALSE)

	A	B	C	D	E	G
1	Warehouse information					
2						
3	**Product:**	fr4	**Location:**	=VLOOKUP	**Cost:**	
4						
5	**Code**	**Warehouse Location**	**Cost**			
6	ab1	1	£2.00			
7	ab2	2	£30.00			
8	ab3	1	£27.00			
9	ab4	1	£14.00			
10	ab5	3	£21.00			
11	ab6	4	£12.00			
12	ab7	1	£7.00			
13	ab8	2	£24.00			
14	ab9	1	£27.00			
15	ab10	5	£50.00			

Product cost lookup:

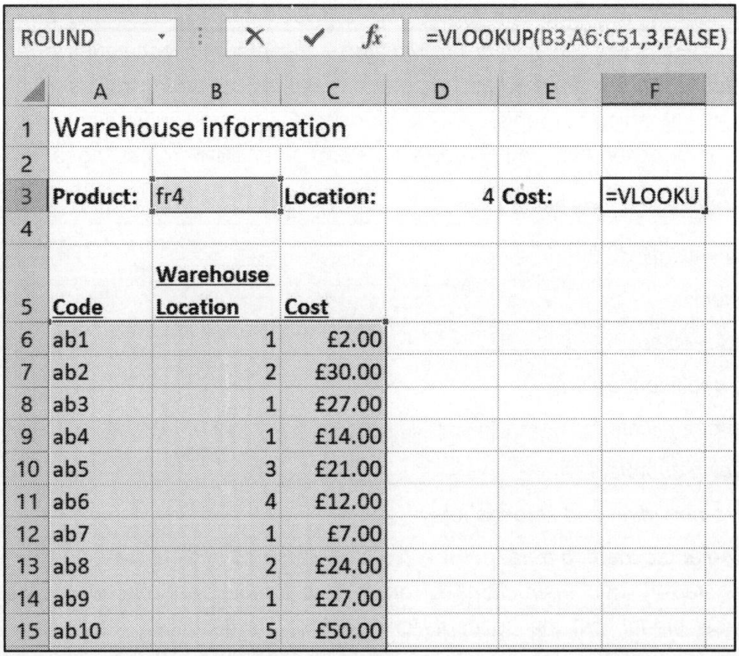

ROUND | =VLOOKUP(B3,A6:C51,3,FALSE)

	A	B	C	D	E	F
1	Warehouse information					
2						
3	**Product:**	fr4	**Location:**	4	**Cost:**	=VLOOKU
4						
5	**Code**	**Warehouse Location**	**Cost**			
6	ab1	1	£2.00			
7	ab2	2	£30.00			
8	ab3	1	£27.00			
9	ab4	1	£14.00			
10	ab5	3	£21.00			
11	ab6	4	£12.00			
12	ab7	1	£7.00			
13	ab8	2	£24.00			
14	ab9	1	£27.00			
15	ab10	5	£50.00			

5 Sorting, checking and importing data

this chapter covers...

This chapter covers the tools which are regularly available within spreadsheet packages, and shows how you can move data between spreadsheets and other documents. It explains and takes you through the concepts and techniques listed below. By the time you have finished this chapter and carried out the exercises which follow, you should be able to organise your spreadsheet to include subtotals, and be able to transfer information between spreadsheets and other software packages.

The concepts and techniques covered are:

- *formula validation*
- *spell check*
- *find and replace*
- *sorting and filtering data*
- *removing duplicates*
- *introducing subtotals*
- *linking, embedding and screenshots*
- *importing and exporting data*

Note that the step-by-step instructions given in this chapter are based on the Microsoft® Excel model, but the concepts and techniques described relate to all spreadsheet packages.

FORMULA AUDITING

We have explained formulas and how to create them earlier in this book. We are now going to explain some of the ways of checking that the formulas we have entered are doing what we expect them to do. The methods which we are going to cover are:

- show formulas
- error checking
- circular references
- trace precedents
- trace dependents

show formulas

This is a simple visual method, where formulas are displayed within the sheet. The example below shows the inventory record worksheet (the Issues columns have been hidden for convenience) displayed in the normal way:

	A	B	C	D	H	I	J	K
1	Inventory Record		Average cost valuation					
2								
3	Item RT12548		Minimum inventory level			100		
4								
5	Date		Receipts			Balance		
6		Quantity	Cost per unit	Total cost	Quantity	Cost per unit	Total cost	Low Balance <100
7	02/04/2021	100	3	300	100	3	300	NO
8	03/04/2021				50	3	150	YES
9	05/04/2021	100	4.5	450	150	4	600	NO
10	06/04/2021				50	4	200	YES
11	21/04/2021	150	4	600	200	4	800	NO
12								
13	Total	350		750				

Select **Show Formulas** from the **Formulas** menu and the screen will display any formulas contained in the cells or the data, as shown below:

	A	B	C	D	H	I	J	K
1	Inventory Record		Average c					
2								
3	Item RT12548		Minimum			100		
4								
5	Date		Receipts			Balance		
6		Quantity	Cost per unit	Total cost	Quantity	Cost per unit	Total cost	Low Balance <100
7	44288	100	3	=C7*B7	=B7-E7	=J7/H7	=D7	=IF(H7<$I$3,"YES","NO")
8	44289				=H7+(B8-E8)	=J8/H8	=J7 +(D8-G8)	=IF(H8<$I$3,"YES","NO")
9	44291	100	4.5	=C9*B9	=H8+(B9-E9)	=J9/H9	=J8 +(D9-G9)	=IF(H9<$I$3,"YES","NO")
10	44292				=H9+(B10-E10)	=J10/H10	=J9 +(D10-G10)	=IF(H10<$I$3,"YES","NO")
11	44307	150	4	=C11*B11	=H10+(B11-E11)	=J11/H11	=J10 +(D11-G11)	=IF(H11<$I$3,"YES","NO")
12								
13	Total	=SUM(B7:B11)		=SUM(D7:D10)				

In column A where we have dates, for example, what we now see is the serial number representation of the date (as described previously). Other columns show the mathematical formulas used to calculate costs and balances.

In a relatively small worksheet, or a particular section of a larger worksheet, it is easy to check that the formulas that have been entered are correct by using the **Show Formulas** option.

It is possible to print the worksheet in this form using the normal print options.

To revert to the normal display, we select **Show Formulas** again from the **Formulas** menu bar and select the appropriate command.

As mentioned, this is a fairly basic way of checking formulas. There is a more automated way using a facility called error checking, which is available in most spreadsheet packages.

error checking

The **error checking** facility checks for common errors which occur in formulas. These include:

- formulas that result in an error, such as dividing by zero
- numbers formatted as text, or preceded by an apostrophe (‘)
- formulas inconsistent with other formulas near them
- formulas which omit cells which are near others which have been included in the formula (eg a range of cells)
- cells containing circular references

Any cells where the formula is in error are flagged with a small green triangle in the upper-left corner of the cell.

In the same way that we can have our word processing package checking for errors as we type, it is possible to set the spreadsheet package options, so that our formulas are checked as we enter them; this is known as **automatic error checking**.

Automatic error checking is normally switched on but if not, it can be activated at any time by selecting the error checking feature from the **Formulas** menu.

If we take the Inventory record spreadsheet shown on the previous page we can modify the formula in cell H9:

from =H8+(B9-E9)

to =H8+(B9+E9)

You can see, in the image on the next page, that when we have automatic checking on, we get a small triangle in the upper left of cell D9, indicating a formula error.

H9 =H8+(B9+E9)

	A	B	C	D	H	I	J	K
1	Inventory Record		Average cost valuation					
2								
3	Item RT12548		Minimum inventory level			100		
4								
5	Date		Receipts			Balance		
6		Quantity	Cost per unit	Total cost	Quantity	Cost per unit	Total cost	Low Balance <100
7	02/04/2021	100	3	300	100	3	300	NO
8	03/04/2021				50	3	150	YES
9	05/04/2021	100	4.5	50	150	4	600	NO
10	06/04/2021				50	4	200	YES
11	21/04/2021	150	4	600	200	4	800	NO
12								
13	Total	350		750				

If we then select cell H9 we get an exclamation icon and a description of the error – 'Inconsistent Formula' – which tells us that this formula does not match the pattern of the formulas above and below (or to either side in the same row). Here, cell H9 is inconsistent with the formulas in column H.

H9 =H8+(B9+E9)

	A	B	C	D	H	I	J	K
1	Inventory Record		Average cost valuation					
2								
3	Item RT12548		Minimum inventory level			100		
4								
5	Date		Receipts			Balance		
6		Quantity	Cost per unit	Total cost	Quantity	Cost per unit	Total cost	Low Balance <100
7	02/04/2021	100	3	300	100	3	300	NO
8	03/04/2021				50	3	150	YES
9	05/04/2021	100	4.5		150	4	600	NO
10	06/04/2021				50	4	200	YES
11	21/04/2021				200	4	800	NO
12								
13	Total							
14								
15								
16								
17								

Inconsistent Formula
Copy Formula from Above
Help on this Error
Ignore Error
Edit in Formula Bar
Error Checking Options...

To set your choices for error checking:

either

- select **Options** from the **File** menu
- select **Formulas**

or, if you have an error, as shown in the example above:

- select **Checking Options** from the drop-down menu shown by clicking the ! (exclamation mark) then:

- either check or uncheck **Enable background error checking** as required
- check or uncheck the **Rules** to configure as you require

Note that if the formula is actually what we want, we can instruct the error check to **ignore the error**.

To perform a full worksheet error check:

- select **Error check** (or its equivalent) from the **Formulas** menu

The rules will be applied as set up in the Options described on the previous page, and any cells with a formula error will be flagged as shown on the previous page.

circular references

As mentioned previously, this occurs when a cell's formula contains a reference to itself. The **Error Checking** menu displays a drop-down list and one of the items in the list is **Circular References**. Clicking this item will cause a list of those cells containing circular references to be displayed. If you click on any of the cells in the list, the cursor will move to that cell and you can edit the formula. When all circular references have been resolved, the list will be empty.

trace precedents

The **Trace Precedents** facility allows you to identify those cells which affect the value of the currently selected cell.

For example, if cell D4 contained the formula

=A3 + B3

both A3 and B3 would be precedents of D4 since they both affect the value of D4.

If we take the Inventory record worksheet illustrated on the last few pages as an example, if we select cell K8, which holds the formula

=IF(H8<$I$3,"YES","NO")

and then select **Trace Precedents** from the **Formulas** menu, we can see the result as shown on the next page.

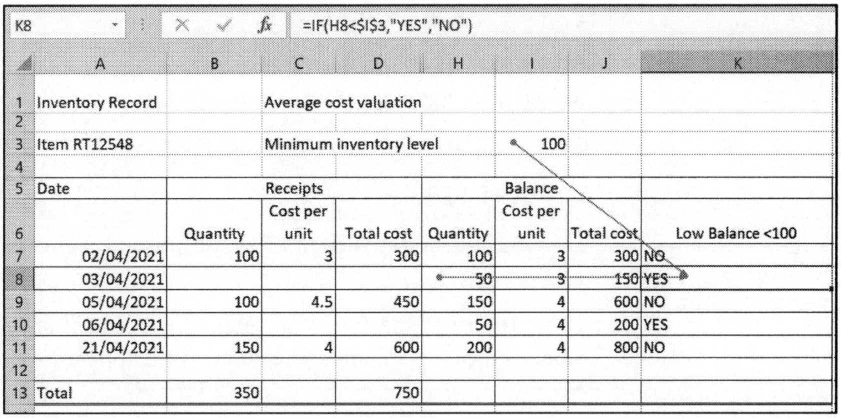

K8 =IF(H8<$I$3,"YES","NO")

	A	B	C	D	H	I	J	K
1	Inventory Record		Average cost valuation					
2								
3	Item RT12548		Minimum inventory level			100		
4								
5	Date		Receipts			Balance		
6		Quantity	Cost per unit	Total cost	Quantity	Cost per unit	Total cost	Low Balance <100
7	02/04/2021	100	3	300	100	3	300	NO
8	03/04/2021				50	3	150	YES
9	05/04/2021	100	4.5	450	150	4	600	NO
10	06/04/2021				50	4	200	YES
11	21/04/2021	150	4	600	200	4	800	NO
12								
13	Total	350		750				

From this image you can see that the arrows indicate that cells H8 and I3 both affect (ie are precedents of) the value K8.

If we were to select **Trace Precedents** for a second time without moving from the selected cell, we would see the cells which are precedents H8 and I3 are added to the picture, as shown below:

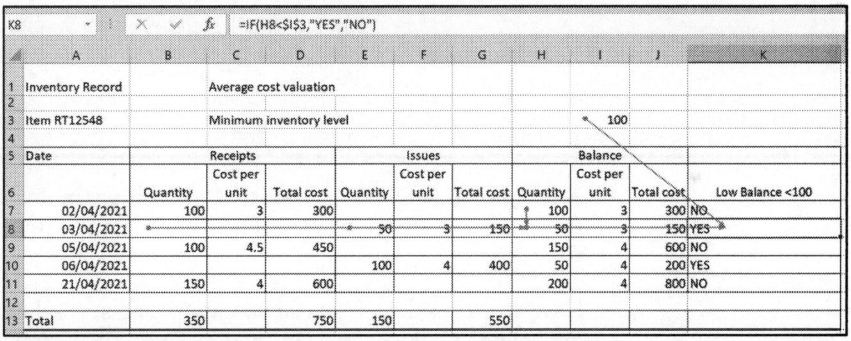

K8 =IF(H8<$I$3,"YES","NO")

	A	B	C	D	E	F	G	H	I	J	K
1	Inventory Record		Average cost valuation								
2											
3	Item RT12548		Minimum inventory level						100		
4											
5	Date		Receipts			Issues			Balance		
6		Quantity	Cost per unit	Total cost	Quantity	Cost per unit	Total cost	Quantity	Cost per unit	Total cost	Low Balance <100
7	02/04/2021	100	3	300				100	3	300	NO
8	03/04/2021				50	3	150	50	3	150	YES
9	05/04/2021	100	4.5	450				150	4	600	NO
10	06/04/2021				100	4	400	50	4	200	YES
11	21/04/2021	150	4	600				200	4	800	NO
12											
13	Total	350		750	150		550				

The extra arrows show that H8 utilises the cells B8 and E8, and I3 is not dependent on any other cell.

This **Trace Precedents** tool is very useful for checking formulas, especially on more complex sheets.

To Trace Precedents for a particular cell:

- select the required cell
- select **Trace Precedents** from the menu bar (usually in the formulas section)
- repeat as required

To remove the arrows generated:

- select **Remove Arrows** from the menu bar

trace dependents

The **Trace Dependents** facility allows you to identify those cells which are affected by the value of the currently selected cell.

For example, if cell D4 contained the formula

=22+F4/20

D4 would be a **dependent** of F4 because its value is dependent on the value of F4.

If we return to the Inventory record worksheet and select cell B7, and then select Trace Dependents, the screen will appear as follows:

B7 fx 100

	A	B	C	D	E	F	G	H	I	J	K
1	Inventory Record		Average cost valuation								
2											
3	Item RT12548		Minimum inventory level						100		
4											
5	Date		Receipts			Issues			Balance		
6		Quantity	Cost per unit	Total cost	Quantity	Cost per unit	Total cost	Quantity	Cost per unit	Total cost	Low Balance <100
7	02/04/2021	100	3	300				100	3	300	NO
8	03/04/2021				50	3	150	50	3	150	YES
9	05/04/2021	100	4.5	450				150	4	600	NO
10	06/04/2021				100	4	400	50	4	200	YES
11	21/04/2021	150	4	600				200	4	800	NO
12											
13	Total	350		750	150		550				

From this image you can see that the arrows indicate that cell B7 is used in formulas in cells B13, D7 and H7, showing that these cells are dependent on B7.

If we were to select Trace Dependents for a second time without moving from the selected cell, we would then see any cells affected by B13, D7 and H7 added to the picture, as shown below:

B7 fx 100

	A	B	C	D	E	F	G	H	I	J	K
1	Inventory Record		Average cost valuation								
2											
3	Item RT12548		Minimum inventory level						100		
4											
5	Date		Receipts			Issues			Balance		
6		Quantity	Cost per unit	Total cost	Quantity	Cost per unit	Total cost	Quantity	Cost per unit	Total cost	Low Balance <100
7	02/04/2021	100	3	300				100	3	300	NO
8	03/04/2021				50	3	150	50	3	150	YES
9	05/04/2021	100	4.5	450				150	4	600	NO
10	06/04/2021				100	4	400	50	4	200	YES
11	21/04/2021	150	4	600				200	4	800	NO
12											
13	Total	350		750	150		550				

There are several additional arrows showing cells D13, H8, I7, J7 and K7 are all dependents on the dependents of B7.

To Trace Dependents for a particular cell:

- select the required cell
- select **Trace Dependents** from the menu bar (usually in the formulas section)
- repeat as required

To remove the arrows generated:

- select **Remove Arrows** from the menu bar

SPELL CHECK

Spreadsheet packages usually provide built-in spell-checking tools to check the text in your worksheets.

For our example, we will use a modified version of our expenditure forecast worksheet, which now contains several typing mistakes. This is illustrated below:

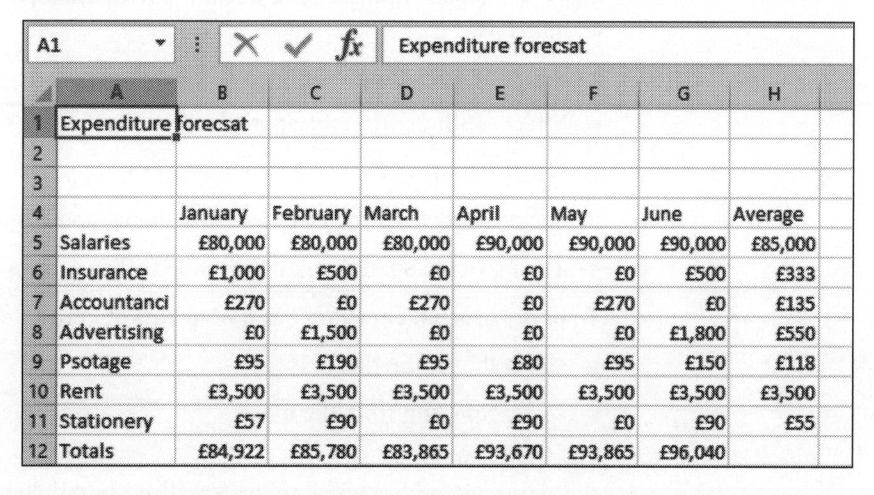

A1 | Expenditure forecsat

	A	B	C	D	E	F	G	H
1	Expenditure forecsat							
2								
3								
4		January	February	March	April	May	June	Average
5	Salaries	£80,000	£80,000	£80,000	£90,000	£90,000	£90,000	£85,000
6	Insurance	£1,000	£500	£0	£0	£0	£500	£333
7	Accountanci	£270	£0	£270	£0	£270	£0	£135
8	Advertising	£0	£1,500	£0	£0	£0	£1,800	£550
9	Psotage	£95	£190	£95	£80	£95	£150	£118
10	Rent	£3,500	£3,500	£3,500	£3,500	£3,500	£3,500	£3,500
11	Stationery	£57	£90	£0	£90	£0	£90	£55
12	Totals	£84,922	£85,780	£83,865	£93,670	£93,865	£96,040	

If we select **Spelling** from the **Review** menu, the first text to be identified will be in cell A1, where we have spelt forecast incorrectly:

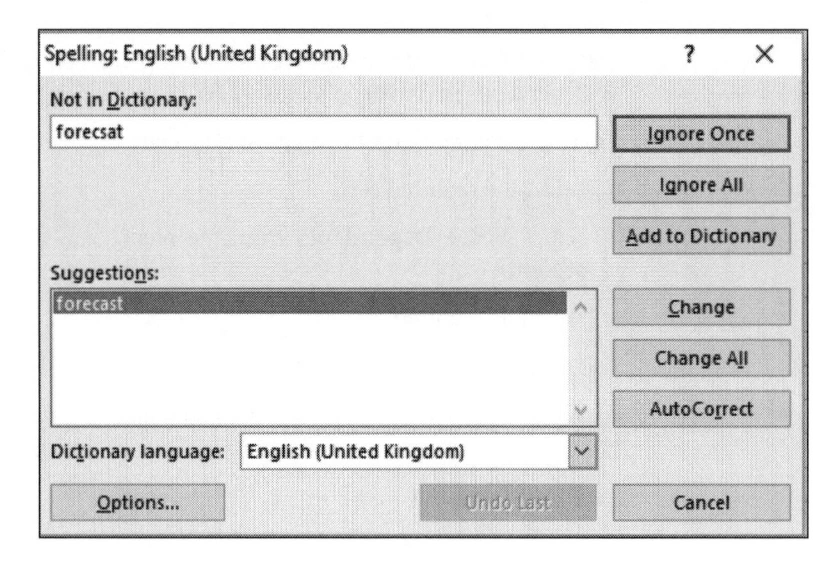

Once identified, you can choose how you want to proceed from the options given, as shown above. The tool can step through and check the spelling in all cells on the worksheet.

Within the spellcheck tool options, you can choose rules which you want to apply when performing a spell check – for example, to ignore words that are all uppercase.

To set your rule choices for Spell check:

- select **Options** from the appropriate menu
- select **Proofing**
- check or uncheck the rules to configure as you require

You can request Spell check on just one cell or a group of cells.

To perform **Spell check** on a **cell** or **group of cells**:

- select the required cell(s)
- select **Spelling** from the menu

The rules will be applied as set up in the Options/Proofing described above, and any cells with a spelling error will be highlighted and suggestions for revised spellings offered.

To perform a full worksheet Spell check:

- select **Spelling** from the menu
- confirm that you wish to check the whole sheet

REMOVE DUPLICATES

If the data within our spreadsheet has come from another program, perhaps via Import, it is possible that some of the rows of data may be repeated. Alternatively, we may have rows which repeat just some values. There is a tool available to **Remove duplicate** rows, or rows containing duplicate values.

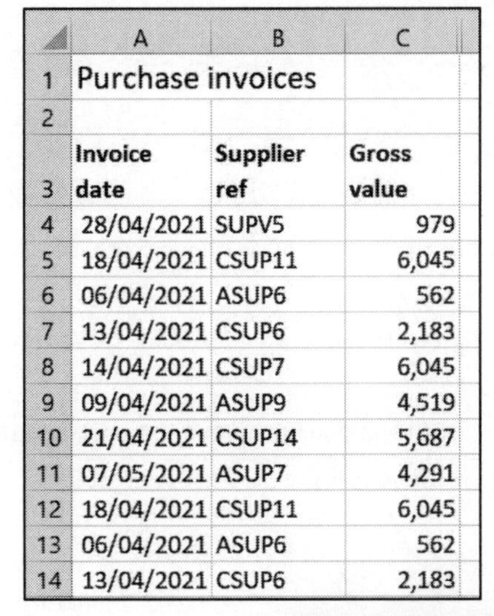

	A	B	C
1	Purchase invoices		
2			
3	Invoice date	Supplier ref	Gross value
4	28/04/2021	SUPV5	979
5	18/04/2021	CSUP11	6,045
6	06/04/2021	ASUP6	562
7	13/04/2021	CSUP6	2,183
8	14/04/2021	CSUP7	6,045
9	09/04/2021	ASUP9	4,519
10	21/04/2021	CSUP14	5,687
11	07/05/2021	ASUP7	4,291
12	18/04/2021	CSUP11	6,045
13	06/04/2021	ASUP6	562
14	13/04/2021	CSUP6	2,183

The Remove Duplicates tool is found in the **Data** menu, Data tools section.

If we look at an example, where we have a list of purchase invoices as shown on the left.

This is the list of purchase invoices used previously, but if we look more closely we can see it has changed, and the entries on rows 5, 6 and 7 appear identical to those on 12, 13 and 14. Somehow the data has been duplicated, we will use the Remove duplicates tool to clean the data.

- Select the data in rows 4 to 14
- Select Remove duplicates from the **Data** menu (as shown on the next page)

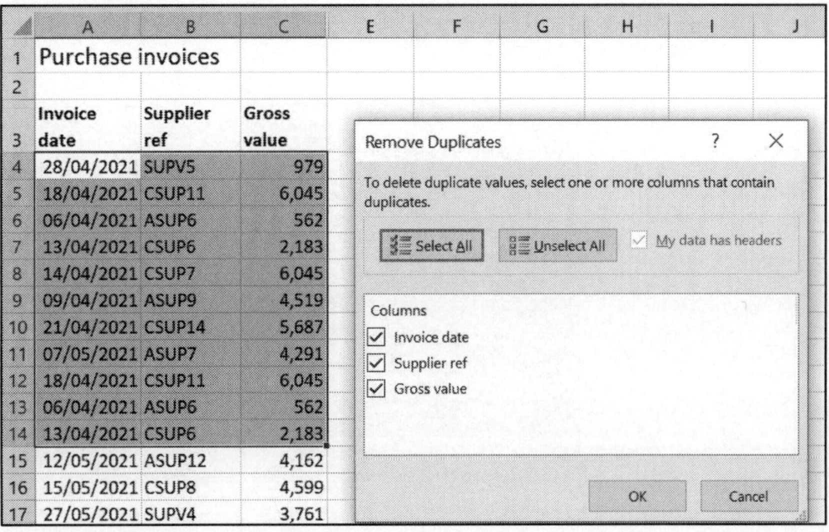

	A	B	C
1	Purchase invoices		
2			
3	Invoice date	Supplier ref	Gross value
4	28/04/2021	SUPV5	979
5	18/04/2021	CSUP11	6,045
6	06/04/2021	ASUP6	562
7	13/04/2021	CSUP6	2,183
8	14/04/2021	CSUP7	6,045
9	09/04/2021	ASUP9	4,519
10	21/04/2021	CSUP14	5,687
11	07/05/2021	ASUP7	4,291
12	18/04/2021	CSUP11	6,045
13	06/04/2021	ASUP6	562
14	13/04/2021	CSUP6	2,183
15	12/05/2021	ASUP12	4,162
16	15/05/2021	CSUP8	4,599
17	27/05/2021	SUPV4	3,761

If we select ok, those rows with identical values in all three columns will be deleted.

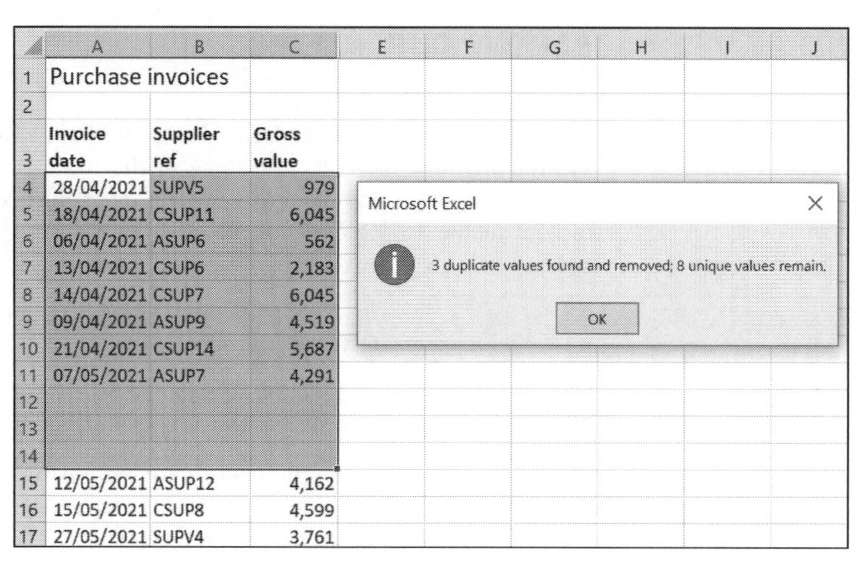

Alternatively, we may wish to only delete those with identical values in a certain column, or column(s).

If we just wanted to delete those rows with the same Gross value, we would select only the Gross value column in the Remove Duplicates options, as shown below:

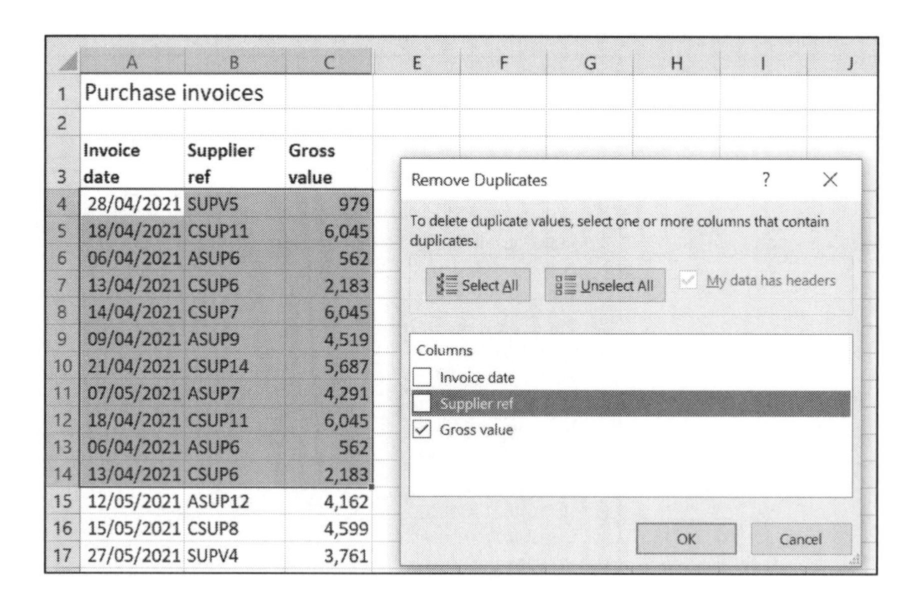

This removes four duplicate values, as can be seen on the next page:

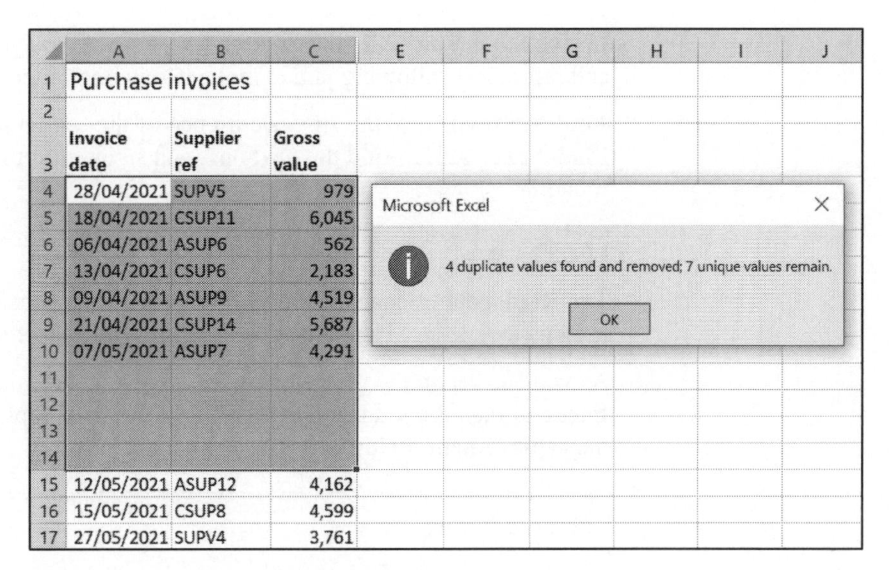

	A	B	C	E	F	G	H	I	J
1	Purchase invoices								
2									
3	Invoice date	Supplier ref	Gross value						
4	28/04/2021	SUPV5	979						
5	18/04/2021	CSUP11	6,045						
6	06/04/2021	ASUP6	562						
7	13/04/2021	CSUP6	2,183						
8	09/04/2021	ASUP9	4,519						
9	21/04/2021	CSUP14	5,687						
10	07/05/2021	ASUP7	4,291						
11									
12									
13									
14									
15	12/05/2021	ASUP12	4,162						
16	15/05/2021	CSUP8	4,599						
17	27/05/2021	SUPV4	3,761						

One more row was deleted than previously, since row 8 matched on value, but not on Invoice date or Supplier.

Note: if you wish to put the rows back into your data, clicking UNDO straight after clicking OK will UNDO the deletions.

FIND AND REPLACE

find

Another powerful facility is the **Find** tool, which can be used to find a specific value or text within the worksheet.

To use **Find**, select the **Find and Select** icon, select **Find** from the **Home** menu. As shown in the screen below, you then specify:

Find what – this will be the value or text which is to be found (known as the **search string**):

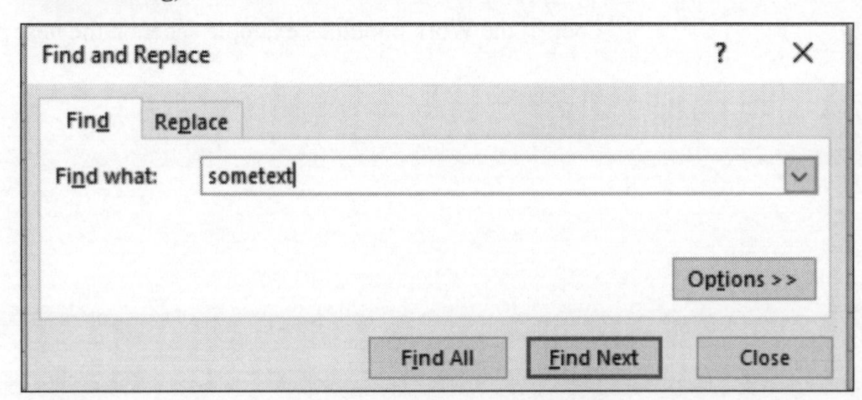

If you chose **Find All**, all occurrences will be displayed together with their cell references, allowing you to move to any one of them.

Find Next will find the first occurrence of the search string. You then click **Find Next** again to find the next one, and so on until there are no more to be found.

replace

The **Replace** tool enables you to find and replace specific text or values. To use this tool, select **Replace** from the **Find and Select** menu.

As you can see in the image below, you specify the value or text you want to find, and then the value or text which you want to replace it with (known as the **replacement string**):

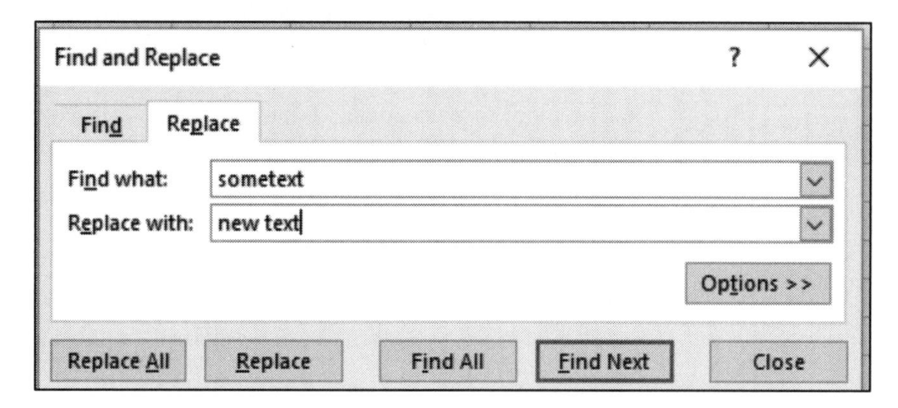

If you chose **Replace All**, all occurrences of the **search string** will automatically be replaced with the **replacement string**.

Sometimes, you may only want to replace certain occurrences of the search string, in which case, you would select **Find Next**, until you find one which you want to change, and then you select **Replace** and then **Find Next** again until you have made all the changes you require.

Look at the Work bookings example sheet on the next page.

	A	B	C	D	E	F
1	Work bookings					
2						
3	Hourly rate	£30				
4						
5	Client	Week1	Week2	Week3	Week4	Total
6	Smiths Ltd	15	15	15	15	60
7	Jones and Partner	12	8	10	9	39
8	Redwoods	13	20	11	7	51
9	Underhills	13	20	11	2	46

We could use **Find and Replace** to change the column titles from Week1, Week2, etc. to be Month1, Month2, and so on. To do this:

- select **Find and Replace** from the menu
- find what – enter **Week**
- replace with – enter **Month**
- click **Replace All**

This is shown in the image on the next page.

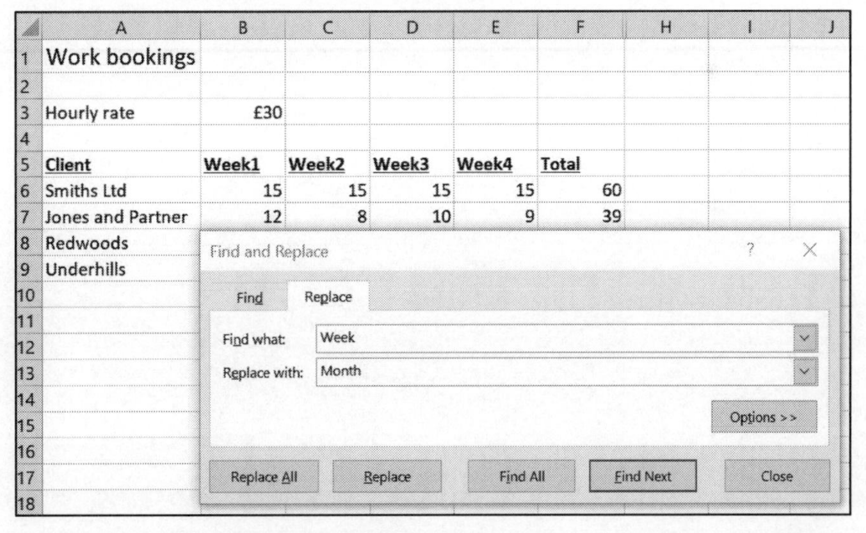

A message will be displayed indicating how many occurrences of the search string have been found and changed.

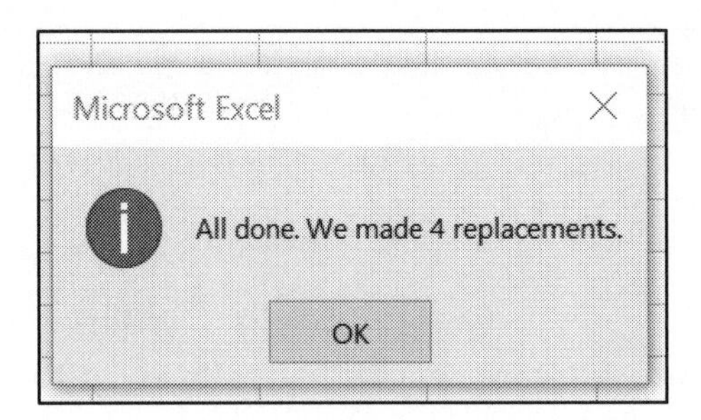

You can see the results in the screen below.

	A	B	C	D	E	F
1	Work bookings					
2						
3	Hourly rate	£30				
4						
5	Client	Month1	Month2	Month3	Month4	Total
6	Smiths Ltd	15	15	15	15	60
7	Jones and Partner	12	8	10	9	39
8	Redwoods	13	20	11	7	51
9	Underhills	13	20	11	2	46

SORTING DATA

In the next few pages we will be working with tools which allow us to manipulate data, such as SORT, FILTER and SUBTOTAL.

The data we use should be in consecutive rows and columns, with each column having a unique heading, and no empty rows or columns.

If we look at worksheet Weekly Pay data shown in the image below, we can see that the employee names are not in alphabetical order.

	A	B	C	D	E	F
1	Weekly Pay data					
2						
3	Std weekly hours	38				
4	Hourly Rate	£16.00				
5	Overtime Rate	£21.50				
6						
7	**Employee**	**Hours worked**	**Overtime hours**	**Basic pay**	**Overtime pay**	**Total pay**
8	Johal	40	2	£608.00	£43.00	£651.00
9	Bhopal	49	11	£608.00	£236.50	£844.50
10	Wakula	50	12	£608.00	£258.00	£866.00
11	Hacek	38	0	£608.00	£0.00	£608.00
12	Young	39.5	1.5	£608.00	£32.25	£640.25
13	White	52	14	£608.00	£301.00	£909.00
14	Jones	38	0	£608.00	£0.00	£608.00
15	Plant	39.5	1.5	£608.00	£32.25	£640.25

Alphabetical sorting is very simple, using a built-in **sort tool**, which allows us to sort data alphabetically A to Z, or reversely Z to A. Numeric data, can also be sorted in ascending or descending order.

When we are doing a sort we have to identify and select the data which is to be sorted. It is very important that we include any associated data in the nearby columns within our selection.

In the example above, because the data in the hours and pay columns is specific to the individual employee, if we change the order of the employees, we must also change the order of the other data in the same way. This will happen automatically if we include the associated columns in our selection, before we select sort.

In the image on the next page, the data in all six columns is selected from row 8 downwards.

	A	B	C	D	E	F
1	Weekly Pay data					
2						
3	Std weekly hours	38				
4	Hourly Rate	£16.00				
5	Overtime Rate	£21.50				
6						
7	Employee	Hours worked	Overtime hours	Basic pay	Overtime pay	Total pay
8	Johal	40	2	£608.00	£43.00	£651.00
9	Bhopal	49	11	£608.00	£236.50	£844.50
10	Wakula	50	12	£608.00	£258.00	£866.00
11	Hacek	38	0	£608.00	£0.00	£608.00
12	Young	39.5	1.5	£608.00	£32.25	£640.25
13	White	52	14	£608.00	£301.00	£909.00
14	Jones	38	0	£608.00	£0.00	£608.00
15	Plant	39.5	1.5	£608.00	£32.25	£640.25

We then select **Sort and Filter** from the **Home** or **Data** menus, choose Sort A to Z to order alphabetically A to Z and get the results below.

	A	B	C	D	E	F
1	Weekly Pay data					
2						
3	Std weekly hours	38				
4	Hourly Rate	£16.00				
5	Overtime Rate	£21.50				
6						
7	Employee	Hours worked	Overtime hours	Basic pay	Overtime pay	Total pay
8	Bhopal	49	11	£608.00	£236.50	£844.50
9	Hacek	38	0	£608.00	£0.00	£608.00
10	Johal	40	2	£608.00	£43.00	£651.00
11	Jones	38	0	£608.00	£0.00	£608.00
12	Plant	39.5	1.5	£608.00	£32.25	£640.25
13	Wakula	50	12	£608.00	£258.00	£866.00
14	White	52	14	£608.00	£301.00	£909.00
15	Young	39.5	1.5	£608.00	£32.25	£640.25

The selected data has been sorted by the first column on the left – Employee, and you can see that all the data has moved with the individual employee name and remains correct.

The data will always be sorted by the first column on the left, unless you use **Custom Sort**, and specifically choose a different column. **Sort** is also available from the **Data** menu, this leads directly into a Custom Sort.

When doing a **sort** to a column containing text, we could choose reverse order Z to A if required.

Columns containing numbers can be sorted in **Ascending** (increasing) or **Descending** (decreasing) order. For columns containing dates, these could be sorted newest to oldest or oldest to newest.

Our headings in row 5 are recognised as column headings or names because they are immediately above the data, so when we select **Custom Sort**, these column names are displayed for us to choose from, as shown below. (The **My data has headers** box is checked to indicate this.)

Within Custom Sort, you can choose the column to sort by.

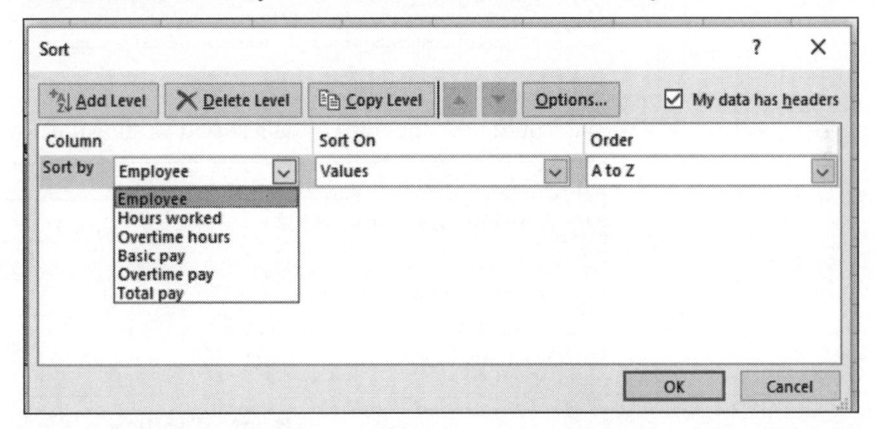

What you want to sort on.

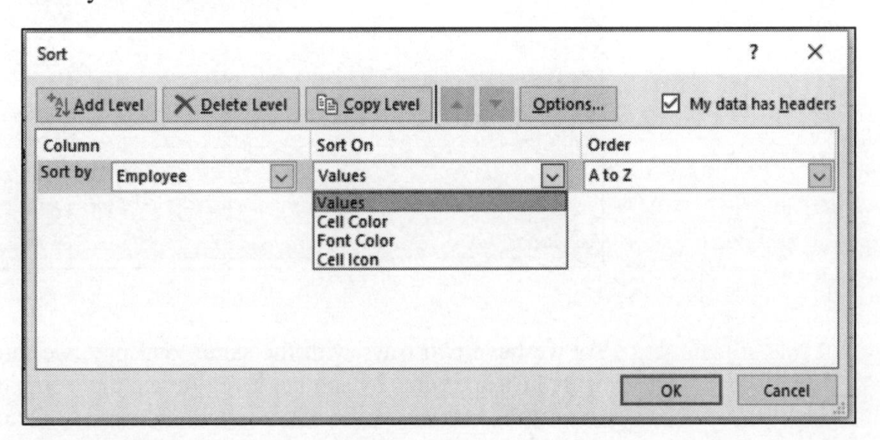

And the order you want to sort by.

If we had chosen to sort by Total pay, a numeric column, we can then select order Smallest to Largest, or Largest to Smallest, as shown on the next page.

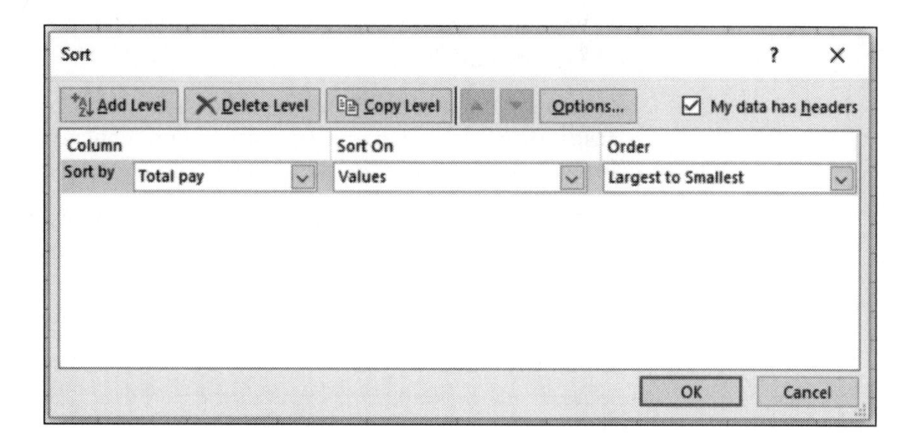

We would have the rows of data sorted as shown below:

	A	B	C	D	E	F
1	Weekly Pay data					
2						
3	Std weekly hours	38				
4	Hourly Rate	£16.00				
5	Overtime Rate	£21.50				
6						
7	Employee	Hours worked	Overtime hours	Basic pay	Overtime pay	Total pay
8	White	52	14	£608.00	£301.00	£909.00
9	Wakula	50	12	£608.00	£258.00	£866.00
10	Bhopal	49	11	£608.00	£236.50	£844.50
11	Johal	40	2	£608.00	£43.00	£651.00
12	Plant	39.5	1.5	£608.00	£32.25	£640.25
13	Young	39.5	1.5	£608.00	£32.25	£640.25
14	Hacek	38	0	£608.00	£0.00	£608.00
15	Jones	38	0	£608.00	£0.00	£608.00

As we have two rows with the same total pay, we might want to sort rows with the same value by another level, for example employee name. To do this, in custom sort we would add a level, and specify the column to sort on and the order, as shown in the example on the next page.

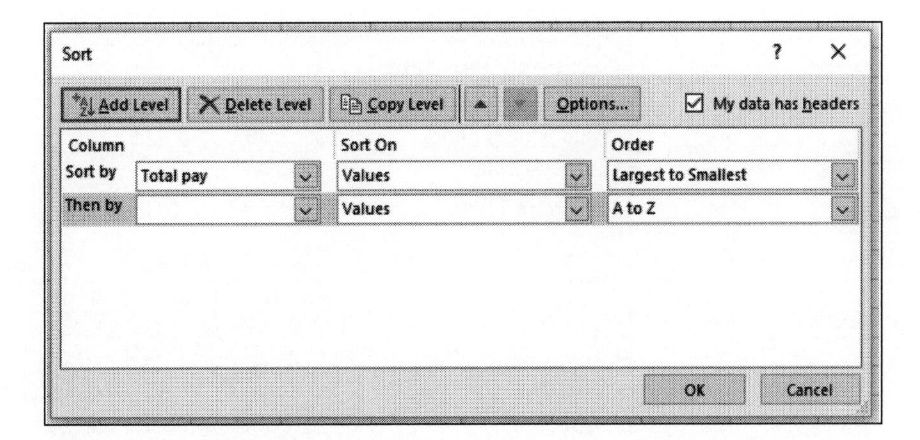

Selecting as shown below:

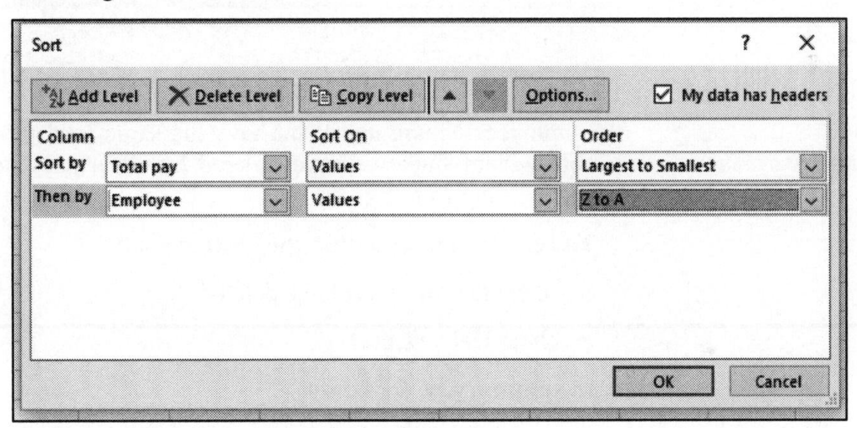

Would give the data sorted as follows:

	A	B	C	D	E	F
1	Weekly Pay data					
2						
3	Std weekly hours	38				
4	Hourly Rate	£16.00				
5	Overtime Rate	£21.50				
6						
7	Employee	Hours worked	Overtime hours	Basic pay	Overtime pay	Total pay
8	White	52	14	£608.00	£301.00	£909.00
9	Wakula	50	12	£608.00	£258.00	£866.00
10	Bhopal	49	11	£608.00	£236.50	£844.50
11	Johal	40	2	£608.00	£43.00	£651.00
12	Young	39.5	1.5	£608.00	£32.25	£640.25
13	Plant	39.5	1.5	£608.00	£32.25	£640.25
14	Jones	38	0	£608.00	£0.00	£608.00
15	Hacek	38	0	£608.00	£0.00	£608.00

Employees Young and Plant have the same total pay. Young now appears above Plant since we have ordered by Total pay, and then by Employees name, going from Z to A.

To remove a level within the custom sort:

- select the **sort level** to be deleted
- click **Delete Level**

In summary, to sort data:

- **select the data** which we want **to sort** (including any associated data)
- select **Sort and Filter** from the menu

either

- choose **Sort** (A to Z, Z to A, Ascending or Descending) as appropriate

or

- select **Custom sort** and make your choices, as described above

filter

If you have a spreadsheet containing a large amount of data, as in the example below (which shows sales by month), the **Filter** facility allows you to filter the data so that you only see rows which contain certain values or combinations of values. For example, **Filter** could show just those rows where Region=North West or a combination such as Region=North West and Manufacturer=Ford (see illustration below).

	A	B	C	D	E
1	Year	Month	Manufacturer	Region	Quantity
2	2020	Jan	Mercedes	South West	220
3	2020	Mar	BMW	North West	155
4	2020	Feb	Toyota	North West	35
5	2020	Jun	VW	South	125
6	2020	Jul	Ford	East	126
7	2020	Jul	Skoda	East	1,345
8	2020	Apr	VW	South West	56
9	2020	Aug	Mercedes	South	68
10	2020	Aug	Toyota	South	100
11	2019	Feb	Ford	South	1,500
12	2019	Feb	Seat	East	220
13	2019	Mar	Seat	South West	155
14	2019	Apr	VW	North West	35
15	2019	Mar	Mercedes	North West	125
16	2019	Jan	Skoda	South	1,260
17	2019	Mar	Toyota	East	45
18	2019	Jul	VW	South West	56
19	2019	Feb	Ford	South West	68

To Filter data:

- place the cursor in the cell containing the leftmost heading text
- select **Filter** from the **Sort and Filter** icon on the **Home** menu or the Filter icon from the DATA menu

You will see something similar to the image below.

	A	B	C	D	E
1	Year	Month	Manufacturer	Region	Quantit
2	2020	Jan	Mercedes	South West	220
3	2020	Mar	BMW	North West	155
4	2020	Feb	Toyota	North West	35
5	2020	Jun	VW	South	125
6	2020	Jul	Ford	East	126
7	2020	Jul	Skoda	East	1,345
8	2020	Apr	VW	South West	56
9	2020	Aug	Mercedes	South	68
10	2020	Aug	Toyota	South	100
11	2019	Feb	Ford	South	1,500
12	2019	Feb	Seat	East	220
13	2019	Mar	Seat	South West	155

You can now choose how you want to filter the data:

- click on the **drop-down arrow** on a column
- select the required values which you wish to analyse from the drop-down menu

- repeat on other columns as required to refine the rows displayed

In the image below, you can see the rows which would be displayed when a filter of Region=North West is applied to the sales data. The funnel symbol next to Region indicates that a filter has been applied to that column.

	A	B	C	D	E
1	Year	Month	Manufacturer	Region	Quantit
3	2020	Mar	BMW	North West	155
4	2020	Feb	Toyota	North West	35
14	2019	Apr	VW	North West	35
15	2019	Mar	Mercedes	North West	125
25	2018	Apr	Ford	North West	56
26	2018	Nov	Seat	North West	125
33	2019	Dec	Ford	North West	34
35	2019	Dec	VW	North West	1,500
36	2019	Nov	Mercedes	North West	220

If we applied a further filter to the Manufacturer, looking only for Ford, we would get only those rows displayed where Region=North West and Manufacturer=Ford, as can be seen below:

	A	B	C	D	E
1	Year	Month	Manufacturer	Region	Quantit
25	2018	Apr	Ford	North West	56
33	2019	Dec	Ford	North West	34

Alternatively, we can filter by numbers.

For example, from the original data shown below, we might want to only see those rows where the Quantity is more than 100 and less than 1000.

	A	B	C	D	E
1	Year	Month	Manufacturer	Region	Quantit
2	2020	Jan	Mercedes	South West	220
3	2020	Mar	BMW	North West	155
4	2020	Feb	Toyota	North West	35
5	2020	Jun	VW	South	125
6	2020	Jul	Ford	East	126
7	2020	Jul	Skoda	East	1,345
8	2020	Apr	VW	South West	56
9	2020	Aug	Mercedes	South	68
10	2020	Aug	Toyota	South	100
11	2019	Feb	Ford	South	1,500
12	2019	Feb	Seat	East	220
13	2019	Mar	Seat	South West	155

To do this:

- click on the drop-down arrow on the Quantity column
- select Number Filters, then Greater Than
- enter the value 100
- ensure AND is selected
- select is less than from the lower drop-down box
- enter the value 1000
- select OK

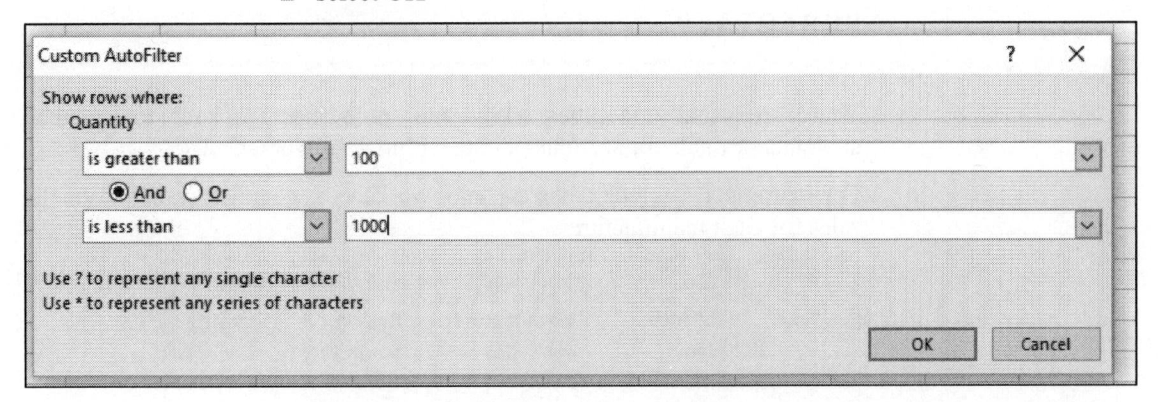

We can see how only those rows with Quantity greater than 100 and less than 1000 are now displayed.

	A	B	C	D	E
1	Year	Month	Manufacturer	Region	Quantit
2	2020	Jan	Mercedes	South West	220
3	2020	Mar	BMW	North West	155
5	2020	Jun	VW	South	125
6	2020	Jul	Ford	East	126
12	2019	Feb	Seat	East	220
13	2019	Mar	Seat	South West	155
15	2019	Mar	Mercedes	North West	125
26	2018	Nov	Seat	North West	125
27	2018	Nov	Seat	South	126
36	2019	Nov	Mercedes	North West	220
37	2019	Sep	Toyota	South	155
39	2019	Dec	BMW	South West	125

It is worth experimenting with Number Filters, since there are many different filters which can be applied.

When filtering is active, to **Turn off** the active filter on a column:

- Click on the **Filter** symbol on the column
- Select **clear filters**

To Remove all Filters:

- Select **Filter** from the **Sort and Filter** menu

(The filter icon will be highlighted in the menu, showing filtering is active.)

SUBTOTALS

There are usually facilities within the spreadsheet package to calculate subtotals or totals for sections of data within your worksheet.

For example, if we look at the car sales worksheet, we might want to total the sales for each manufacturer.

	A	B	C	D	E
1	**Year**	**Month**	**Manufacturer**	**Region**	**Quantity**
2	2020	Jan	Mercedes	South West	220
3	2020	Mar	BMW	North West	155
4	2020	Feb	Toyota	North West	35
5	2020	Jun	VW	South	125
6	2020	Jul	Ford	East	126
7	2020	Jul	Skoda	East	1,345
8	2020	Apr	VW	South West	56
9	2020	Aug	Mercedes	South	68
10	2020	Aug	Toyota	South	100
11	2019	Feb	Ford	South	1,500
12	2019	Feb	Seat	East	220
13	2019	Mar	Seat	South West	155

The first step is to order/sort the data, so that it is arranged by the column for which we want subtotals. For example, if we want subtotals by manufacturer we will sort the data by that column, if we want subtotals by Region, we will sort the data by that column.

Let us assume we want to create **Subtotals** by **manufacturer**, ie we want to know how many cars each manufacturer has sold.

We will first sort the data as shown below, using **Custom Sort**, and selecting the **manufacturer column**. The data is then shown in alphabetical order by **manufacturer**.

	A	B	C	D	E
1	Year	Month	Manufacturer	Region	Quantity
2	2020	Mar	BMW	North West	155
3	2018	Sep	BMW	East	1,460
4	2018	Sep	BMW	South West	34
5	2019	Oct	BMW	South West	68
6	2019	Nov	BMW	East	56
7	2019	Oct	BMW	South West	35
8	2019	Dec	BMW	South West	125
9	2020	Jul	Ford	East	126
10	2019	Feb	Ford	South	1,500
11	2019	Feb	Ford	South West	68
12	2018	Apr	Ford	North West	56
13	2019	Dec	Ford	North West	34
14	2020	Jan	Mercedes	South West	220

The next step is to select all the data including our column headings, either:

- select **Subtotal** from the **Data** menu

or

- select **Outline**, then **Subtotal** from the **Data** menu

The Subtotal options then appear, and we have to make some choices:

1 The first choice is the column for which we need a subtotal.

  The default choice is the column on the left – the 'Year' column.

  Because we want to create a Subtotal for each manufacturer, we use the 'Manufacturer' column. For **At each change in** we select 'Manufacturer'.

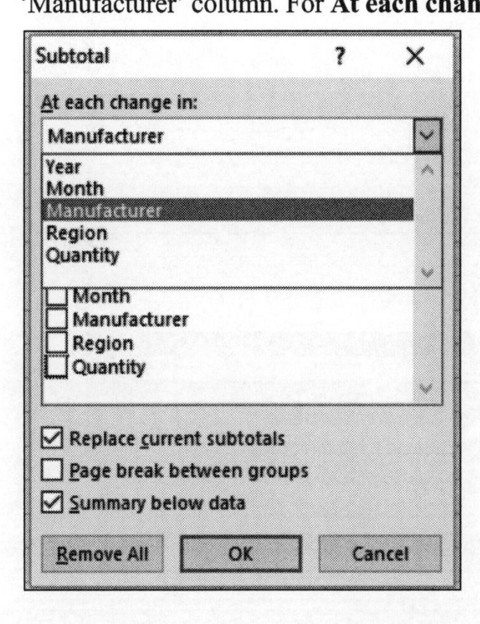

2 The next choice is the **function** we want to use, with a wide range of possibilities eg COUNT, AVERAGE, MAX, MIN etc.

We select **SUM**, because we want to total the number of cars sold by each manufacturer.

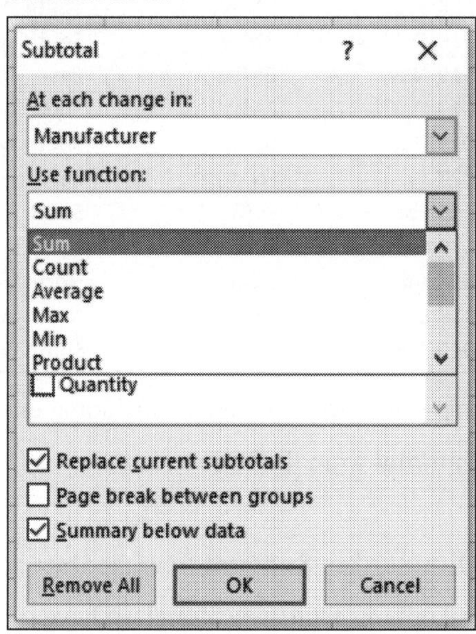

3 The final choice is the column we are adding up and the column to which we want to add a Subtotal.

We select the **Quantity** column.

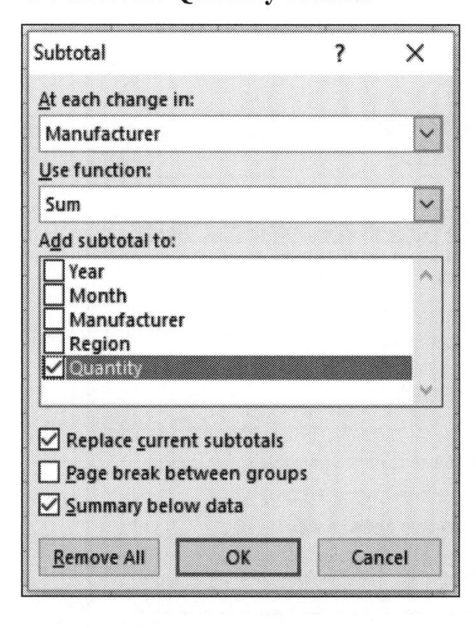

4 You should keep the defaults for the remaining options.

The results are shown in the screen below.

	A	B	C	D	E
1	**Year**	**Month**	**Manufacturer**	**Region**	**Quantity**
2	2020	Mar	BMW	North West	155
3	2018	Sep	BMW	East	1,460
4	2018	Sep	BMW	South West	34
5	2019	Oct	BMW	South West	68
6	2019	Nov	BMW	East	56
7	2019	Oct	BMW	South West	35
8	2019	Dec	BMW	South West	125
9			**BMW Total**		1,932
10	2020	Jul	Ford	East	126
11	2019	Feb	Ford	South	1,500
12	2019	Feb	Ford	South West	68
13	2018	Apr	Ford	North West	56
14	2019	Dec	Ford	North West	34
15			**Ford Total**		1,784
16	2020	Jan	Mercedes	South West	220

Looking at the image above, on the left-hand side, you can see minus (-) symbols and lines, these are known as outlines, which allow us to see all the detail rows making up the subtotals.

We can choose to just see the summary of subtotals in outline, either by selecting individual minus (-) symbols on the left or selecting all the data, and then **Hide Detail** from the **Outline** option on the **Data** menu, the red minus symbol, (found to the right of the Subtotal option) or by selecting 1, 2, or 3 from the symbols shown on the top left, indicating levels of detail to be displayed. As shown in the image below, you can see that the minus signs are now replaced by plus signs (+).

	A	B	C	D	E
1	**Year**	**Month**	**Manufacturer**	**Region**	**Quantity**
9			**BMW Total**		1,932
15			**Ford Total**		1,784
21			**Mercedes Total**		689
28			**Seat Total**		2,185
31			**Skoda Total**		2,605
37			**Toyota Total**		434
46			**VW Total**		4,777
47			**Grand Total**		14,406

If we had wanted the **average** number of cars sold by each manufacturer, we would have just chosen the AVERAGE function within the subtotal options, as shown below:

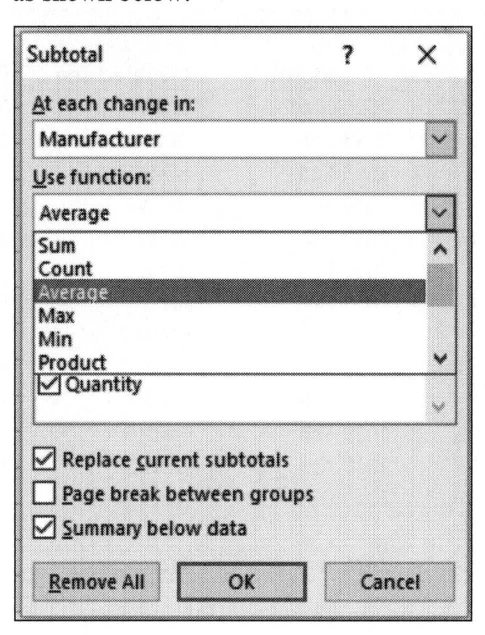

Which would give us the following:

	A	B	C	D	E
1	Year	Month	Manufacturer	Region	Quantity
2	2020	Mar	BMW	North West	155
3	2018	Sep	BMW	East	1,460
4	2018	Sep	BMW	South West	34
5	2019	Oct	BMW	South West	68
6	2019	Nov	BMW	East	56
7	2019	Oct	BMW	South West	35
8	2019	Dec	BMW	South West	125
9			**BMW Average**		276
10	2020	Jul	Ford	East	126
11	2019	Feb	Ford	South	1,500
12	2019	Feb	Ford	South West	68
13	2018	Apr	Ford	North West	56
14	2019	Dec	Ford	North West	34
15			**Ford Average**		357
16	2020	Jan	Mercedes	South West	220

Alternatively, we could use SUBTOTAL to give us the COUNT, MAX or MIN for each manufacturer.

As you can see from the screens on the previous page, the SUBTOTAL function is extremely useful when we have large amounts of data, and only want to look at a summary.

If you need to revert to full detail, either select individual plus signs (+), or select all the data and then show detail from the menu, or by selecting 3 from the symbols shown on the top left, indicating levels of detail to be displayed.

To remove the subtotals:

- select all the data
- select **Subtotal** from the **Outline** option on the **Data** menu
- click on **Remove All**

It is possible to have subtotals within subtotals, for example, how many cars within each car manufacturer, within each region.

To do this, the data should be sorted by Manufacturer, and then by Region.

As before, create subtotals by Manufacturer, then create additional subtotals within the manufacturer by region, by selecting the options as shown below, making sure that Replace current subtotals is not ticked.

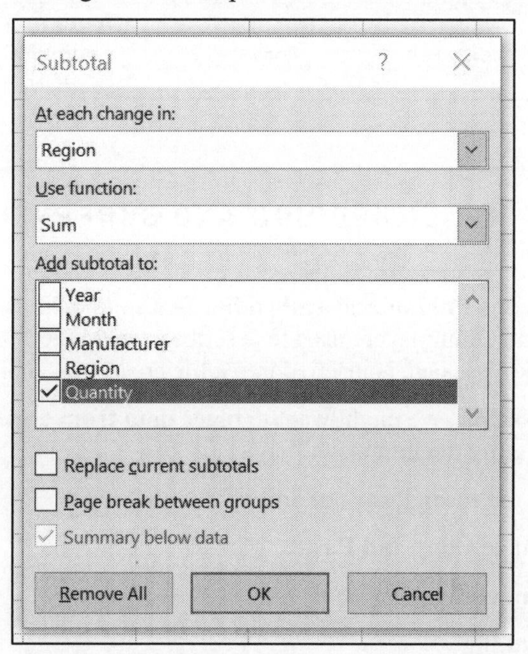

This will produce subtotals as shown on the next page:

	A	B	C	D	E
1	**Year**	**Month**	**Manufacturer**	**Region**	**Quantity**
2	2018	Sep	BMW	East	1,460
3	2019	Nov	BMW	East	56
4				**East Total**	1,516
5	2020	Mar	BMW	North West	155
6				**North West T**	155
7	2018	Sep	BMW	South West	34
8	2019	Oct	BMW	South West	68
9	2019	Oct	BMW	South West	35
10	2019	Dec	BMW	South West	125
11				**South West T**	261
12			**BMW Total**		1,932
13	2020	Jul	Ford	East	126
14				**East Total**	126
15	2018	Apr	Ford	North West	56
16	2019	Dec	Ford	North West	34
17				**North West T**	90
18	2019	Feb	Ford	South	1,500
19				**South Total**	1,500
20	2019	Feb	Ford	South West	68
21				**South West T**	68

LINKING, EMBEDDING AND SCREENSHOTS

The terms **linking and embedding** – also known as **OLE** (Object Linking and Embedding) – are used to describe a technique where data created by one software package is inserted into a file created by another software package.

For example, we might want to **place data from a spreadsheet into a word processing document**.

There are several ways of doing this:

- simple **Copy and Paste**
- **Embedding**
- **Linking**

copy and paste

Copy and Paste would just put a copy of the spreadsheet data in the word processing document, but if anything changed in the original spreadsheet, the data would not change in the document.

embedding

If we **Embed** the data in the word processing document, it creates a static copy of the spreadsheet data as a table in the word processing document, so if anything changed in the original spreadsheet, the data would not change in the document. This can be useful if you don't want the document to reflect changes in the spreadsheet.

If you select to edit this table of spreadsheet data within the word processing document (usually by DOUBLE CLICK), it will automatically open up the spreadsheet software and display the data ready to be changed.

To insert spreadsheet data as embedded:

Select and copy the data in the original spreadsheet, switch to the word processing package with the document open, select **Paste Special**, and paste as a worksheet object.

linking

If the spreadsheet data were **linked** in the word processing document, then if it changed in the original spreadsheet, it would automatically update in the word processing document the next time the word processing document was opened, or if it were open when the original spreadsheet were changed.

To link data:

First select the data in the original worksheet to copy, switch to the word processing package with a document open, select **Paste Special**, paste as a worksheet object, and select **Paste Link**.

This is an area where you should experiment with your software packages, since detailed key-strokes will vary from package to package.

screenshots

There are several ways to create a screenshot:

- select **Illustrations** from the **Insert** menu
- select **Screenshot**

either

- choose from one of the windows displayed

or

- use the clipping tool to clip the area you want to include

The window or clipped image will be inserted into your spreadsheet.

Alternatively, if you wish to create a screenshot of your spreadsheet to insert into another package, or onto a new sheet in Excel:

either

- select the appropriate spreadsheet window
- press ALT and PrintScreen buttons together

or

- select the appropriate spreadsheet window
- open the Microsoft Snipping Tool®
- select New
- left-click at the top left of the area, hold down the left mouse key and drag the cursor over the area you want to capture, release the left key when you have it all selected, then
- select the application window where you want to place the screenshot
- select PASTE, or press CTRL and V

EXPORT, IMPORT AND SAVE AS

In this section we will be looking at the concepts of importing, exporting and saving files in different formats.

The normal file format when you save your spreadsheet is .xlsx which is based on the Open XML Format.

Historically, if you wanted to move data from one software package to another, and the software packages were produced by different companies, you would take the data out of the first package – **export** – into a text file format, and then load or **import** the data as a text file into the second package.

The need to export and import has greatly reduced as software packages have become more sophisticated; however, you may still need to do it.

There are two commonly used text file formats:

- **Delimited text files** (.txt), in which the TAB character typically separates each field of text.
- **Comma separated values** text files (.csv), in which the comma character (,) typically separates each field of text.

An example CSV file based on part of the car sales spreadsheet is shown below.

```
Year,Month,Manufacturer,Region,Quantity,
2020,Mar,BMW,North West,155,
2018,Sep,BMW,East,"1,460",
2018,Sep,BMW,South West,34,
2019,Oct,BMW,South West,68,
2019,Nov,BMW,East,56,
2019,Oct,BMW,South West,35,
2019,Dec,BMW,South West,125,
2020,Jul,Ford,East,126,
2019,Feb,Ford,South,"1,500",
2019,Feb,Ford,South West,68,
2018,Apr,Ford,North West,56,
2019,Dec,Ford,North West,34,
2020,Jan,Mercedes,South West,220,
2020,Aug,Mercedes,South,68,
2019,Mar,Mercedes,North West,125,
2018,Dec,Mercedes,South West,56,
2019,Nov,Mercedes,North West,220,
2019,Feb,Seat,East,220,
2019,Mar,Seat,South West,155,
2019,Jan,Seat,South,100,
2019,Apr,Seat,South,"1,460",
```

You can see each cell of data is separated by a comma, and each row of data is output on a fresh line.

To export data from a spreadsheet as a text file:

- select **Save as** from the **File** menu
- from the **Format** or **Save as type** select **Text** (tab delimited), or **CSV** (comma separated)

or

- select **Export** from the **File** menu
- select **Change File Type**
- select **Text** or **CSV** from the list of file types

then

- select the folder and specify the file name which you wish to use for the file

Note that only the current worksheet will be exported from a workbook, and formatting will not be carried through into the text file.

To import the data to create a spreadsheet:

- select **Open** from the **File** menu
- select **Browse**
- change **All Excel Files** to **Text** files

As shown below:

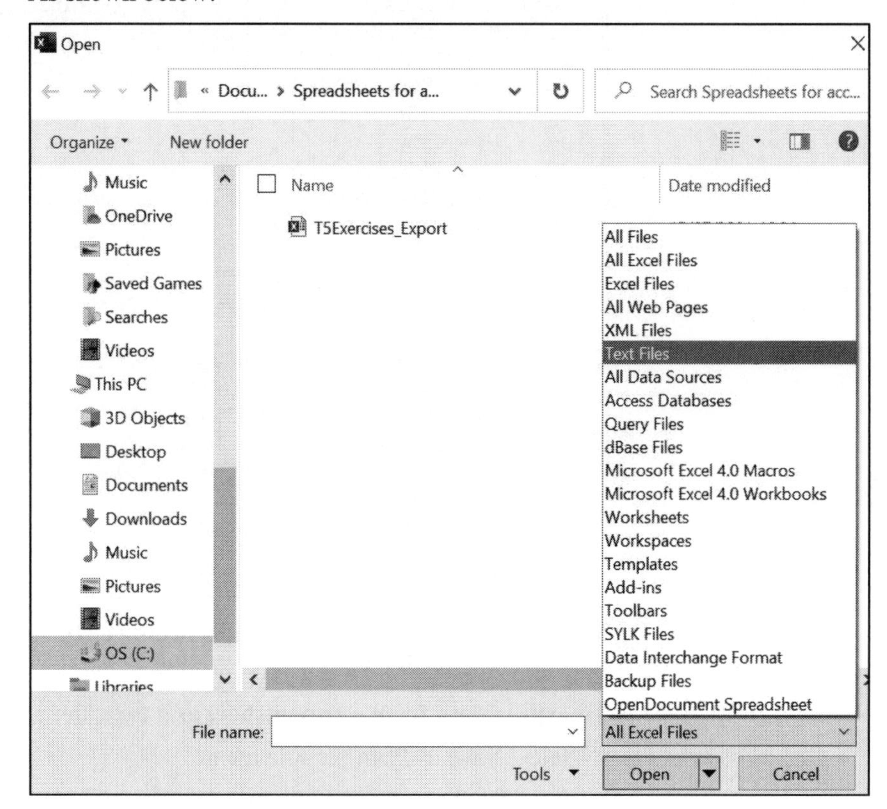

- select the folder and the file name to import

An imported CSV file will open as a new Excel workbook automatically.

If the data you are importing is a text file, rather than a CSV file, you may need to step through the Text Import Wizard, to describe your data with steps, as shown on the next page.

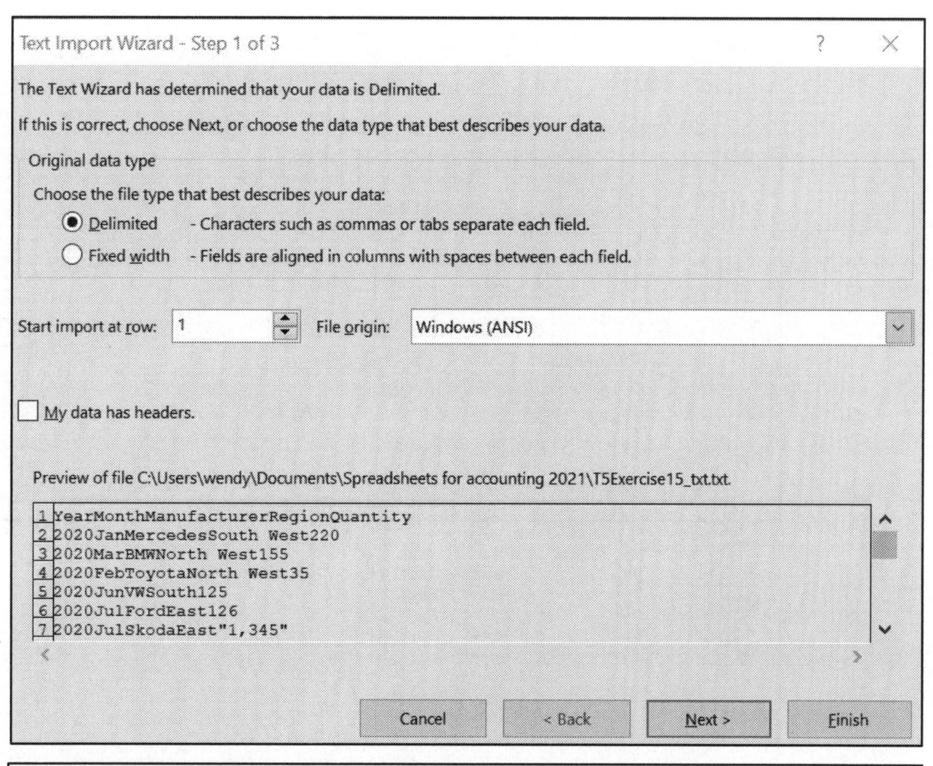
Text Import Wizard - Step 1 of 3
The Text Wizard has determined that your data is Delimited.
If this is correct, choose Next, or choose the data type that best describes your data.
Original data type
Choose the file type that best describes your data:
Delimited - Characters such as commas or tabs separate each field.
Fixed width - Fields are aligned in columns with spaces between each field.
Start import at row: 1
File origin: Windows (ANSI)
My data has headers.
Preview of file C:\Users\wendy\Documents\Spreadsheets for accounting 2021\T5Exercise15_txt.txt.
1 YearMonthManufacturerRegionQuantity
2 2020JanMercedesSouth West220
3 2020MarBMWNorth West155
4 2020FebToyotaNorth West35
5 2020JunVWSouth125
6 2020JulFordEast126
7 2020JulSkodaEast"1,345"
Cancel
< Back
Next >
Finish

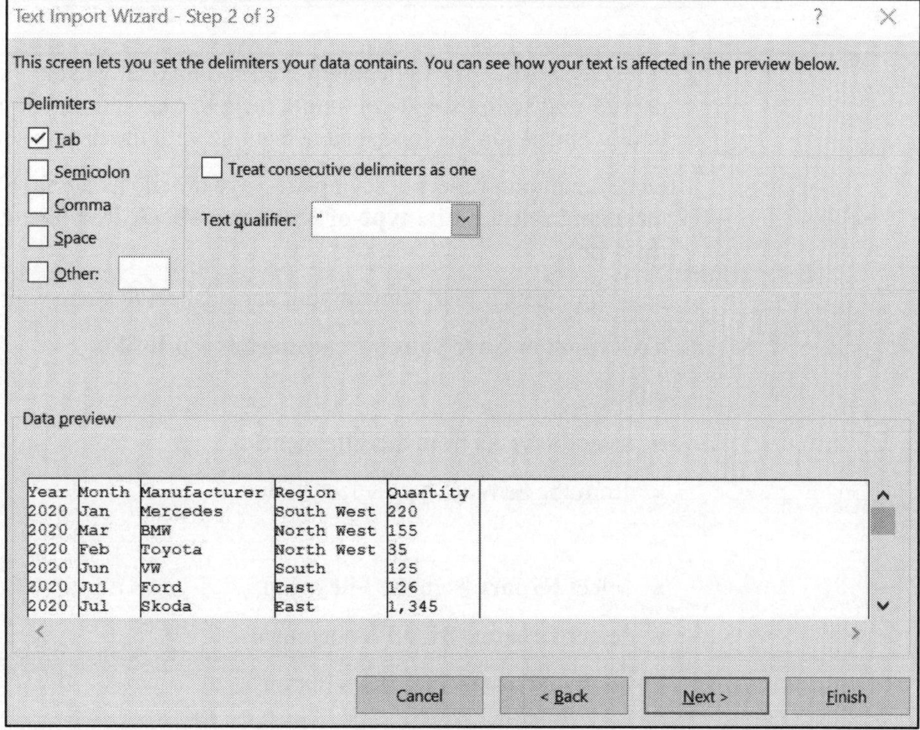
Text Import Wizard - Step 2 of 3
This screen lets you set the delimiters your data contains. You can see how your text is affected in the preview below.
Delimiters
Tab
Semicolon
Comma
Space
Other:
Treat consecutive delimiters as one
Text qualifier: "
Data preview
Year Month Manufacturer Region Quantity
2020 Jan Mercedes South West 220
2020 Mar BMW North West 155
2020 Feb Toyota North West 35
2020 Jun VW South 125
2020 Jul Ford East 126
2020 Jul Skoda East 1,345
Cancel
< Back
Next >
Finish

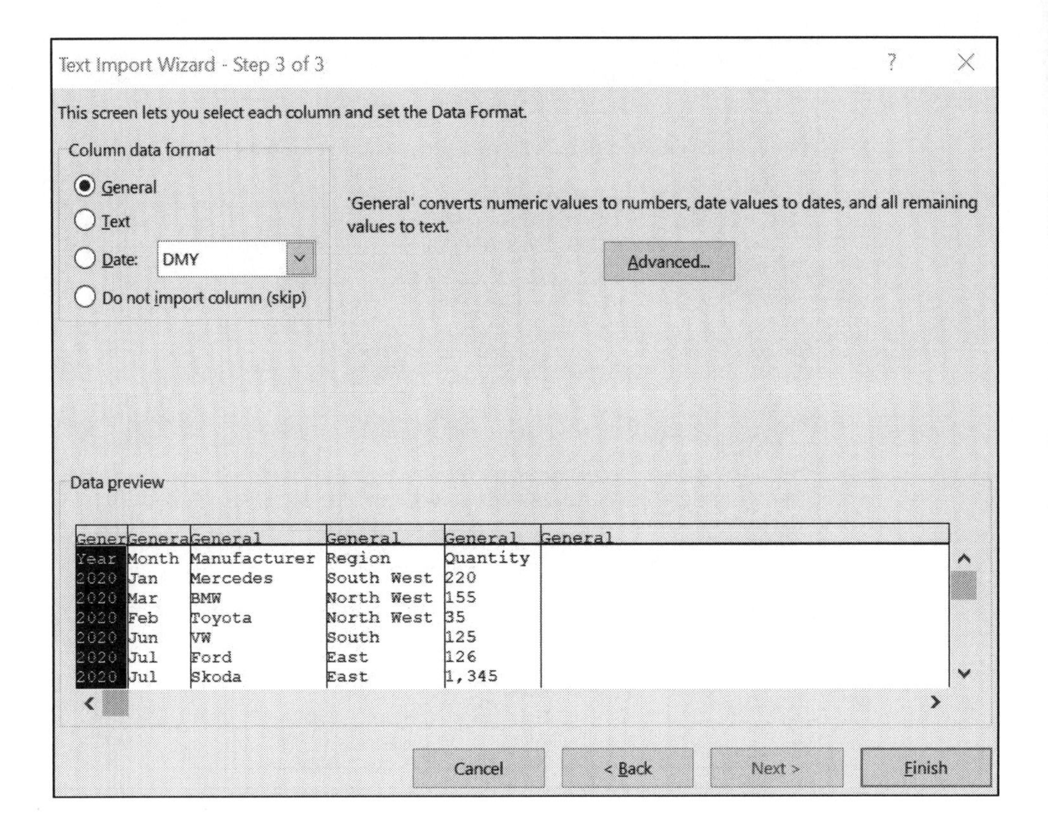

If it is a CSV file, it will be interpreted automatically using the current default data format settings, but you might need to tick and untick different options until it appears in the format shown above with the data in separate columns.

Once the import process is complete, save the file using **Save as** from the **File** menu and select a **File type of Excel workbook** from the drop-down list of file types.

You can create a PDF copy of your spreadsheet to share with other people.

To Export or Save your spreadsheet as a pdf file:

either

- select **Save as** from the **File** menu
- from the **Save as type** select **PDF**

or

- select **Export** from the **File** menu
- select **Create PDF/XPS** document
- click on **Create PDF/XPS** button

Then

- select the folder and specify the file name for the new file
- click on **Publish**

The file will automatically be displayed in whatever PDF reader is installed on your computer. This may be Adobe reader or your web browser.

If you wished to save your file as a web page (HTML):

- select **Save as** from the **File** menu
- from the **Save as type** select **Web Page**
- select the folder and specify the file name for the new file

The **Save as** option offers a variety of different formats. We will not be covering them all here, but you should experiment with the different outputs available.

Chapter Summary

In this chapter we have covered the following spreadsheet concepts and techniques:

- formula validation
- spell check
- find and replace
- sorting and filtering data
- removing duplicates
- introducing subtotals
- linking, embedding and screenshots
- exporting and importing data

You should now carry out some or all of the exercises on the next few pages in order to practise and reinforce your learning.

Activities

Here are a group of exercises to allow you to practise the topics covered in this chapter; they can be done individually, or as a sequence, working your way through them.

If you choose to work your way through them, you may not need to open the exercise workbook as suggested at the start of each exercise, as it may already be open.

The saving at the end of each exercise is also optional, although it serves as a reminder to regularly save your work. You can also save to different file names and may choose to keep using the same name to avoid having lots of files.

Exercise 1

> Spreadsheet skills:
>
> - Auditing tools - show formulas

1. Open workbook T5Exercises
2. Select worksheet Exercise 1
3. Select Show Formulas from the menu bar

	A	B	C	D	E	F
1	Employees wages information					
2						
3	Average productivity bonus %		=SUM(E7:E15)/9			
4						
5	Surname	Basic pay	Gross pay	Productivity bonus	Productivity bonus %	Weekly productivity bonus
6		£	£	£	%	£
7	Patel	31200	32620.5	=C7-B7	=D7/B7	=D7/52
8	Johnson	28900	31425.33	=C8-B8	=D8/B8	=D8/52
9	Singh	31200	31500	=C9-B9	=D9/B9	=D9/52
10	Gregory	24900	28950.31	=C10-B10	=D10/B10	=D10/52
11	Williams	24900	26750.5	=C11-B11	=D11/B11	=D11/52
12	Reed	28900	31850.67	=C12-B12	=D12/B12	=D12/52
13	Khan	28900	31450.72	=C13-B13	=D13/B13	=D13/52
14	Begum	24900	28650	=C14-B14	=D14/B14	=D14/52
15	Sheppard	28900	31400.5	=C15-B14	=D15/B15	=D15/52
16	Total	=SUM(B7:B14)	=SUM(C8:C15)			

4. Move from formula to formula and you will see the cells making up that formula highlighted
5. Select Show Formulas again, so the formulas are now hidden

Exercise 2

Spreadsheet skills:

- Auditing tools - error checking

1. Open Excel, Select Formulas, Error checking, Options and change Background Error Checking to Off
2. Open workbook T5Exercises
3. Select worksheet Exercise 2
4. Select Formulas, Error checking, Options and change Background Error Checking to On. You should now see some green error triangles appear in the top left-hand corner of those cells which may contain an error (Cells B16 and C16)
5. Select Error Checking from the menu bar. Follow the process as it steps through each cell. Where it identifies a possible error, change as appropriate, as shown in the example below

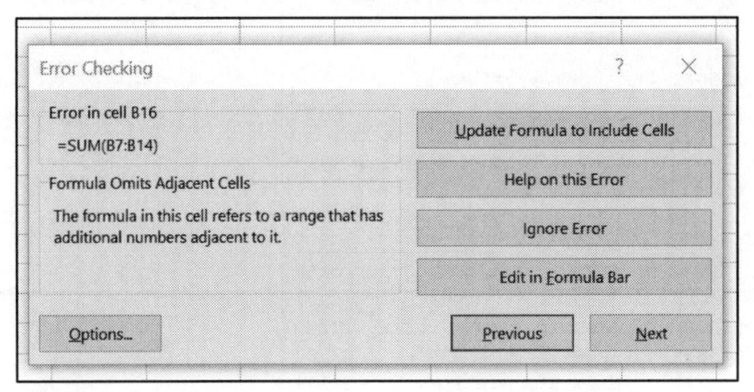

6. Save the workbook with the name Chapter5_Exercise2

   It should have the same values as the image shown below:

	A	B	C	D	E	F
1	Employees wages information					
2						
3	Average productivity bonus %		10.504%			
4						
5	Surname	Basic pay	Gross pay	Productivity bonus	Productivity bonus %	Weekly productivity bonus
6		£	£	£	%	£
7	Patel	£31,200.00	£32,620.50	£1,420.50	4.553%	£27.32
8	Johnson	£28,900.00	£31,425.33	£2,525.33	8.738%	£48.56
9	Singh	£31,200.00	£31,500.00	£300.00	0.962%	£5.77
10	Gregory	£24,900.00	£28,950.31	£4,050.31	16.266%	£77.89
11	Williams	£24,900.00	£26,750.50	£1,850.50	7.432%	£35.59
12	Reed	£28,900.00	£31,850.67	£2,950.67	10.210%	£56.74
13	Khan	£28,900.00	£31,450.72	£2,550.72	8.826%	£49.05
14	Begum	£24,900.00	£28,650.00	£3,750.00	15.060%	£72.12
15	Sheppard	£28,900.00	£31,400.50	£6,500.50	22.493%	£125.01
16	Total	£252,700.00	£274,598.53			

Exercise 3

Spreadsheet skills:

- Auditing tools - Trace Precedents

1. Open workbook T5Exercises
2. Select worksheet Exercise 3
3. Select cell D7, and select Trace Precedents
4. Select cell D14, and select Trace Precedents
5. Select cell D15, and select Trace Precedents

You should notice something strange with cell D15, there is an inconsistent formula, but this was not picked up by the Error Checking.

	A	B	C	D	E	F
1	Employees wages information					
2						
3	Average productivity bonus %		10.504%			
4						
5	Surname	Basic pay	Gross pay	Productivity bonus	Productivity bonus %	Weekly productivity bonus
6		£	£	£	%	£
7	Patel	£31,200.00	£32,620.50	£1,420.50	4.553%	£27.32
8	Johnson	£28,900.00	£31,425.33	£2,525.33	8.738%	£48.56
9	Singh	£31,200.00	£31,500.00	£300.00	0.962%	£5.77
10	Gregory	£24,900.00	£28,950.31	£4,050.31	16.266%	£77.89
11	Williams	£24,900.00	£26,750.50	£1,850.50	7.432%	£35.59
12	Reed	£28,900.00	£31,850.67	£2,950.67	10.210%	£56.74
13	Khan	£28,900.00	£31,450.72	£2,550.72	8.826%	£49.05
14	Begum	£24,900.00	£28,650.00	£3,750.00	15.060%	£72.12
15	Sheppard	£28,900.00	£31,400.50	£6,500.50	22.493%	£125.01
16	Total	£252,700.00	£274,598.53			

6. Select Remove Arrows to clear the trace arrows
7. Correct the formula in cell D15
8. Select cell D15, and select Trace Precedents
9. Save the workbook with the name Chapter5_Exercise3

It should now look as follows:

	A	B	C	D	E	F
1	Employees wages information					
2						
3	Average productivity bonus %		8.967%			
4						
5	Surname	Basic pay	Gross pay	Productivity bonus	Productivity bonus %	Weekly productivity bonus
6		£	£	£	%	£
7	Patel	£31,200.00	£32,620.50	£1,420.50	4.553%	£27.32
8	Johnson	£28,900.00	£31,425.33	£2,525.33	8.738%	£48.56
9	Singh	£31,200.00	£31,500.00	£300.00	0.962%	£5.77
10	Gregory	£24,900.00	£28,950.31	£4,050.31	16.266%	£77.89
11	Williams	£24,900.00	£26,750.50	£1,850.50	7.432%	£35.59
12	Reed	£28,900.00	£31,850.67	£2,950.67	10.210%	£56.74
13	Khan	£28,900.00	£31,450.72	£2,550.72	8.826%	£49.05
14	Begum	£24,900.00	£28,650.00	£3,750.00	15.060%	£72.12
15	Sheppard	£28,900.00	£31,400.50	£2,500.50	8.652%	£48.09
16	Total	£252,700.00	£274,598.53			

Exercise 4

Spreadsheet skills:

- Auditing tools - Trace Dependents

1. Open workbook T5Exercises
2. Select worksheet Exercise 4
3. Select cell B7, and select Trace Dependents
4. Select cell B14, and select Trace Dependents
5. Select cell B15, and select Trace Dependents

Again, you can see an inconsistency affecting B15 and D15.

	A	B	C	D	E	F
1	Employees wages information					
2						
3	Average productivity bonus %		10.504%			
4						
5	Surname	Basic pay	Gross pay	Productivity bonus	Productivity bonus %	Weekly productivity bonus
6		£	£	£	%	£
7	Patel	£31,200.00	£32,620.50	£1,420.50	4.553%	£27.32
8	Johnson	£28,900.00	£31,425.33	£2,525.33	8.738%	£48.56
9	Singh	£31,200.00	£31,500.00	£300.00	0.962%	£5.77
10	Gregory	£24,900.00	£28,950.31	£4,050.31	16.266%	£77.89
11	Williams	£24,900.00	£26,750.50	£1,850.50	7.432%	£35.59
12	Reed	£28,900.00	£31,850.67	£2,950.67	10.210%	£56.74
13	Khan	£28,900.00	£31,450.72	£2,550.72	8.826%	£49.05
14	Begum	£24,900.00	£28,650.00	£3,750.00	15.060%	£72.12
15	Sheppard	£28,900.00	£31,400.50	£6,500.50	22.493%	£125.01
16	Total	£252,700.00	£274,598.53			

6. Select Remove Arrows to clear the trace arrows
7. Correct the formula in cell D15
8. Select cell B14, and select Trace Dependents
9. Select cell B15, and select Trace Precedents
10. Save the workbook with the name Chapter5_Exercise4

It should now look as follows:

	A	B	C	D	E	F
1	Employees wages information					
2						
3	Average productivity bonus %		8.967%			
4						
5	Surname	Basic pay	Gross pay	Productivity bonus	Productivity bonus %	Weekly productivity bonus
6		£	£	£	%	£
7	Patel	£31,200.00	£32,620.50	£1,420.50	4.553%	£27.32
8	Johnson	£28,900.00	£31,425.33	£2,525.33	8.738%	£48.56
9	Singh	£31,200.00	£31,500.00	£300.00	0.962%	£5.77
10	Gregory	£24,900.00	£28,950.31	£4,050.31	16.266%	£77.89
11	Williams	£24,900.00	£26,750.50	£1,850.50	7.432%	£35.59
12	Reed	£28,900.00	£31,850.67	£2,950.67	10.210%	£56.74
13	Khan	£28,900.00	£31,450.72	£2,550.72	8.826%	£49.05
14	Begum	£24,900.00	£28,650.00	£3,750.00	15.060%	£72.12
15	Sheppard	£28,900.00	£31,400.50	£2,500.50	8.652%	£48.09
16	Total	£252,700.00	£274,598.53			

Exercise 5

Spreadsheet skills:

- Spell Check

1. Open workbook T5Exercises
2. Select worksheet Exercise 5
3. Select cells B4 to B10 in the Product column
4. Select the Spelling option from the **Review** menu
5. Step through the individual checks, making corrections as appropriate, choosing the correct spelling from the choices offered as illustrated below

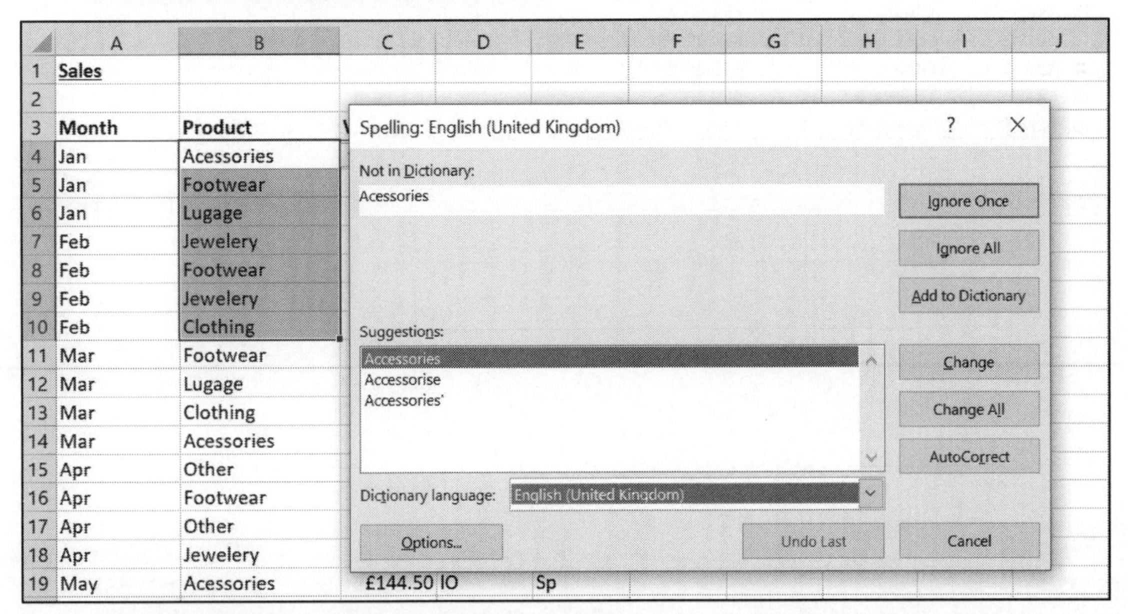

6. Select the whole of the Product column (column B)
7. Select the Spelling option from the menu
8. Step through the individual checks, choosing the correct spelling from the choices offered, and this time select Change All, to correct all occurrences in column B which are spelt incorrectly
9. Save the workbook with the name Chapter5_Exercise5

Your spreadsheet should now look as shown below:

	A	B	C	D	E
1	Sales				
2					
3	**Month**	**Product**	**Value**	**Sales Rep**	**Country**
4	Jan	Accessories	£125.75	TP	UK
5	Jan	Footwear	£99.95	SM	UK
6	Jan	Luggage	£220.00	py	ger
7	Feb	Jewellery	£1,500.00	TP	UK
8	Feb	Footwear	£220.00	py	Fr
9	Feb	Jewellery	£67.75	IO	ger
10	Feb	Clothing	£34.90	SM	Sp
11	Mar	Footwear	£154.50	py	ger
12	Mar	Luggage	£124.60	SM	Sp
13	Mar	Clothing	£44.75	py	Fr
14	Mar	Accessories	£154.50	IO	Sp
15	Apr	Other	£34.90	IO	Sp
16	Apr	Footwear	£1,460.40	TP	UK
17	Apr	Other	£56.25	IO	ger
18	Apr	Jewellery	£56.00	IO	Sp
19	May	Accessories	£144.50	IO	Sp

Exercise 6

Spreadsheet skills:

- Remove duplicates

1. Open workbook T5Exercises
2. Select worksheet Exercise 6
3. Select all the data and using Remove Duplicates, delete all rows with a duplicate Gross value

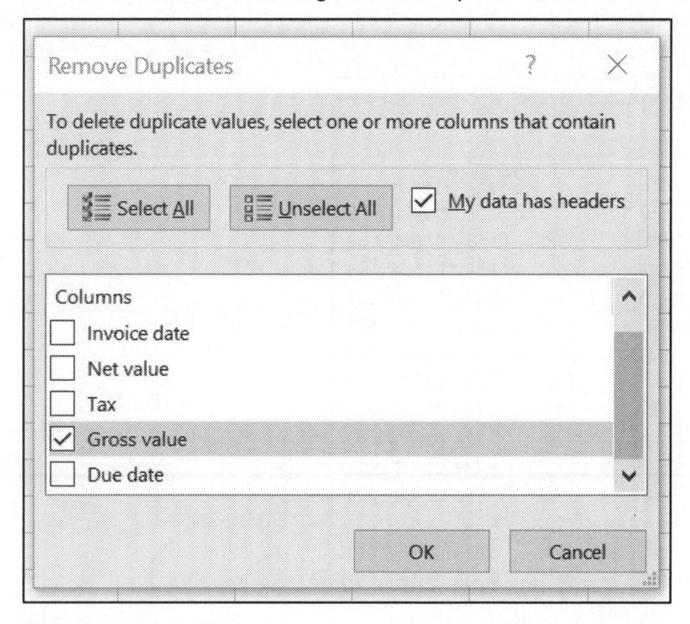

The message:

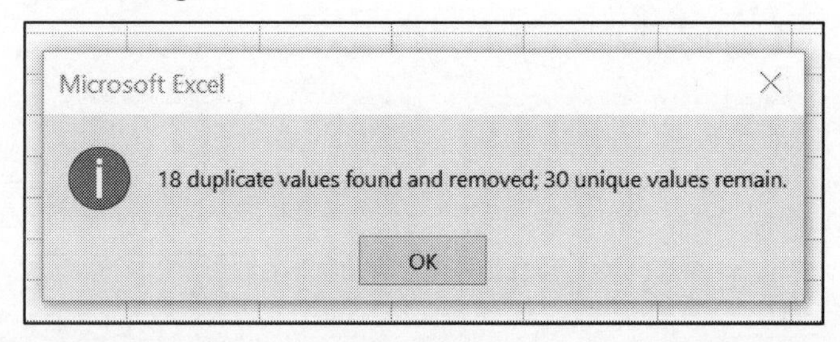

This isn't really what we need, since some rows have been deleted with the same values but different customers.

4. Click UNDO to return the rows

   The last row should be row 51

5. Now use Remove duplicates again, to delete any invoice records which match across each of the six columns

The message:

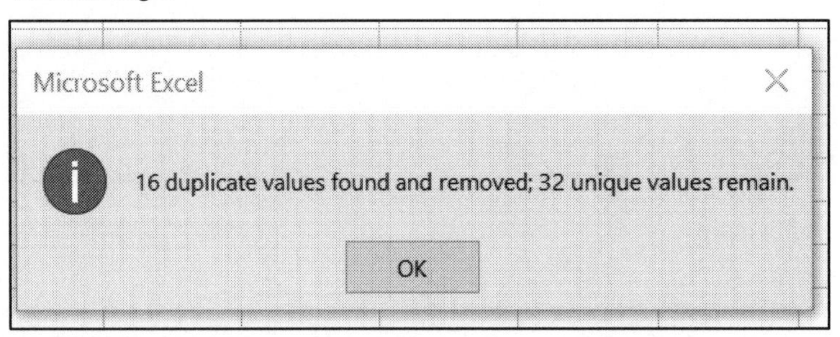

should appear and the first few rows of the data should now look as shown below, with the last row being row 35.

	A	B	C	D	E	F
1	Sales invoices					
2						
3	Customer ref	Invoice date	Net value	Tax	Gross value	Due date
4	ACUST1	30/06/2021	2,983	596	3,579	01/08/2021
5	ACUST10	09/06/2021	2,525	505	3,030	01/07/2021
6	ACUST11	11/05/2021	3,703	741	4,444	01/07/2021
7	ACUST12	12/05/2021	3,468	694	4,162	01/07/2021
8	ACUST2	01/07/2021	542	108	650	01/08/2021
9	ACUST3	02/06/2021	713	142	855	01/07/2021
10	ACUST4	03/07/2021	1,750	350	2,100	01/08/2021
11	ACUST5	04/07/2021	1,023	205	1,228	01/08/2021
12	ACUST5	29/07/2021	5,610	1,122	6,732	01/08/2021
13	ACUST6	06/04/2021	468	94	562	01/06/2021
14	ACUST7	07/05/2021	3,576	715	4,291	01/07/2021
15	ACUST9	09/04/2021	3,766	753	4,519	01/06/2021
16	CCUST11	18/04/2021	5,038	1,007	6,045	01/06/2021

7. Save your spreadsheet with the name: Chapter5_Exercise6

Exercise 7

Spreadsheet skills:

- Find
- Find and Replace

1. Open workbook T5Exercises
2. Select worksheet Exercise 7
3. Use the Find facility to find a sale of Value 67.75 in column C where Country (column E) is UK, select next until you find the required row

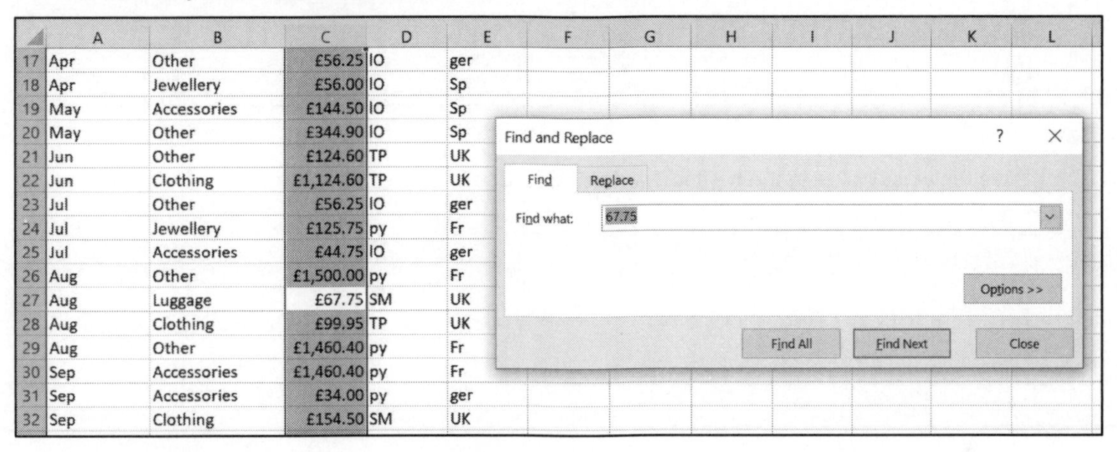

A B C D E F G H I J K L
17 Apr Other £56.25 IO ger
18 Apr Jewellery £56.00 IO Sp
19 May Accessories £144.50 IO Sp
20 May Other £344.90 IO Sp
21 Jun Other £124.60 TP UK
22 Jun Clothing £1,124.60 TP UK
23 Jul Other £56.25 IO ger
24 Jul Jewellery £125.75 py Fr
25 Jul Accessories £44.75 IO ger
26 Aug Other £1,500.00 py Fr
27 Aug Luggage £67.75 SM UK
28 Aug Clothing £99.95 TP UK
29 Aug Other £1,460.40 py Fr
30 Sep Accessories £1,460.40 py Fr
31 Sep Accessories £34.00 py ger
32 Sep Clothing £154.50 SM UK
Find and Replace
?
Find
Replace
Find what:
67.75
Options >>
Find All
Find Next
Close

4. Use the Find and Replace facility to change all occurrences of py in the Sales Rep column (column D) to all capitals – PY

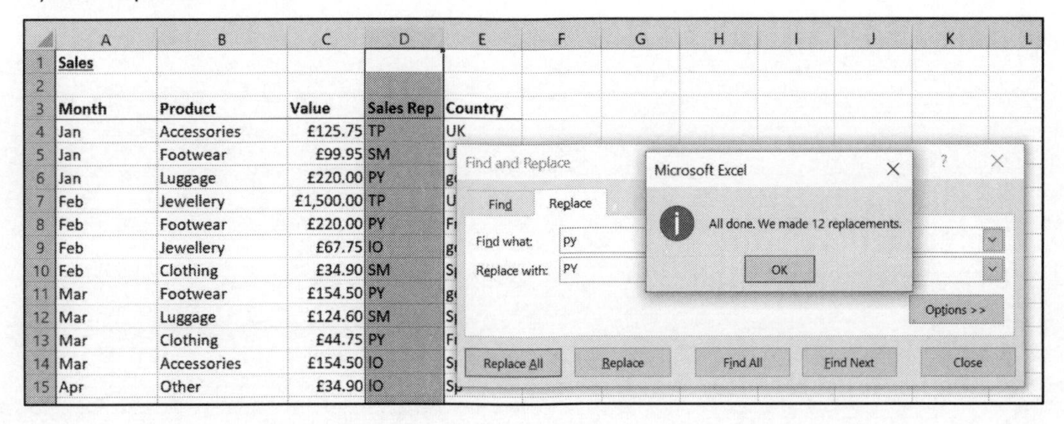

5. Use the Find and Replace facility to change all occurrences of Fr in the Country column (column E) to all capitals – FR

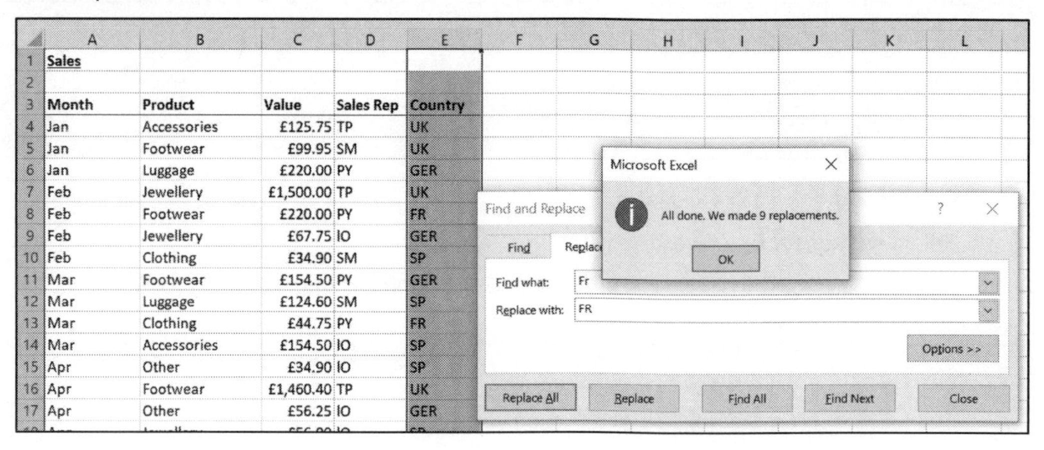

	A	B	C	D	E
1	Sales				
2					
3	Month	Product	Value	Sales Rep	Country
4	Jan	Accessories	£125.75	TP	UK
5	Jan	Footwear	£99.95	SM	UK
6	Jan	Luggage	£220.00	PY	GER
7	Feb	Jewellery	£1,500.00	TP	UK
8	Feb	Footwear	£220.00	PY	FR
9	Feb	Jewellery	£67.75	IO	GER
10	Feb	Clothing	£34.90	SM	SP
11	Mar	Footwear	£154.50	PY	GER
12	Mar	Luggage	£124.60	SM	SP
13	Mar	Clothing	£44.75	PY	FR
14	Mar	Accessories	£154.50	IO	SP
15	Apr	Other	£34.90	IO	SP
16	Apr	Footwear	£1,460.40	TP	UK
17	Apr	Other	£56.25	IO	GER

6. Save the workbook with the name Chapter5_Exercise7

Exercise 8

Spreadsheet skills:

- Data sort - multiple criteria

1. Open workbook T5Exercises
2. Select worksheet Exercise 8
3. Select all the data and Sort by Product (column B) alphabetically A -> Z

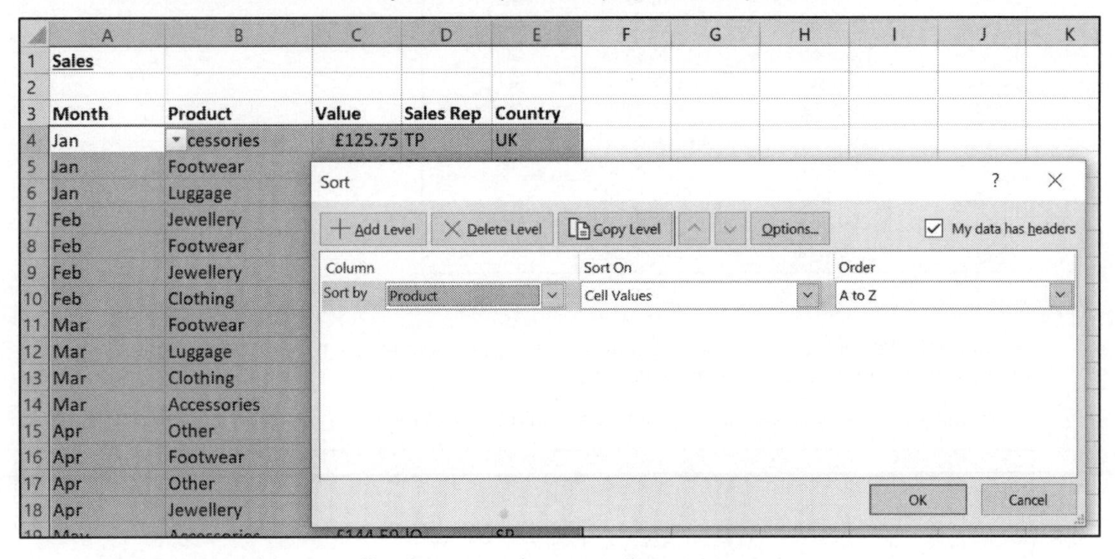

Your spreadsheet should appear like the screen image on the next page.

	A	B	C	D	E
1	Sales				
2					
3	Month	Product	Value	Sales Rep	Country
4	Jan	Accessories	£125.75	TP	UK
5	Mar	Accessories	£154.50	IO	SP
6	May	Accessories	£144.50	IO	SP
7	Jul	Accessories	£44.75	IO	GER
8	Sep	Accessories	£1,460.40	PY	FR
9	Sep	Accessories	£34.00	PY	GER
10	Oct	Accessories	£67.75	IO	GER
11	Oct	Accessories	£34.90	PY	GER
12	Nov	Accessories	£56.00	PY	FR
13	Dec	Accessories	£124.60	MP	GER
14	Feb	Clothing	£34.90	SM	SP
15	Mar	Clothing	£44.75	PY	FR
16	Jun	Clothing	£1,124.60	TP	UK
17	Aug	Clothing	£99.95	TP	UK
18	Sep	Clothing	£154.50	SM	UK
19	Oct	Clothing	£99.95	SM	UK
20	Jan	Footwear	£99.95	SM	UK

4. Within each Product, we now want to sort by the Value (column C) in descending order (largest to smallest), by adding another level to the sort.

   In the image below, you can see the settings within the sort facility.

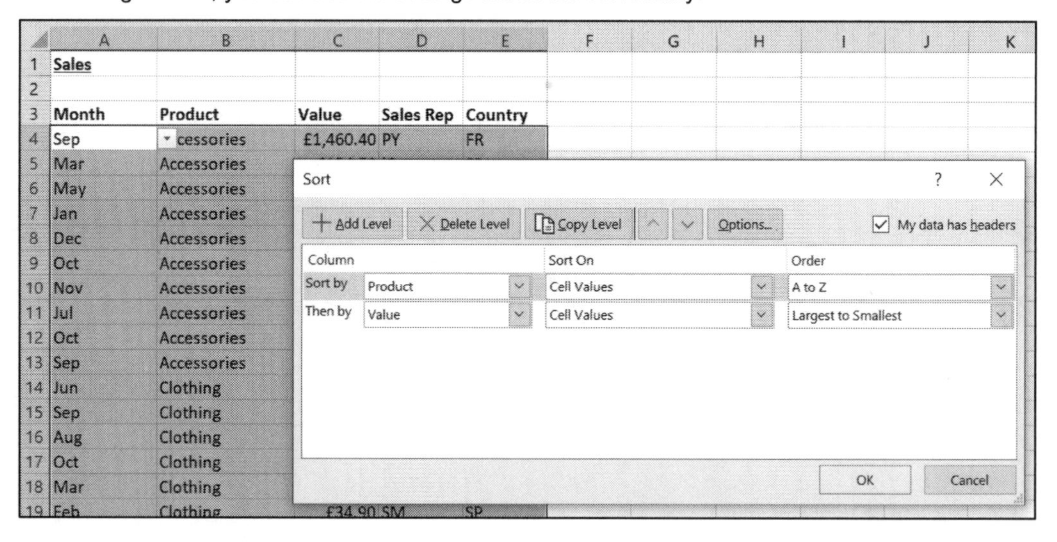

Here are the results of the sort:

	A	B	C	D	E
1	Sales				
2					
3	Month	Product	Value	Sales Rep	Country
4	Sep	Accessories	£1,460.40	PY	FR
5	Mar	Accessories	£154.50	IO	SP
6	May	Accessories	£144.50	IO	SP
7	Jan	Accessories	£125.75	TP	UK
8	Dec	Accessories	£124.60	MP	GER
9	Oct	Accessories	£67.75	IO	GER
10	Nov	Accessories	£56.00	PY	FR
11	Jul	Accessories	£44.75	IO	GER
12	Oct	Accessories	£34.90	PY	GER
13	Sep	Accessories	£34.00	PY	GER
14	Jun	Clothing	£1,124.60	TP	UK
15	Sep	Clothing	£154.50	SM	UK
16	Aug	Clothing	£99.95	TP	UK
17	Oct	Clothing	£99.95	SM	UK
18	Mar	Clothing	£44.75	PY	FR
19	Feb	Clothing	£34.90	SM	SP
20	Apr	Footwear	£1,460.40	TP	UK

5. Save the workbook with the name Chapter5_Exercise8

Exercise 9

Spreadsheet skills:

- Data sort
- Subtotals - SUM

1. Open workbook T5Exercises
2. Select worksheet Exercise 9
3. Select all the data and Sort by Sales Rep (column D), alphabetically A -> Z

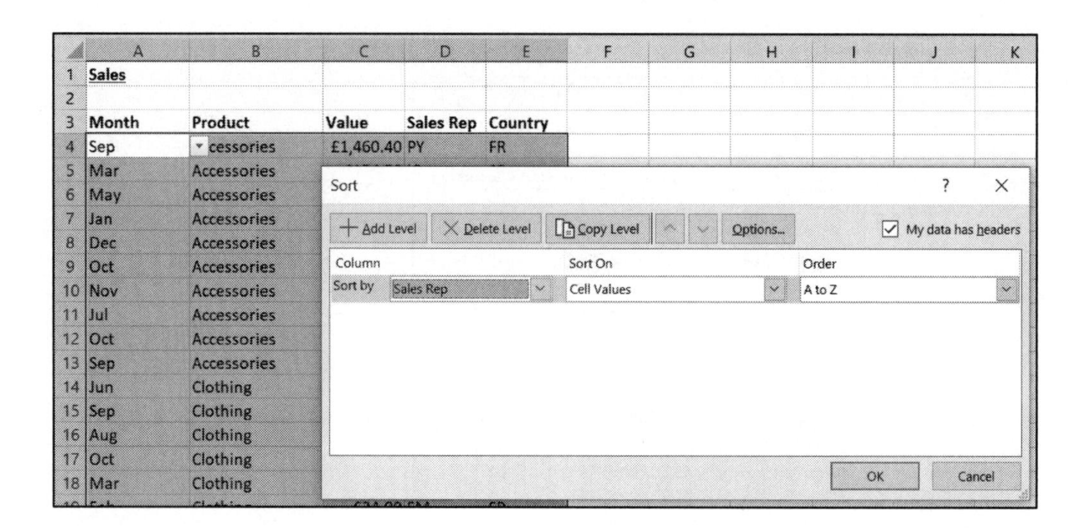

4. Using the Subtotal facility to subtotal:

   At each change of Sales Rep

   Use function SUM

   Add subtotal to Value

   Replace current subtotals (yes)

   Summary below data (yes)

   As illustrated below

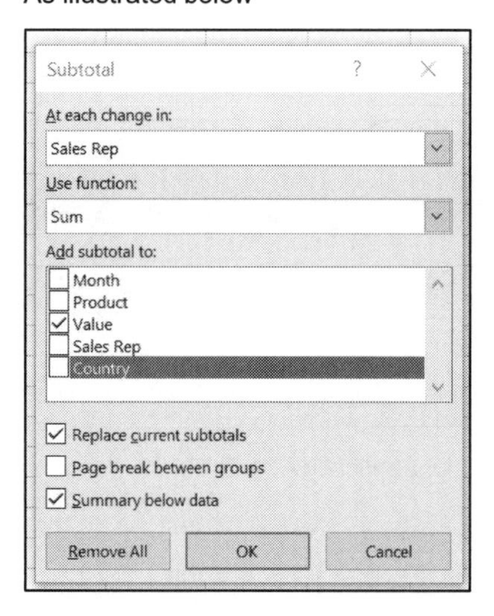

5. Select the Hide Detail option or click on the number 2 in the left-hand side bar

6. Widen the Value column so that all data displays in full

Your spreadsheet should appear as shown in the image below.

	A	B	C	D	E
3	**Month**	**Product**	**Value**	**Sales Rep**	**Country**
17			£2,803.80	**IO Total**	
20			£158.60	**MP Total**	
33			£5,355.45	**PY Total**	
41			£706.25	**SM Total**	
49			£4,561.05	**TP Total**	
50			£13,585.15	**Grand Total**	

7. Select the IO total row (row 17), and either click on the plus sign (+) to the left of the row, or select the Show Detail option from the menu bar

Your spreadsheet should appear as shown in the image below.

	A	B	C	D	E
3	**Month**	**Product**	**Value**	**Sales Rep**	**Country**
4	Mar	Accessories	£154.50	IO	SP
5	May	Accessories	£144.50	IO	SP
6	Oct	Accessories	£67.75	IO	GER
7	Jul	Accessories	£44.75	IO	GER
8	Feb	Jewellery	£67.75	IO	GER
9	Apr	Jewellery	£56.00	IO	SP
10	Nov	Luggage	£220.00	IO	SP
11	Dec	Luggage	£56.25	IO	GER
12	Dec	Other	£1,500.00	IO	FR
13	May	Other	£344.90	IO	SP
14	Apr	Other	£56.25	IO	GER
15	Jul	Other	£56.25	IO	GER
16	Apr	Other	£34.90	IO	SP
17			£2,803.80	**IO Total**	
20			£158.60	**MP Total**	
33			£5,355.45	**PY Total**	
41			£706.25	**SM Total**	
49			£4,561.05	**TP Total**	
50			£13,585.15	**Grand Total**	

8. Remove the Subtotals
9. Save the workbook with the name Chapter5_Exercise9

Exercise 10

Spreadsheet skills:

- Data filter - multiple criteria

1. Open workbook T5Exercises
2. Select worksheet Exercise 10
3. Select all the data, then select the filter tool to apply a filter
4. On the Country column, apply a filter so that you can only see rows where Country is GER

The worksheet should look as shown below:

	A	B	C	D	E
1	Sales				
2					
3	Month	Product	Value	Sales Re	Country
8	Dec	Accessories	£124.60	MP	GER
9	Oct	Accessories	£67.75	IO	GER
11	Jul	Accessories	£44.75	IO	GER
12	Oct	Accessories	£34.90	PY	GER
13	Sep	Accessories	£34.00	PY	GER
22	Mar	Footwear	£154.50	PY	GER
28	Feb	Jewellery	£67.75	IO	GER
31	Jan	Luggage	£220.00	PY	GER
35	Dec	Luggage	£56.25	IO	GER
41	Apr	Other	£56.25	IO	GER
42	Jul	Other	£56.25	IO	GER

5. Apply an additional filter to the rows, using the product column, so that only the rows for Product = Accessories and Country = GER are to be shown

The worksheet should look as shown below:

	A	B	C	D	E
1	Sales				
2					
3	Month	Product	Value	Sales Re	Country
8	Dec	Accessories	£124.60	MP	GER
9	Oct	Accessories	£67.75	IO	GER
11	Jul	Accessories	£44.75	IO	GER
12	Oct	Accessories	£34.90	PY	GER
13	Sep	Accessories	£34.00	PY	GER

6. Save the workbook with the name Chapter5_Exercise10

Exercise 11

Spreadsheet skills:

- Embed Excel data in a Word document

1. Open workbook T5Exercises
2. Select worksheet Exercise 11
3. Select and copy the text in I3 to I5
4. Open a new word document and paste this text, selecting the 'Keep Text Only' option which shows as a clipboard with a capital A on it

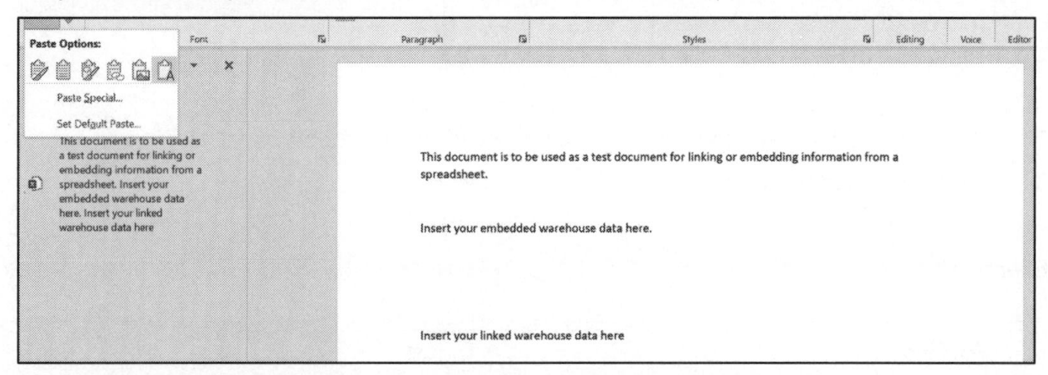

5. Within the open Excel worksheet, copy all cells in the range A4:C14
6. In the word processing document, move down the document, so that the cursor is below the text relating to embedding the data. Select Paste Special and paste as Microsoft Excel Worksheet Object.

This is illustrated below:

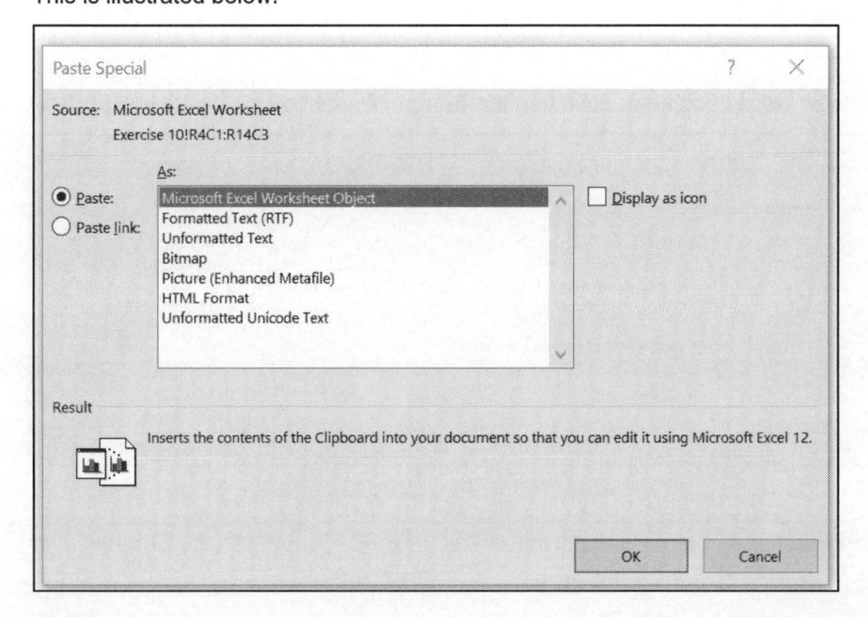

The document should appear as follows:

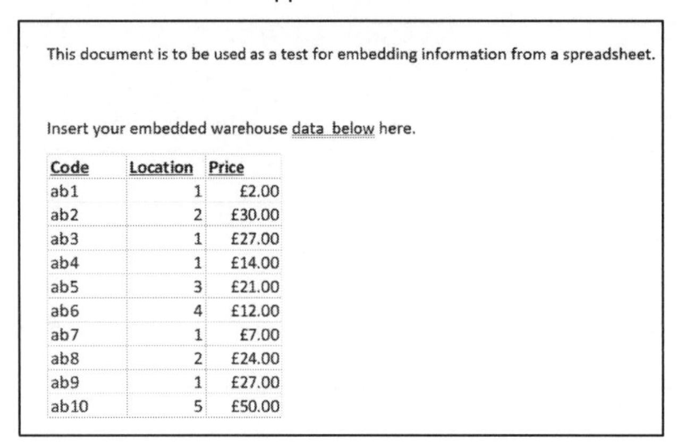

This document is to be used as a test for embedding information from a spreadsheet.

Insert your embedded warehouse data below here.

Code	Location	Price
ab1	1	£2.00
ab2	2	£30.00
ab3	1	£27.00
ab4	1	£14.00
ab5	3	£21.00
ab6	4	£12.00
ab7	1	£7.00
ab8	2	£24.00
ab9	1	£27.00
ab10	5	£50.00

7. Switching back to the worksheet, change the price for ab1 to £2.50
8. Within the word document, notice nothing changes

Exercise 12

Spreadsheet skills:

- Link Excel data in a Word document

1. Open workbook T5Exercises
2. Select worksheet Exercise 12
3. Select the text in I3 to I5
4. Paste this text in a new word document, selecting the far right Paste option A, with a clipboard

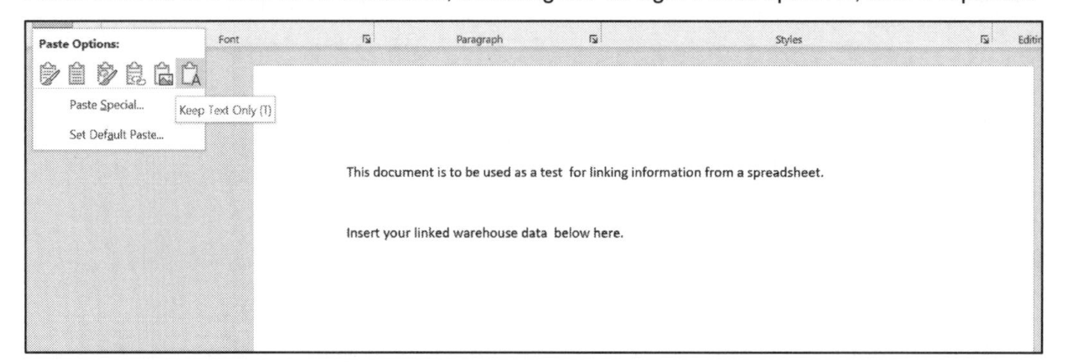

5. Within the open worksheet, select all cells in the range A4:C14, select Copy from the **Edit** menu, or use CTRL and C to copy the data

6. In word, move down the document, so that the cursor is below the text relating to linking the data, select Paste Special, Paste as Microsoft Excel Worksheet Object and click the Paste Link button

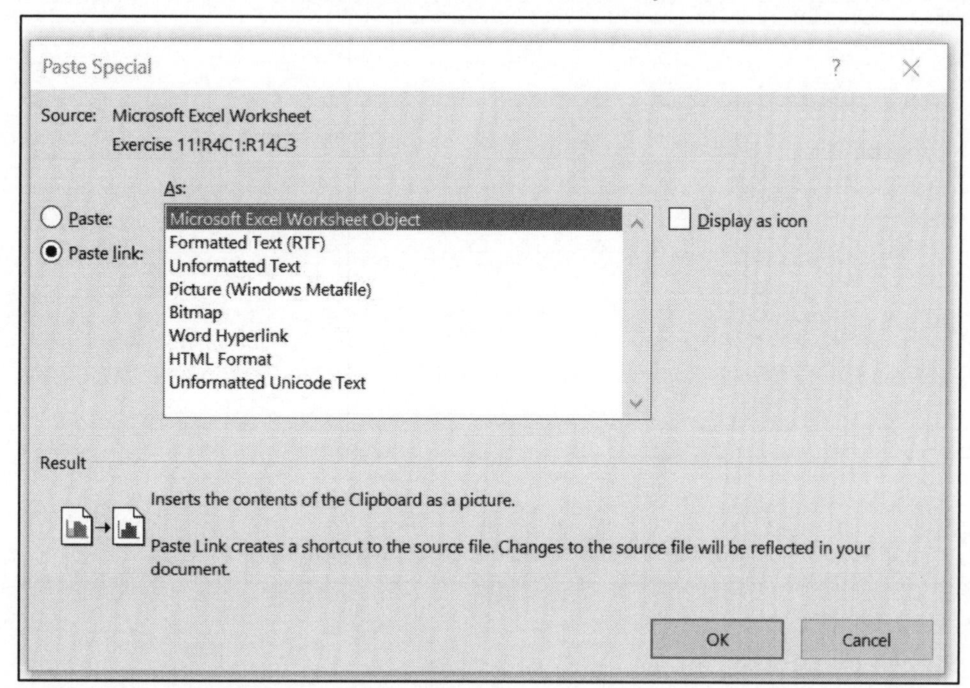

The document should appear as shown below:

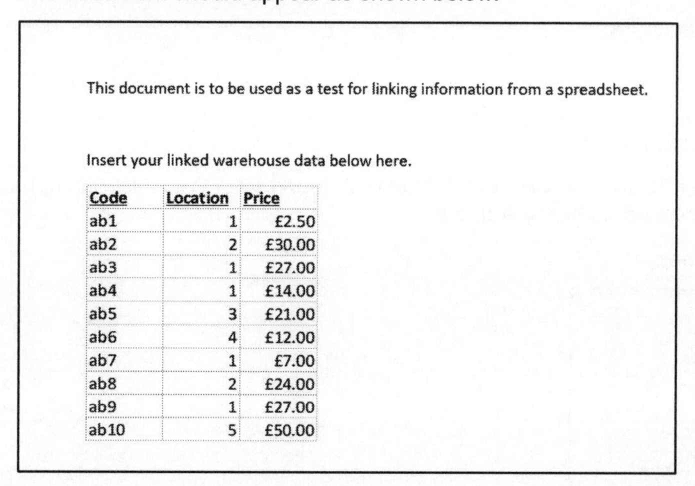

This document is to be used as a test for linking information from a spreadsheet.

Insert your linked warehouse data below here.

Code	Location	Price
ab1	1	£2.50
ab2	2	£30.00
ab3	1	£27.00
ab4	1	£14.00
ab5	3	£21.00
ab6	4	£12.00
ab7	1	£7.00
ab8	2	£24.00
ab9	1	£27.00
ab10	5	£50.00

7. Within the word document, double click on the inserted data, which will take you to the spreadsheet package, change the price for ab1 to £2.50, swap back to the word processing package, right-click on the linked data table, and select Update Link, if it has not automatically updated

The document should appear as shown below:

This document is to be used as a test for linking information from a spreadsheet.

Insert your linked warehouse data below here.

Code	Location	Price
ab1	1	£2.50
ab2	2	£30.00
ab3	1	£27.00
ab4	1	£14.00
ab5	3	£21.00
ab6	4	£12.00
ab7	1	£7.00
ab8	2	£24.00
ab9	1	£27.00
ab10	5	£50.00

Exercise 13

Spreadsheet skills:

- Save As text or Export

1. Open workbook T5Exercises_Export
2. Select worksheet Export
3. Using Save as or Export, save the worksheet as a Text (Tab delimited) file, with name Chapter5_Exercise13. Close the workbook
4. Open the file Chapter5_Exercise13 in Microsoft® Notepad (found from the **Start** Menu, under All Programs, Accessories, Notepad) or equivalent file

The file should appear as shown below:

```
Code    Location        Price
ab1     1       £2.00
ab2     2       £30.00
ab3     1       £27.00
ab4     1       £14.00
ab5     3       £21.00
ab6     4       £12.00
ab7     1       £7.00
ab8     2       £24.00
ab9     1       £27.00
ab10    5       £50.00
```

Exercise 14

Spreadsheet skills:

- Save As CSV or Export

1. Open workbook T5Exercises_Export
2. Select worksheet Export
3. Using Save as or Export, save the worksheet as a CSV (Comma delimited) file, with name Chapter5_Exercise14. Close the workbook
4. Open the file Chapter5_Exercise14 in Microsoft® Notepad (found from the **Start** Menu, under All Programs, Accessories, Notepad) or equivalent file

The file should appear as shown below:

```
Code,Location,Price
ab1,1,£2.00
ab2,2,£30.00
ab3,1,£27.00
ab4,1,£14.00
ab5,3,£21.00
ab6,4,£12.00
ab7,1,£7.00
ab8,2,£24.00
ab9,1,£27.00
ab10,5,£50.00
```

Exercise 15

Spreadsheet skills:

- Export to PDF

1. Open workbook T5Exercises
2. Select worksheet Exercise 15
3. Export the worksheet As a PDF, with name Chapter5_Exercise15, make sure Open file after publishing is ticked
4. The PDF file will then automatically open in a browser window, as shown below

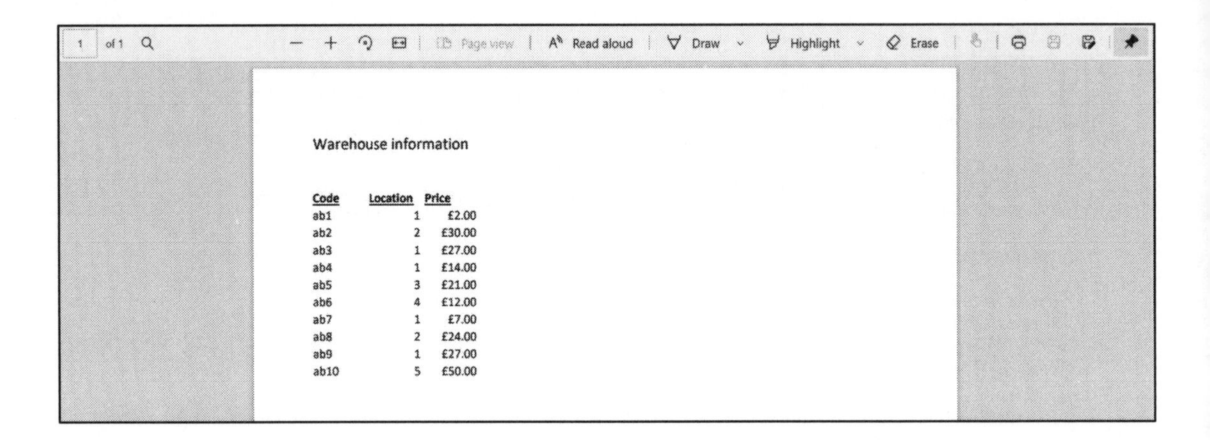

Warehouse information

Code	Location	Price
ab1	1	£2.00
ab2	2	£30.00
ab3	1	£27.00
ab4	1	£14.00
ab5	3	£21.00
ab6	4	£12.00
ab7	1	£7.00
ab8	2	£24.00
ab9	1	£27.00
ab10	5	£50.00

Exercise 16

Spreadsheet skills:

- Import TXT files
- Import CSV files

1. Open Excel
2. From the **File** menu select Open, then Browse. Change the Files of Type drop-down to All files, and select the workbook T5Exercise16_CSV

The file should automatically open, showing the appropriate data in Excel, as shown below:

	A	B	C
1	Code	Location	Price
2	ab1	1	£2.00
3	ab2	2	£30.00
4	ab3	1	£27.00
5	ab4	1	£14.00
6	ab5	3	£21.00
7	ab6	4	£12.00
8	ab7	1	£7.00
9	ab8	2	£24.00
10	ab9	1	£27.00
11	ab10	5	£50.00

3. Save the worksheet displayed, as type Excel Workbook, and name it Chapter5_Exercise16csv
4. Select File, Open, Browse, change Files of Type to All Files, find and select the workbook T5Exercise16_TXT

5. Step through the import options

   On step 1, make sure the File Origin is Windows (ANSI)

   Check My data has headers

   On Step 2 of 3, the Delimiters, make sure the tab box is checked

   The workbook should appear as shown below:

	A	B	C	D	E
1	Year	Month	Manufactu	Region	Quantity
2	2020	Jan	Mercedes	South We:	220
3	2020	Mar	BMW	North We:	155
4	2020	Feb	Toyota	North We:	35
5	2020	Jun	VW	South	125
6	2020	Jul	Ford	East	126
7	2020	Jul	Skoda	East	1,345
8	2020	Apr	VW	South We:	56
9	2020	Aug	Mercedes	South	68
10	2020	Aug	Toyota	South	100
11	2019	Feb	Ford	South	1,500
12	2019	Feb	Seat	East	220
13	2019	Mar	Seat	South We:	155
14	2019	Apr	VW	North We:	35
15	2019	Mar	Mercedes	North We:	125
16	2019	Jan	Skoda	South	1,260
17	2019	Mar	Toyota	East	45
18	2019	Jul	VW	South We:	56

6. Save the worksheet displayed, as type Excel Workbook, and name it Chapter5_Exercise16txt

this chapter covers...

This chapter covers the use of statistical formulas. It explains and takes you through the concepts and techniques listed below.

By the time you have finished this chapter and carried out the exercises which follow, you should be able to produce spreadsheets which perform a variety of statistical calculations.

The concepts and techniques covered are:

- *simple statistical functions*
- *formulas – absolute addresses*
- *rounding functions*
- *notes*
- *comments*

Note that the step-by-step instructions given in this chapter are based on the Microsoft® Excel model, but the concepts and techniques described generally relate to all spreadsheet packages.

STATISTICAL FUNCTIONS

The functions we are going to cover in this section are as follows:

- COUNT
- COUNTA
- MAX
- MIN
- AVERAGE
- COUNTIF
- SUMIF

COUNT

The COUNT function counts the number of cells that contain numbers within a group of cells specified by the user. The formula is:

=COUNT(value1,[value2],...)

The COUNT function has these arguments:

- **value1**

  This is required and can be the first item, cell reference, or range within which you want to count numbers
- **value2**

  This is optional

You can specify up to 255 arguments. Each 'argument' can be either a number, cell reference, or range of cells.

Here are some examples:

=COUNT(B1:B16)

This would tell us how many cells in the range B1 to B16 contain numbers.

=COUNT(B1:B16,C20:C36)

This would return the total of how many cells in the range B1 to B16, and C20 to C36 contain numbers.

A simple illustration of customer sales is shown in the screen image on the next page, where we are counting out of the six months, how many months the customers bought something, and record the result in column H.

We use the formula =COUNT(B4:G4) entered in cell H4 to tell us how many months Farmhouse Foods made a purchase. This formula can then be copied to the remaining customer rows.

H4	=COUNT(B4:G4)						
	A	B	C	D	E	F	G	H

	A	B	C	D	E	F	G	H
1		Monthly Sales Value						
2								Months made
3	Customer Name	Month1	Month2	Month3	Month4	Month5	Month6	a purchase
4	Farmhouse Foods		£112				£26	2
5	Engineering Services					£67		1
6	Another Food Service				£58	£116		2
7	Top Quality Supplies		£56					1
8	Halal Foods							0
9	Edwards Farm					£40		1
10	Allen and co	£45	£68	£231	£0	£331	£37	6
11	Ahmed and son							0

COUNTA

The COUNTA function counts the number of cells that are not empty within a group of cells specified by the user. The formula is:

=COUNTA(value1,[value2],...)

The COUNTA function has these arguments:

- **value1**

  This is required and can be the first item, cell reference, or range within which you want to count numbers

- **value2**

  This is optional

You can specify up to 255 arguments. Each 'argument' can be either a number, cell reference, or range of cells.

Very similar to COUNT,

=COUNTA(B1:B16)

would tell us how many cells in the range B1 to B16 are not empty.

=COUNTA(B1:B16,C20:C36)

would return how many cells in the range B1 to B16, and C20 to C36 are not empty.

We have an example on the next page; with the list of customers and sales, together with their postcode, we can use the COUNTA function to tell us how many customers have the postcode specified, using formula =COUNTA(B4:B15) as shown in cell B16.

B16 =COUNTA(B4:B15)

	A	B	C	D	E	F	G	H	I
1			Monthly Sales Value						
2									Months made
3	Customer Name	Postcode	Month1	Month2	Month3	Month4	Month5	Month6	a purchase
4	*Farmhouse Foods*	*WR15 2AA*		£112				£26	2
5	*Engineering Services*	*SR12 T12*					£67		1
6	*Another Food Service*					£58	£116		2
7	*Top Quality Supplies*	*TH2 J11*		£56					1
8	*Halal Foods*	*KL1 C34*							0
9	*Edwards Farm*	*LM1 6LL*					£40		1
10	*Allen and co*		£45	£68	£231	£0	£331	£37	6
11	*Ahmed and son*	*L11 5GG*							0
12	*Green & Sons Wholesalers*	*MN12 1RT*	£700		£104				2
13	*Higginbottom and son*								0
14	*W B Meats*	*WW1 3HH*		£45					1
15	*The Halal Centre*	*DD12 3DF*			£50			£0	2
16	Postcode Specified	9							

MAX

'MAX' is an abbreviation of 'maximum'. The MAX function returns the maximum (largest) number within a group of cells specified by the user.

The formula is:

=MAX(number1,number2,...)

The MAX function has these arguments:

- **number1 – this is required**
- **number2 – this is optional**

You can specify up to 255 arguments for which you want to find the maximum value. Each argument can be either a number, cell reference, or range.

Here are some examples:

=MAX(B1:B6)

This would return the largest of the numbers in the range B1 to B6.

=MAX(B1:B6,80)

This would return the largest of the numbers in the range B1 to B6, and 80, ie if none of the numbers within the range is greater than 80 it would return a value of 80.

In the customer sales spreadsheet shown on the next page, we have setup column H to show the maximum (highest) monthly spend by each customer, the formula is put in H4, and copied to H5 through to H15.

H4 =MAX(B4:G4)

	A	B	C	D	E	F	G	H
1		**Monthly Sales Value**						
2								**Max**
3	**Customer Name**	**Month1**	**Month2**	**Month3**	**Month4**	**Month5**	**Month6**	**Purchase**
4	*Farmhouse Foods*		£112				£26	£112
5	*Engineering Services*					£67		£67
6	*Another Food Service*				£58	£116		£116
7	*Top Quality Supplies*		£56					£56
8	*Halal Foods*							£0
9	*Edwards Farm*					£40		£40
10	*Allen and co*	£45	£68	£231	£0	£331	£37	£331
11	*Ahmed and son*							£0
12	*Green & Sons Wholesalers*	£700		£104				£700
13	*Higginbottom and son*							£0
14	*W B Meats*		£45					£45
15	*The Halal Centre*			£50			£0	£50

MIN

'MIN' is an abbreviation of 'minimum'. The MIN function returns the smallest number within a group of cells specified by the user.

The formula is:

=MIN(number1,number2,...)

The MIN function has these arguments:

- **number1 – this is required**
- **number2 – this is optional**

You can specify up to 255 arguments for which you want to find the minimum value. Each argument can be either a number, or cell reference, or range.

Here are some examples:

=MIN(C2:C16)

This would return the smallest of the numbers in the range C2 to C16.

=MIN(C2:C16,10)

This would return the smallest of the numbers in the range C2 to C16, and 10, ie if none of the numbers within the range is smaller than 10 it would return a value of 10.

In the customer sales spreadsheet shown on the next page, we have this time setup column H to show the minimum (lowest) monthly purchase for each customer. The formula has been input in cell H4 and copied to H5 through to H15.

H4 =MIN(B4:G4)

	A	B	C	D	E	F	G	H
1		Monthly Sales Value						
2								Min
3	Customer Name	Month1	Month2	Month3	Month4	Month5	Month6	Purchase
4	*Farmhouse Foods*		£112				£26	£26
5	*Engineering Services*					£67		£67
6	*Another Food Service*				£58	£116		£58
7	*Top Quality Supplies*		£56					£56
8	*Halal Foods*							£0
9	*Edwards Farm*					£40		£40
10	*Allen and co*	£45	£68	£231	£0	£331	£37	£0
11	*Ahmed and son*							£0
12	*Green & Sons Wholesalers*	£700		£104				£104
13	*Higginbottom and son*							£0
14	*W B Meats*		£45					£45
15	*The Halal Centre*			£50			£0	£0

AVERAGE

The AVERAGE function returns the average (arithmetic mean) of a group of cells specified by the user. Other functions such as MODE and MEDIAN are also available, but will not be covered by this book.

The formula is:

=AVERAGE(number1,number2,...)

The AVERAGE function has these arguments:

- **number1 – this is required**
- **number2 – this is optional**

You can specify up to 255 arguments for which you want to find the AVERAGE value. Each argument can be either a number, or cell reference, or range.

Here are some examples:

=AVERAGE (C2:C16)

This would return the average of the numbers in the cell range C2 to C16.

=AVERAGE (C2:C16,10)

This would return the average of the numbers in the cell range C2 to C16 and 10.

In the example on the next page, we have calculated the average amount spent by each customer over the six months. The formula used for row 4 is =AVERAGE(B4:G4)

H4 =AVERAGE(B4:G4)

	A	B	C	D	E	F	G	H
1		Monthly Sales Value						
2								Average
3	Customer Name	Month1	Month2	Month3	Month4	Month5	Month6	Purchase
4	Farmhouse Foods		£112				£26	£69
5	Engineering Services					£67		
6	Another Food Service				£58	£116		
7	Top Quality Supplies		£56					
8	Halal Foods							
9	Edwards Farm					£40		
10	Allen and co	£45	£68	£231	£0	£331	£37	
11	Ahmed and son							
12	Green & Sons Wholesalers	£700		£104				
13	Higginbottom and son							
14	W B Meats		£45					
15	The Halal Centre			£50			£0	

Notice what happens when this formula is copied to the other rows:

	A	B	C	D	E	F	G	H
1		Monthly Sales Value						
2								Average
3	Customer Name	Month1	Month2	Month3	Month4	Month5	Month6	Purchase
4	Farmhouse Foods		£112				£26	£69
5	Engineering Services					£67		£67
6	Another Food Service				£58	£116		£87
7	Top Quality Supplies		£56					£56
8	Halal Foods							#DIV/0!
9	Edwards Farm					£40		£40
10	Allen and co	£45	£68	£231	£0	£331	£37	£119
11	Ahmed and son							#DIV/0!
12	Green & Sons Wholesalers	£700		£104				£402
13	Higginbottom and son							#DIV/0!
14	W B Meats		£45					£45
15	The Halal Centre			£50			£0	£25

We get errors in those rows where the customer has not made any purchases over the six months. Any cells containing a value, even if it is zero, will be included in the Average.

This can be corrected by changing our formula to only calculate the average, if the customer has made a purchase in the six months, ie use an IF statement, together with the COUNT function to see if there are any values greater than 0 in the 6 months. This is illustrated in the image on the next page.

H4 =IF(COUNT(B4:G4)>0,AVERAGE(B4:G4),0)

	A	B	C	D	E	F	G	H
1		Monthly Sales Value						
2								Average
3	Customer Name	Month1	Month2	Month3	Month4	Month5	Month6	Purchase
4	*Farmhouse Foods*		£112				£26	£69
5	*Engineering Services*					£67		£67
6	*Another Food Service*				£58	£116		£87
7	*Top Quality Supplies*		£56					£56
8	*Halal Foods*							£0
9	*Edwards Farm*					£40		£40
10	*Allen and co*	£45	£68	£231	£0	£331	£37	£119
11	*Ahmed and son*							£0
12	*Green & Sons Wholesalers*	£700		£104				£402
13	*Higginbottom and son*							£0
14	*W B Meats*		£45					£45
15	*The Halal Centre*			£50			£0	£25

COUNTIF

The COUNTIF function counts the number of cells within a group of cells specified by the user which meet certain criteria. The formula is:

=COUNTIF(range, criteria)

The COUNTIF function has these arguments:

- **range**

  This is required, it is the range within which you want to count, eg B4:B15

- **criteria**

  defines the condition that tells the function which cells to count. It can be a number, text, cell reference or expression.

  =COUNTIF(B1:B16, 10)

would tell us how many cells in the range B1 to B16 have the value 10.

=COUNTIF(B1:B16, “>10”)

would return how many cells in the range B1 to B16 are bigger than 10.

=COUNTIF(B1:B16, A1)

would return how many cells in the range B1 to B16 contain the value held in cell A1.

In the customers' sales example below, new customers are identified with a 'Y" so we can use the COUNTIF function to tell us how many customers are new. We would use the formula:

=COUNTIF(B4:B15,“Y”)

as shown in cell B16:

B16 =COUNTIF(B4:B15,"Y")

	A	B	C	D	E	F	G	H
1			Monthly Sales Value					
2		New						
3	Customer Name	Customer	Month1	Month2	Month3	Month4	Month5	Month6
4	*Farmhouse Foods*	*Y*		£112				£26
5	*Engineering Services*	*N*					£67	
6	*Another Food Service*	*N*				£58	£116	
7	*Top Quality Supplies*	*N*		£56				
8	*Halal Foods*	*N*						
9	*Edwards Farm*	*Y*					£40	
10	*Allen and co*	*N*	£45	£68	£231	£0	£331	£37
11	*Ahmed and son*	*N*						
12	*Green & Sons Wholesalers*	*Y*	£700		£104			
13	*Higginbottom and son*	*N*						
14	*W B Meats*	*Y*		£45				
15	*The Halal Centre*	*Y*			£50			£0
16	**New Customers**	5						

SUMIF

The SUMIF function totals the cells within a group of cells specified by the user which meet certain criteria. The formula is:

=SUMIF(range, criteria,[sum_range])

The SUMIF function has these arguments:

- **range**

  This is required, it is the range within which you want to count, eg B4:B15

- **criteria**

  defines the condition that tells the function which cells to include in the total. It can be a number, text, cell reference or expression.

- **sum_range**

  this is optional, and defines the actual cells to add, if you want to add cells other than those specified in the range argument. If the sum_range argument is omitted, the cells that are specified in the range argument (the same cells to which the criteria is applied) are added together.

  =SUMIF(C1:C16, ">50")

  would add together those cells in the range C1 to C16 which have a value greater than 50.

  =SUMIF(B1:B16, "Y",C1:C16)

  would add together those cells in the range C1 to C16 where the corresponding value in column B is Y, ie if the value in B1 is Y, C1 would be included in the total.

Similarly if the value in B2 is Y, C2 would be included, and so on.

In the customers' sales example below, new customers are identified with a "Y" so we can use the SUMIF function to create a monthly total for each month for new customers. We would use the formula:

=SUMIF(B4:B15,"Y", C4:C15)

as shown in cell C16:

C16 | =SUMIF(B4:B15,"Y",C4:C15)

	A	B	C	D	E	F	G	H
1				Monthly Sales Value				
2		New						
3	Customer Name	Customer	Month1	Month2	Month3	Month4	Month5	Month6
4	*Farmhouse Foods*	*Y*		£112				£26
5	*Engineering Services*	*N*					£67	
6	*Another Food Service*	*N*				£58	£116	
7	*Top Quality Supplies*	*N*		£56				
8	*Halal Foods*	*N*						
9	*Edwards Farm*	*Y*					£40	
10	*Allen and co*	*N*	£45	£68	£231	£0	£331	£37
11	*Ahmed and son*	*N*						
12	*Green & Sons Wholesalers*	*Y*	£700		£104			
13	*Higginbottom and son*	*N*						
14	*W B Meats*	*Y*		£45				
15	*The Halal Centre*	*Y*			£50			£0
16	New Customers Monthly Total		£700					

FORMULAS

absolute addressing

As discussed in chapter 4, the use of absolute cell referencing is a very important concept when copying formulas.

Sometimes we do not want the cell, row or column reference to change as we copy a formula – we want to keep a reference to an original cell, column or row. To do this we use the **dollar sign: $.**

For example:

$B$3

would refer to **cell** B3, and, when placed in a formula and copied, the copies would all also refer to B3.

In our previous example, if we just copy the formula in cell C16 into D16, we would get the formula:

=SUMIF(C4:C15,"Y",D4:D15)

Which isn't what we want, we need to use absolute addressing, so that we are always comparing the values in column B:

=SUMIF($B$4:$B$15,"Y",C4:C15)

This will now copy across to the other cells to produce the required result, as can be seen below:

D16 =SUMIF($B$4:$B$15,"Y",D4:D15)

	A	B	C	D	E	F	G	H
1			Monthly Sales Value					
2		New						
3	Customer Name	Customer	Month1	Month2	Month3	Month4	Month5	Month6
4	*Farmhouse Foods*	Y		£112				£26
5	*Engineering Services*	N					£67	
6	*Another Food Service*	N				£58	£116	
7	*Top Quality Supplies*	N		£56				
8	*Halal Foods*	N						
9	*Edwards Farm*	Y					£40	
10	*Allen and co*	N	£45	£68	£231	£0	£331	£37
11	*Ahmed and son*	N						
12	*Green & Sons Wholesalers*	Y	£700		£104			
13	*Higginbottom and son*	N						
14	*W B Meats*	Y		£45				
15	*The Halal Centre*	Y			£50			£0
16	**New Customers Monthly Total**		£700	£157	£154	£0	£40	£26

A **row** example could be:

B$3

which would mean when the formula was copied, the column would change, but not the row, it would always refer to row 3.

If we were just referring to a row in a range, we would use:

$3:$3

On other occasions, we may want to keep the same **column**, but move down the rows, in this instance, we would use

$B3 in our formula.

Similarly for a column range:

$B:$B

would keep column B in the formula, as you copied it.

Here are some more examples:

In this example, in cell G3 we are using the COUNTIF function, looking down column A for the value in F3.

G3 =COUNTIF(A:A,F3)

	A	B	C	D	E	F	G
1	W/c 02/04/2021						
2	Name		Day	Product		Name	No of items produced
3	Simon Lee		Friday	Blouse		Simon Lee	27
4	Shaiyan Kumar		Thursday	Dress		Shaiyan Kumar	0
5	Shannon Bradley		Monday	Blouse		Shannon Bradley	0
6	Sue Parker		Tuesday	Skirt		Sue Parker	0
7	Simon Lee		Wednesday	Skirt		Nikki Gali	0
8	Nikki Gali		Wednesday	Skirt		Pablo Bernardi	0
9	Simon Lee		Monday	Dress		Petra Robinson	
10	Shaiyan Kumar		Wednesday	Blouse			

For G4, we want to look for the value in F4, so within the formula, we want to keep to the same column – F but move down to the next row. To achieve this, we would use $F3 in our formula, and then copy it.

G3 =COUNTIF(A:A,$F3)

	A	B	C	D	E	F	G
1	W/c 02/04/2021						
2	Name		Day	Product		Name	No of items produced
3	Simon Lee		Friday	Blouse		Simon Lee	27
4	Shaiyan Kumar		Thursday	Dress		Shaiyan Kumar	0
5	Shannon Bradley		Monday	Blouse		Shannon Bradley	0
6	Sue Parker		Tuesday	Skirt		Sue Parker	0
7	Simon Lee		Wednesday	Skirt		Nikki Gali	0
8	Nikki Gali		Wednesday	Skirt		Pablo Bernardi	0
9	Simon Lee		Monday	Dress		Petra Robinson	
10	Shaiyan Kumar		Wednesday	Blouse			

The effects of copying this formula are shown below:

Name	No of items produced
Simon Lee	=COUNTIF(A:A,$F3)
Shaiyan Kumar	=COUNTIF(A:A,$F4)
Shannon Bradley	=COUNTIF(A:A,$F5)
Sue Parker	=COUNTIF(A:A,$F6)
Nikki Gali	=COUNTIF(A:A,$F7)
Pablo Bernardi	=COUNTIF(A:A,$F8)
Petra Robinson	=COUNTIF(A:A,$F9)

If our table of names went in the other direction, across columns:

	A	B	C	D	E	F	G	H	I
1	W/c 02/04/2021								
2									Name
3	Name		Day	Product		Simon Lee	Shaiyan Kumar	Shannon Bradley	Sue Parker
4	Simon Lee		Friday	Blouse					

When we copy our formulas, we would want to keep the row the same and change the column.

We start with:

F4 =COUNTIF($A:$A,F$3)

	A	B	C	D	E	F	G	H	I
1	W/c 02/04/2021								
2									Name
3	Name		Day	Product		Simon Lee	Shaiyan Kumar	Shannon Bradley	Sue Parker
4	Simon Lee		Friday	Blouse		27	0	0	0

Notice how we have $A:$A, as we always want to count down column A.

When we copy the formula in F4 we get:

F	G	H	I
			Name
Simon Lee	Shaiyan Kumar	Shannon Bradley	Sue Parker
=COUNTIF($A:$A,F$3)	=COUNTIF($A:$A,G$3)	=COUNTIF($A:$A,H$3)	=COUNTIF($A:$A,I$3)

ROUNDING FUNCTIONS

The functions we are going to cover in this section are as follows:

- ROUND
- ROUNDUP
- ROUNDDOWN

ROUND

The ROUND function is used to round a number in a cell to a given number of decimal places.

You will be used to using the formatting feature to display your figures to a certain number of decimal places, but this doesn't alter the actual figure. To alter the figure and use it rounded in subsequent calculations, the ROUND functions are essential.

The formula is:

=ROUND (number, num_digits)

The ROUND function has two arguments

- **number** – the number which you wish to round up
- **num_digits** – the position of the digit to which you want to round the number, relative to the decimal point. Positive numbers will cause rounding after the decimal point, 0 will remove the decimal point and round on the last digit before the decimal point, and negative numbers will cause rounding on digits preceding the decimal point.

Note: digits 0 to 4 are rounded down, 5 to 9 are rounded up.

Both arguments must be included in the function.

Some simple examples are shown below:

=ROUND(125.1456, 1) would return 125.1

=ROUND(125. 1456, 2) would return 125.15

=ROUND(125. 1456, 3) would return 125.146

If you enter 0 for the num_digits argument, this would ROUND to the nearest integer, for example:

= ROUND(125.9, 0) would return 126

If you enter a number less than 0 for the num_digits argument, this would ROUND to the nearest ten, hundred or thousand as shown below:

=ROUND(125.1, -1) would return 130

=ROUND(125.1, -2) would return 100

=ROUND(125.1, -3) would return 0

ROUNDUP

The ROUNDUP function is used to round a number in a cell **UP**.

The formula is:

=ROUNDUP(number, num_digits)

The ROUNDUP function has two arguments:

- **number** – the number which you wish to round up
- **num_digits** – the position of the digit to which you want to round the number, relative to the decimal point. Positive numbers will cause rounding after the decimal point, 0 will remove the decimal point and round on the last digit before the decimal point, and negative numbers will cause rounding on digits preceding the decimal point.

Both arguments must be included in the function.

Some simple examples are shown below:

=ROUNDUP(125.1543, 1) would return 125.2

=ROUNDUP(125.1543, 2) would return 125.16

=ROUNDUP(125.1543, 3) would return 125.155

If you enter 0 for the num_digits argument, this would ROUNDUP to the nearest integer, for example:

= ROUNDUP(125.1543, 0) would return 126

If you enter a number less than 0 for the num_digits argument, this would ROUNDUP to the nearest ten, hundred or thousand as shown below:

=ROUNDUP(125.1543, -1) would return 130

=ROUNDUP(125.1543, -2) would return 200

=ROUNDUP(125.1543, -3) would return 1000

ROUNDOWN

The ROUNDDOWN function is used to round a number in a cell **DOWN**.

The formula is:

=ROUNDDOWN (number, num_digits)

The ROUNDDOWN function has two arguments:

- **number** – the number which you wish to round down
- **num_digits** – the position of the digit to which you want to round the number, relative to the decimal point. Positive numbers will cause rounding after the decimal point, 0 will remove the decimal point and round on the last digit before the decimal point, and negative numbers will cause rounding on digits preceding the decimal point.

Both arguments must be included in the function.

Some simple examples are shown below:

=ROUNDDOWN(125.1543, 1) would return 125.1

=ROUNDDOWN(125.1543, 2) would return 125.15

=ROUNDDOWN(125.1543, 3) would return 125.154

If you enter 0 for the num_digits argument, this would ROUNDDOWN to the nearest integer, for example:

= ROUNDDOWN(125.1543, 0) would return 125

If you enter a number less than 0 for the num_digits argument, this would ROUNDDOWN to the nearest ten, hundred or thousand as shown below:

= ROUNDDOWN(125.1543, -1) would return 120

= ROUNDDOWN(125.1543, -2) would return 100

= ROUNDDOWN(125.1543, -3) would return 0

NOTES

It is possible to add a note to a cell. This is a useful way of recording a note which relates to the cell content, perhaps when or why it was last changed or noting its previous value.

Any cell which has a NOTE attached to it will display a red indicator in the top right corner of the cell, as can be seen on cell C8 below.

Note: in earlier versions of Excel, these were known as comments. Comments now have a different role, as explained in the next section.

	A	B	C	E
1	Purchase invoices			
2				
3	**Invoice date**	**Supplier ref**	**Gross value**	
4	28/04/2021	SUPV5	979	
5	18/04/2021	CSUP11	6,045	
6	06/04/2021	ASUP6	562	
7	13/04/2021	CSUP6	2,183	
8	14/04/2021	CSUP7	6,045	
9	09/04/2021	ASUP9	4,519	
10	21/04/2021	CSUP14	5,687	
11	07/05/2021	ASUP7	4,291	

When the cursor is on the cell with the red indicator, the comment will be displayed.

	A	B	C	E	F
1	Purchase invoices				
2					
3	**Invoice date**	**Supplier ref**	**Gross value**		
4	28/04/2021	SUPV5	979		
5	18/04/2021	CSUP11	6,045		
6	06/04/2021	ASUP6	562		
7	13/04/2021	CSUP6	2,183		
8	14/04/2021	CSUP7	6,045	**Wendy Yates:** Is this the correct value	
9	09/04/2021	ASUP9	4,519		
10	21/04/2021	CSUP14	5,687		
11	07/05/2021	ASUP7	4,291		

It is also possible to adjust the size of the comment box – this is described later in the section.

To ADD a Note:

either

- right-click on the required cell
- select **New Note**

or

- select the cell
- select New Note from the **Review** menu, Notes option

then

- enter your text
- click away from the note box when you have finished

To keep a note SHOWING:

either

- right-click on the required cell
- select Show/Hide Note

or

- select the cell
- select Show/Hide Note from the **Review** menu, Notes option

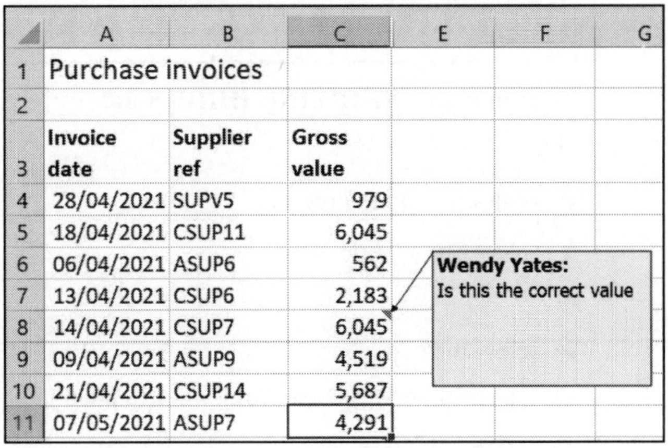

	A	B	C	E	F	G
1	Purchase invoices					
2						
3	**Invoice date**	**Supplier ref**	**Gross value**			
4	28/04/2021	SUPV5	979			
5	18/04/2021	CSUP11	6,045			
6	06/04/2021	ASUP6	562			
7	13/04/2021	CSUP6	2,183			
8	14/04/2021	CSUP7	6,045			
9	09/04/2021	ASUP9	4,519			
10	21/04/2021	CSUP14	5,687			
11	07/05/2021	ASUP7	4,291			

Wendy Yates:
Is this the correct value

To SHOW all notes:

- Select Show All Notes from the **Review** menu, Notes option

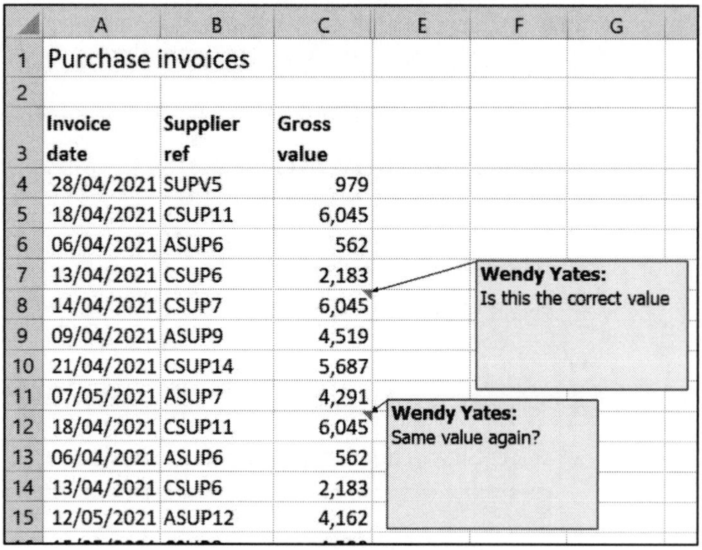

	A	B	C	E	F	G
1	Purchase invoices					
2						
3	Invoice date	Supplier ref	Gross value			
4	28/04/2021	SUPV5	979			
5	18/04/2021	CSUP11	6,045			
6	06/04/2021	ASUP6	562			
7	13/04/2021	CSUP6	2,183			
8	14/04/2021	CSUP7	6,045			
9	09/04/2021	ASUP9	4,519			
10	21/04/2021	CSUP14	5,687			
11	07/05/2021	ASUP7	4,291			
12	18/04/2021	CSUP11	6,045			
13	06/04/2021	ASUP6	562			
14	13/04/2021	CSUP6	2,183			
15	12/05/2021	ASUP12	4,162			

Wendy Yates:
Is this the correct value

Wendy Yates:
Same value again?

To stop a note SHOWING (HIDE a note):

either

- right-click on the required cell
- select Show/Hide Note

or

- select the cell
- select Show/Hide Note from the **Review** menu, Notes option

To HIDE all notes:

- select Show All Notes again from the **Review** menu, Notes option

To EDIT a Note:

either

- right-click on the required cell
- select Edit Note

or

- select the cell
- select Edit Note from the **Review** menu, Notes option

then

- modify your text
- click away from the note box when you have finished

To RESIZE the note box:

- right-click on the required cell
- select Edit Note

The sizing handles appear.

- drag the handles on the sides or corners of the box to adjust the size

To MOVE the note box:

- click on the required cell
- move the cursor to the edge of the note box
- when the four headed arrow symbol appears, drag the Note box to a new position

To DELETE a note:

- right-click on the required cell
- select Delete Note

COMMENTS

Another option is to add a comment to a cell, this will allow other comments to be added, starting a conversation with other users about a particular cell.

Any cell which has a comment(s) attached to it will display a purple indicator in the top right corner of the cell, as can be seen on cell C8 on the next page.

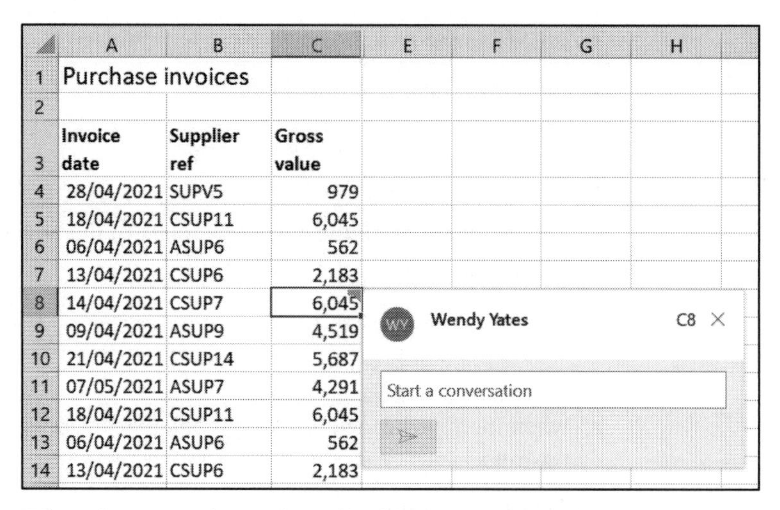

	A	B	C
1	Purchase invoices		
2			
3	**Invoice date**	**Supplier ref**	**Gross value**
4	28/04/2021	SUPV5	979
5	18/04/2021	CSUP11	6,045
6	06/04/2021	ASUP6	562
7	13/04/2021	CSUP6	2,183
8	14/04/2021	CSUP7	6,045
9	09/04/2021	ASUP9	4,519
10	21/04/2021	CSUP14	5,687
11	07/05/2021	ASUP7	4,291
12	18/04/2021	CSUP11	6,045
13	06/04/2021	ASUP6	562
14	13/04/2021	CSUP6	2,183

When the cursor is on the cell with the purple indicator, any comments will be displayed.

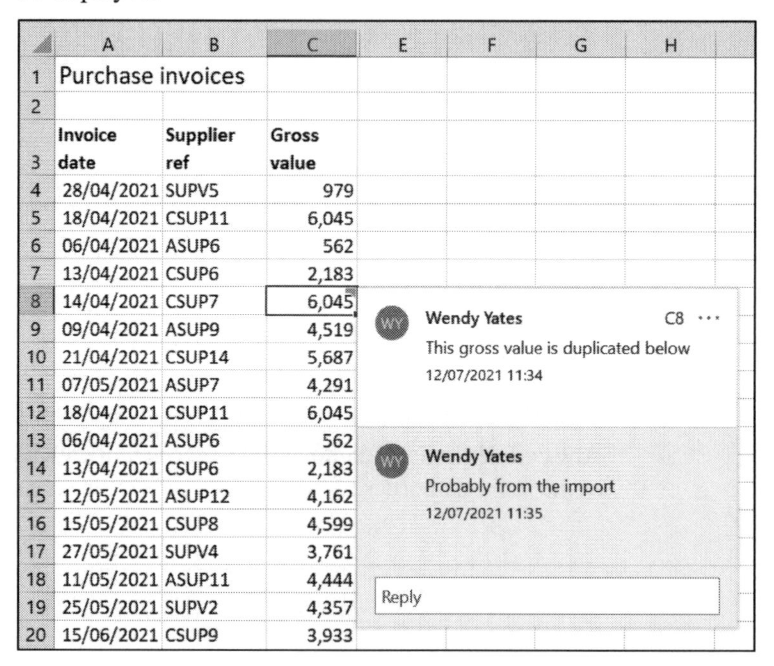

	A	B	C
1	Purchase invoices		
2			
3	**Invoice date**	**Supplier ref**	**Gross value**
4	28/04/2021	SUPV5	979
5	18/04/2021	CSUP11	6,045
6	06/04/2021	ASUP6	562
7	13/04/2021	CSUP6	2,183
8	14/04/2021	CSUP7	6,045
9	09/04/2021	ASUP9	4,519
10	21/04/2021	CSUP14	5,687
11	07/05/2021	ASUP7	4,291
12	18/04/2021	CSUP11	6,045
13	06/04/2021	ASUP6	562
14	13/04/2021	CSUP6	2,183
15	12/05/2021	ASUP12	4,162
16	15/05/2021	CSUP8	4,599
17	27/05/2021	SUPV4	3,761
18	11/05/2021	ASUP11	4,444
19	25/05/2021	SUPV2	4,357
20	15/06/2021	CSUP9	3,933

To ADD a comment:

either

- right-click on the required cell
- select New Comment

or

- select the cell
- select New comment from the **Review** menu

then

- enter your text
- click the green icon below the text box, or press CTRL and ENTER

To EDIT a comment:

- right-click on the required cell
- select Edit on the comment to be changed
- modify your text
- click Save when you have finished

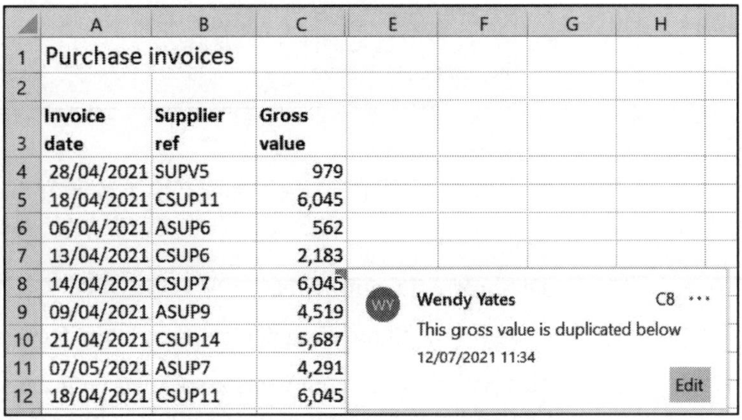

	A	B	C	E	F	G	H
1	Purchase invoices						
2							
3	**Invoice date**	**Supplier ref**	**Gross value**				
4	28/04/2021	SUPV5	979				
5	18/04/2021	CSUP11	6,045				
6	06/04/2021	ASUP6	562				
7	13/04/2021	CSUP6	2,183				
8	14/04/2021	CSUP7	6,045				
9	09/04/2021	ASUP9	4,519				
10	21/04/2021	CSUP14	5,687				
11	07/05/2021	ASUP7	4,291				
12	18/04/2021	CSUP11	6,045				

WY **Wendy Yates** C8 ···
This gross value is duplicated below
12/07/2021 11:34
Edit

To DELETE a comment:

either

- right-click on the required cell
- select Delete on the comment to be deleted

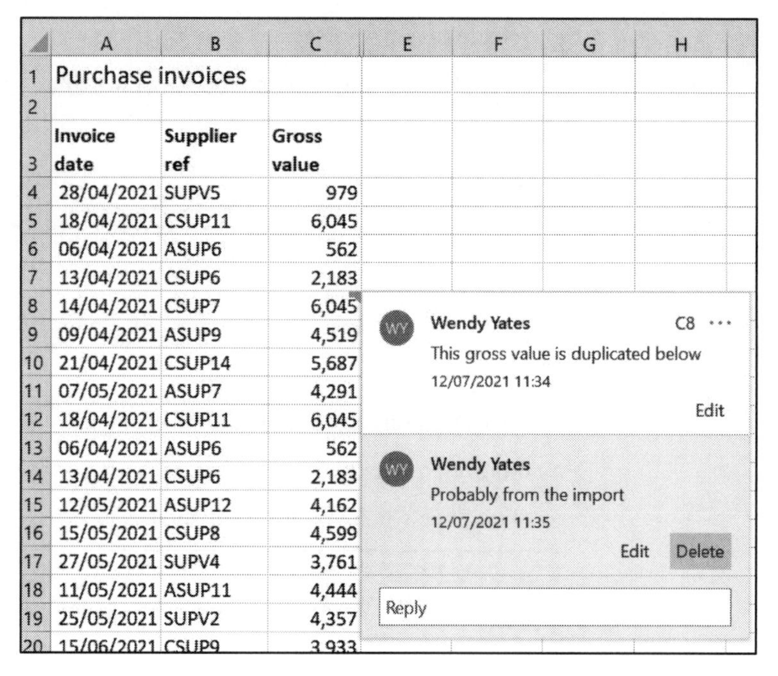

	A	B	C
1	Purchase invoices		
2			
3	**Invoice date**	**Supplier ref**	**Gross value**
4	28/04/2021	SUPV5	979
5	18/04/2021	CSUP11	6,045
6	06/04/2021	ASUP6	562
7	13/04/2021	CSUP6	2,183
8	14/04/2021	CSUP7	6,045
9	09/04/2021	ASUP9	4,519
10	21/04/2021	CSUP14	5,687
11	07/05/2021	ASUP7	4,291
12	18/04/2021	CSUP11	6,045
13	06/04/2021	ASUP6	562
14	13/04/2021	CSUP6	2,183
15	12/05/2021	ASUP12	4,162
16	15/05/2021	CSUP8	4,599
17	27/05/2021	SUPV4	3,761
18	11/05/2021	ASUP11	4,444
19	25/05/2021	SUPV2	4,357
20	15/06/2021	CSUP9	3,933

- select the cell
- select Delete from the Comments section of the **Review** menu

To Show All Comments:

- select the Show Comments option in the **Review** menu

This will show all comments associated with the worksheet in a panel to the right of the worksheet; in our example below we have comments on cells C8 and C10.

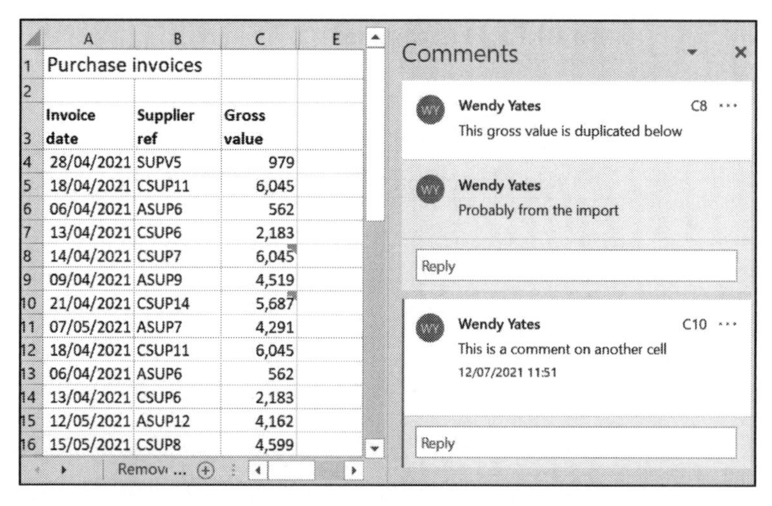

	A	B	C
1	Purchase invoices		
2			
3	**Invoice date**	**Supplier ref**	**Gross value**
4	28/04/2021	SUPV5	979
5	18/04/2021	CSUP11	6,045
6	06/04/2021	ASUP6	562
7	13/04/2021	CSUP6	2,183
8	14/04/2021	CSUP7	6,045
9	09/04/2021	ASUP9	4,519
10	21/04/2021	CSUP14	5,687
11	07/05/2021	ASUP7	4,291
12	18/04/2021	CSUP11	6,045
13	06/04/2021	ASUP6	562
14	13/04/2021	CSUP6	2,183
15	12/05/2021	ASUP12	4,162
16	15/05/2021	CSUP8	4,599

To stop Show All Comments:

- deselect the Show Comments option in the **Review** menu

CONVERT NOTES TO COMMENTS

If you change your mind, it is possible to convert any notes to comments, so that you can have a conversation relating to a cell.

To Convert all notes to Comments:

- select Convert to Comments from the **Review** menu, Notes option
- select Convert all notes as shown in the image below

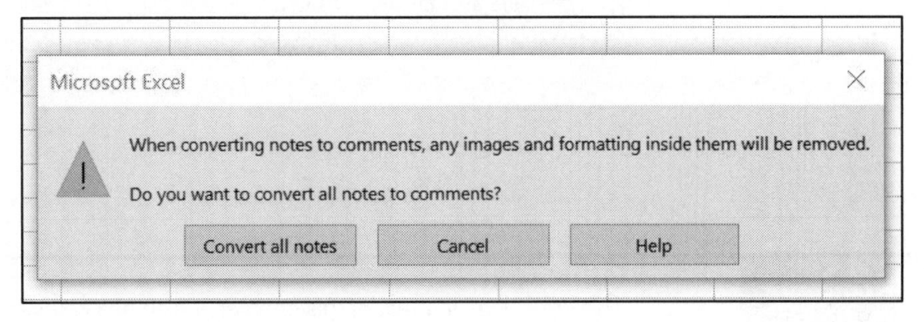

If we look at the previous example, with notes on cells C8 and C12:

	A	B	C	E
1	Purchase invoices			
2				
3	**Invoice date**	**Supplier ref**	**Gross value**	
4	28/04/2021	SUPV5	979	
5	18/04/2021	CSUP11	6,045	
6	06/04/2021	ASUP6	562	
7	13/04/2021	CSUP6	2,183	
8	14/04/2021	CSUP7	6,045	
9	09/04/2021	ASUP9	4,519	
10	21/04/2021	CSUP14	5,687	
11	07/05/2021	ASUP7	4,291	
12	18/04/2021	CSUP11	6,045	

If we select Convert Notes to Comments, then click on Convert all notes, then select Show comments, we see the notes appearing as comments in the right panel, as shown below:

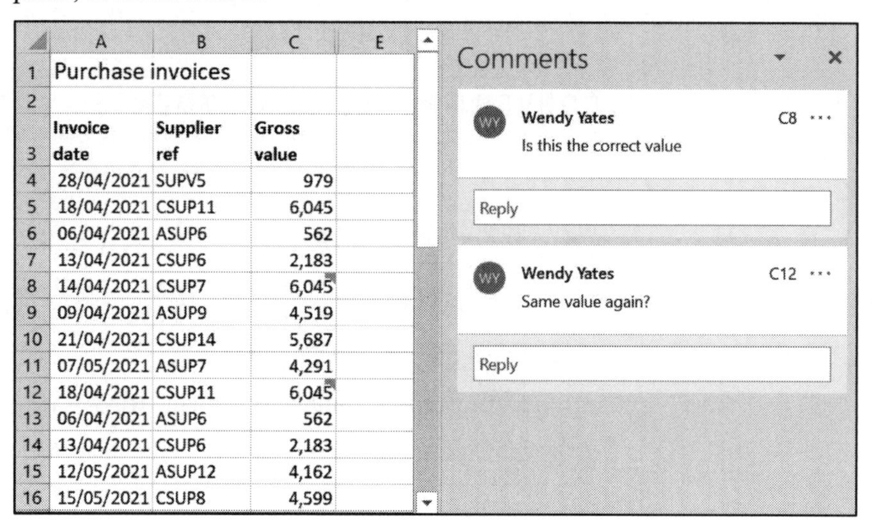

	A	B	C	E
1	Purchase invoices			
2				
3	**Invoice date**	**Supplier ref**	**Gross value**	
4	28/04/2021	SUPV5	979	
5	18/04/2021	CSUP11	6,045	
6	06/04/2021	ASUP6	562	
7	13/04/2021	CSUP6	2,183	
8	14/04/2021	CSUP7	6,045	
9	09/04/2021	ASUP9	4,519	
10	21/04/2021	CSUP14	5,687	
11	07/05/2021	ASUP7	4,291	
12	18/04/2021	CSUP11	6,045	
13	06/04/2021	ASUP6	562	
14	13/04/2021	CSUP6	2,183	
15	12/05/2021	ASUP12	4,162	
16	15/05/2021	CSUP8	4,599	

Chapter Summary

This concludes the text of this chapter, which has covered:

- simple statistical functions
- formulas – absolute addresses
- rounding functions
- notes
- comments

You should now carry out some or all of the exercises on the next few pages in order to practise and reinforce your learning.

Activities

Here are a group of exercises to allow you to practise the topics covered in this chapter. They can be done individually, or as a sequence, working your way through them.

If you choose to work your way through them, you may not need to open the exercise workbook as suggested at the start of each exercise, as it may already be open.

The saving at the end of each exercise is also optional, although it serves as a reminder to regularly save your work. You can also save to different file names and may choose to keep using the same name to avoid having lots of files.

Exercise 1

Spreadsheet skills:

- Function - COUNT
- Function - COUNTA

1. Open workbook T6Exercises
2. Select worksheet Exercise 1
3. In cell F4, enter a formula to calculate how many invoices there are in the data using the COUNT function on the Gross Value column
4. In cell G4, enter a formula to calculate how many invoices have a Supplier reference using the COUNTA function on the Supplier ref column
5. In cell H4, enter a formula to calculate how many invoices are missing a Supplier reference using both the COUNT and COUNTA functions
6. Save your spreadsheet with the name: Chapter6_Exercise1

Note: we could easily have made the formula for missing suppliers in cell H4 =F4 – G4 but it is useful to practise combining several functions in one formula.

	A	B	C	D	E	F	G	H
1	Purchase invoices							
2								
3	**Invoice date**	**Supplier ref**	**Gross value**	**Date paid**		**Total no of invoices**	**Invoices with Supplier ref**	**Invoices with no supplier ref**
4	28/04/2021	SUPV5	979	01/06/2021		46	42	4
5	18/04/2021	CSUP11	6,045	01/06/2021				
6	06/04/2021	ASUP6	562	01/06/2021				

With formulas:

	A	B	C	D	E	F	G	H
1	Purchase in							
2								
3	**Invoice date**	**Supplier ref**	**Gross value**	**Date paid**		**Total no of invoices**	**Invoices with Supplier ref**	**Invoices with no supplier ref**
4	44314	SUPV5	979	44348		=COUNT(C4:C49)	=COUNTA(B4:B49)	=COUNT(C4:C49)-COUNTA(B4:B49)
5	44304	CSUP11	6045	44348				
6	44292	ASUP6	562	44348				

Exercise 2

Spreadsheet skills:

- Function - MAX (maximum)
- Function - MIN (minimum)
- Function - AVERAGE

1. Open workbook T6Exercises
2. Select worksheet Exercise 2
3. In cell C3, enter a formula to calculate the highest Wages and salaries across all six months using the MAX function
4. In cell F3, enter a formula to calculate the lowest Postage value using the MIN function
5. In column H enter a formula to calculate the average value for the last three months for each of the payment rows, if background error checking is on, you may see a green triangle on each 3 month figure, step through and choose to ignore the warnings

   Note: the warnings occur because you have six columns of numbers and are choosing to add only three columns.
6. In column I enter a formula to calculate the average value over the six months for each of the payment rows, format to 0 decimal places (notice no green triangles this time)
7. Save your spreadsheet with the name: Chapter6_Exercise2

	A	B	C	D	E	F	G	H	I
1	Cash Payments								
2									
3		**Max wages value**	60000		**Min postage value**	1000			
4					**£**			**Average £**	
5		**Jan**	**Feb**	**Mar**	**Apr**	**May**	**Jun**	**3 month**	**6 month**
6	**Wages and salaries**	25090	25000	60000	25010	30900	24000	26637	31667
7	**Motor Expenses**	13200	6150	3900	1530	1504	16090	6375	7062
8	**Postage**	1000	1500	2500	1000	1000	2000	1333	1500
9	**Insurance**	1200	2800	4000		2130	1770	1950	2380
10	**Advertising**	7000		25600	9230		11800	10515	13408
11	**Rent and rates**	22000	22000	22000	22000	22000	22000	22000	22000
12	**Heat and light**	3200	3200	3200	3200	3200	3200	3200	3200

With formulas:

	A	B	C	D	E	F	G	H	I
1	Cash Payments								
2									
3		**Max wages value**	=MAX(B6:G6)		**Min postage value**	=MIN(B8:G8)			
4					**£**			**Average £**	
5		**Jan**	**Feb**	**Mar**	**Apr**	**May**	**Jun**	**3 month**	**6 month**
6	**Wages and salaries**	25090	25000	60000	25010	30900	24000	=AVERAGE(E6:G6)	=AVERAGE(B6:H6)
7	**Motor Expenses**	13200	6150	3900	1530	1504	16090	=AVERAGE(E7:G7)	=AVERAGE(B7:H7)
8	**Postage**	1000	1500	2500	1000	1000	2000	=AVERAGE(E8:G8)	=AVERAGE(B8:H8)
9	**Insurance**	1200	2800	4000		2130	1770	=AVERAGE(E9:G9)	=AVERAGE(B9:H9)
10	**Advertising**	7000		25600	9230		11800	=AVERAGE(E10:G10)	=AVERAGE(B10:H10)
11	**Rent and rates**	22000	22000	22000	22000	22000	22000	=AVERAGE(E11:G11)	=AVERAGE(B11:H11)
12	**Heat and light**	3200	3200	3200	3200	3200	3200	=AVERAGE(E12:G12)	=AVERAGE(B12:H12)

Exercise 3

Spreadsheet skills:

- Function - COUNTIF

1. Open workbook T6Exercises
2. Select worksheet Exercise 3

We are going to calculate how many of each type of clothing product has been produced this week.

3. In cell G4, enter a formula to calculate how many of the product "Blouse" have been produced in this week, use the COUNTIF function
4. In cell G5, enter a formula to calculate how many of the product "Skirt" have been produced in this week
5. In cell G6, enter a formula to calculate how many of the product "Dress" have been produced in this week

G4 =COUNTIF(D3:D164,"Blouse")

	A	B	C	D	E	F	G
1	W/c 02/04/2021						
2	**Name**		**Day**	**Product**			**Total**
3	Sue Parker		Monday	Skirt		**Items produced**	
4	Sue Parker		Monday	Skirt		Blouse	52
5	Sue Parker		Monday	Skirt		Skirt	40
6	Sue Parker		Monday	Dress		Dress	70
7	Sue Parker		Monday	Skirt			
8	Sue Parker		Monday	Skirt			

With formulas:

	Total
Items produced	
Blouse	=COUNTIF(D3:D164,"Blouse")
Skirt	=COUNTIF(D3:D164,"Skirt")
Dress	=COUNTIF(D3:D164,"Dress")

6. Modify the formulas in cells G4, G5, G6, to use cells F4, F5, F6 (as appropriate), rather than putting the text such as "Blouse" in the formula

7. Modify again, to use the whole of column D as the range, as an absolute address

   The results shouldn't change, but the formulas are simpler and allow for changes to the data.

G4 =COUNTIF($D:$D,F4)

	A	B	C	D	E	F	G
1	W/c 02/04/2021						
2	**Name**		**Day**	**Product**			**Total**
3	Sue Parker		Monday	Skirt		**Items produced**	
4	Sue Parker		Monday	Skirt		Blouse	52
5	Sue Parker		Monday	Skirt		Skirt	40
6	Sue Parker		Monday	Dress		Dress	70

	Total
Items produced	
Blouse	=COUNTIF($D:$D,F4)
Skirt	=COUNTIF($D:$D,F5)
Dress	=COUNTIF($D:$D,F6)

8. Save your spreadsheet with the name: Chapter6_Exercise3

Exercise 4

Spreadsheet skills:

- Function - COUNTIF
- Formulas - absolute cell references (addresses)

1. Open workbook T6Exercises
2. Select worksheet Exercise 4

We are going to calculate how many items were produced each day this week.

3. In cell G3, enter a formula to calculate how many items were produced on Monday this week, use absolute cell references (addresses) as appropriate
4. Similarly for cells H3 to K3, create formulas for each of the other weekdays, ideally copying the formula in G3
5. Save your spreadsheet with the name: Chapter6_Exercise4

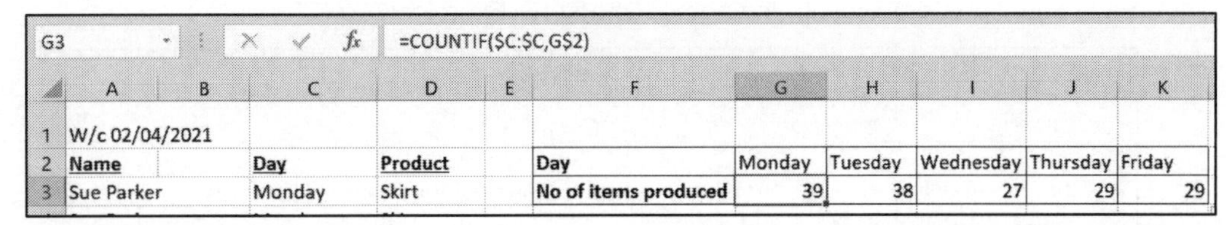

G3 =COUNTIF($C:$C,G$2)

	A	B	C	D	E	F	G	H	I	J	K
1	W/c 02/04/2021										
2	Name		Day	Product		Day	Monday	Tuesday	Wednesday	Thursday	Friday
3	Sue Parker		Monday	Skirt		No of items produced	39	38	27	29	29

With formulas:

Day	Monday	Tuesday	Wednesday	Thursday	Friday
No of items produced	=COUNTIF($C:$C,G$2)	=COUNTIF($C:$C,H$2)	=COUNTIF($C:$C,I$2)	=COUNTIF($C:$C,J$2)	=COUNTIF($C:$C,K$2)

Exercise 5

Spreadsheet skills:

- Function - SUMIF
- Formulas - absolute cell references (addresses)

1. Open workbook T6Exercises
2. Select worksheet Exercise 5

We are going to calculate the Gross pay for each person.

3. In cell I3, enter a formula, using SUMIF and absolute cell referencing, to calculate the Gross pay for Anya Salenko using the Gross wages column
4. Copy the formula created above to cells I4 to I10 for the other staff members
5. Total the Gross pay in cell I11
6. Save your spreadsheet with the name: Chapter6_Exercise5

I3 =SUMIF(C$3:C$42,H3,F$3:F$42)

	A	B	C	D	E	F	G	H	I
1									
2	Date	Job	Person name	Hours	Wage rat	Gross wages		Summary	Gross pay
3	01/08/2021	Harvey party	Anya Salenko	6	£14.50	£87.00		Anya Salenko	£391.50
4	01/08/2021	Harvey party	Tim Woodward	6	£14.50	£87.00		Tim Woodward	£362.50
5	01/08/2021	Harvey party	Cara Wilson	3	£14.50	£43.50		Cara Wilson	£290.00
6	01/08/2021	Harvey party	Kevin Dudek	8	£17.00	£136.00		Kevin Dudek	£663.00
7	01/08/2021	Harvey party	Lisa Salem	4	£14.50	£58.00		Lisa Salem	£319.00
8	01/08/2021	Harvey party	Mia Taylor	6	£14.50	£87.00		Mia Taylor	£362.50
9	01/08/2021	Harvey party	Phil Wing	8	£15.50	£124.00		Phil Wing	£589.00
10	01/08/2021	Harvey party	Ed Owen	4	£14.50	£58.00		Ed Owen	£333.50
11	08/08/2021	Bhatt Party	Anya Salenko	6	£14.50	£87.00			£3,311.00

With formulas:

H	I
Summary	Gross pay
Anya Salenko	=SUMIF(C$3:C$42,H3,F$3:F$42)
Tim Woodward	=SUMIF(C$3:C$42,H4,F$3:F$42)
Cara Wilson	=SUMIF(C$3:C$42,H5,F$3:F$42)
Kevin Dudek	=SUMIF(C$3:C$42,H6,F$3:F$42)
Lisa Salem	=SUMIF(C$3:C$42,H7,F$3:F$42)
Mia Taylor	=SUMIF(C$3:C$42,H8,F$3:F$42)
Phil Wing	=SUMIF(C$3:C$42,H9,F$3:F$42)
Ed Owen	=SUMIF(C$3:C$42,H10,F$3:F$42)
	=SUM(I3:I10)

Exercise 6

Spreadsheet skills:

- Function - IF (nested)
- Function - SUMIF
- Formulas - absolute cell references (addresses)

1. Open workbook T6Exercises
2. Select worksheet Exercise 6

The rates paid per item are in cells H3 to H5.

3. Using a Nested IF statement in column E insert the appropriate rate from cells H3 to H5 for each product produced

   The logic to use:

   If the product is Blouse (G3), then the rate is H3

   If the product is Skirt (G4) then the rate is H4

   Otherwise, the product can only be Dress so the rate is H5

   Because we are copying the formula we must use absolute addressing.

E3 =IF(D3=$G$3,$H$3, IF(D3=$G$4,$H$4, $H$5))

	A	B	C	D	E	F	G	H
1	W/c 02/04/2021							
2	Name		Day	Product	Rate		Rate paid per item	
3	Sue Parker		Monday	Skirt	£6		Blouse	£12
4	Sue Parker		Monday	Skirt	£6		Skirt	£6
5	Sue Parker		Monday	Skirt	£6		Dress	£15

With formulas:

	A	B	C	D	E
1	W/c 02/04/2021				
2	Name		Day	Product	Rate
3	Sue Parker		Monday	Skirt	=IF(D3=$G$3,$H$3, IF(D3=$G$4,$H$4, $H$5))
4	Sue Parker		Monday	Skirt	=IF(D4=$G$3,$H$3, IF(D4=$G$4,$H$4, $H$5))
5	Sue Parker		Monday	Skirt	=IF(D5=$G$3,$H$3, IF(D5=$G$4,$H$4, $H$5))
6	Sue Parker		Monday	Dress	=IF(D6=$G$3,$H$3, IF(D6=$G$4,$H$4, $H$5))
7	Sue Parker		Monday	Skirt	=IF(D7=$G$3,$H$3, IF(D7=$G$4,$H$4, $H$5))
8	Sue Parker		Monday	Skirt	=IF(D8=$G$3,$H$3, IF(D8=$G$4,$H$4, $H$5))
9	Sue Parker		Monday	Blouse	=IF(D9=$G$3,$H$3, IF(D9=$G$4,$H$4, $H$5))

4. Use the SUMIF function in cells K3 to K5 to calculate the weekly costs for the production of each product, based on the rate now calculated in column E

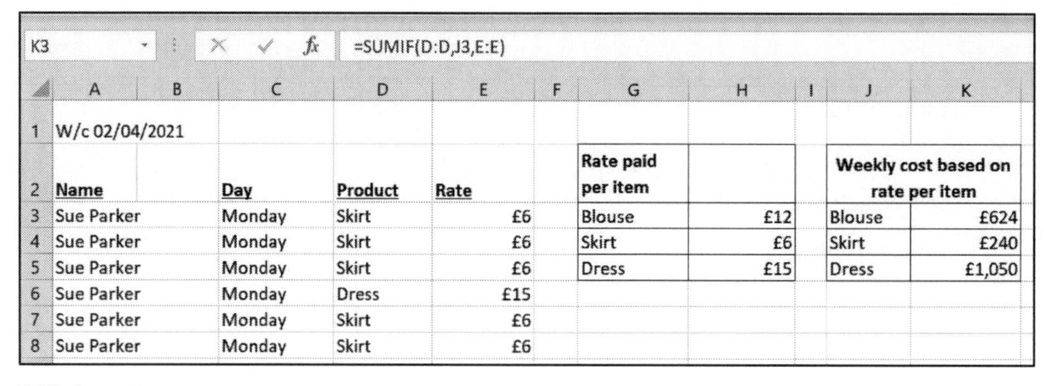

K3 =SUMIF(D:D,J3,E:E)

	A	B	C	D	E	F	G	H	I	J	K
1	W/c 02/04/2021										
2	**Name**		**Day**	**Product**	**Rate**		**Rate paid per item**			**Weekly cost based on rate per item**	
3	Sue Parker		Monday	Skirt	£6		Blouse	£12		Blouse	£624
4	Sue Parker		Monday	Skirt	£6		Skirt	£6		Skirt	£240
5	Sue Parker		Monday	Skirt	£6		Dress	£15		Dress	£1,050
6	Sue Parker		Monday	Dress	£15						
7	Sue Parker		Monday	Skirt	£6						
8	Sue Parker		Monday	Skirt	£6						

With formulas:

Weekly cost based on rate per item	
Blouse	=SUMIF(D:D,J3,E:E)
Skirt	=SUMIF(D:D,J4,E:E)
Dress	=SUMIF(D:D,J5,E:E)

5. Save your spreadsheet with the name: Chapter6_Exercise6

Exercise 7

Spreadsheet skills:

- Function - ROUND
- Function - ROUNDUP
- Function - ROUNDDOWN

1. Open workbook T6Exercises
2. Select worksheet Exercise 7
3. In column F apply the ROUND function to the Productivity bonus (Column D), rounding to 0 decimal places
4. In column G apply the ROUNDUP function to the Productivity bonus, rounding to 0 decimal places
5. In column H apply the ROUNDDOWN function to the Productivity bonus, rounding to 0 decimal places
6. Hide the Productivity bonus % column, column E
7. Save your spreadsheet with the name: Chapter6_Exercise7

F7 =ROUND(D7,0)

	A	B	C	D	F	G	H
1	Employees wages information						
2							
3	Average productivity bonus %		8.967%				
4							
5	Surname	Basic pay	Gross pay	Productivity bonus	Bonus ROUND	Bonus ROUNDUP	Bonus ROUNDDOWN
6		£	£	£			
7	Patel	£31,200.00	£32,620.50	£1,420.50	£1,421.00	£1,421.00	£1,420.00
8	Johnson	£28,900.00	£31,425.33	£2,525.33	£2,525.00	£2,526.00	£2,525.00
9	Singh	£31,200.00	£31,500.00	£300.00	£300.00	£300.00	£300.00
10	Gregory	£24,900.00	£28,950.31	£4,050.31	£4,050.00	£4,051.00	£4,050.00
11	Williams	£24,900.00	£26,750.50	£1,850.50	£1,851.00	£1,851.00	£1,850.00
12	Reed	£28,900.00	£31,850.67	£2,950.67	£2,951.00	£2,951.00	£2,950.00
13	Khan	£28,900.00	£31,450.72	£2,550.72	£2,551.00	£2,551.00	£2,550.00
14	Begum	£24,900.00	£28,650.00	£3,750.00	£3,750.00	£3,750.00	£3,750.00
15	Sheppard	£28,900.00	£31,400.50	£2,500.50	£2,501.00	£2,501.00	£2,500.00
16	Total						

Exercise 8

Spreadsheet skills:

- Notes - add, show and resize

1. Open workbook T6Exercises
2. Select worksheet Exercise 8
3. Add a note to cell D8 – Premium increased by 20%

	A	B	C	D	E	F	G
1	Cash Payments						
2							
3				£			
4		Jan	Feb	Mar	Apr	May	Jun
5	**Wages and salaries**	25090	25000	60000	25010	30900	24000
6	**Motor Expenses**	13200	6150	3900	1530	1504	16090
7	**Postage**	1000	1500	2500	1000	1000	2000
8	**Insurance**	1200	2800	4000			1770
9	**Advertising**	7000		25600			11800
10	**Rent and rates**	22000	22000	22000			22000
11	**Heat and light**	3200	3200	3200			3200

Wendy Yates:
Premium increased by 20%

4. Edit the note to say Premium increased by 20%, but now fixed for two years, and move the note to the right of all the figures
5. Adjust the size of the note box, so that the text fits on two lines
6. Select Show notes

	A	B	C	D	E	F	G	H	I	J
1	Cash Payments									
2										
3				£						
4		Jan	Feb	Mar	Apr	May	Jun			
5	**Wages and salaries**	25090	25000	60000	25010	30900	24000			
6	**Motor Expenses**	13200	6150	3900	1530	1504	16090			
7	**Postage**	1000	1500	2500	1000	1000	2000			
8	**Insurance**	1200	2800	4000		2130	1770			
9	**Advertising**	7000		25600	9230		11800			
10	**Rent and rates**	22000	22000	22000	22000	22000	22000			
11	**Heat and light**	3200	3200	3200	3200	3200	3200			

Wendy Yates:
Premium increased by 20%, but now fixed for 2 years

7. Save your spreadsheet with the name: Chapter6_Exercise8

Exercise 9

> Spreadsheet skills:
>
> - Comments - add, delete and show
> - Notes - convert to comments

1. Open workbook T6Exercises
2. Select worksheet Exercise 9
3. Add a comment to cell D9 – Investigating why this value is so high
4. Add to the conversation – Spoke to Agency 1st July, awaiting response
5. Add to the conversation – 15th July still nothing
6. Select Show comments

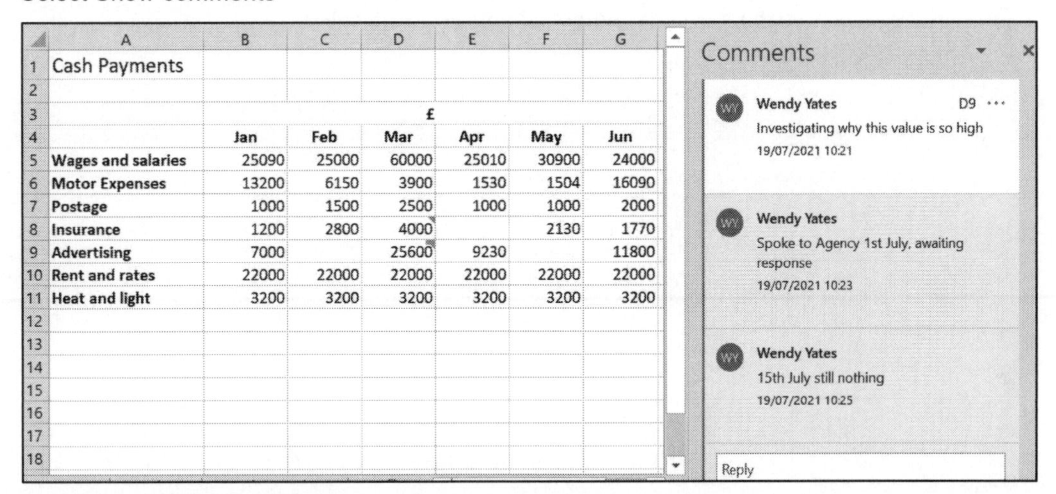

	A	B	C	D	E	F	G
1	Cash Payments						
2							
3				£			
4		Jan	Feb	Mar	Apr	May	Jun
5	Wages and salaries	25090	25000	60000	25010	30900	24000
6	Motor Expenses	13200	6150	3900	1530	1504	16090
7	Postage	1000	1500	2500	1000	1000	2000
8	Insurance	1200	2800	4000		2130	1770
9	Advertising	7000		25600	9230		11800
10	Rent and rates	22000	22000	22000	22000	22000	22000
11	Heat and light	3200	3200	3200	3200	3200	3200
12							
13							
14							
15							
16							
17							
18							

7. Delete the last comment in the conversation on cell D9
8. Convert all notes to comments

   You should now have the following:

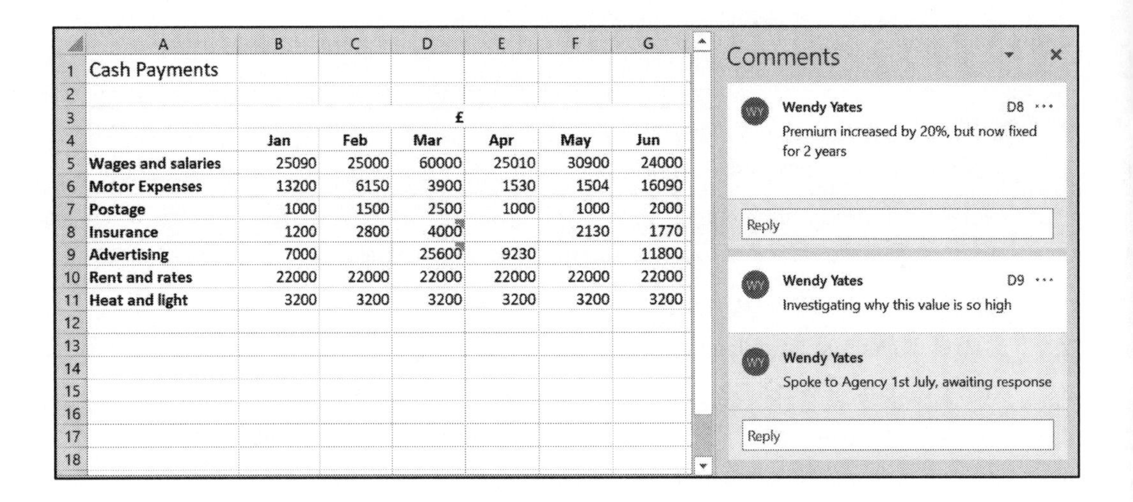

	A	B	C	D	E	F	G
1	Cash Payments						
2							
3				£			
4		**Jan**	**Feb**	**Mar**	**Apr**	**May**	**Jun**
5	**Wages and salaries**	25090	25000	60000	25010	30900	24000
6	**Motor Expenses**	13200	6150	3900	1530	1504	16090
7	**Postage**	1000	1500	2500	1000	1000	2000
8	**Insurance**	1200	2800	4000		2130	1770
9	**Advertising**	7000		25600	9230		11800
10	**Rent and rates**	22000	22000	22000	22000	22000	22000
11	**Heat and light**	3200	3200	3200	3200	3200	3200
12							
13							
14							
15							
16							
17							
18							

9. Save your spreadsheet with the name: Chapter6_Exercise9

this chapter covers...

This chapter covers creating and modifying charts. It explains and takes you through the concepts and techniques listed below.

By the time you have finished this chapter and carried out the exercises which follow, you should be able to produce spreadsheets which contain appropriate charts to illustrate worksheet data.

The concepts and techniques covered are:

- *types of charts*
- *parts of a chart*
- *creating charts*
- *data tables and data series*
- *modification of charts*
- *pie charts*
- *3D or exploded charts*

Note that the step-by-step instructions given in this chapter are based on the Microsoft® Excel model, but the concepts and techniques described generally relate to all spreadsheet packages.

TYPES OF CHARTS

Within spreadsheet packages, there are a variety of different chart types available for the visual representation of data. In this section we are going to illustrate the following types of chart. Instructions for the creation of charts will follow in a separate section at the end of this chapter.

- Column (bar)
- Pie
- Line
- Scatter

column (bar) chart

The bar chart is probably the most commonly used chart and can be applied to data that is arranged in columns or rows on a worksheet. In the image below, you can see that we have taken six months of sales data, represented as a vertical bar chart, also known as column chart, showing how the value of sales has changed over the period of six months.

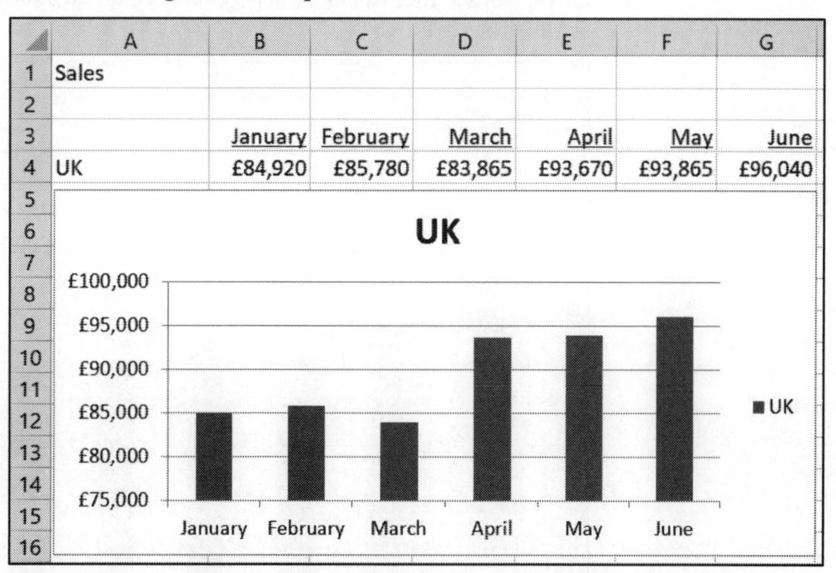

	A	B	C	D	E	F	G
1	Sales						
2							
3		January	February	March	April	May	June
4	UK	£84,920	£85,780	£83,865	£93,670	£93,865	£96,040

This is a bar chart in its simplest form, with only one set of data values. With two sets of data, sales in the UK and sales in China, we can show the values side by side, this is known as **Clustered**.

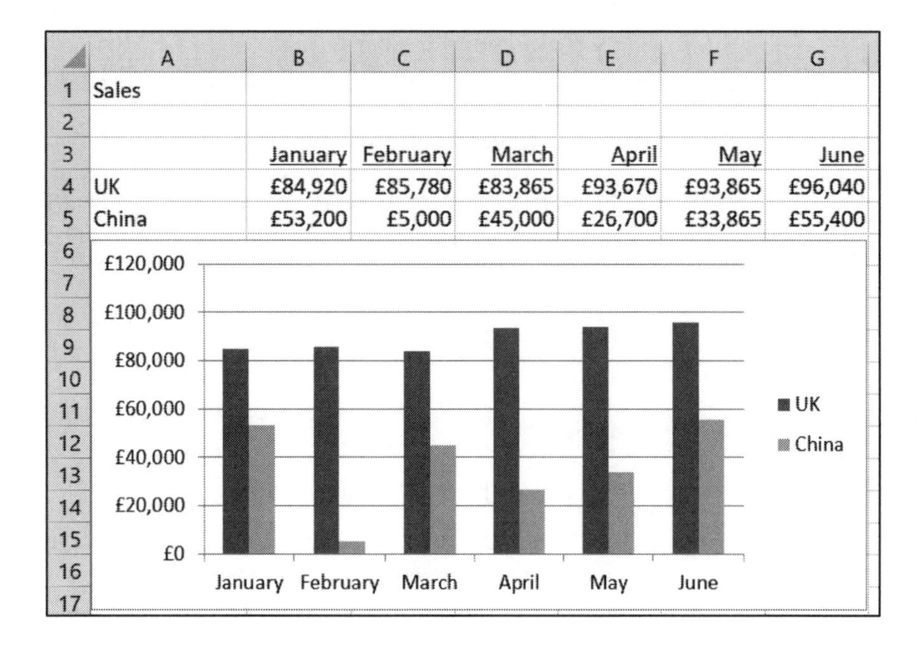

Or we can see them stacked, where both values are shown in the same column, as illustrated below:

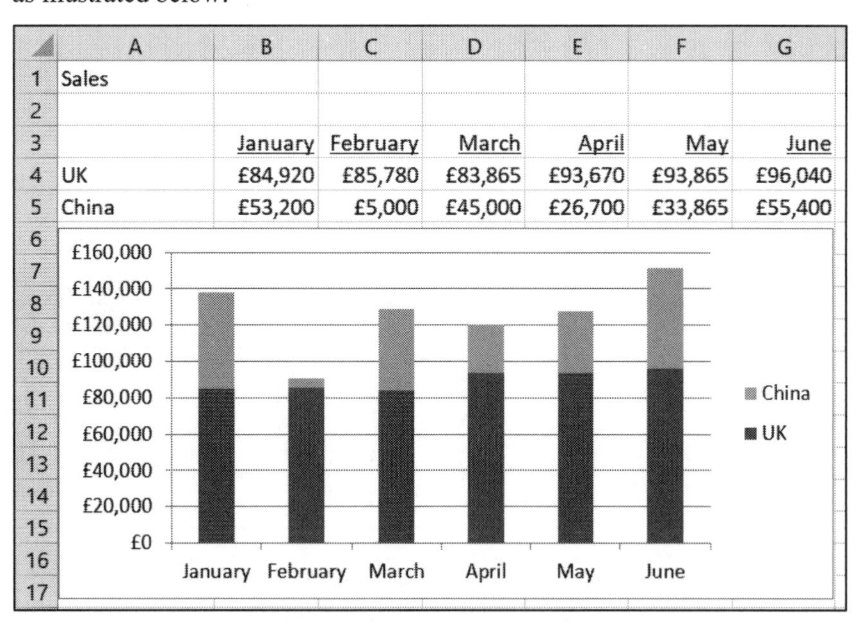

We are also able to **switch the row and column axes** over so that instead of the x (horizontal) axis being the months, and the series being UK and China, the x axis becomes UK and China, and the series becomes the months. This is illustrated on the next page.

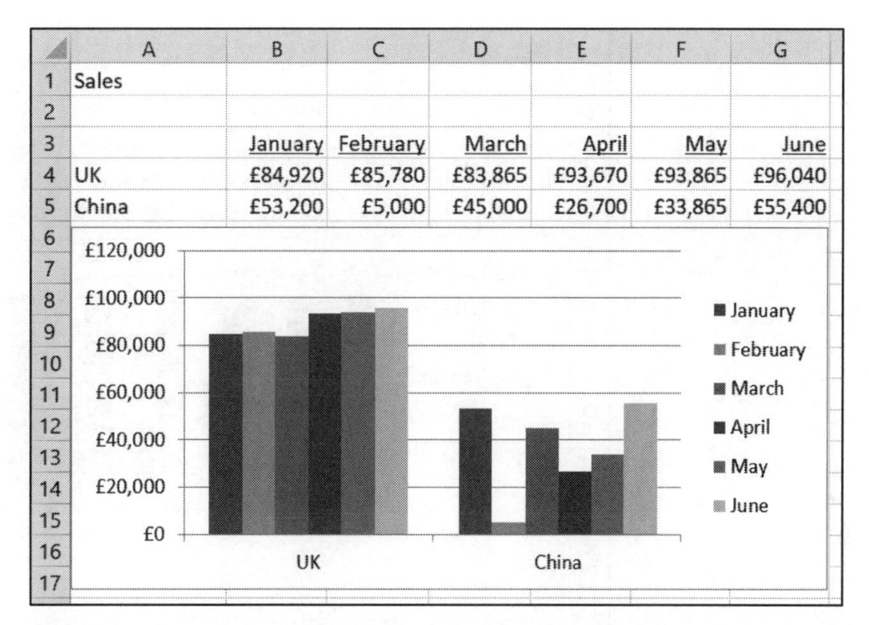

	A	B	C	D	E	F	G
1	Sales						
2							
3		January	February	March	April	May	June
4	UK	£84,920	£85,780	£83,865	£93,670	£93,865	£96,040
5	China	£53,200	£5,000	£45,000	£26,700	£33,865	£55,400

Bar charts can also be created with horizontal bars, as shown in the example below:

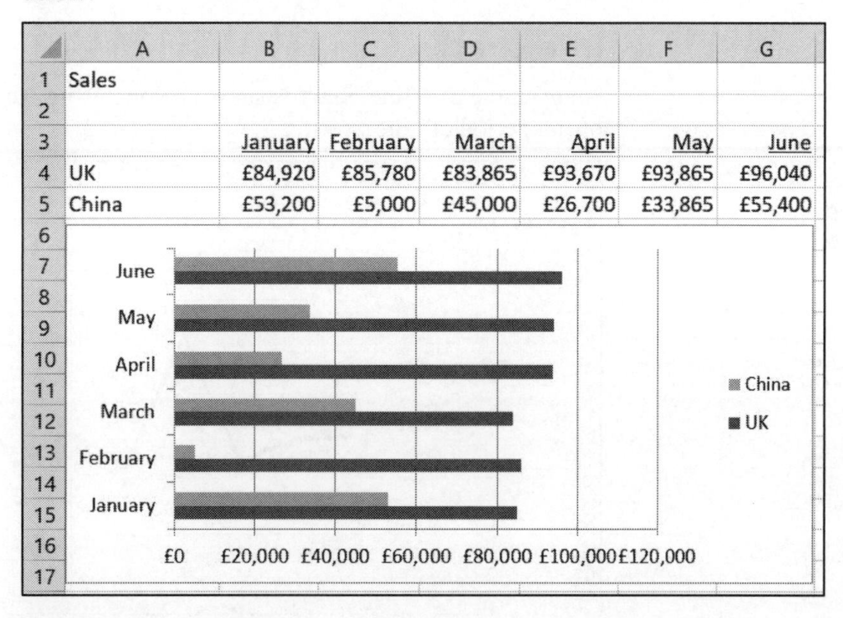

	A	B	C	D	E	F	G
1	Sales						
2							
3		January	February	March	April	May	June
4	UK	£84,920	£85,780	£83,865	£93,670	£93,865	£96,040
5	China	£53,200	£5,000	£45,000	£26,700	£33,865	£55,400

Note: within the **Chart** menu, **Column** is used to create vertical bar charts, and **Bar** to create horizontal bar charts.

Both **column** and **bar** type **charts** can also be created in **3D** (3 dimensional), by selecting the appropriate style from the choices available.

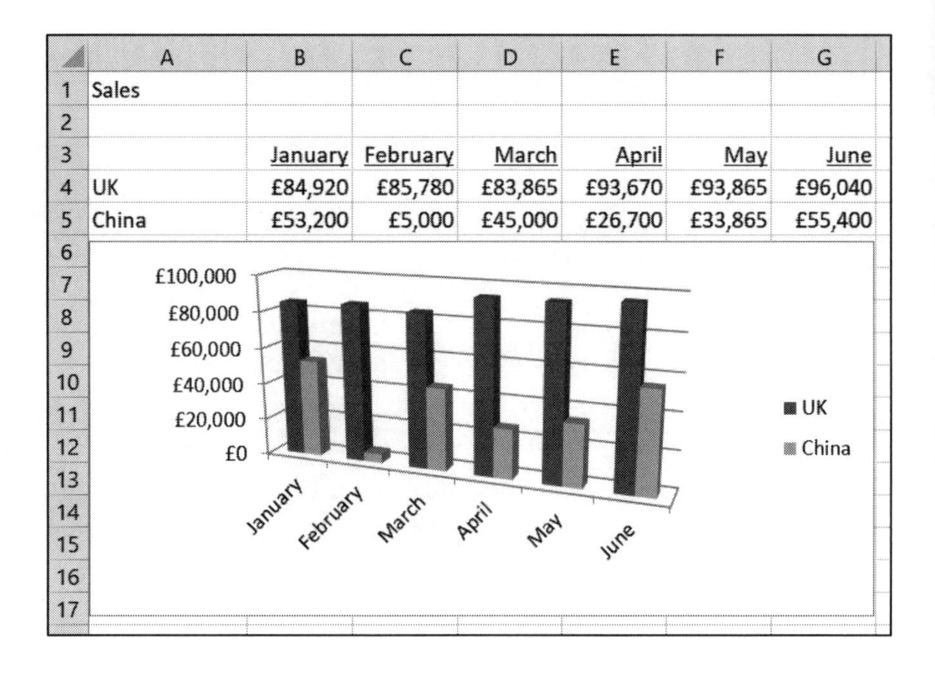

	A	B	C	D	E	F	G
1	Sales						
2							
3		January	February	March	April	May	June
4	UK	£84,920	£85,780	£83,865	£93,670	£93,865	£96,040
5	China	£53,200	£5,000	£45,000	£26,700	£33,865	£55,400

line chart

An example of a **line chart** is shown below, using Annual Expenses figures over a period of nine years.

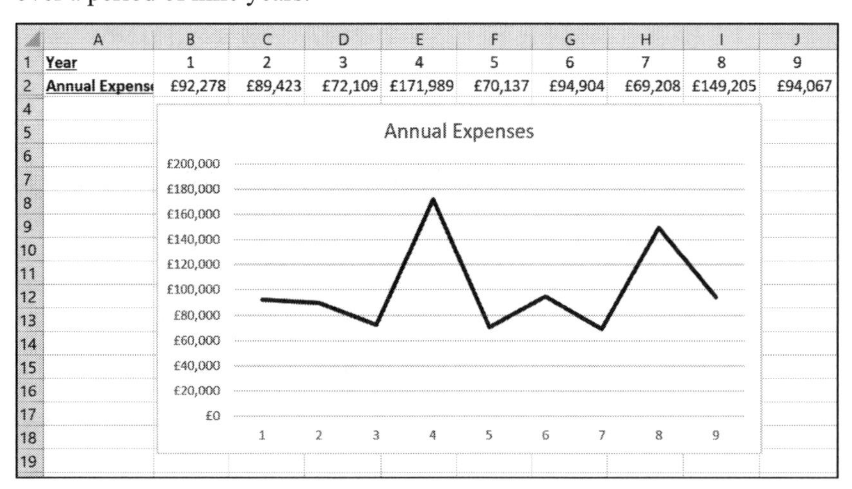

	A	B	C	D	E	F	G	H	I	J
1	Year	1	2	3	4	5	6	7	8	9
2	Annual Expens	£92,278	£89,423	£72,109	£171,989	£70,137	£94,904	£69,208	£149,205	£94,067

If our line chart has two sets of data, Annual Expenses and Sales, as shown at the top of the next page:

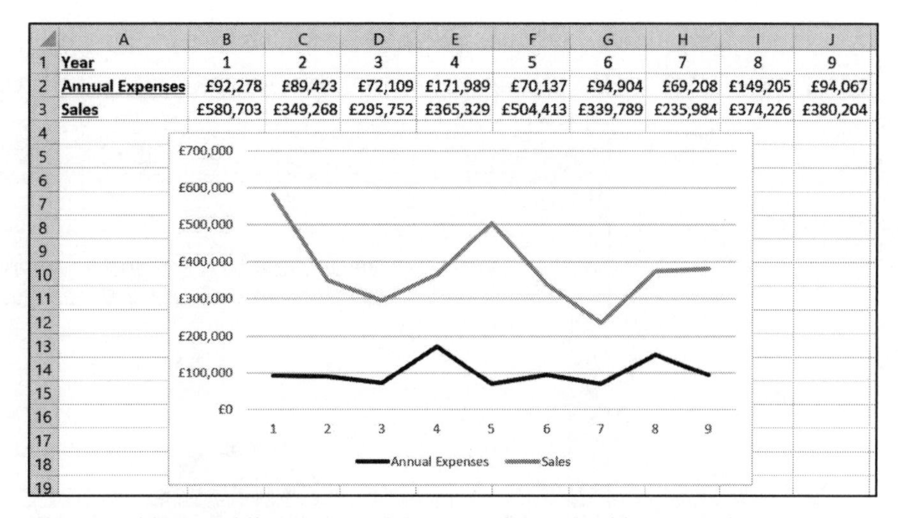

	A	B	C	D	E	F	G	H	I	J
1	Year	1	2	3	4	5	6	7	8	9
2	Annual Expenses	£92,278	£89,423	£72,109	£171,989	£70,137	£94,904	£69,208	£149,205	£94,067
3	Sales	£580,703	£349,268	£295,752	£365,329	£504,413	£339,789	£235,984	£374,226	£380,204

We can add a trend line to one of the sets of data, in this case Sales:

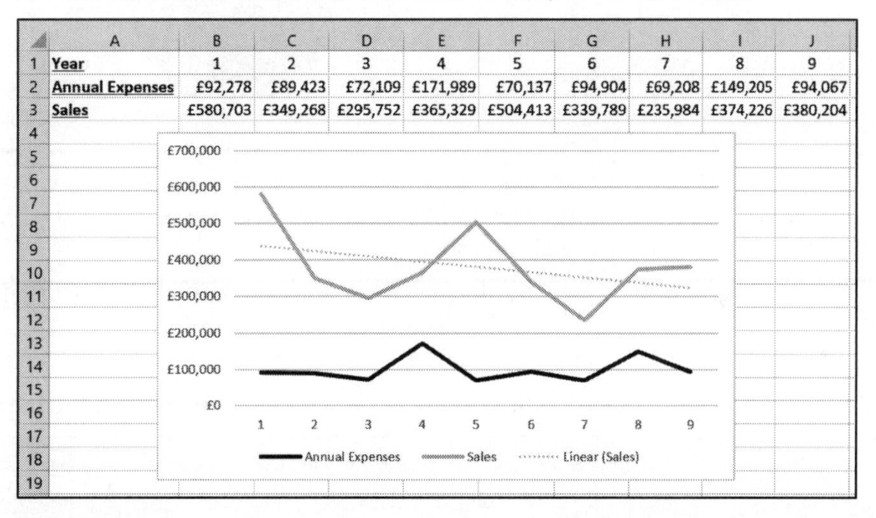

	A	B	C	D	E	F	G	H	I	J
1	Year	1	2	3	4	5	6	7	8	9
2	Annual Expenses	£92,278	£89,423	£72,109	£171,989	£70,137	£94,904	£69,208	£149,205	£94,067
3	Sales	£580,703	£349,268	£295,752	£365,329	£504,413	£339,789	£235,984	£374,226	£380,204

pie chart

A **pie chart** can be produced for only one set of data values, arranged in one column or row on a worksheet. It is known as a ‘pie chart’ because it looks like a pie divided into a number of ‘slices’.

Pie charts show the data values relative to the total of the values. Each data value is shown in a pie chart as a percentage or proportion of the whole ‘pie’.

A pie chart can be used when:

- you only have one set of data values that you want to plot
- none of the values that you want to plot is negative
- very few of the values that you want to plot are zero
- you do not have more than seven values

- the data values represent all the parts of the whole

In the image below, you can see an example of a **pie chart** where the values represent sales in China for each of the six months:

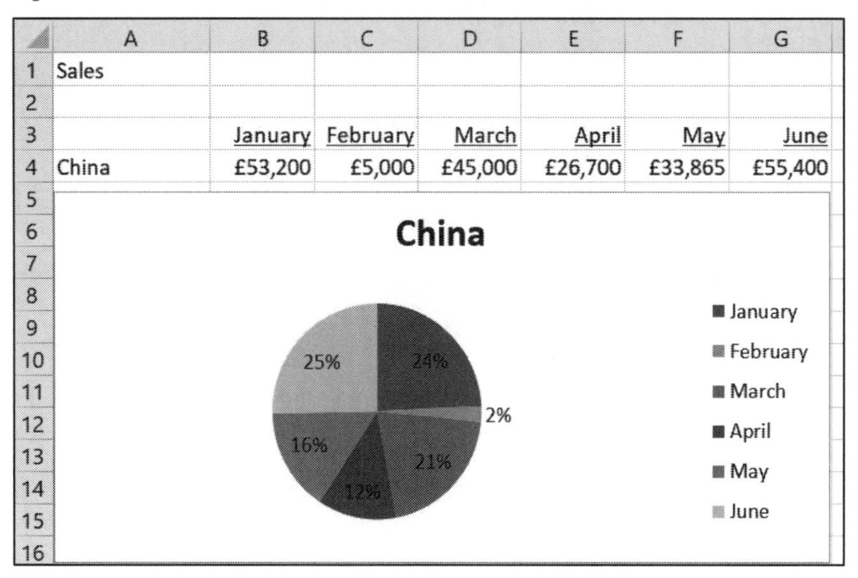

	A	B	C	D	E	F	G
1	Sales						
2							
3		January	February	March	April	May	June
4	China	£53,200	£5,000	£45,000	£26,700	£33,865	£55,400

Each value is represented as a percentage of the whole, which would be the total sales for the six months and can be labelled with the percentage or the actual values.

To make the pie chart more visual, it is possible to select a **3D** chart and the slices will be shown as three dimensional or exploded where the individual slices are separated. These options can add to a chart's clarity.

The China sales data is shown as a **3D pie** chart in the image below.

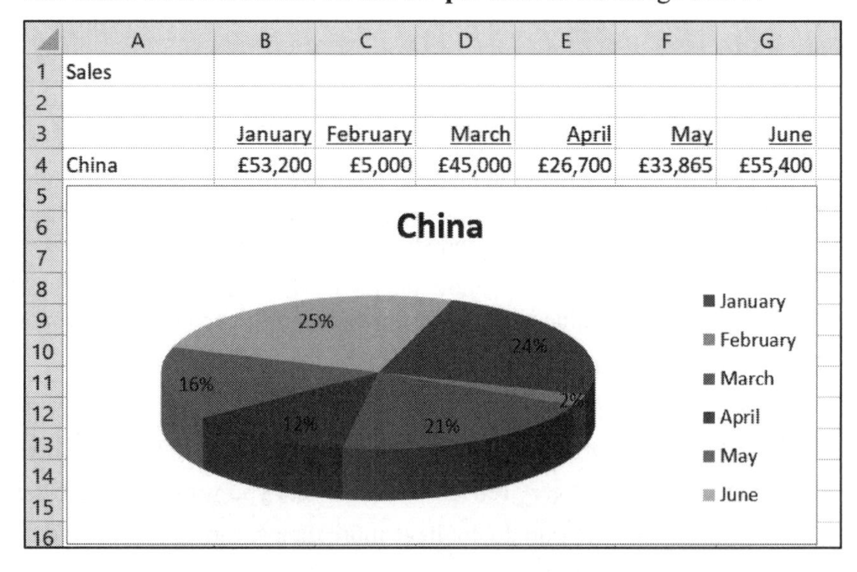

	A	B	C	D	E	F	G
1	Sales						
2							
3		January	February	March	April	May	June
4	China	£53,200	£5,000	£45,000	£26,700	£33,865	£55,400

The China sales data is shown as a **3D Exploded pie** chart in the image below.

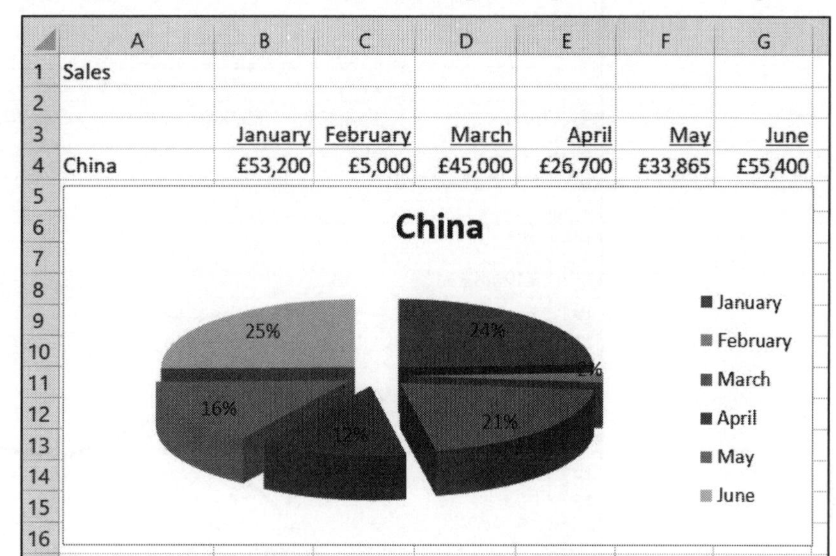

	A	B	C	D	E	F	G
1	Sales						
2							
3		January	February	March	April	May	June
4	China	£53,200	£5,000	£45,000	£26,700	£33,865	£55,400

PARTS OF A CHART

Before we create a chart, we will look at some of the basic elements which make up a chart.

data series

This is the set or sets of data which you wish to display in the chart. In the example below, we have two series of data, one for the UK, and one for China. We can use just one, or both in our charts. In the image on the next page, you can see the top line in the chart is based on the UK data series and the bottom line is based on the China data series.

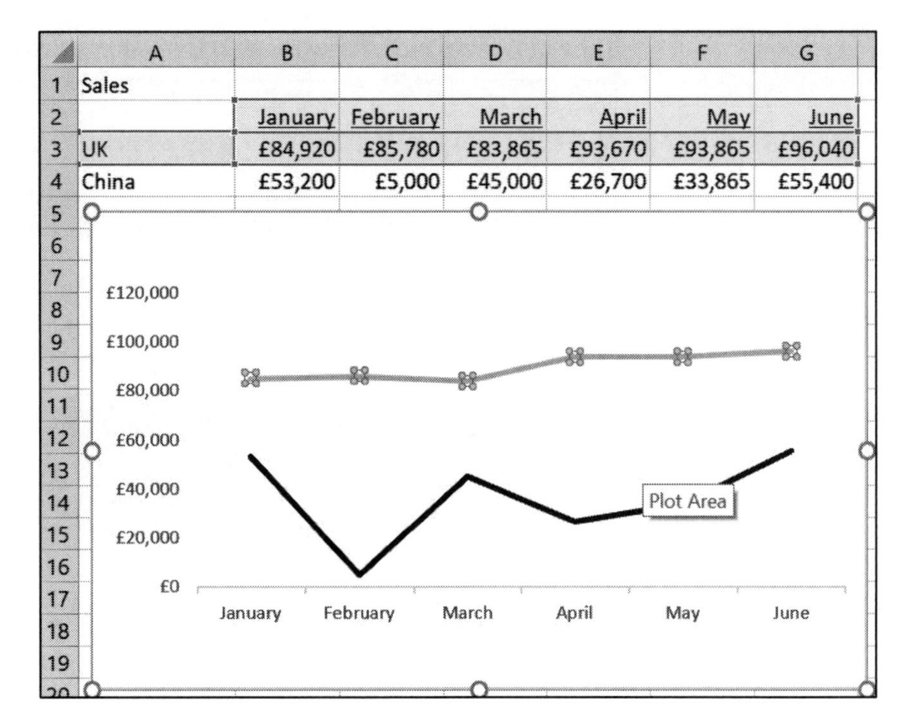

chart type

Such as bar, column, pie.

chart title

A useful short description of the purpose of the chart.

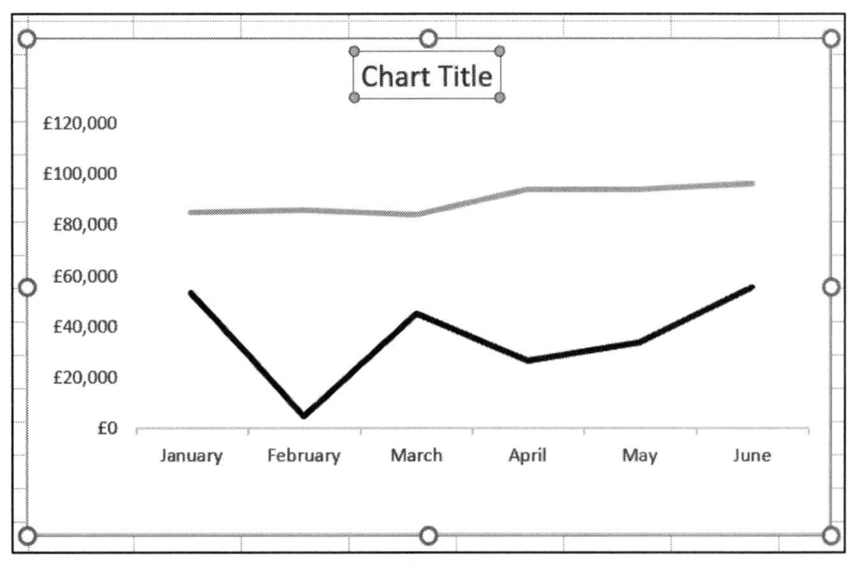

axes

In the example below, we have the months along the x (horizontal) axis, and a scale on the y (vertical) axis, which covers the range of values within the sales data.

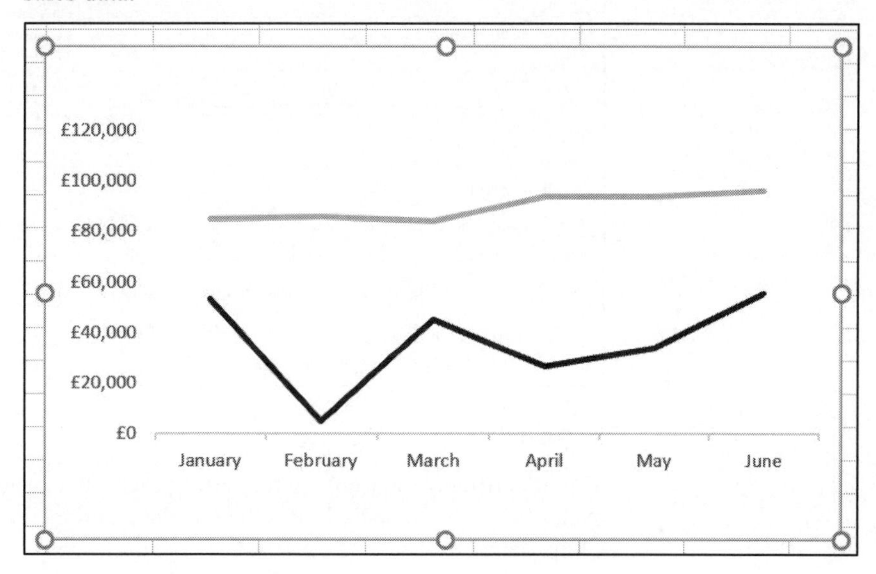

axis scale

When a chart is created, a scale for the numeric values is automatically generated to cover the range of values in the data. How the scale is displayed can be changed. In the example below, we have changed to use number, with no commas for the thousands. We can also change the scaling maximum and minimum.

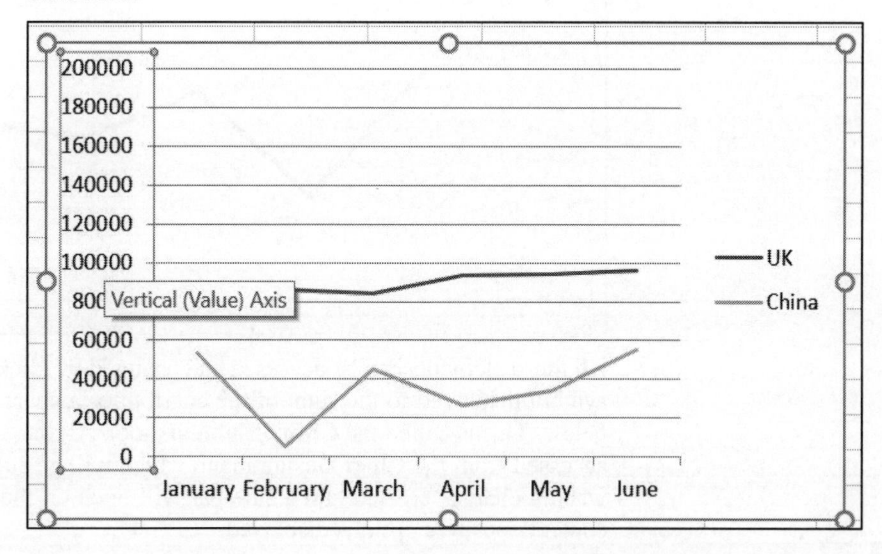

axis title

A simple label to describe what the data represents. In the chart below, the x axis label could say 'Months' and the y axis label could say 'Sales value'.

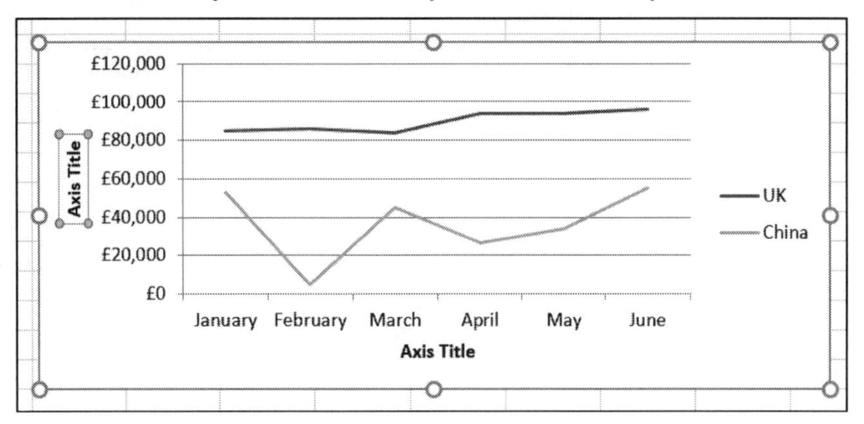

legend

This identifies which colour represents each data series in the chart. In our example below, the pale line is the UK data, and the black line represents the China data.

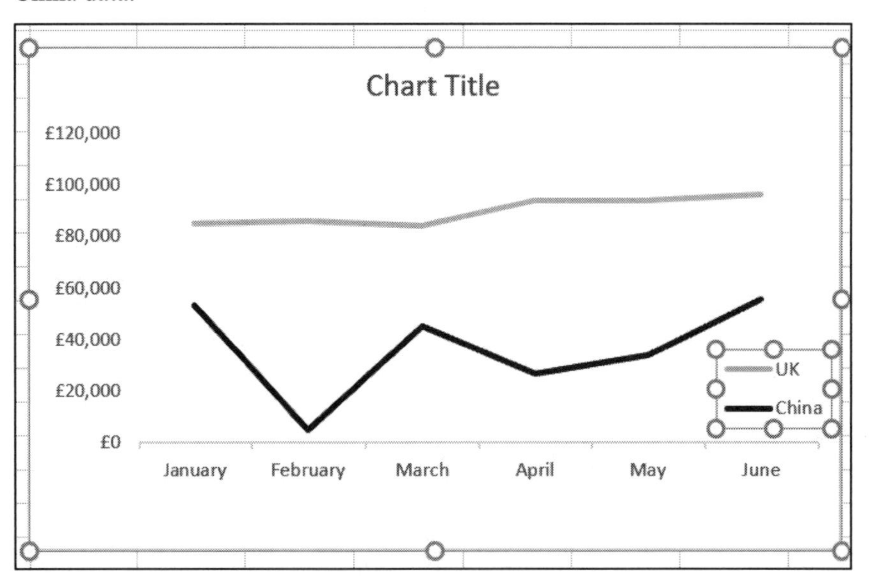

All these elements can be accessed and changed by clicking on the green plus symbol displayed to the right of the chart, once a chart is selected, as shown below. This is called the **Chart Elements** tool. All these elements can also be accessed from the Chart Design menu which will be automatically displayed when a chart is created and a side bar will open on the right-hand side with context-sensitive options displayed.

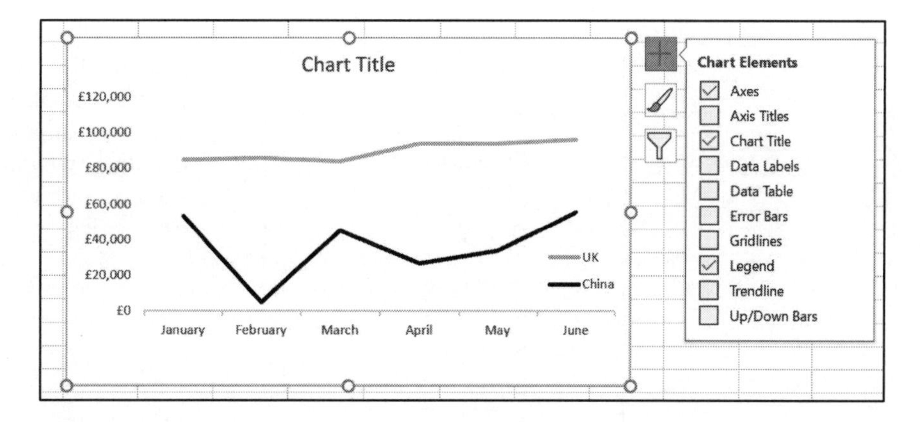

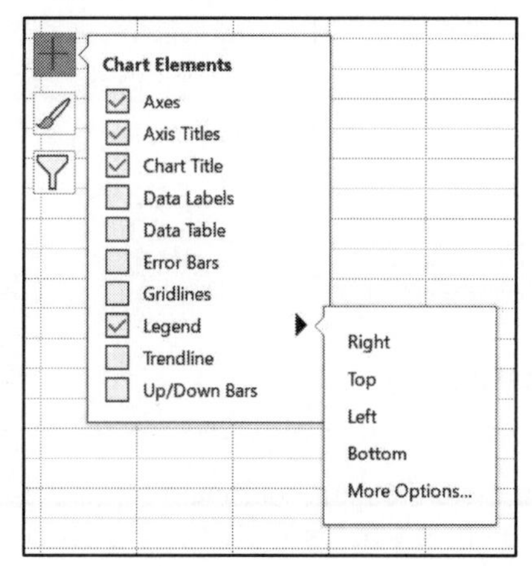

Note: if you move the mouse over the text of some of the elements in this list, a small arrow appears.

Clicking on the small arrow reveals options relating to the element, such as positioning.

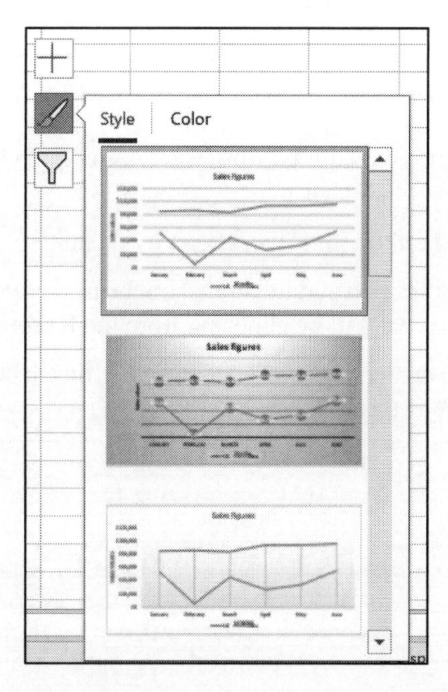

The second tool – **Chart Styles** – the paint brush symbol, as shown on the left, lets you easily change the style of the chart and the colours used.

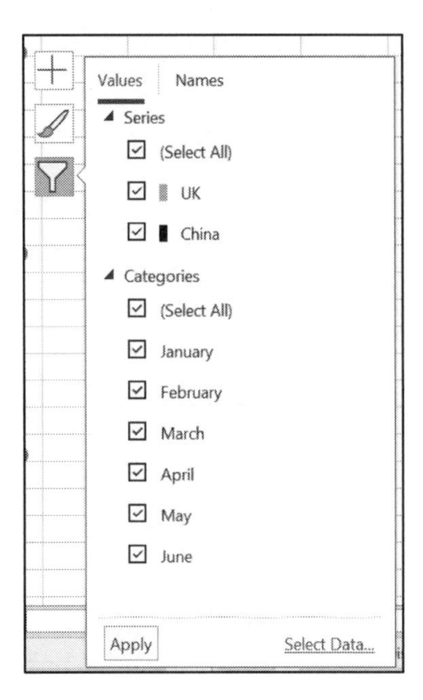

And finally – **Chart Filters** – the funnel symbol, as shown left, allows you to manipulate the data series, deciding which series should be shown, and which cells make up each series.

CREATING CHARTS

We have seen that there are numerous chart types available to use. However, the basic steps which can be used to create a chart from a worksheet are applicable to most chart types:

- select the data and headings on the worksheet to be presented in the chart
- select INSERT
- select the chart type required from **Recommended charts**, the appropriate icon, or the list of all charts

A chart is created on the same worksheet by default.

These steps are described and illustrated on the next page, using the sales data for UK and China; we will be choosing from the **Recommended** charts.

You may wish to create a spreadsheet and enter this data yourself, so that you can follow the steps through.

	A	B	C	D	E	F	G
1	Sales						
2							
3		January	February	March	April	May	June
4	UK	£84,920	£85,780	£83,865	£93,670	£93,865	£96,040
5	China	£53,200	£5,000	£45,000	£26,700	£33,865	£55,400

Step 1 – select the data

Select the data, including the text which relates to the data. We are going to select both rows of data, since we want to compare the two rows of sales values. Each row of data represents one **data series**. The data can be selected as shown below:

	January	February	March	April	May	June
UK	£84,920	£85,780	£83,865	£93,670	£93,865	£96,040
China	£53,200	£5,000	£45,000	£26,700	£33,865	£55,400

Note that if you need to specify the range of your data for any reason, this can be done by either moving to the data and selecting as shown in the image above, or manually specifying the range, in this case $A$3:$G$5, always using absolute cell addresses.

Step 2 – create the chart

- select INSERT from the menu
- select the Chart type required from **Recommended** charts and the chart will be created representing your data series

In our example we are going to create a line chart, which we have placed below our rows of data.

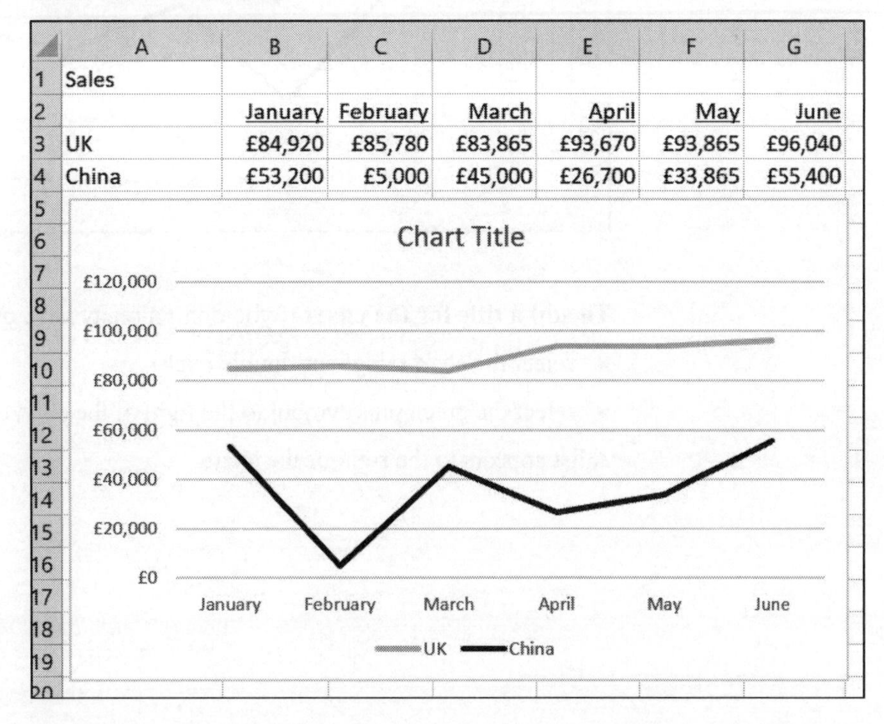

	A	B	C	D	E	F	G
1	Sales						
2		January	February	March	April	May	June
3	UK	£84,920	£85,780	£83,865	£93,670	£93,865	£96,040
4	China	£53,200	£5,000	£45,000	£26,700	£33,865	£55,400

The chart axes are automatically created with scales based on the ranges of values in the data. The legend has been automatically displayed at the bottom of the chart.

Step 3 – add or change the chart title

To change the title for the chart:

Click the Chart Title text and enter the required title.

We will enter the title 'Sales figures'.

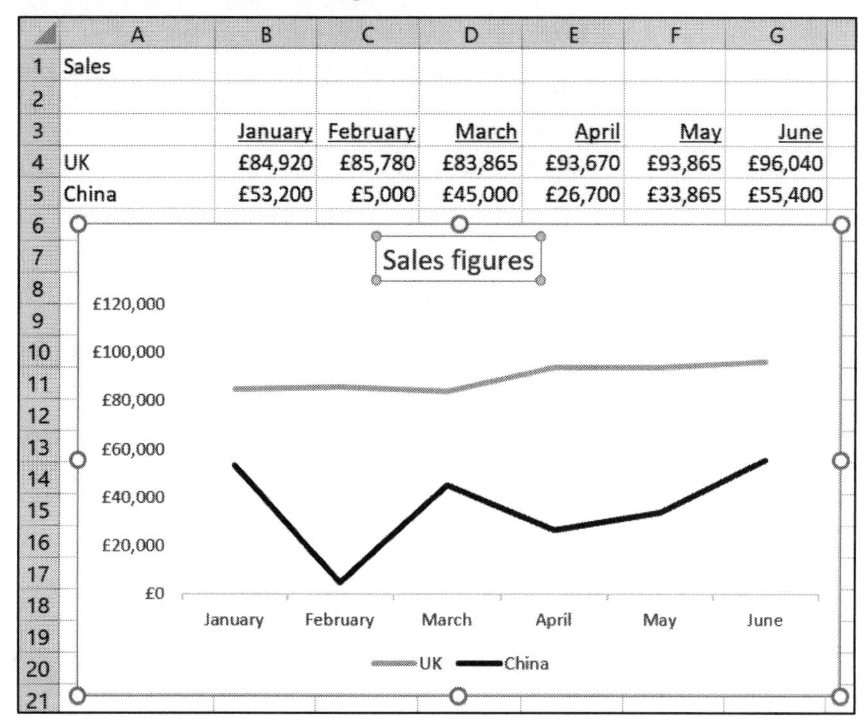

To add a title for the chart if you don't already have one:

- select the chart (single or double click)
- select the green plus symbol to the right of the chart (Chart Elements tool)

A list appears to the right of the chart:

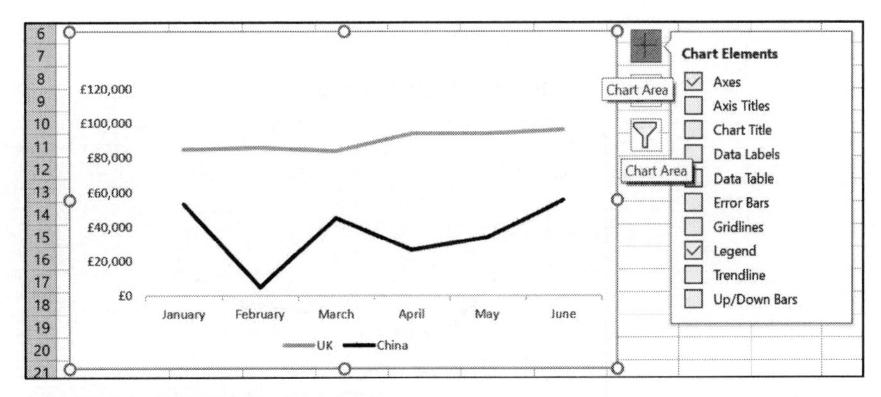

- ensure **Chart Title** is ticked

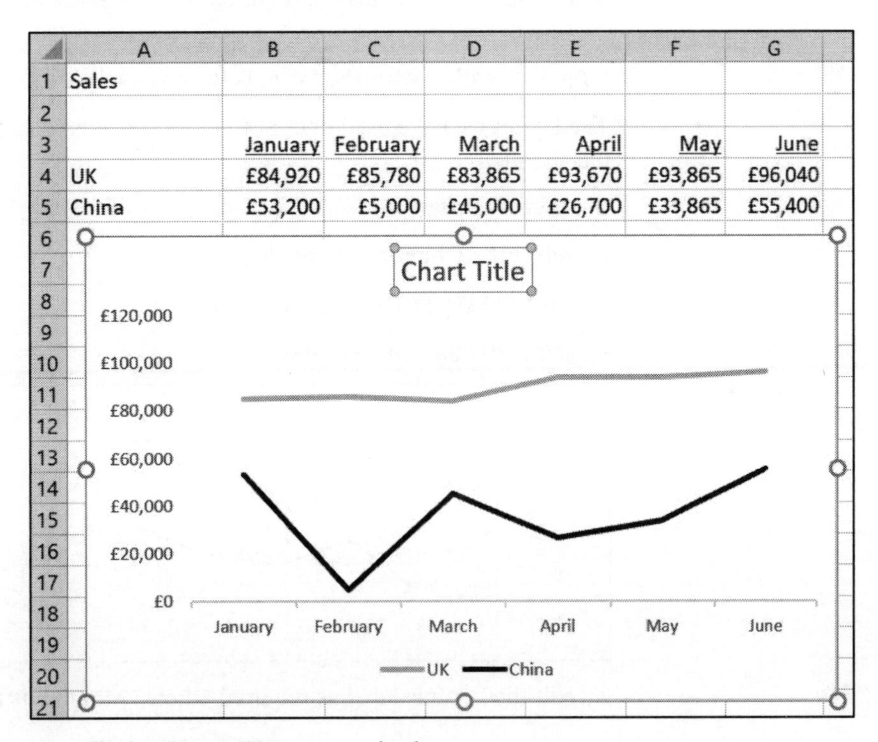

- edit the **Chart Title** as required

Step 4 – dealing with the 'y' axis (vertical axis)

If the chart layout you use does not include an axis label for the y axis:

- select the chart
- select the **Chart Elements** tool

- ensure **Axis Titles** is ticked
- select **Primary vertical**

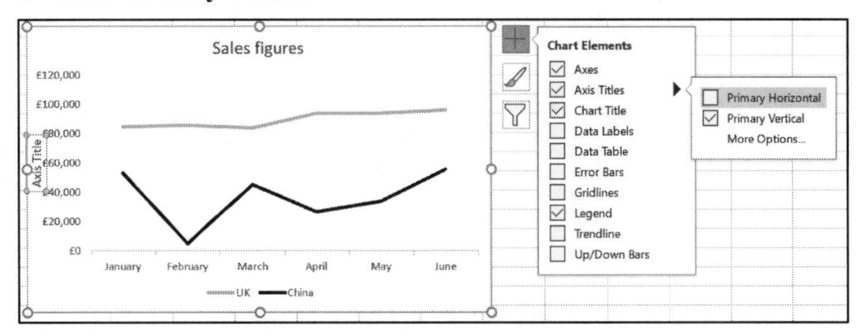

- edit the 'y' axis label as required – here 'Sales Value' is the chosen axis title

Step 5 – dealing with the 'x' axis (horizontal axis)

The layout we have used does not include an axis label for the x axis. To add this manually:

- select the chart
- select the **Chart Elements** tool
- ensure **Axis Titles** is ticked
- select **Primary horizontal**

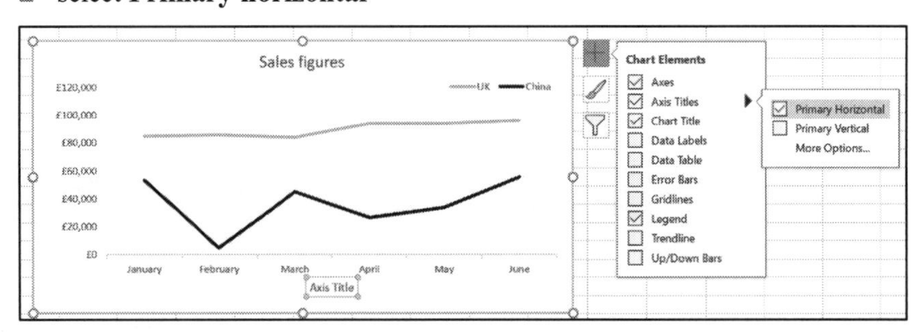

- edit the 'x' axis label as required – here 'Months' is the chosen axis title

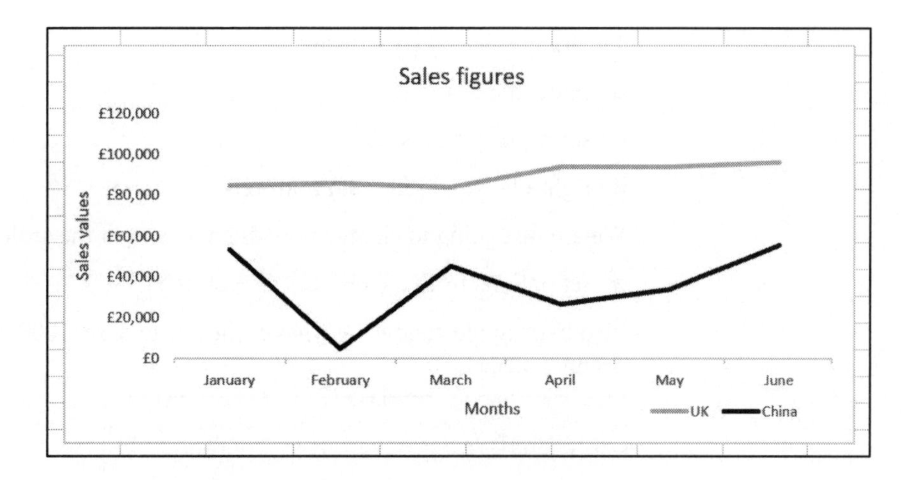

Step 6 – dealing with the chart legend

The legend lists the name and the colour used to represent each data series in the chart. It is usually automatically added to the chart when the chart is created. It is possible to choose whether or not a legend should be displayed and if so, where it should be positioned within the chart.

To manipulate the chart legend:

- select the chart
- select the **Chart Elements** tool
- ensure **Legend** is ticked
- select **More Options**

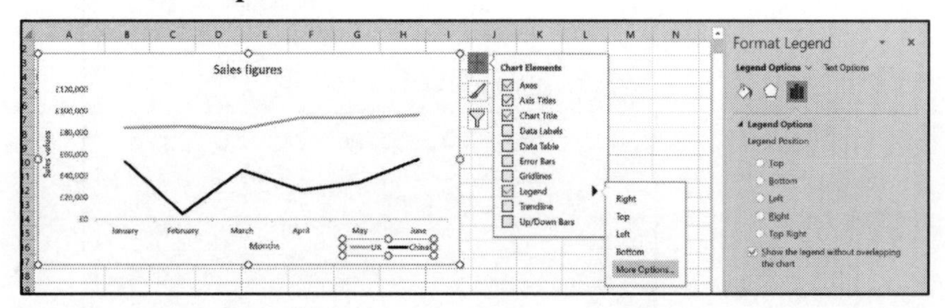

Format Legend will provide you with options which allow you to change the position and appearance.

Step 7 – changing an axis scale

When a chart is created, the scale for the numeric values is automatically generated to cover the range of values in the data; how the scale is displayed can be changed, we will look at the numeric values on the y (vertical axis) in the example on the next page.

To change the y axis scaling:

- select the chart
- select the y axis scale
- right-click and select **format axis**

We are just going to change how the numbers of the scale are displayed.

- set options from the choices as required

In our example below, we have chosen to Use 1000 Separator, and two decimal places.

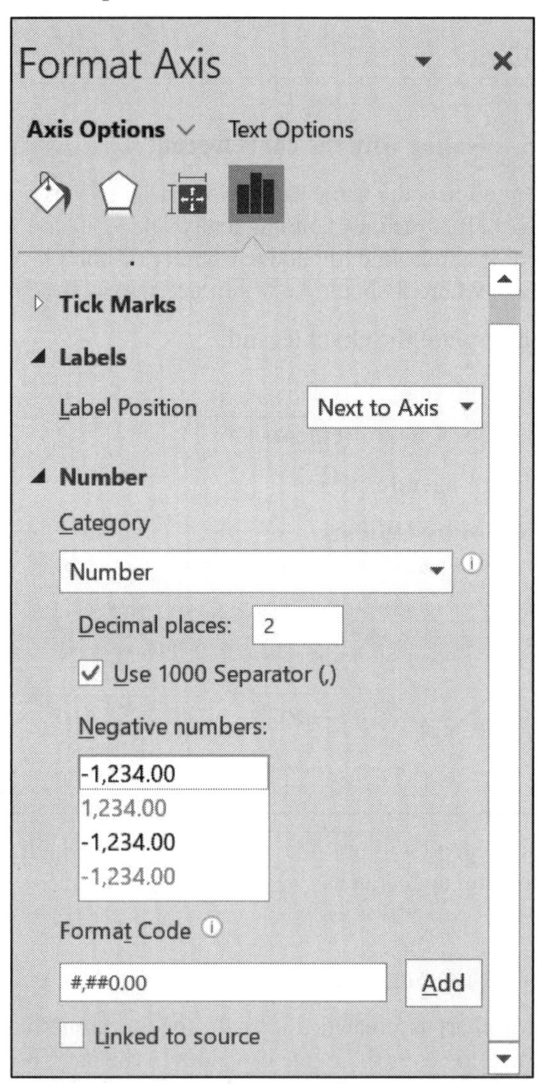

As you can see there are many options which can be changed.

DATA TABLES AND DATA SERIES

An additional element which we can add to our chart is a **Data table**. This table displays the data series used in our chart, and will be particularly useful if the chart is on a separate page to the original data.

For ease of viewing, we have changed the chart type to Column within our example shown below:

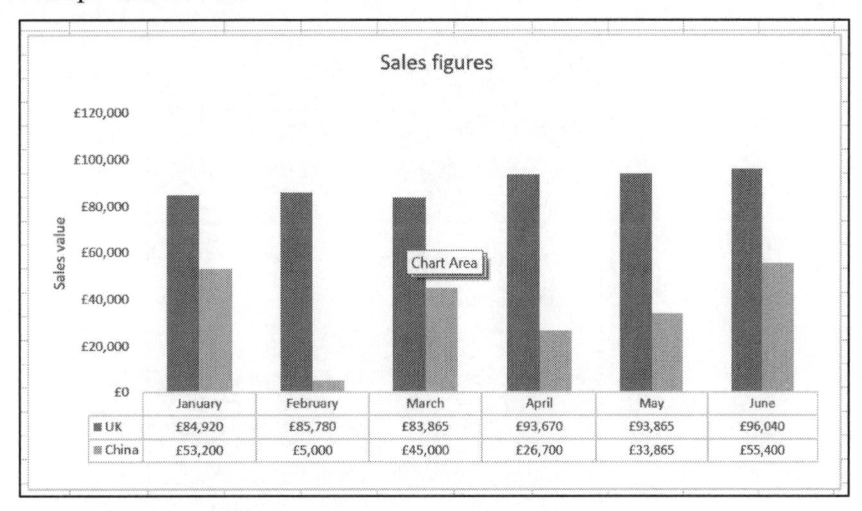

To add a Data table to a chart:

- select the chart
- select the **Chart Elements** tool
- select or tick **Data Table**

The table will automatically be added at the bottom of the chart.

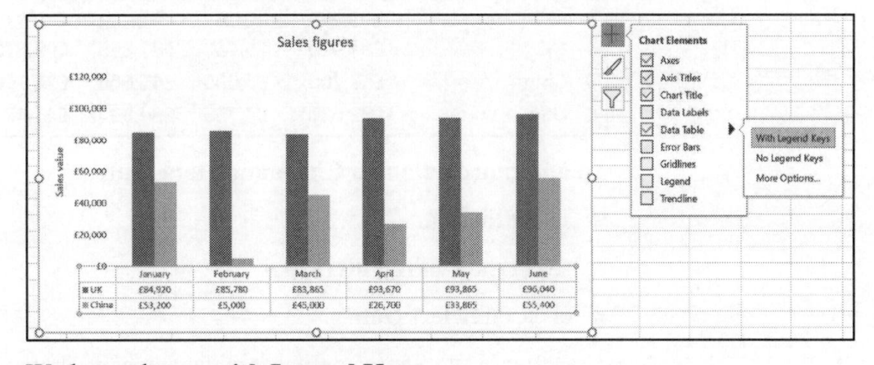

We have chosen **with Legend Keys**.

To change the format of a Data table:

- select the chart
- select the **Chart Filters** tool
- click the **right arrow**
- select **More options**

You will see the Format Data Table menu as shown below:

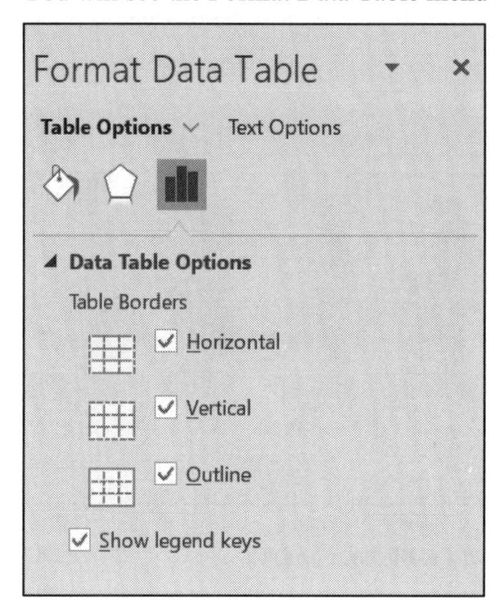

In our example, we have now got a third row of Sales data for the USA.

	A	B	C	D	E	F	G
1	Sales						
2							
3		January	February	March	April	May	June
4	UK	£84,920	£85,780	£83,865	£93,670	£93,865	£96,040
5	China	£53,200	£5,000	£45,000	£26,700	£33,865	£55,400
6	USA	£82,630	£7,766	£69,894	£41,470	£52,599	£86,047

To add more data to a Chart and Data table:

- select the chart
- select the **Chart Filters** tool
- click on **Select Data**

The Select Data Source options are displayed as shown on the next page.

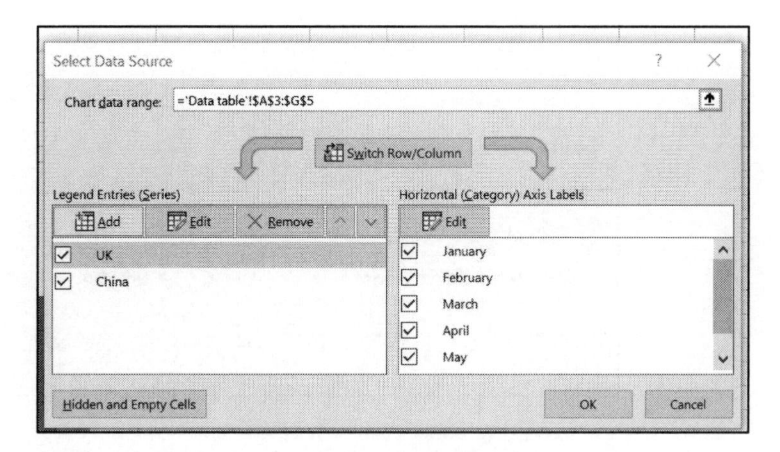

There are two ways of including more data:

either:

- edit the chart data range to include the new row of data

change ='Sales sheet'!$A$3:$G$5

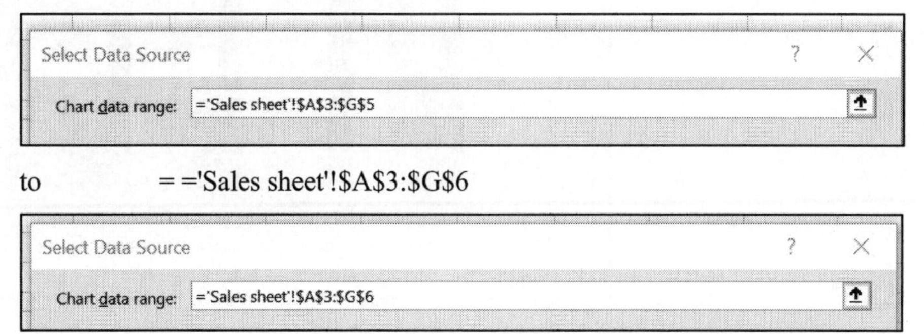

to = ='Sales sheet'!$A$3:$G$6

or:

- select Add
- select cell A6 for Series name
- select cells B6 to G6 Series values

As shown on the next page.

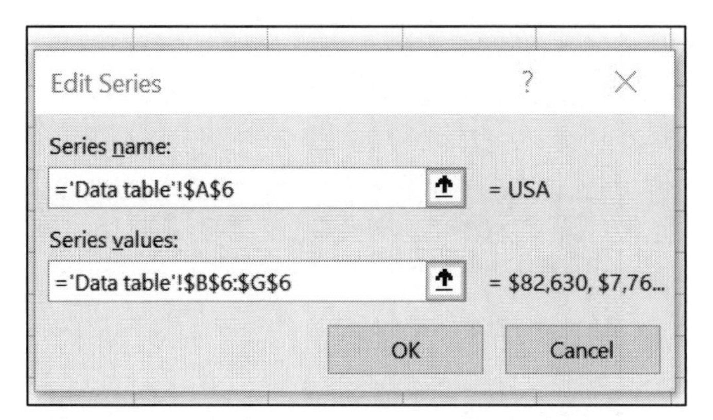

The resulting chart is shown below:

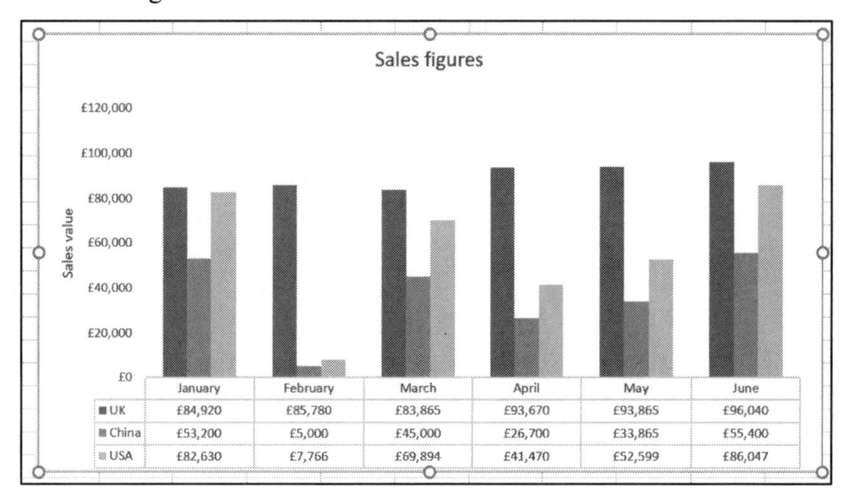

To remove a data series from a Chart and Data table:

- select the chart
- select the **Chart Filters** tool
- **deselect** the **series** you want to remove eg USA, as shown on the right

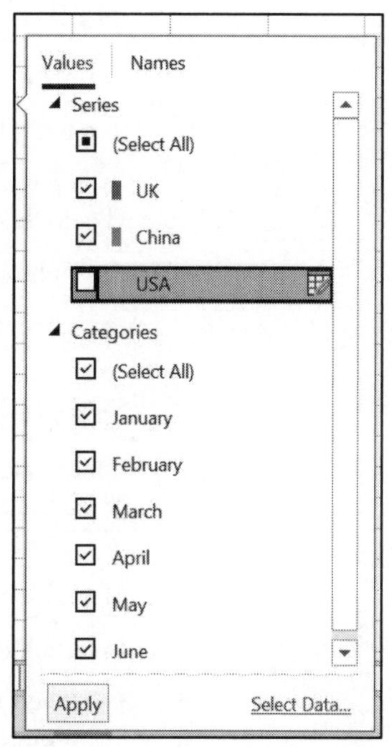

To remove a category from a Chart and Data table:

- select the chart
- select the **Chart Filters** tool
- **deselect** the **Category** you want to remove eg January, as shown on the right

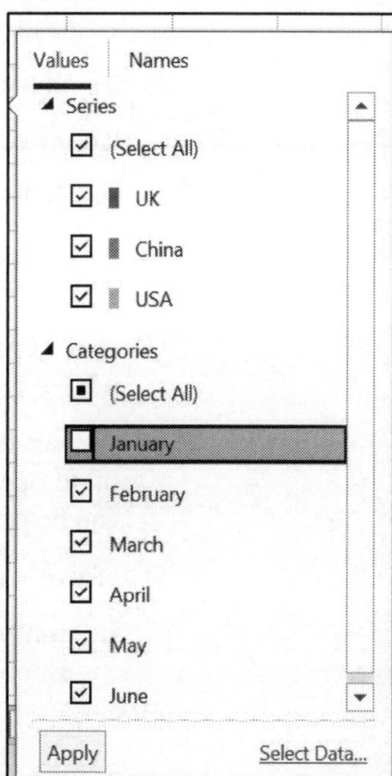

To remove a Data table:

- select the chart
- select the **Chart Elements** tool
- untick **Data Table**

The table will automatically be removed from the chart.

MODIFYING CHARTS

changing font size and style for a chart element

It is possible to change the font size and style for any of the titles or labels. To do this:

- right-click on the item
- select **font** and make the changes you require

moving or resizing

Once you have created a chart as described in the previous steps, you may wish to resize or move the chart to a different location either on the same or a different worksheet, for example to avoid it covering some of the data.

To resize a chart:

- click on the chart to select it
- place the cursor over one of the corners of the chart frame, or the dots around the edges of the frame (you will see the cursor changes to a double headed arrow)
- click and drag to the required size

To move a chart:

- click on the chart to select it
- click and drag the chart to its new position

moving charts, embedded charts and chart sheets

A chart can be on a **chart sheet**, which contains nothing but the chart scaled up to occupy a full page. All the chart options still apply and the chart sheet can be printed as normal.

If you want to move the chart to a new sheet:

- right-click within the space surrounding the chart, but still within the chart frame
- select **Move chart** from the menu

The following screen is displayed:

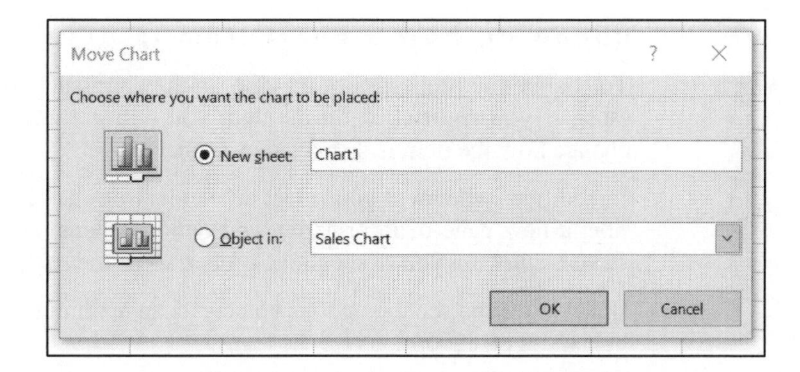

To select an existing worksheet and place the chart on it:

- click **Object in** radio button
- select the worksheet to which the chart is to move from the drop-down list

To create a new chart sheet and place the chart on it:

- click **New sheet** radio button
- enter a name for the new sheet, or leave it as Chart1

An example of chart sheet is shown below:

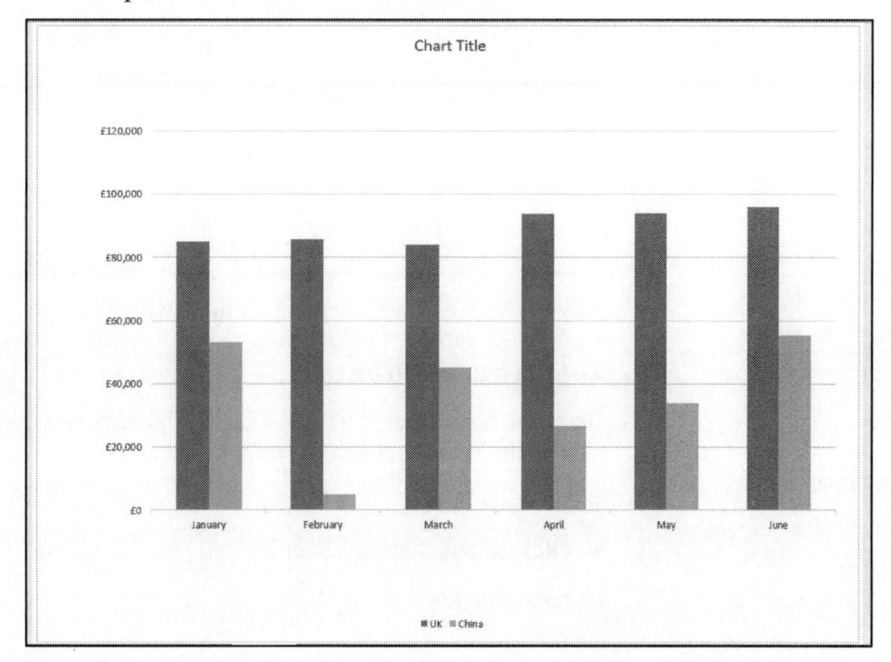

changing how a chart item is displayed

To change the properties of an item on the chart such as Chart Title or axis label, if you **right**-click on the item you will get a menu allowing you to change how the item is displayed or formatted.

In addition, whenever you select an element on the chart, such as the chart title, a new pane of information and options opens on the right side of the screen, allowing you to set all the properties of the selected element.

Below, you can see the options you can change relating to the position of the title and then the options for the text.

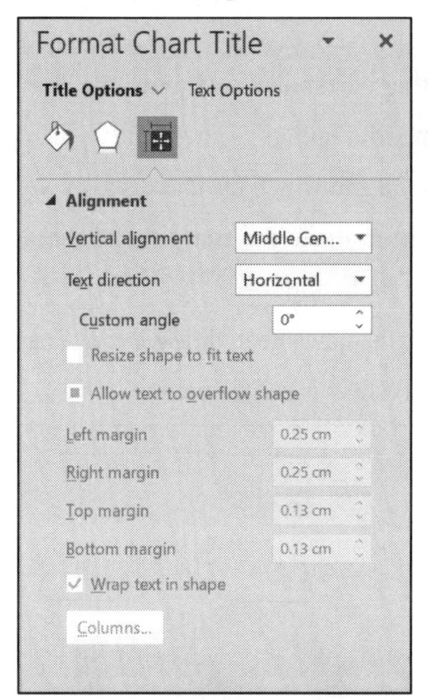

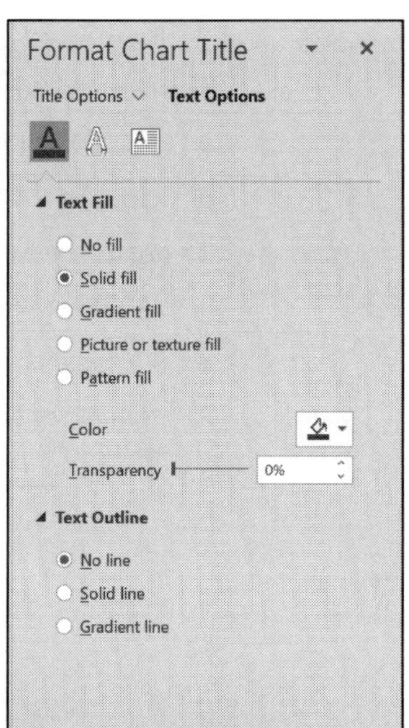

As you can see, there are many options which can be changed.

deleting a chart

Once you have created a chart it is possible that you may wish to delete it and start again, or just remove it from the sheet.

To delete a chart:

- click on the chart to select it
- press delete

printing a chart

Once you have created a chart it is possible that you may wish to print just the chart.

To print a chart:

- click on the chart to select it
- select **Print** and adjust **Page Setup** as required

PIE CHARTS

In the case of a pie chart, to make it more meaningful we would like each slice to show the value or percentage of the whole, as shown in the examples earlier in the chapter. To do this we would need to add data labels as follows:

To label a pie chart:

- right-click on the centre of the pie chart to select all slices
- select **add data labels**

The values represented by each sector are now displayed.

To change whether we see values or percentages or both:

- right-click on the centre of the pie chart to select all slices
- select **format data labels**
- under **Label Options**, check or uncheck Value and Percentage as required

Alternatively, you can:

- select the chart
- select the **Chart Elements** tool
- ensure **Data labels** is ticked
- click on the **right arrow**, and select **More Options**
- select **Label Options**, and set accordingly

3D AND EXPLODED CHARTS

Several of the chart types we have mentioned, can also be created in 3D, such as bar and pie.

To create a 3D chart:

- select the chart
- right-click on the chart

- select **Change Chart Type**
- select one of the types which displays in 3D

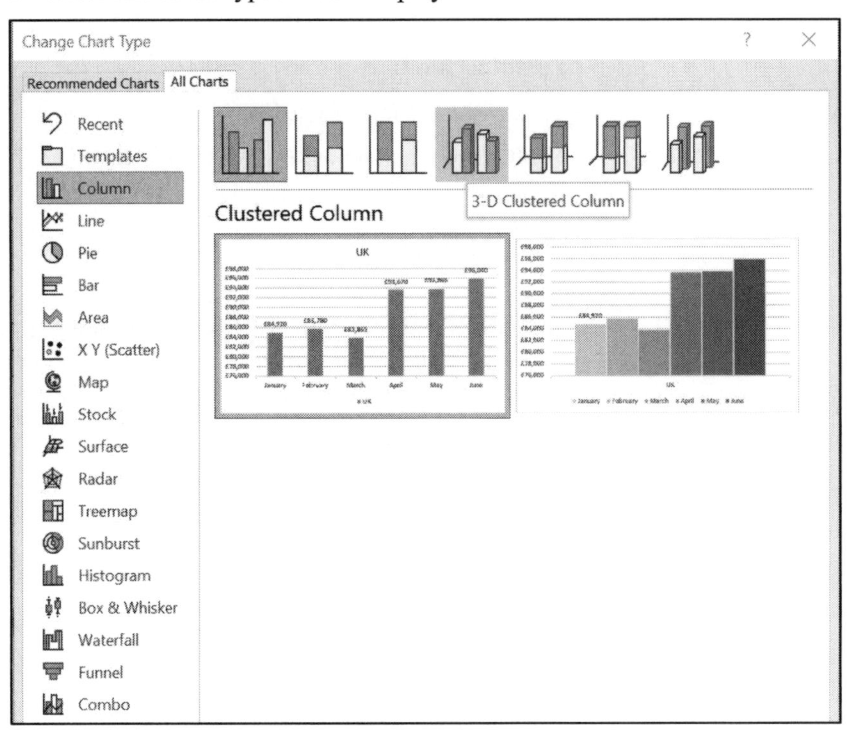

The effect is shown below:

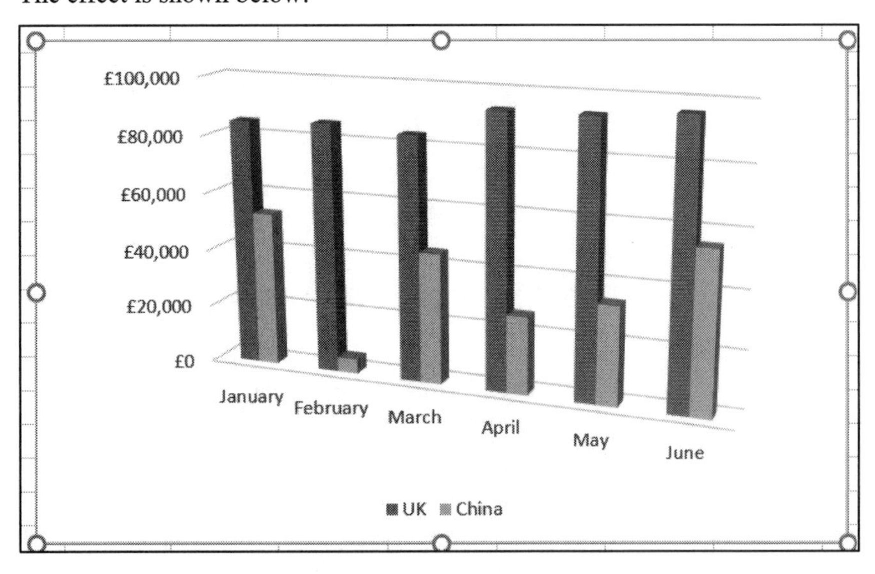

To change the 3D angles:

- right-click on the chart
- select 3-D rotation
- enter the X rotation and Y rotation as required

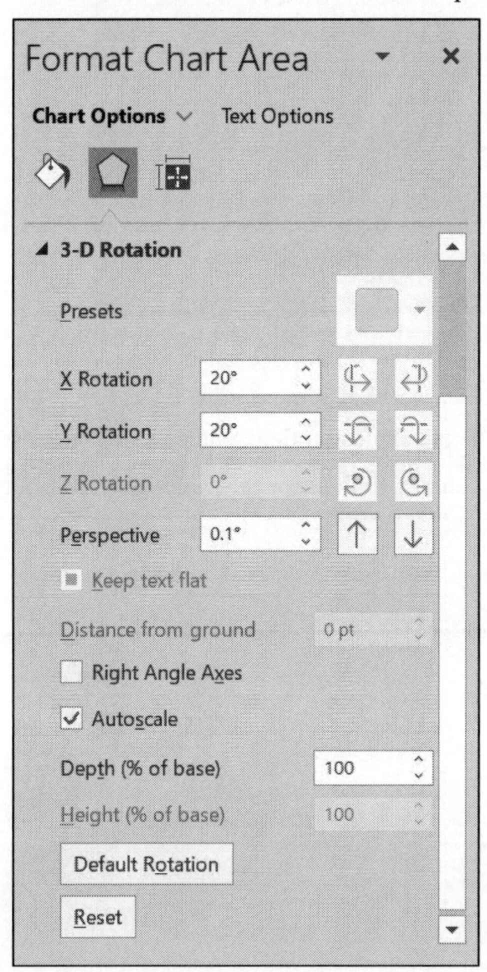

To create an exploded pie chart:

- create a normal pie chart for your data
- right-click on the pie chart
- select **Format Data Series**

The Format Data Series pane opens on the right as shown on the next page:

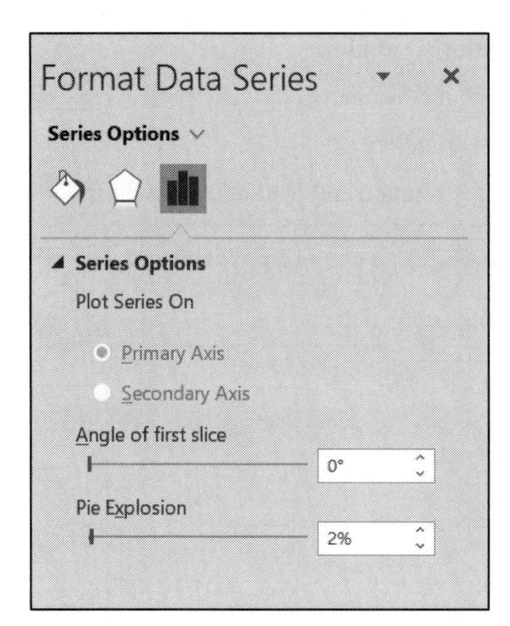

- in the pie explosion field, enter a value such as 20%

The pie chart will then appear exploded as illustrated below.

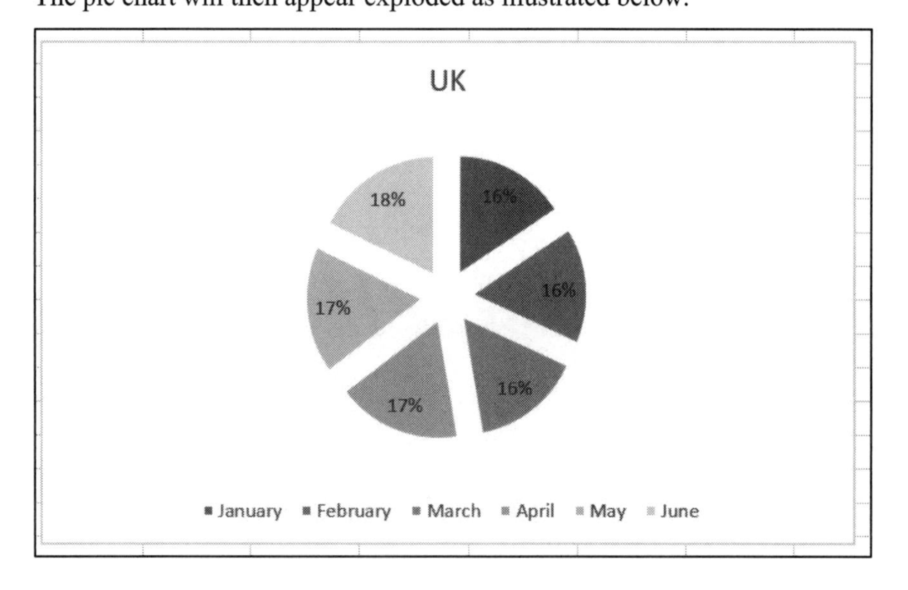

To explode one section of the pie chart:

- select the chart
- left-click on the pie chart
- left-click on the slice you want to move and drag out

As can be seen in the image below:

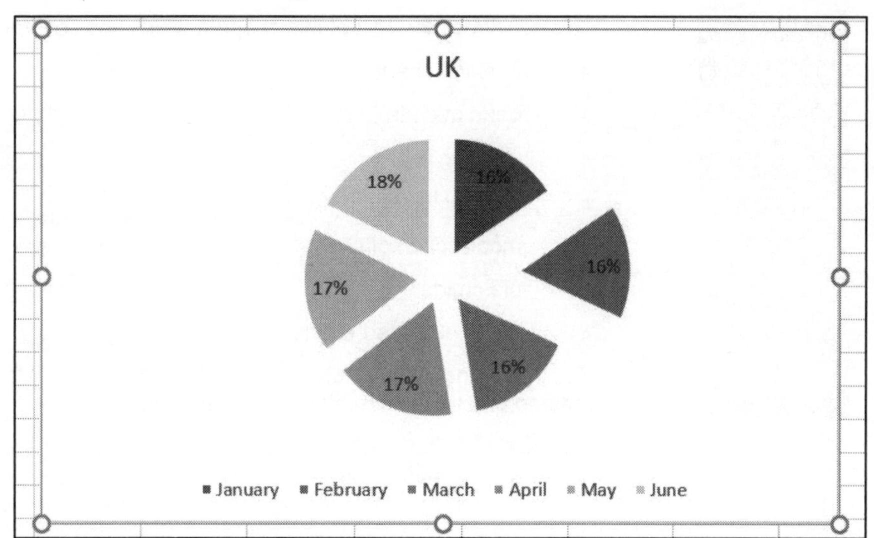

To change the colour of a slice:

- select the chart
- left-click on the pie chart
- left-click on the slice you want to change
- select the required colours from the format options

charts – learning about the software

As you will see from reading this chapter and experimenting with the spreadsheet software, there are many things which can be changed within the chart layout itself, such as:

- the position of the legend
- displaying gridlines
- how the scales are to be shown
- how data points are to be shown on the lines

As you will see, not all these areas are covered in this text, but you are strongly recommended to experiment with your own data.

Spreadsheet software is an essentially practical 'hands on' subject. As previously mentioned, different software packages will step through the chart creation process in different ways, so it is important to familiarise yourself with the processes involved.

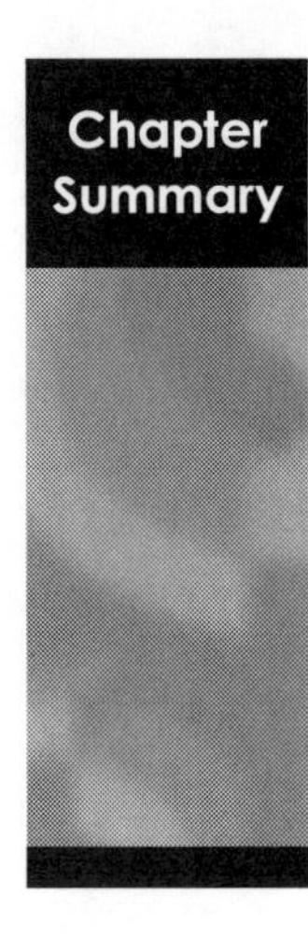

This concludes the text of this chapter, which has covered:

- types of charts
- parts of chart
- creating charts
- data tables and data series
- modification of charts
- pie charts
- 3D or exploded charts

You should now carry out some or all of the exercises on the next few pages in order to practise and reinforce your learning.

Activities

Here are a group of exercises to allow you to practise the topics covered in this chapter. They can be done individually, or as a sequence, working your way through them.

If you choose to work your way through them, you may not need to open the exercise workbook as suggested at the start of each exercise, as it may already be open.

The saving at the end of each exercise is also optional, although it serves as a reminder to regularly save your work. You can also save to different file names and may choose to keep using the same name to avoid having lots of files.

Exercise 1

Spreadsheet skills:

- Charts - create a Bar chart
- Chart alteration - move a chart
- Format charts - edit the chart title

1. Open workbook T7Exercises
2. Select worksheet Exercise 1
3. Select the cells A2 through to G5, this includes the column headings, row headings and data for the six months for each product
4. Insert a vertical bar (column) chart to represent this data
5. Move the chart and position it below the data. Resize it to the same width as the data
6. Change the Chart Title to Sales January to June
7. Save your spreadsheet with the name: Chapter7_Exercise1

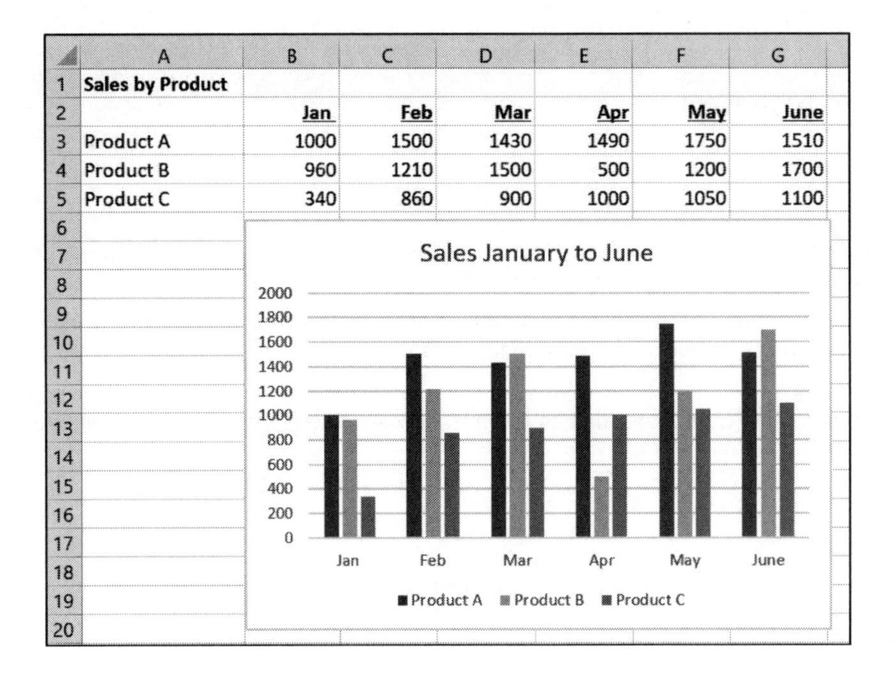

	A	B	C	D	E	F	G
1	**Sales by Product**						
2		**Jan**	**Feb**	**Mar**	**Apr**	**May**	**June**
3	Product A	1000	1500	1430	1490	1750	1510
4	Product B	960	1210	1500	500	1200	1700
5	Product C	340	860	900	1000	1050	1100

Exercise 2

Spreadsheet skills:

- Format charts - axes, labels

1. Open workbook T7Exercises
2. Select worksheet Exercise 2
3. Using Chart Elements, add a title to the Vertical axis
4. Edit the label to Qty
5. Using Chart Elements, change the position of the Legend to be right of the chart
6. Add a title to the Horizotal axis - Months
7. Save your spreadsheet with the name: Chapter7_Exercise2

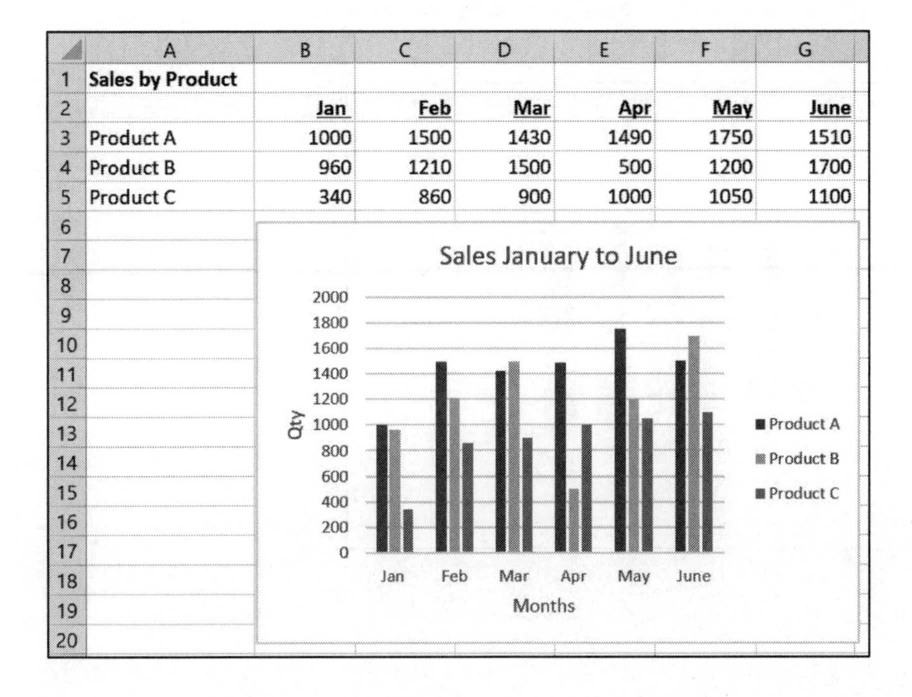

	A	B	C	D	E	F	G
1	**Sales by Product**						
2		**Jan**	**Feb**	**Mar**	**Apr**	**May**	**June**
3	Product A	1000	1500	1430	1490	1750	1510
4	Product B	960	1210	1500	500	1200	1700
5	Product C	340	860	900	1000	1050	1100

Exercise 3

Spreadsheet skills:

- Format charts - axis scale
- Chart alteration - change chart type
- Changing data series - change chart element colour

1. Open workbook T7Exercises
2. Select worksheet Exercise 3
3. Modify the vertical axis scale to be a number, comma for thousands, and no decimal places
4. Change the colour of the Chart title text to grey
5. Change the Chart Type to 3D Column
6. Save your spreadsheet with the name: Chapter7_Exercise3

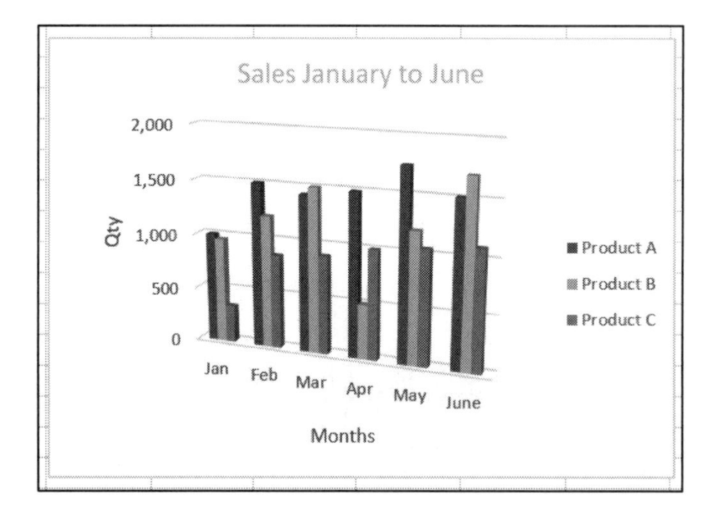

Exercise 4

Spreadsheet skills:

- Chart alteration - move a chart
- Chart alteration - change to line chart
- Print a chart

1. Open workbook T7Exercises
2. Select worksheet Exercise 4
3. Move the chart onto a new worksheet with name MyChart
4. Change the chart type to line
5. Print the chart
6. Save your spreadsheet with the name: Chapter7_Exercise4

   Your print preview should look as shown below:

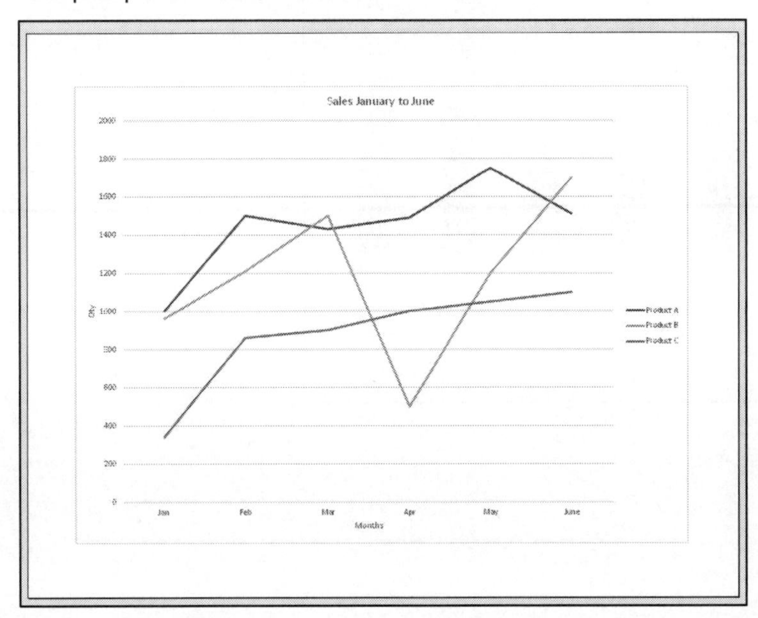

Exercise 5

Spreadsheet skills:

- Charts - create a stacked bar chart
- Format chart - add a data table

1. Open workbook T7Exercises
2. Select worksheet Exercise 5
3. Create a stacked bar chart with data for products A and B only
4. The chart title should be Sales by Product
5. The vertical axis label should be Qty
6. Add the data table to your chart, positioned below the chart
7. Save your spreadsheet with the name: Chapter7_Exercise5

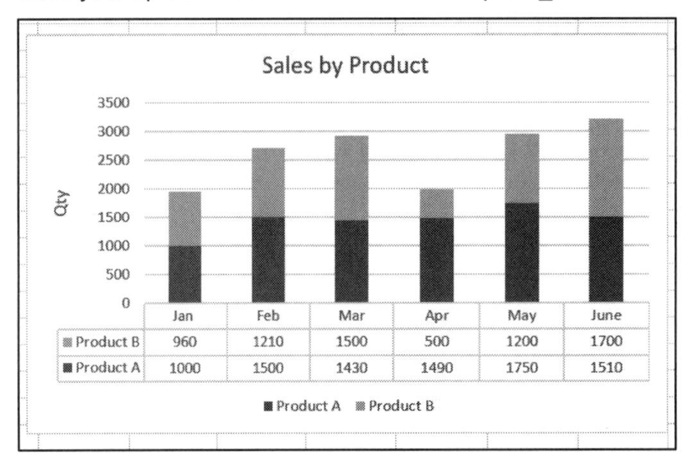

	Jan	Feb	Mar	Apr	May	June
Product B	960	1210	1500	500	1200	1700
Product A	1000	1500	1430	1490	1750	1510

Exercise 6

Spreadsheet skills:

- Changing data series - chart filter
- Changing data series - change the data included in a chart

1. Open workbook T7Exercises
2. Select worksheet Exercise 6
3. Add the data for Product C to the chart, using Chart Filter

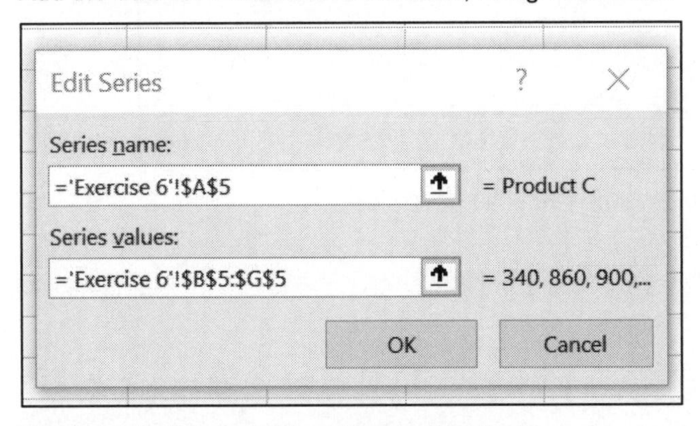

The data for Product C is added to the chart.

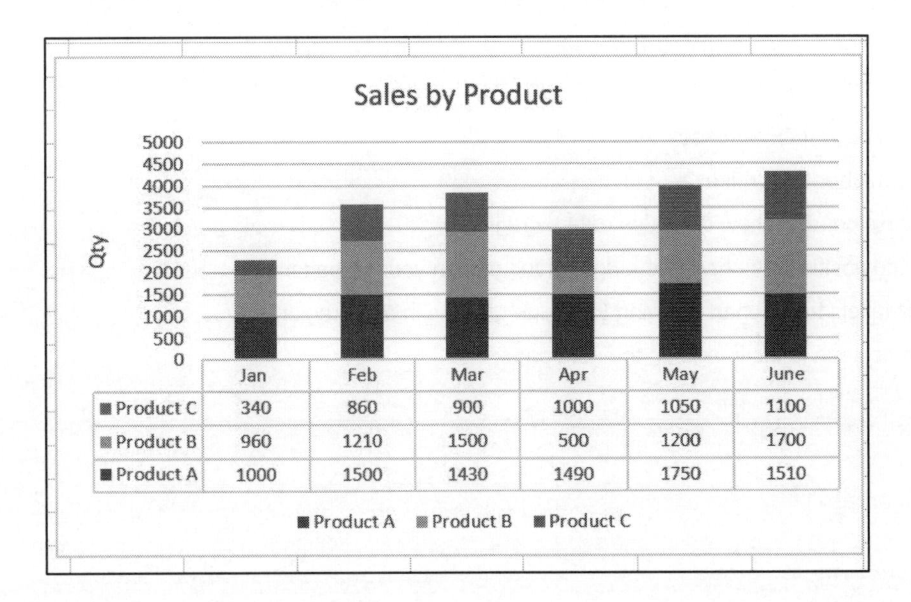

	Jan	Feb	Mar	Apr	May	June
Product C	340	860	900	1000	1050	1100
Product B	960	1210	1500	500	1200	1700
Product A	1000	1500	1430	1490	1750	1510

4. Remove the January data from the chart

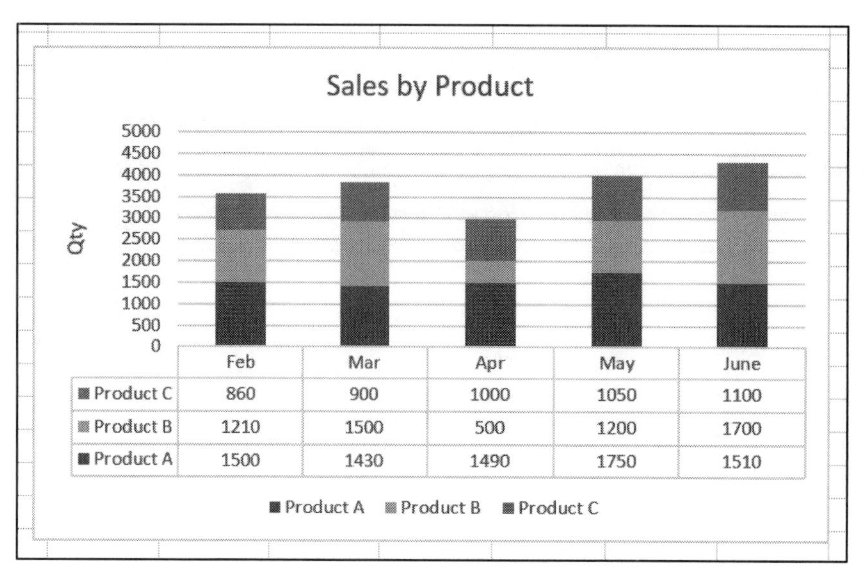

5. Save your spreadsheet with the name: Chapter7_Exercise6

Exercise 7

> Spreadsheet skills:
> - Charts - create a Pie chart
> - Chart alteration - move and resize a chart

1. Open workbook T7Exercises
2. Select worksheet Exercise 7
3. Create a pie chart to show the sales data by region
4. Resize and position the chart to the right of the data in your spreadsheet
5. Add data labels to the chart showing the value of sales in each region

   This can be seen in the image on the next page:

	A	B
1	Company ABC ltd	
2		
3	Region	Sales
4	South	210,000
5	West	155,000
6	Central	412,000
7	North	327,000
8	East	523,000

6. Format the data labels on the chart to just show percentages.

   This is shown in the image below:

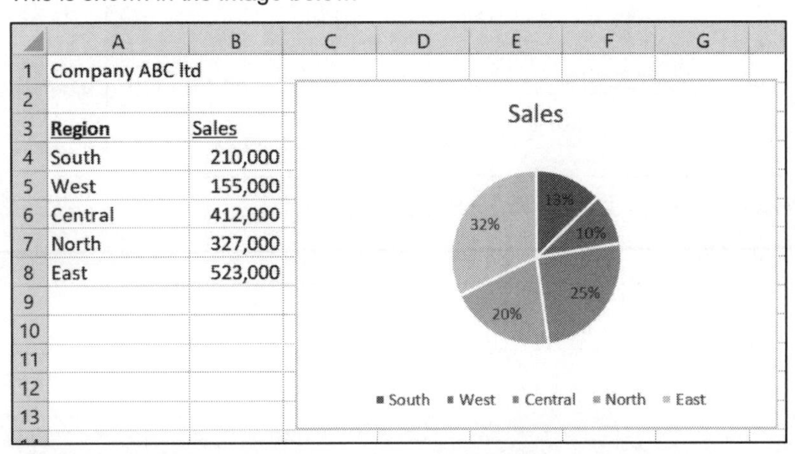

	A	B
1	Company ABC ltd	
2		
3	Region	Sales
4	South	210,000
5	West	155,000
6	Central	412,000
7	North	327,000
8	East	523,000

7. Save your spreadsheet with the name: Chapter7_Exercise7

Exercise 8

Spreadsheet skills:

- Chart alteration - explode a pie chart
- Charts - create a 3D pie chart
- Changing data series - add data to a chart

1. Open workbook T7Exercises
2. Select worksheet Exercise 8

3. Modify the chart data series to include the extra data A9, B9
4. Explode the pie chart to 20%
5. Adjust the Series Legend so that it is to the right of the pie chart

   Your worksheet should look as shown below:

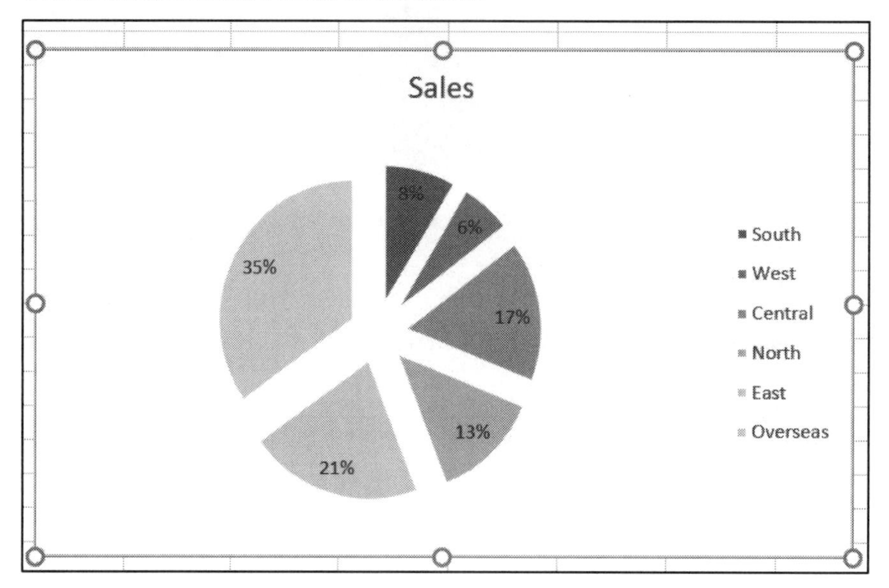

6. Change the pie chart style to be 3D, with X and Y rotation at 20%

   Your worksheet should look as shown below:

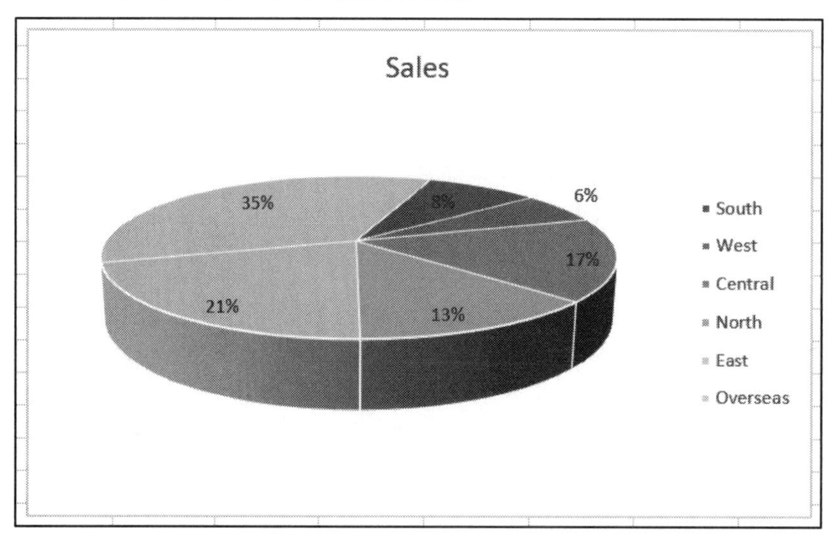

7. Save your spreadsheet with the name: Chapter7_Exercise8

8 Pivot tables and workbook management

this chapter covers...

This chapter covers some further spreadsheet techniques such as window management using Freeze Panes. It also explains the use of pivot tables and describes how they are created and formatted. By the time you have finished this chapter and carried out the exercises which follow, you should be able to produce spreadsheets which are very comprehensive, easy to read and contain pivot tables.

The concepts and techniques covered are:

- *managing windows – using freeze panes*
- *using the Paste Special function*
- *working with multiple worksheets and workbooks*
- *creating a simple pivot table*
- *using subsets of data*
- *formatting pivot tables*
- *goal seeking*
- *what-if scenarios*
- *FORECAST*
- *hyperlinks*

Note that the step-by-step instructions given in this chapter are based on the Microsoft® Excel model, but the concepts and techniques described generally relate to all spreadsheet packages.

WINDOW – FREEZE PANES

As we have seen in earlier chapters, we can scroll up, down and across our worksheet using the scroll bars positioned around the working area of the worksheet.

However, sometimes if we have a large amount of data, we still want to be able to see our row or column text headings so that we know what data we are looking at. The problem is illustrated in the next two screen images.

If we look at the image below, we can see the top portion of a large spreadsheet recording customer sales. The headings are clearly visible.

	A	B	C	D	E	F	G	H	I
1	Name	Total	Month1	Month2	Month3	Month4	Month5	Month6	Month7
2	*Farmhouse Foods*	£154	£0	£112	£0	£0	£0	£26	£0
3	*Engineering Services*	£554	£0	£0	£0	£0	£67	£0	£0
4	*Another Food Service*	£790	£0	£0	£0	£58	£116	£0	£0
5	*Top Quality Supplies*	£56	£0	£56	£0	£0	£0	£0	£0
6	*Halal Foods*	£36	£0	£0	£0	£0	£0	£0	£0
7	*Edwards Farm*	£195	£0	£0	£0	£0	£40	£0	£65
8	*Allen and co*	£1,412	£45	£68	£231	£0	£331	£37	£49
9	*Ahmed and son*	£340	£0	£0	£0	£0	£0	£0	£0
10	*Green & Sons Wholesalers*	£1,827	£700	£0	£104	£0	£0	£0	£0
11	*Higginbottom and son*	£389	£0	£0	£0	£0	£0	£0	£300
12	*W B Meats*	£135	£0	£45	£0	£0	£0	£0	£0

If we use the scroll bars to move around the data, we can end up in a situation where we cannot see the text at the top of the column, or at the start of the row. This is not very helpful, as you can see in the image shown below:

	D	E	F	G	H	I	J	K	L	M
4	£0	£0	£58	£116	£0	£0	£174	£0	£0	£0
5	£56	£0	£0	£0	£0	£0	£0	£0	£0	£0
6	£0	£0	£0	£0	£0	£0	£0	£0	£0	£36
7	£0	£0	£0	£40	£0	£65	£0	£0	£0	£0
8	£68	£231	£0	£331	£37	£49	£0	£0	£100	£115
9	£0	£0	£0	£0	£0	£0	£0	£0	£0	£0
10	£0	£104	£0	£0	£0	£0	£0	£363	£0	£0
11	£0	£0	£0	£0	£0	£300	£0	£0	£0	£89
12	£45	£0	£0	£0	£0	£0	£0	£0	£0	£0
13	£0	£50	£0	£0	£0	£0	£25	£0	£0	£0
14	£166	£583	£225	£414	£365	£470	£490	£244	£423	£354
15	£40	£0	£0	£0	£0	£0	£0	£0	£0	£0

To get over this problem we can use a facility called **Freeze Panes**. This facility is found under the **View** menu.

There are several choices within **Freeze Panes**, but the simplest is to select the first data cell (B2 in our example), then select **Freeze Panes** from the

View menu, and this will freeze the row(s) directly above and the column(s) directly to the left of the chosen cell.

You are now able to scroll up and down with row and column headings staying in view, as can be seen in the image below, where we have scrolled both right and down. The slightly more solid lines at the bottom of row1 and to the right of column A indicate they are frozen and will not disappear out of view as you scroll around the worksheet.

	A	G	H	I	J	K	L	M	N
1	Name	Month5	Month6	Month7	Month8	Month9	Mont10	Month11	Month12
4	*Another Food Service*	£116	£0	£0	£174	£0	£0	£0	£0
5	*Top Quality Supplies*	£0	£0	£0	£0	£0	£0	£0	£0
6	*Halal Foods*	£0	£0	£0	£0	£0	£0	£36	£0
7	*Edwards Farm*	£40	£0	£65	£0	£0	£0	£0	£90
8	*Allen and co*	£331	£37	£49	£0	£0	£100	£115	£77
9	*Ahmed and son*	£0	£0	£0	£0	£0	£0	£0	£0
10	*Green & Sons Wholesalers*	£0	£0	£0	£0	£363	£0	£0	£0
11	*Higginbottom and son*	£0	£0	£300	£0	£0	£0	£89	£0
12	*W B Meats*	£0	£0	£0	£0	£0	£0	£0	£0
13	*The Halal Centre*	£0	£0	£0	£25	£0	£0	£0	£0
14	*T F Curries*	£414	£365	£470	£490	£244	£423	£354	£560
15	*Fiber Optical Services*	£0	£0	£0	£0	£0	£0	£0	£0

It is also possible to freeze just the row headings, or just the column headings as follows:

To Freeze row or column headings:

from the **View** menu,

- select **Freeze Panes**

either

- select **Freeze Top Row**

or

- select **Freeze First Column**

To turn off Freeze Panes:

From the **View** menu,

- select **Freeze Panes**
- select **Unfreeze Panes**

PASTE SPECIAL

This is an extremely useful facility when we are copying data, whether it be a formula, just some text in a cell or group of cells or the way cells are formatted.

Paste Special allows us to decide exactly how we want to paste this copied information into its new location.

For example, if it is some text we are copying, formatted in Bold and Underlined, we may not want the copied text to be formatted in the same way. Or perhaps we have a formula which we are copying, and we don't want to copy the formula but the actual value it produces instead, to paste in to the new location.

Looking at the image below, we have selected five cells of text, A5 to E5.

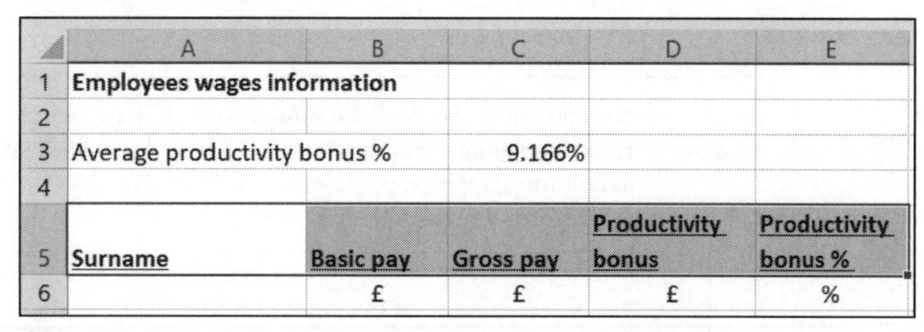

	A	B	C	D	E
1	**Employees wages information**				
2					
3	Average productivity bonus %		9.166%		
4					
5	Surname	Basic pay	Gross pay	Productivity bonus	Productivity bonus %
6		£	£	£	%

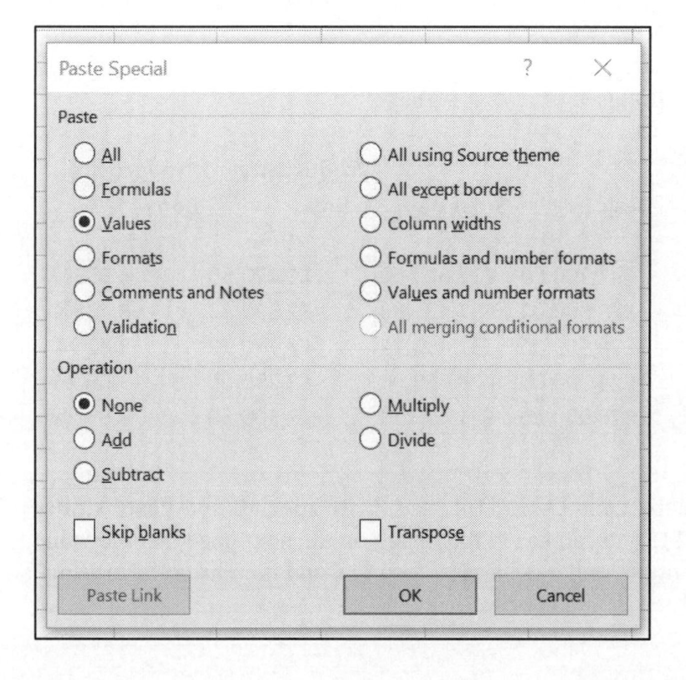

Then:

- select **Copy**
- move to where you want to place the copy – in this case, cell A14
- select **Paste Special** from **Paste** on the **Home** menu

The **Paste Special** options appear as shown on the left.

In this case we just want to copy the **values**, without formats, so we select Values, and OK. The results are shown in the screen image on the next page, with the copy of the unformatted text shown in cells A14:E14.

	A	B	C	D	E	F
1	**Employees wages information**					
2						
3	Average productivity bonus %		9.166%			
4						
5	**Surname**	**Basic pay**	**Gross pay**	**Productivity bonus**	**Productivity bonus %**	
6		£	£	£	%	
7	Patel	£31,200.00	£32,620.50	£1,420.50	4.553%	
8	Johnson	£28,900.00	£31,425.33	£2,525.33	8.738%	
9	Khan	£28,900.00	£31,450.72	£2,550.72	8.826%	
10	Begum	£24,900.00	£28,650.00	£3,750.00	15.060%	
11	Sheppard	£28,900.00	£31,400.50	£2,500.50	8.652%	
12	Total					
13						
14	Surname	Basic pay	Gross pay	Productivity bo	Productivity bonus %	

By choosing the **Values** button you will paste the values resulting from formulas (rather than the formulas themselves) without formatting. If we look at column D, which contains some formulas. The formula in D7 can be seen in the formula bar in the next image.

D7 =C7-B7

	A	B	C	D	E
1	**Employees wages information**				
2					
3	Average productivity bonus %		9.166%		
4					
5	**Surname**	**Basic pay**	**Gross pay**	**Productivity bonus**	**Productivity bonus %**
6		£	£	£	%
7	Patel	£31,200.00	£32,620.50	£1,420.50	4.553%
8	Johnson	£28,900.00	£31,425.33	£2,525.33	8.738%
9	Khan	£28,900.00	£31,450.72	£2,550.72	8.826%
10	Begum	£24,900.00	£28,650.00	£3,750.00	15.060%
11	Sheppard	£28,900.00	£31,400.50	£2,500.50	8.652%
12	Total				

If we choose to copy cells D7 to D11, use **Paste special**, and **Paste values** into cells F7 to F11, you can see in the image on the next page that the value in F7 is correct, but no longer contains a formula, and there is no formatting.

F7 | fx 1420.5

	A	B	C	D	E	F
1	**Employees wages information**					
2						
3	Average productivity bonus %		9.166%			
4						
5	**Surname**	**Basic pay**	**Gross pay**	**Productivity bonus**	**Productivity bonus %**	***Productivity bonus***
6		£	£	£	%	***Paste values***
7	Patel	£31,200.00	£32,620.50	£1,420.50	4.553%	1420.5
8	Johnson	£28,900.00	£31,425.33	£2,525.33	8.738%	2525.33
9	Khan	£28,900.00	£31,450.72	£2,550.72	8.826%	2550.72
10	Begum	£24,900.00	£28,650.00	£3,750.00	15.060%	3750
11	Sheppard	£28,900.00	£31,400.50	£2,500.50	8.652%	2500.5
12	Total					

To add formatting, we can copy cells D7 to D11, use **Paste special**, and **Paste Formats** into cells F7 to F11.

	A	B	C	D	E	F
1	**Employees wages information**					
2						
3	Average productivity bonus %		9.166%			
4						
5	**Surname**	**Basic pay**	**Gross pay**	**Productivity bonus**	**Productivity bonus %**	***Productivity bonus***
6		£	£	£	%	***Paste values***
7	Patel	£31,200.00	£32,620.50	£1,420.50	4.553%	£1,420.50
8	Johnson	£28,900.00	£31,425.33	£2,525.33	8.738%	£2,525.33
9	Khan	£28,900.00	£31,450.72	£2,550.72	8.826%	£2,550.72
10	Begum	£24,900.00	£28,650.00	£3,750.00	15.060%	£3,750.00
11	Sheppard	£28,900.00	£31,400.50	£2,500.50	8.652%	£2,500.50
12	Total					

Paste special offers many options when copying cells; one other which we are going to look at is **Paste Link**. This option pastes a direct link to the cell(s) being copied, so that if that cell changes so does the copy.

Using the same example, copying cells D7 to D11, if we use **Paste Special**, then **Paste Link**, F7 now contains a direct link to D7, ie the formula =D7.

As can be seen on the next page:

F7 =D7

	A	B	C	D	E	F
1	**Employees wages information**					
2						
3	Average productivity bonus %		9.166%			
4						
5	**Surname**	**Basic pay**	**Gross pay**	**Productivity bonus**	**Productivity bonus %**	***Productivity bonus***
6		£	£	£	%	***Paste link***
7	Patel	£31,200.00	£32,620.50	£1,420.50	4.553%	£1,420.50
8	Johnson	£28,900.00	£31,425.33	£2,525.33	8.738%	£2,525.33
9	Khan	£28,900.00	£31,450.72	£2,550.72	8.826%	£2,550.72
10	Begum	£24,900.00	£28,650.00	£3,750.00	15.060%	£3,750.00
11	Sheppard	£28,900.00	£31,400.50	£2,500.50	8.652%	£2,500.50
12	Total					

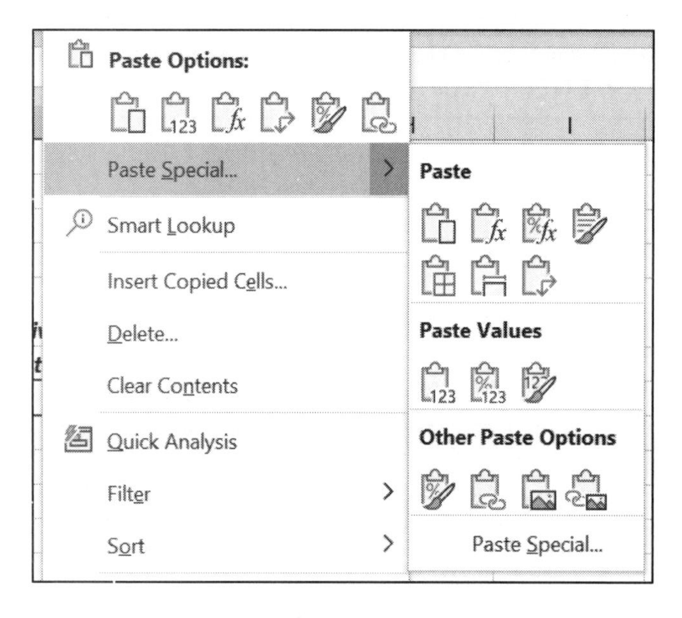

To paste the actual formulas without formatting, choose the **Paste formulas** option from the Paste special options.

Note: once we have selected some cells to copy and moved to where we want to place the copy, we can right-click to access the paste special options as illustrated on the left.

WORKING WITH MULTIPLE WORKSHEETS

When creating a formula, it is possible to use or reference data on another worksheet within the same workbook by including the worksheet name within the formula.

If we look at the images on the next page, we have a workbook with two worksheets, one named **Summary**, the other named **Productivity Bonus**.

The **Productivity** worksheet (shown below) contains Bonus figures which need to be incorporated in the employees' wages information on the **Summary** sheet.

	A	B
1	**Employees wages information**	
2		
3	**Surname**	**Productivity bonus**
4		£
5	Patel	£1,420.50
6	Johnson	£2,525.33
7	Singh	£300.00
8	Gregory	£4,050.31
9	Williams	£1,850.50
10	Reed	£2,950.67
11	Khan	£2,550.72
12	Begum	£3,750.00
13	Sheppard	£2,500.50
14	Total	£21,898.53
15		

... Summary | **Productivity Bonus**

The **Summary** worksheet shows Employees' wages information.

	A	B	C	D
1	**Employees' wages information**			
2				
3	**Surname**	**Basic Pay**	**Productivity bonus**	**Gross Pay**
4		£	£	£
5	Patel	£31,200.00		£31,200.00
6	Johnson	£28,900.00		£28,900.00
7	Singh	£31,200.00		£31,200.00
8	Gregory	£24,900.00		£24,900.00
9	Williams	£24,900.00		£24,900.00
10	Reed	£28,900.00		£28,900.00
11	Khan	£28,900.00		£28,900.00
12	Begum	£24,900.00		£24,900.00
13	Sheppard	£28,900.00		£28,900.00
14	Total	£252,700.00	£0.00	£252,700.00
15				

... **Summary** | Productivity Bonus

In this case, we want cell **C5** on worksheet **Summary** to contain the Productivity Bonus value for Patel, found in cell **B5** on worksheet **Productivity Bonus**. To do this:

- move to cell C5 on worksheet **Summary**
- enter = (to indicate a formula)
- move to cell B5 on worksheet **Productivity Bonus**
- press **RETURN** to complete the formula

Looking at the image below we can see the formula created in cell B5 in the formula bar of worksheet Summary:

='Productivity Bonus'!B5

The formula contains a direct reference to the worksheet Productivity Bonus, followed by an exclamation mark (!) to indicate that this is a worksheet name, and then the cell reference B5 in the worksheet Productivity Bonus.

Notice that the worksheet name is enclosed in single quotes (') this is because the name has a space in it.

C5 | fx ='Productivity Bonus'!B5

	A	B	C	D
1	**Employees' wages information**			
2				
3	**Surname**	**Basic Pay**	**Productivity bonus**	**Gross Pay**
4		£	£	£
5	Patel	£31,200.00	£1,420.50	£32,620.50
6	Johnson	£28,900.00		£28,900.00
7	Singh	£31,200.00		£31,200.00
8	Gregory	£24,900.00		£24,900.00
9	Williams	£24,900.00		£24,900.00
10	Reed	£28,900.00		£28,900.00
11	Khan	£28,900.00		£28,900.00
12	Begum	£24,900.00		£24,900.00
13	Sheppard	£28,900.00		£28,900.00
14	Total	£252,700.00	£1,420.50	£254,120.50

Alternatively, we could use the **Paste special**, **Paste link** option in cell C5 to insert a direct link to cell B5 on worksheet Productivity Bonus.

To do this:

- move to cell B5 on worksheet Productivity Bonus
- select **Copy**
- move to cell C5 on worksheet Summary
- select **Paste special**
- select **Paste link**

The resultant formula in cell C5 is illustrated below:

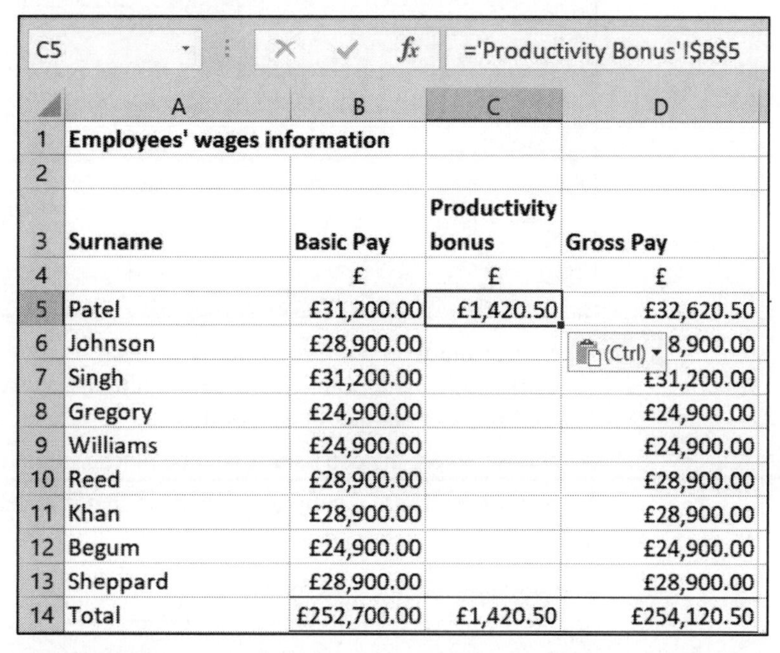

C5 | ='Productivity Bonus'!$B$5

	A	B	C	D
1	**Employees' wages information**			
2				
3	**Surname**	**Basic Pay**	**Productivity bonus**	**Gross Pay**
4		£	£	£
5	Patel	£31,200.00	£1,420.50	£32,620.50
6	Johnson	£28,900.00		8,900.00
7	Singh	£31,200.00		£31,200.00
8	Gregory	£24,900.00		£24,900.00
9	Williams	£24,900.00		£24,900.00
10	Reed	£28,900.00		£28,900.00
11	Khan	£28,900.00		£28,900.00
12	Begum	£24,900.00		£24,900.00
13	Sheppard	£28,900.00		£28,900.00
14	Total	£252,700.00	£1,420.50	£254,120.50

The only difference using this method is that the formula contains an absolute cell reference.

copying a worksheet

It is very simple to make a copy of a worksheet:

- select the worksheet you want to copy
- right-click on the worksheet name tab
- select **Move** or **Copy**

This operation can be seen in the screen image on the next page.

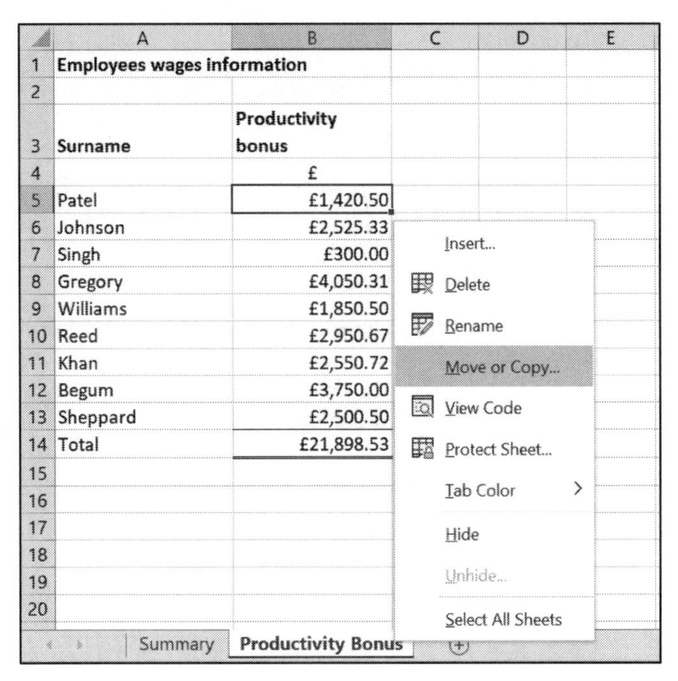

- choose the workbook to which you wish to move or copy the selected worksheet. (This can either be within the current workbook, a new workbook or another open workbook)
- choose where the copy sheet is to be placed in the workbook
- select the **Create a copy** check box, so that it is ticked
- press OK

The screen will appear as follows:

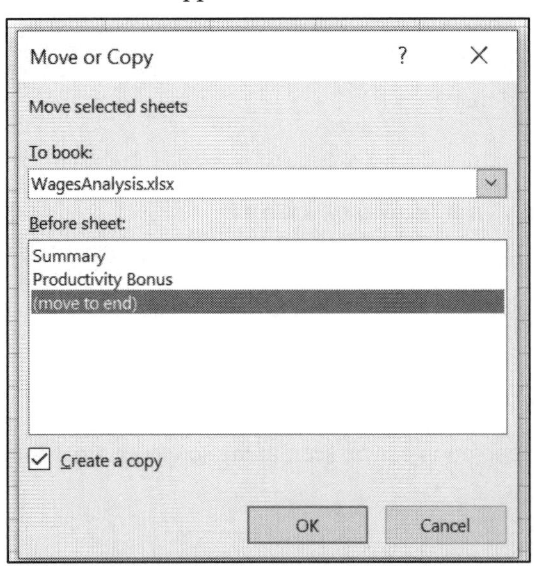

In the example shown above, a copy of the worksheet will be placed at the end of the workbook, named Productivity Bonus (2), as shown below. This worksheet can be renamed by double clicking on the worksheet name tab and entering the required name.

	A	B	C	D	E	F
1	**Employees wages information**					
2						
3	**Surname**	**Productivity bonus**				
4		£				
5	Patel	£1,420.50				
6	Johnson	£2,525.33				
7	Singh	£300.00				
8	Gregory	£4,050.31				
9	Williams	£1,850.50				
10	Reed	£2,950.67				
11	Khan	£2,550.72				
12	Begum	£3,750.00				
13	Sheppard	£2,500.50				
14	Total	£21,898.53				

Summary | Productivity Bonus | **Productivity Bonus (2)**

WORKING WITH MULTIPLE WORKBOOKS

We may regularly want to work with more than one workbook open. In Excel® each workbook is opened in a separate window. To switch between open workbooks, right-click on the Excel icon in the taskbar, and select the required workbook from the list.

It is also possible to move or copy a worksheet from one workbook to another workbook. The procedure is very similar to moving worksheets within a single workbook. To move or copy a worksheet from one workbook to another workbook:

- in the **To book** box, select the name of the workbook where the worksheet is to be moved or copied to (in the example which follows we select **new book** from the drop-down list)
- choose where the copy sheet is to be placed in the selected workbook
- select the **Create a copy** check box, so that it is ticked, and press OK

The screen will appear as shown on the next page. If a worksheet is copied or moved in this way, any formulas will stay exactly as they were in the original sheet.

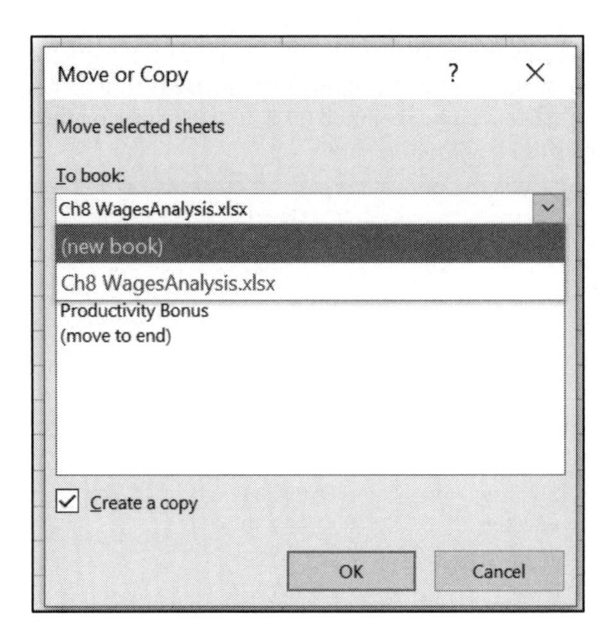

using Copy and Paste to move data

Moving or copying a worksheet as described above is an easy way of moving data from one worksheet to another, whether in the same or in different workbooks.

It is also possible to use the normal Copy and Paste to copy all or part of the data from a worksheet in one open workbook to a worksheet in another open workbook. In the image on the next page, you can see the Wages data on worksheet Summary in our file which is named **WagesAnalysis** (the file name is not visible on the image.)

	A	B	C	D
1	**Employees' wages information**			
2				
3	**Surname**	**Basic Pay**	**Productivity bonus**	**Gross Pay**
4		£	£	£
5	Patel	£31,200.00	£1,420.50	£32,620.50
6	Johnson	£28,900.00	£2,525.33	£31,425.33
7	Singh	£31,200.00	£300.00	£31,500.00
8	Gregory	£24,900.00	£4,050.31	£28,950.31
9	Williams	£24,900.00	£1,850.50	£26,750.50
10	Reed	£28,900.00	£2,950.67	£31,850.67
11	Khan	£28,900.00	£2,550.72	£31,450.72
12	Begum	£24,900.00	£3,750.00	£28,650.00
13	Sheppard	£28,900.00	£2,500.50	£31,400.50
14	Total	£252,700.00	£21,898.53	£274,598.53

Suppose we want to copy some of the wages data to a worksheet in another workbook. To do this we select cells A3:C13, and **Copy and Paste** onto **Sheet1** in another workbook, which is already open, as shown below:

C4 ='[WagesAnalysis.xlsx]Productivity Bonus'!B4

	A	B	C	D	E	F	G
1	Surname	Basic Pay	Productivity bonus				
2		£	£				
3	Patel	£31,200.00	Productivity bonus				
4	Johnson	£28,900.00	£				
5	Singh	£31,200.00	£1,420.50				
6	Gregory	£24,900.00	£2,525.33				
7	Williams	£24,900.00	£300.00				
8	Reed	£28,900.00	£4,050.31				
9	Khan	£28,900.00	£1,850.50				
10	Begum	£24,900.00	£2,950.67				
11	Sheppard	£28,900.00	£2,550.72				

We can see that it hasn't quite gone to plan. Cell C4 is now linked to B4 on WagesAnalysis.xlsx, worksheet Productivity Bonus.

Alternatively, if we use **Copy** and then **Paste Special**, **Paste Link**, it would look as shown below, with each cell holding a direct link to the appropriate cell in workbook WagesAnalysis, although we no longer have the formatting.

Notice how the workbook name is included in the formula, enclosed in square brackets, then the worksheet name followed by an exclamation mark, then the cell on that worksheet.

Looking at cell C3:

C3 =[WagesAnalysis.xlsx]Summary!C5

	A	B	C	D	E	F	G
1	Surname	Basic Pay	Productivity bonus				
2	0	£	£				
3	Patel	31200	1420.5				
4	Johnson	28900	2525.33				
5	Singh	31200	300				
6	Gregory	24900	4050.31				
7	Williams	24900	1850.5				
8	Reed	28900	2950.67				
9	Khan	28900	2550.72				
10	Begum	24900	3750				
11	Sheppard	28900	2500.5				

We can see that it takes its value from cell C5, on worksheet Summary, in workbook WagesAnalysis.

Should any of the original values in the WagesAnalysis workbook change, the values in this workbook will change to match.

PIVOT TABLES – AN INTRODUCTION

what is a pivot table?

A **pivot table** is a very powerful reporting tool found in spreadsheet packages. Pivot tables allow us to generate and extract meaningful information from a large table of information within a matter of minutes, by creating an interactive summary from a worksheet containing numerous rows of data. This summary is known as a **pivot table**.

advantages of a pivot table

Instead of having to analyse vast amounts of data, a pivot table can sort, count, subtotal and total your numeric information. It can allow you to look at the data in different ways very quickly and easily.

It is possible to expand and collapse levels of data and drill down to details from the summary data to look at areas in more detail.

Changing the format in which the data is summarised, by moving rows to columns or columns to rows (pivoting) allows you to see different summaries of the same source data.

examples of pivot tables

If we look at the image on the next page, we can see a small part of some extended sales data relating to the sales generated by individual sales reps:

	A	B	C	D	E
1	**Sales**				
2					
3	**Month**	**Product**	**Value**	**Sales Rep**	**Country**
4	Apr	Other	£34.90	IO	SP
5	Apr	Footwear	£1,460.40	TP	UK
6	Apr	Other	£56.25	IO	IND
7	Apr	Jewellery	£56.00	IO	SP
8	Aug	Other	£1,500.00	IY	FR
9	Aug	Luggage	£67.75	SM	PKN
10	Aug	Clothing	£99.95	TP	UK
11	Aug	Other	£1,460.40	IY	FR
12	Dec	Luggage	£56.25	IO	GER
13	Dec	Jewellery	£34.00	MP	SP
14	Dec	Other	£1,500.00	IO	SP
15	Dec	Accessories	£124.60	MP	GER
16	Feb	Jewellery	£1,500.00	TP	UK

In the example pivot table below, we are showing for each sales rep, the value of each product type sold (eg Accessories, Clothing etc) created from the sales data and summarised in a simple table.

	A	B	C	D	E	F	G	H
1								
2								
3	**Sum of Value**	**Column Labels**						
4	**Row Labels**	**Accessories**	**Clothing**	**Footwear**	**Jewellery**	**Luggage**	**Other**	**Grand Total**
5	IY	1585.3	44.75	374.5	125.75	220	4705.55	7055.85
6	IO	334.75	1180		182.75	552.5	1647.4	3897.4
7	MP	124.6		253	34	2800		3211.6
8	SM		443.85	224.55	240	192.35		1100.75
9	TP	213.75	99.95	1586.15	1500		124.6	3524.45
10	**Grand Total**	**2258.4**	**1768.55**	**2438.2**	**2082.5**	**3764.85**	**6477.55**	**18790.05**

If we then wanted to see the detail of the Accessories sales made by sales rep IY, we could select cell B5, and 'drill down' to show the detailed sales which make up this subtotal, as can be seen in the image below.

	A	B	C	D	E
1	Month	Product	Value	Sales Rep	Country
2	Sep	Accessorie:	34	IY	GER
3	Sep	Accessorie:	1460.4	IY	FR
4	Oct	Accessorie:	34.9	IY	PKN
5	Nov	Accessorie:	56	IY	FR

You can see that a pivot table provides a very powerful analysis and reporting tool.

CREATING A PIVOT TABLE

The techniques for creating a pivot table will vary greatly between spreadsheet packages, and even between versions of the same package, but the principles remain the same. In the steps that follow we will be creating a pivot table in Microsoft® Excel.

We will work with the sales data used in the examples above.

Step 1 – Setting up the data

The data should be set out in columns going down the worksheet.

The columns of data should be adjacent and start in the same row.

Each column of data should have a unique title (name) which relates to the data it contains. In our example we have the following titles:

- Month
- Product
- Value
- Sales Rep
- Country

These titles are normal pieces of text and should be placed in the cell directly above the first data cell, for each column.

The titles are also known as fields (of data) within the pivot table environment and are used extensively in the creation of a pivot table. For the pivot table to work, at least one of the columns must contain data that repeats eg Sales Rep, Product, Country so that the data can be summarised effectively.

Step 2 – Selecting the data

Select all your data, including the column titles, but be careful not to select any total rows that might be present.

Step 3 – Creating the pivot table

You have two choices when creating a pivot table, you can either choose to create a recommended pivot table based on your data set or create a blank pivot table which you will set up yourself. We will cover both options.

Creating a pivot table from scratch:

- select **PivotTable** from the **Insert** menu

The following message box should appear:

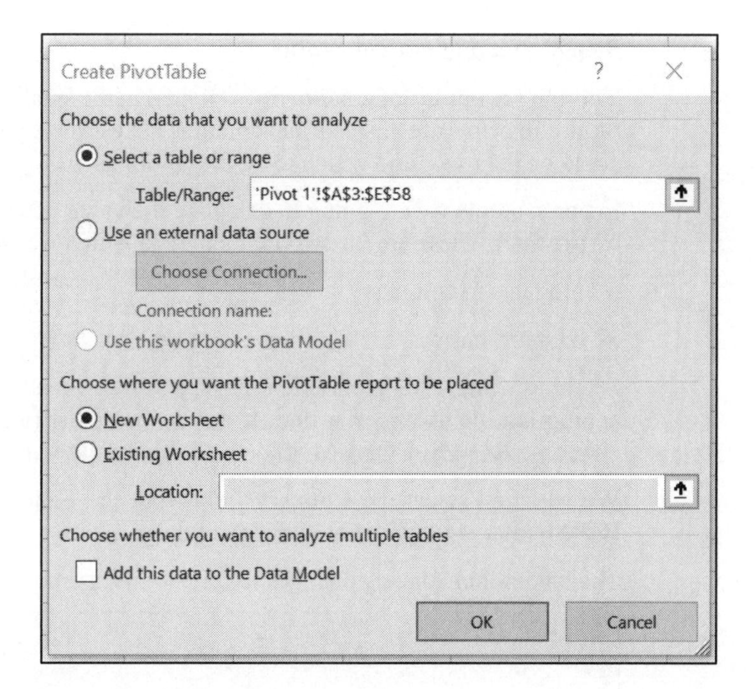

Check that the range entered in the **Table/Range** box is correct and includes all your data cells.

Leave the **New Worksheet** button selected – this will automatically create the pivot table on a new worksheet within your current workbook.

Select OK to continue, a screen like the one below is displayed.

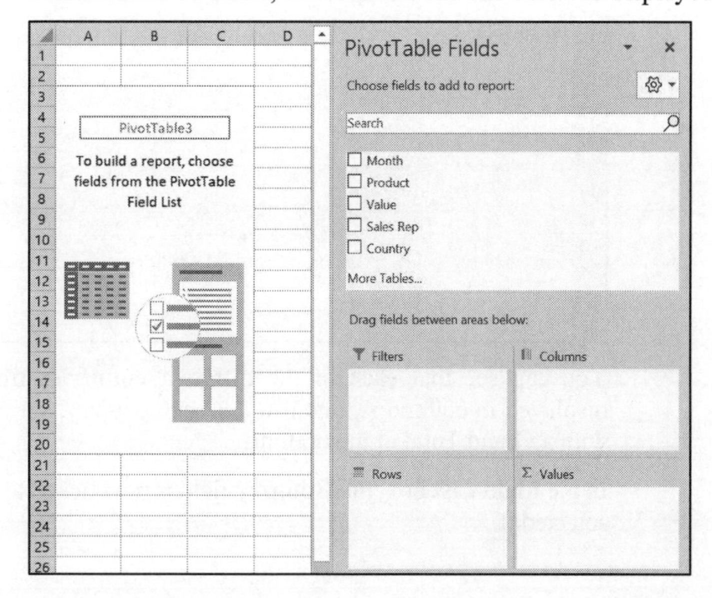

Step 4 – Laying out your table

You can see our list of column titles (fields) in the small box (**Fields List**) top right, and below are the rows and columns boxes where we define which fields are to be the rows, and which to be the columns.

In our example we are going to calculate the value of sales for each **country** by **product**. These are the two fields of data which we want to display:

- products in columns
- country in rows

Working within the PivotTable Fields pane shown on the right, we select the appropriate fields one at a time from the fields list (top right), and drag to either the **ROWS**, **COLUMNS** or **VALUES** areas within the pane.

We will first select the **Country** field from the **Field List** and drag to the **ROWS** area, if not already there, and release.

The layout immediately changes to reflect this, as shown below:

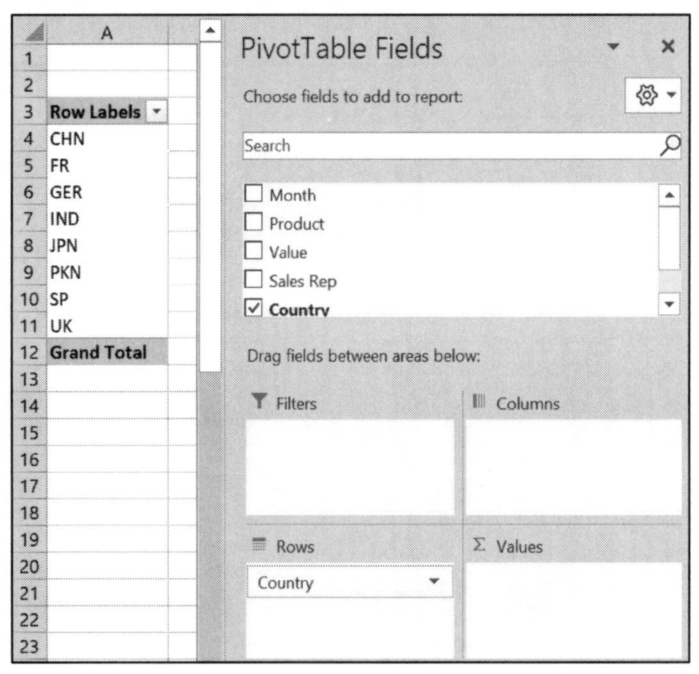

You can see that each of the different **countries** from our sales data is displayed in column A, one row for each country, sorted alphabetically, and with a Grand Total at the bottom.

In the **Field List** box, the **Country** field is now ticked to indicate that we have selected it.

Now, we select the **Product** field from the **Field List**, and drag it to the **COLUMNS** area and release. The screen then appears as shown below:

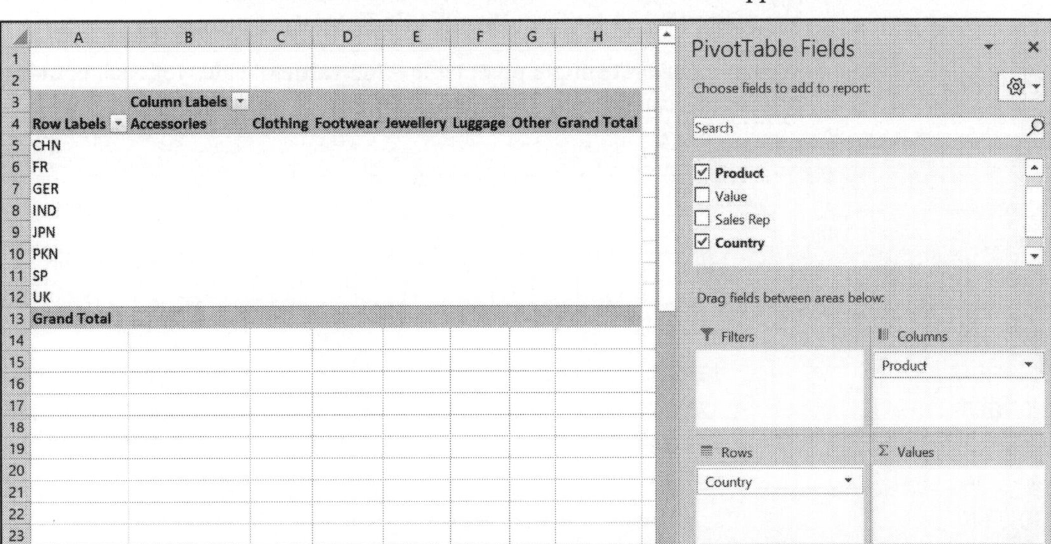

You can see that the titles for the different products from within our data are displayed in Row 4, starting from Column B. There is one column for each product, sorted alphabetically, and with a Grand Total at the end. In the Field List box, the **Product** field is now ticked to indicate that we have selected it. As you can see, the layout structure is becoming clearer.

One further step is now required to include the sales value data so that we can analyse the sales.

To include this field, we select the **Value** field from the **Field List** and drag it to the ∑ **VALUES** area, then release.

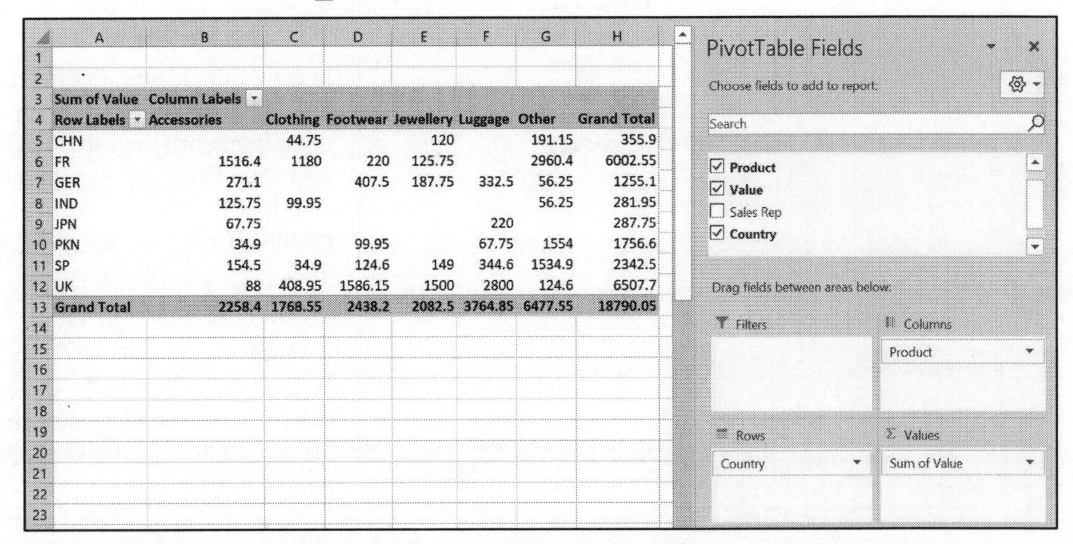

Sum of Value	Column Labels						
Row Labels	Accessories	Clothing	Footwear	Jewellery	Luggage	Other	Grand Total
CHN		44.75		120		191.15	355.9
FR	1516.4	1180	220	125.75		2960.4	6002.55
GER	271.1		407.5	187.75	332.5	56.25	1255.1
IND	125.75	99.95				56.25	281.95
JPN	67.75				220		287.75
PKN	34.9		99.95		67.75	1554	1756.6
SP	154.5	34.9	124.6	149	344.6	1534.9	2342.5
UK	88	408.95	1586.15	1500	2800	124.6	6507.7
Grand Total	2258.4	1768.55	2438.2	2082.5	3764.85	6477.55	18790.05

As our pivot table has now taken shape, we can close the PivotTable Fields pane on the right-hand side of the screen. If you want the box visible again, just select **Field List** from **PivotTABLE Analyze** menu.

We have our first simple pivot table – the **value** of sales for each **country** by **product** as can be seen in the image below.

	A	B	C	D	E	F	G	H
1								
2								
3	Sum of Value	Column Labels						
4	Row Labels	Accessories	Clothing	Footwear	Jewellery	Luggage	Other	Grand Total
5	CHN		44.75		120		191.15	355.9
6	FR	1516.4	1180	220	125.75		2960.4	6002.55
7	GER	271.1		407.5	187.75	332.5	56.25	1255.1
8	IND	125.75	99.95				56.25	281.95
9	JPN	67.75				220		287.75
10	PKN	34.9		99.95		67.75	1554	1756.6
11	SP	154.5	34.9	124.6	149	344.6	1534.9	2342.5
12	UK	88	408.95	1586.15	1500	2800	124.6	6507.7
13	Grand Total	2258.4	1768.55	2438.2	2082.5	3764.85	6477.55	18790.05

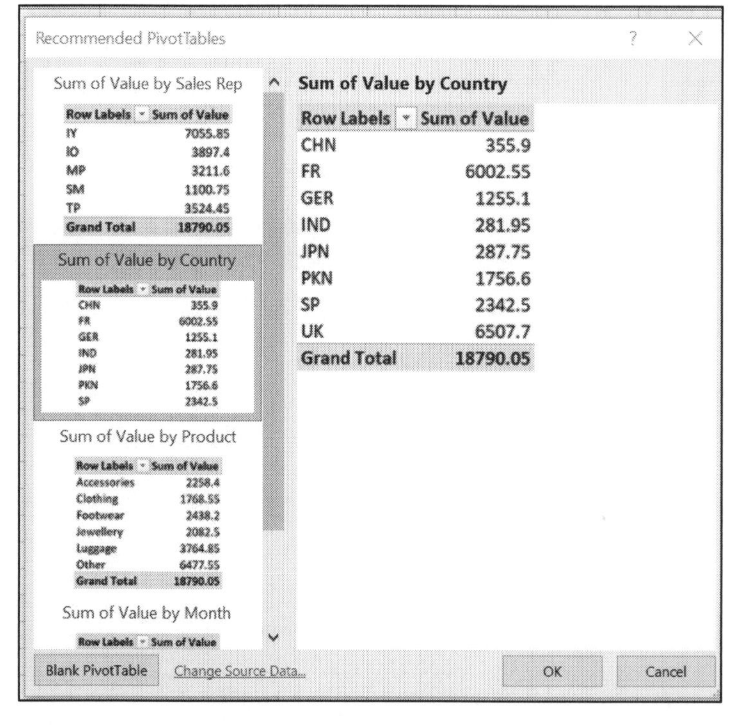

Creating a pivot table using recommended PivotTables:

- select **Recommended PivotTables** from the **Insert** menu
- choose the layout which suits your analysis

In our example, we are offered a pivot table summary by each of our column headings ie by Sales Rep, by Country, by Product and by Month, not by Value since it is what we are going to total.

We choose Sum of Value by Country.

When we select OK, a new worksheet is added containing the pivot table, as shown on the opposite page.

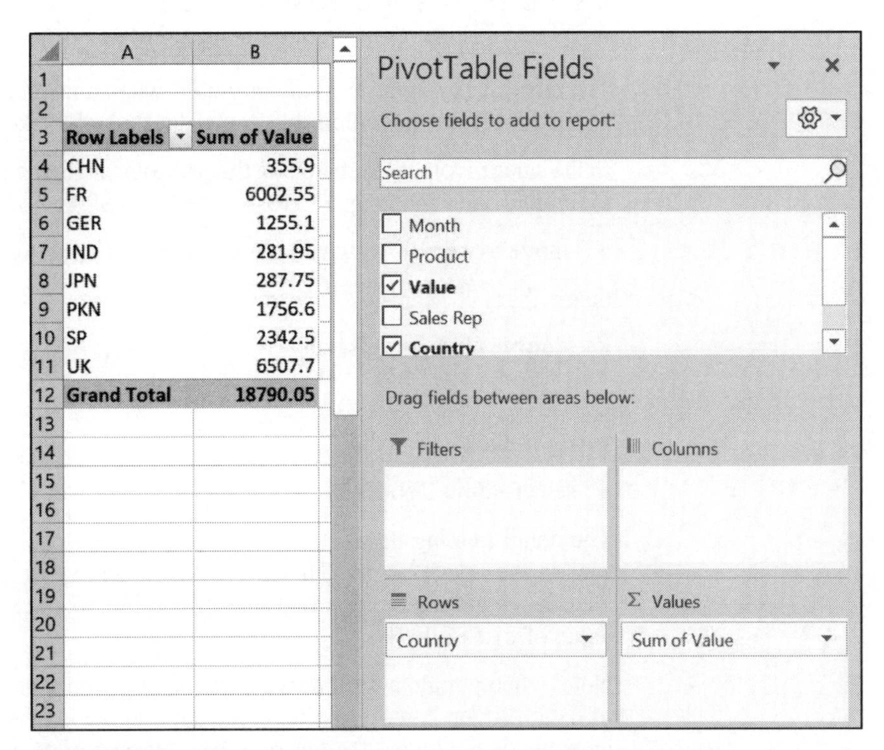

Row Labels	Sum of Value
CHN	355.9
FR	6002.55
GER	1255.1
IND	281.95
JPN	287.75
PKN	1756.6
SP	2342.5
UK	6507.7
Grand Total	18790.05

You can now adjust this layout as described in the layout section above. To achieve the same pivot table as previously, we would tick **Product** in the field list, and drag it to the **COLUMNS** area, as can be seen below.

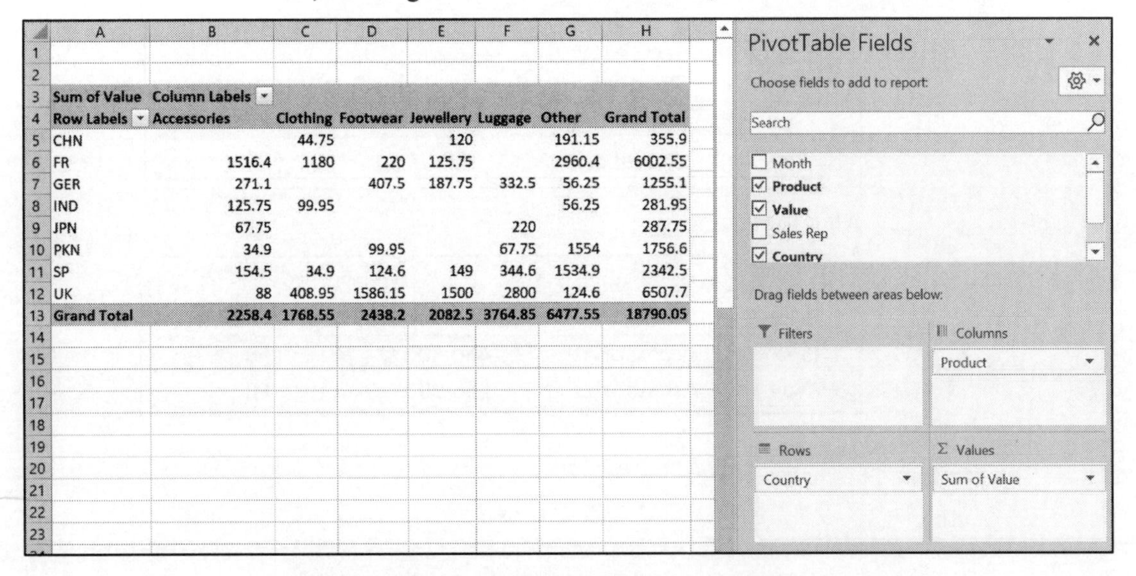

Sum of Value	Column Labels						
Row Labels	Accessories	Clothing	Footwear	Jewellery	Luggage	Other	Grand Total
CHN		44.75		120		191.15	355.9
FR	1516.4	1180	220	125.75		2960.4	6002.55
GER	271.1		407.5	187.75	332.5	56.25	1255.1
IND	125.75	99.95				56.25	281.95
JPN	67.75				220		287.75
PKN	34.9		99.95		67.75	1554	1756.6
SP	154.5	34.9	124.6	149	344.6	1534.9	2342.5
UK	88	408.95	1586.15	1500	2800	124.6	6507.7
Grand Total	2258.4	1768.55	2438.2	2082.5	3764.85	6477.55	18790.05

Achieving the same result as before, but with fewer steps.

DRILL DOWN – SHOW DETAIL

The term 'drill down' is frequently used when analysing data to describe the ability to display the underlying data values which make up a total or subtotal.

In the sales pivot table created on the previous page, if we wanted to see which individual sales made up £1516.40, the value of **Accessories** sales in **FR**:

- move to cell B6 which shows the total value for Accessories sales in FR

then either

- **double click** on this cell

or

- right-click
- select **Show Details**

The detail making up this total is displayed on a fresh worksheet, as can be seen in the image below. This shows that when we **drill down** into the data, we can see that there were two sales of £1,460.40 and £56.00 making up this value of £1,516.40.

Note, when you do a **drill down** there is, by default, no automatic formatting of data. As you can see in the Value column below, for example, the money amounts do not have '£' signs or a fixed number of decimal places. These can be formatted subsequently as required.

Column C before formatting:

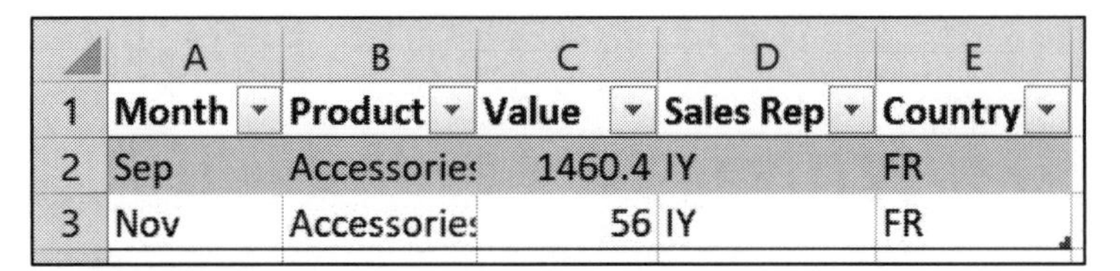

	A	B	C	D	E
1	Month	Product	Value	Sales Rep	Country
2	Sep	Accessorie:	1460.4	IY	FR
3	Nov	Accessorie:	56	IY	FR

After formatting:

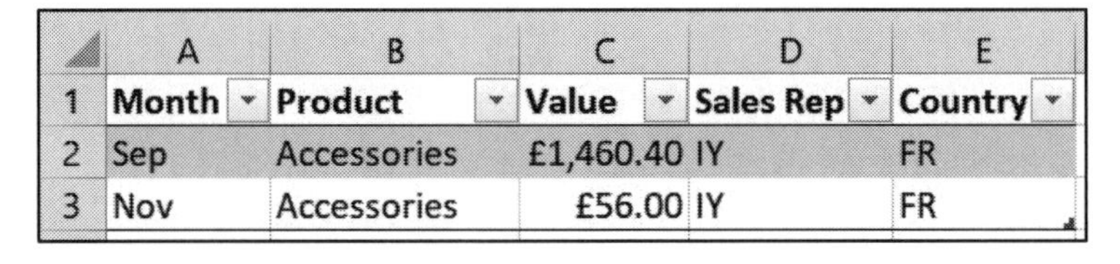

	A	B	C	D	E
1	Month	Product	Value	Sales Rep	Country
2	Sep	Accessories	£1,460.40	IY	FR
3	Nov	Accessories	£56.00	IY	FR

REMOVING OR CHANGING A PIVOT TABLE

changing fields

If you want to change which fields you are including in the pivot table, within the PivotTable Fields pane:

either

- deselect the field in the field list box

or

- select the field from the ROWS, COLUMNS or VALUE areas and drag it back to the field list box

The effect of removing the country field from the pivot table is shown below:

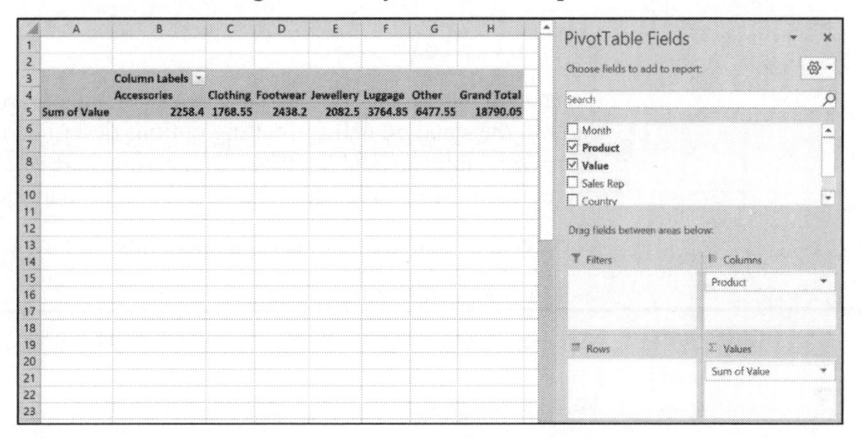

	Column Labels						
	Accessories	Clothing	Footwear	Jewellery	Luggage	Other	Grand Total
Sum of Value	2258.4	1768.55	2438.2	2082.5	3764.85	6477.55	18790.05

If we wanted Product sales by Sales rep, we would select Sales rep, drag it to COLUMNS, and drag Product to ROWS, we would get the screen illustrated below:

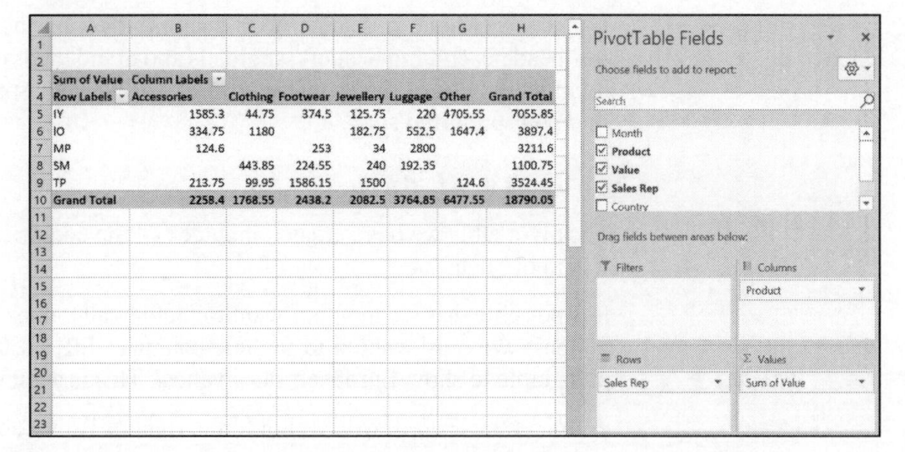

Sum of Value	Column Labels						
Row Labels	Accessories	Clothing	Footwear	Jewellery	Luggage	Other	Grand Total
IY	1585.3	44.75	374.5	125.75	220	4705.55	7055.85
IO	334.75	1180		182.75	552.5	1647.4	3897.4
MP	124.6		253	34	2800		3211.6
SM		443.85	224.55	240	192.35		1100.75
TP	213.75	99.95	1586.15	1500		124.6	3524.45
Grand Total	2258.4	1768.55	2438.2	2082.5	3764.85	6477.55	18790.05

clearing a pivot table

If you have started or created a pivot table, and you want to clear what you have done and start again:

- select **PivotTable Analyze**
- select **Clear** from the **Actions** menu

Note: to access PivotTable Analyze and DESIGN tabs, click within your pivot table.

FORMATTING PIVOT TABLES

There are a variety of ways in which you can change the format or appearance of your table.

cell display

To change the way individual data values are displayed within the table, you can use the standard cell formatting options described in Chapters 2 and 3. In the pivot table created in this chapter, our sales values are displayed as decimal numbers, rather than the £ (UK pound) currency. To change this:

- select all the numeric data cells, including the Grand Total row and column
- select **Format cells**
- select **Currency**, with the pound (£) symbol, and 2 decimal places

table style

Within the pivot table **Design** Menu there are a variety of styles which can be used for the table layout, colouring, and shading, all of which change the appearance of the table.

It is also possible to change other factors affecting the layout, for example row headers, column headers, subtotals and grand totals. This is an area where it is recommended that you experiment within your spreadsheet package to find your preferred style.

subsets of data

The pivot table we have created includes all the countries and products found within our data set.

It is possible that we may not want to include all values of one or other field. Suppose we only wanted to include countries FR, GER, SP and UK in our pivot table to show European sales values. This is achieved as follows:

- select the drop-down symbol to the right of Row Labels (cell A4)

The list of selected row labels appears, as shown below:

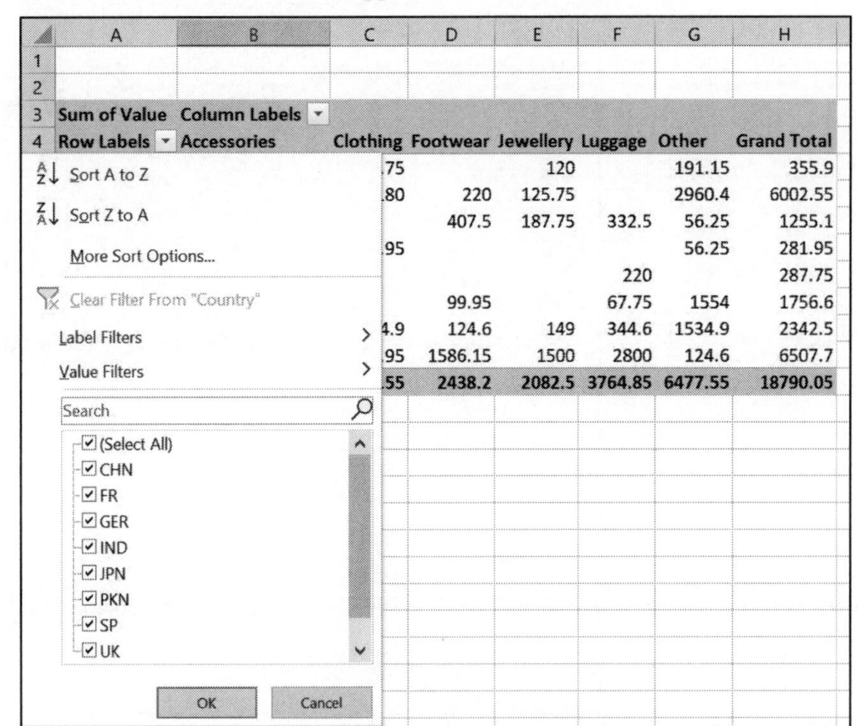

- deselect CHN, IND, JPN, PKN from the list (as shown on the next page)
- select OK

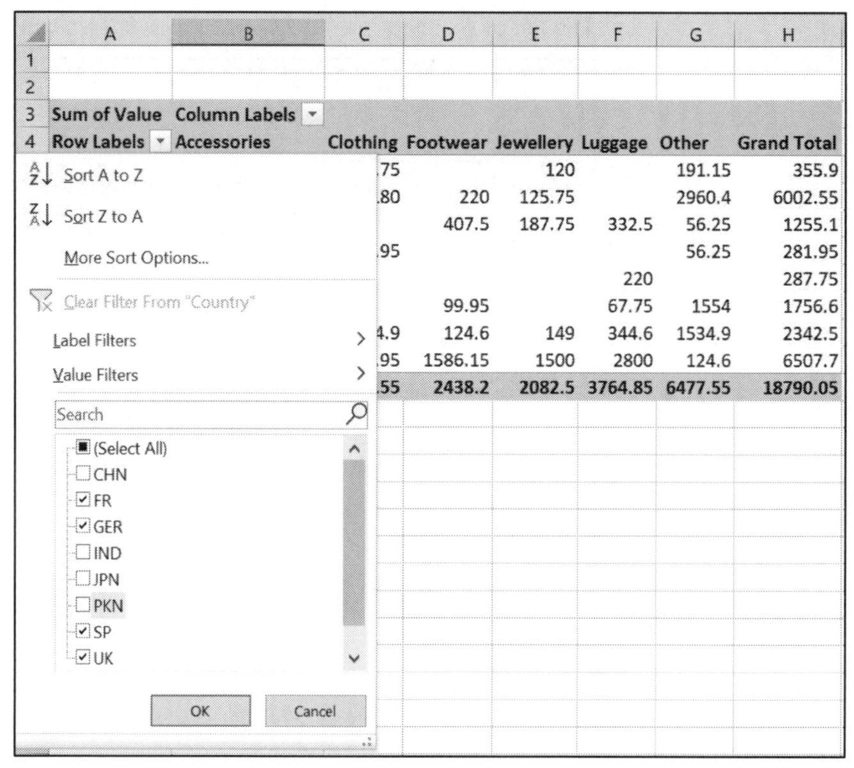

The pivot table adjusts to reflect these choices, as shown in the image below.

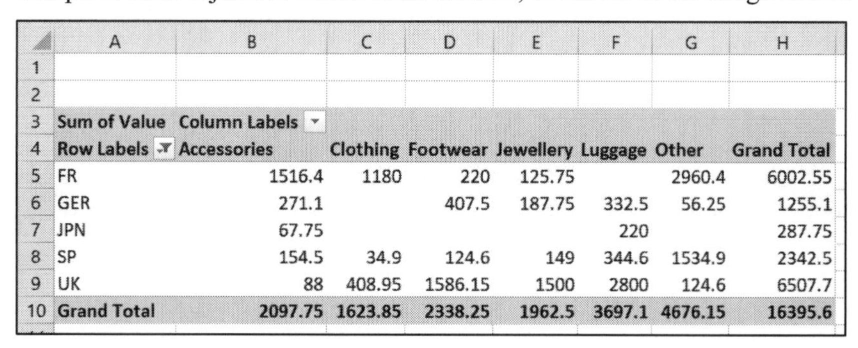

Sum of Value	Column Labels						
Row Labels	Accessories	Clothing	Footwear	Jewellery	Luggage	Other	Grand Total
FR	1516.4	1180	220	125.75		2960.4	6002.55
GER	271.1		407.5	187.75	332.5	56.25	1255.1
JPN	67.75				220		287.75
SP	154.5	34.9	124.6	149	344.6	1534.9	2342.5
UK	88	408.95	1586.15	1500	2800	124.6	6507.7
Grand Total	2097.75	1623.85	2338.25	1962.5	3697.1	4676.15	16395.6

This technique is a quick and easy way of displaying a **subset** of the data.

pivot charts

From the pivot table which we have created, it is possible to produce an interactive chart, which allows you to view subsets of the data graphically. **Note:** if you know you will want a chart as well as a pivot table it's quicker to select the Insert Pivot Chart option from the charts area of the **Insert** menu.

To create a pivot chart for your table:

- select the pivot table, by clicking on any cell within the pivot table
- select **Insert**

- select **PivotChart**
- select your chart type eg column

A chart will be created as shown in the image below:

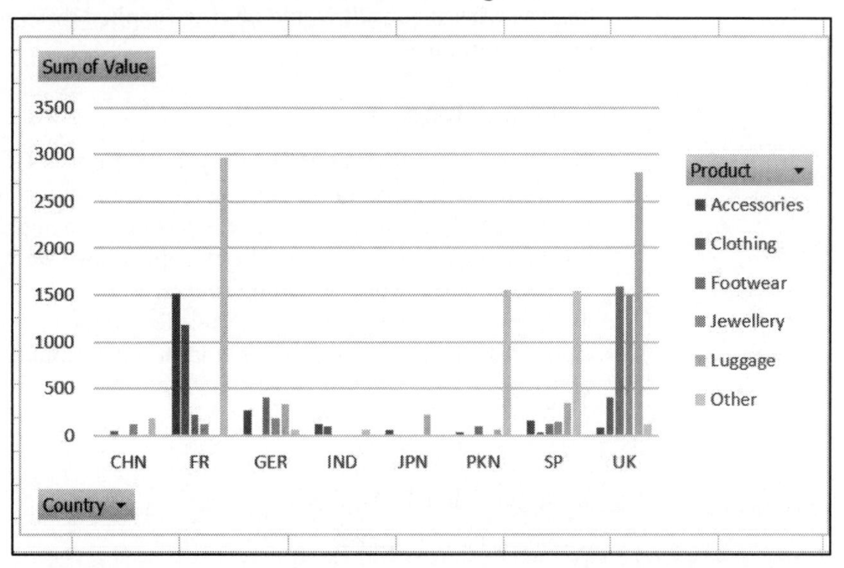

Bottom left you can see a button Country, and top right a button Product. Each of these buttons provides a drop-down list so that you can refine the data that is included in the graph.

In the example below we have chosen to show all Products, and only country UK.

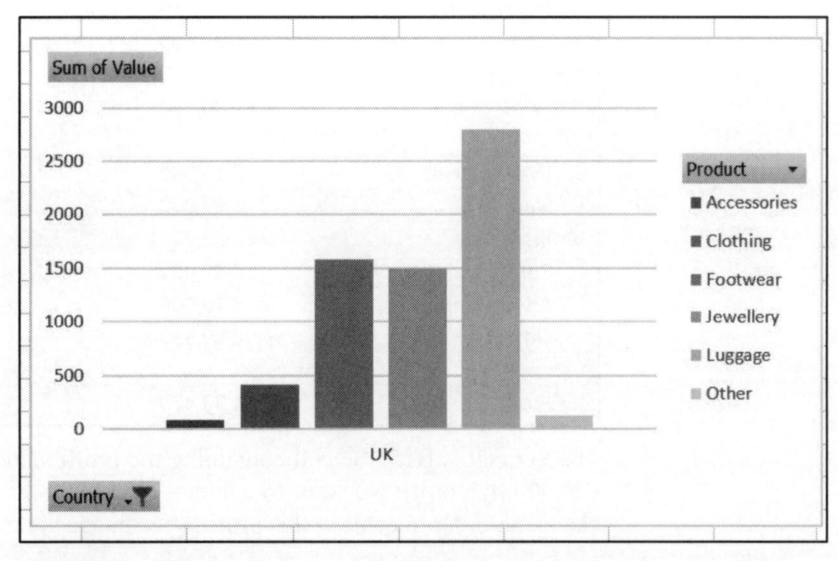

As you can see pivot tables and pivot charts offer a great deal of flexibility in your presentation.

WHAT-IF ANALYSIS

Spreadsheets are created to serve many purposes. One use is to have Excel analyse what the result would be if we applied different sets of values to one or more formulas.

GOAL SEEK

One tool within the **What-If analysis toolpak** is **GOAL SEEK**. This tool allows us to specify an outcome which we require, for example a profit of €40,000, and then a value (cell) which can be changed by the tool to achieve this outcome. So using our profit example above we want to know how big a loan we could take out, assuming an interest rate of 15% and sales of €200,000 to achieve a profit of €40,000. For this technique to work, the cells used in the GOAL SEEK must be linked by at least one formula.

To do this:

- select cell B15
- select **What-If Analysis**
- select **GOAL SEEK**

And the **GOAL SEEK** option box is displayed as shown below:

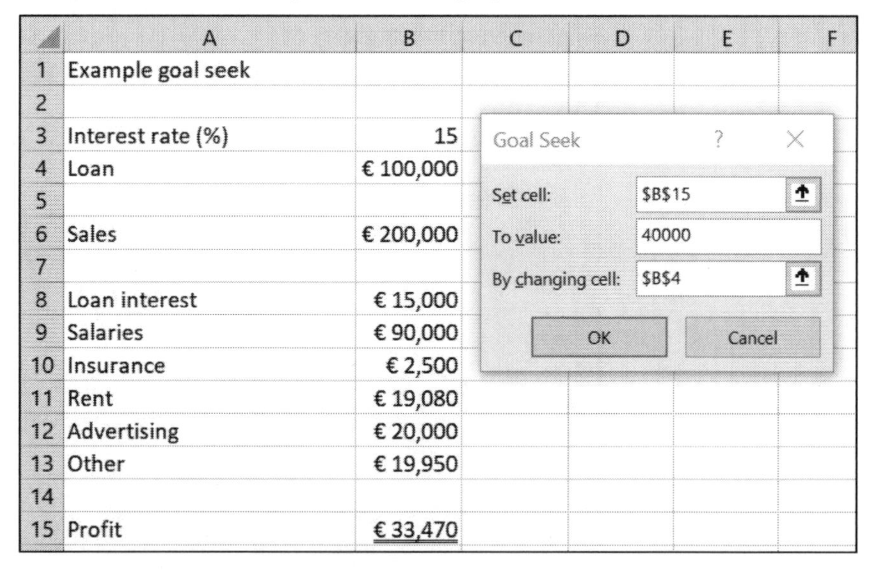

	A	B
1	Example goal seek	
2		
3	Interest rate (%)	15
4	Loan	€ 100,000
5		
6	Sales	€ 200,000
7		
8	Loan interest	€ 15,000
9	Salaries	€ 90,000
10	Insurance	€ 2,500
11	Rent	€ 19,080
12	Advertising	€ 20,000
13	Other	€ 19,950
14		
15	Profit	€ 33,470

The **Set cell** is B15, the cell containing the profit value, and the **To value** is €40,000, the profit we want to achieve. We allow the loan value cell B4 to change in order to achieve this profit. (See image at the top of the next page.)

This shows that a solution has been found, a loan value of €56,467 would achieve a profit of €40,000. (See illustration on the next page.)

	A	B	C	D	E	F
1	Example goal seek					
2						
3	Interest rate (%)	15				
4	Loan	€ 56,467				
5						
6	Sales	€ 200,000				
7						
8	Loan interest	€ 8,470				
9	Salaries	€ 90,000				
10	Insurance	€ 2,500				
11	Rent	€ 19,080				
12	Advertising	€ 20,000				
13	Other	€ 19,950				
14						
15	Profit	€ 40,000				

Goal Seek Status

Goal Seeking with Cell B15 found a solution.

Target value: 40000

Current value: € 40,000

Step | Pause | OK | Cancel

If you don't want to change your spreadsheet to the values in the solution, click Cancel, otherwise click OK to accept the solution.

What-If scenarios

One example might be to see how different interest rates might change the loan repayments, and subsequently the profit, of a business. This could be achieved by having the interest rate built into a formula and manually changing it one value at a time, as required. However, Excel provides a powerful tool which allows us to offer up multiple scenarios and then automatically produce a report showing the various outcomes – these are known as **What-If scenarios**.

	A	B
1	Example what if scenarios	
2		
3	Interest rate (%)	15
4	Loan	€ 100,000
5		
6	Sales	€ 200,000
7		
8	Loan repayments	€ 15,000
9	Salaries	€ 90,000
10	Insurance	€ 2,500
11	Rent	€ 19,080
12	Advertising	€ 20,000
13	Other	€ 19,950
14		
15	Profit	€ 33,470

In the example on the left, we have a summary showing the calculated profit, based on a loan interest repayment rate of 15% and expected sales of €200,000. Cell B8 contains a formula to calculate the annual interest charge based on the interest rate in cell B3, and Cell B15 contains the formula necessary to calculate the profit. We want to see the effect on profit if we have higher or lower interest rates, or if sales don't meet our expectations.

To achieve this we will create our first scenario as follows:

- select **What-If analysis** from the **Data** menu
- select **Scenario Manager**
- select **Add**
- **Scenario Name** enter High interest
- **Changing Cells** – enter or select B3 and B6 separated by commas (the cells containing the values for the interest rate and sales)
- click OK

As shown below:

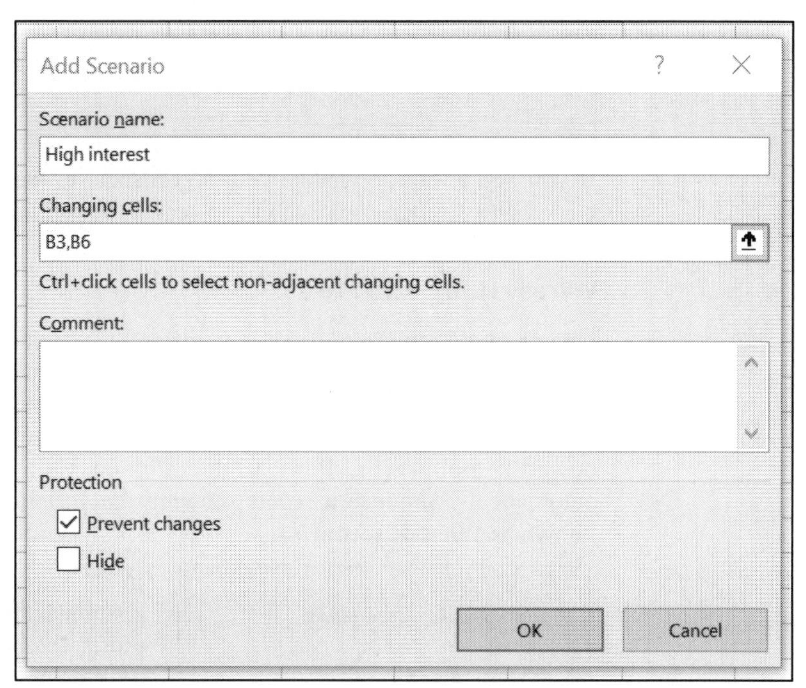

Now we enter the **values** for these cells for this scenario:

- enter 20 for B3, leave B6 unchanged, and click OK

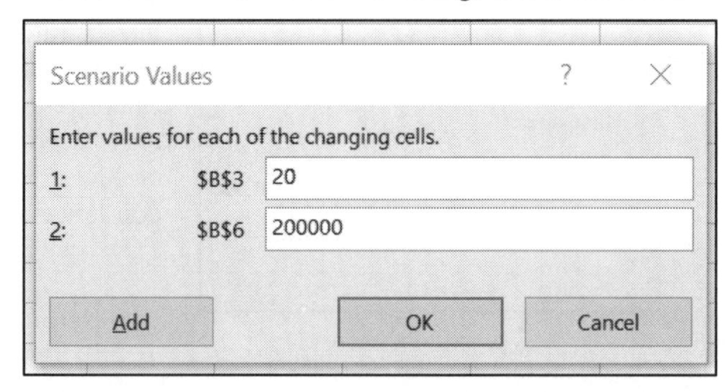

We now select **Add** (another scenario):

- **scenario name** enter Low interest
- continue as before and enter 10 as the value for B3 but leave B6 unchanged at 200,000

Create two more scenarios:

Poor sales entering 150,000 in cell B6 and 15 in cell B3.

High interest and Poor sales entering 150,000 in cell B6 and 20 in cell B3. The list of scenarios should appear as shown below:

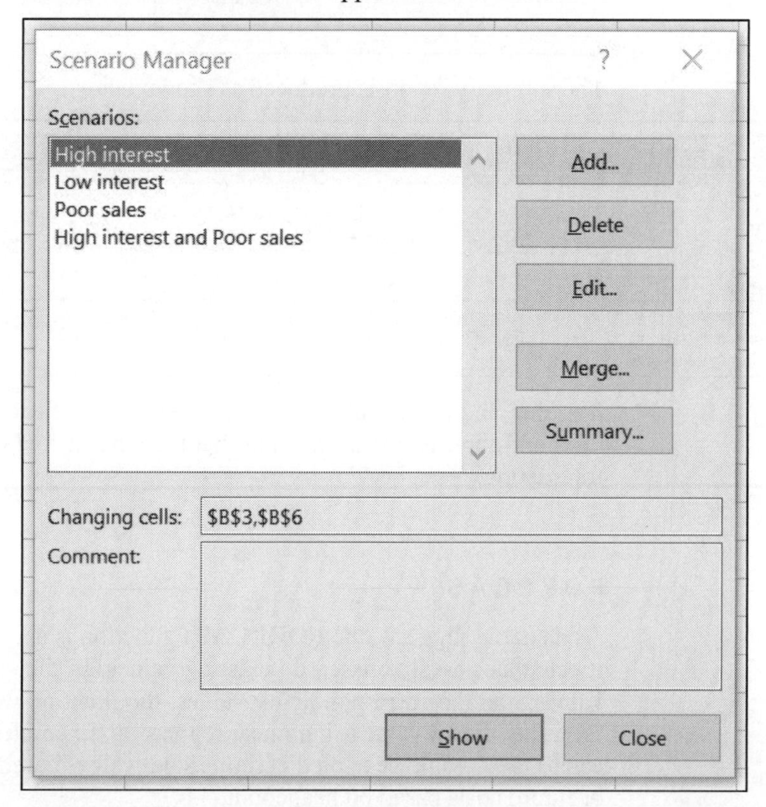

Now that we have defined the scenarios we wish to consider, we select **summary** to produce a report. This can take the form of a scenario summary or a PivotTable report.

We define the **Result** cell, which in this case will be $B$15 (the profit cell). We select **Scenario summary**.

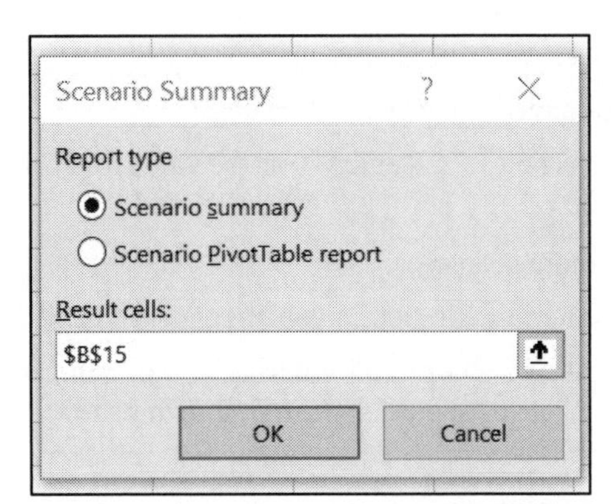

The summary report is produced as shown below:

Scenario Summary	Current Values:	High interest	Low interest	Poor sales	High interest and Poor sales
Changing Cells:					
$B$3	15	20	10	15	20
$B$6	€ 200,000	€ 200,000	€ 200,000	€ 150,000	€ 150,000
Result Cells:					
$B$15	€ 33,470	€ 28,470	€ 38,470	-€ 16,530	-€ 21,530

Notes: Current Values column represents values of changing cells at time Scenario Summary Report was created. Changing cells for each scenario are highlighted in gray.

It is showing us the values we can expect for profit for the different interest rates and forecast sales, showing that the what-if tool can be very useful for forecasting.

FORECAST

As its name suggests, the **FORECAST** function is used to forecast figures, ie it calculates a value based on existing values. In the context of a range of x values, and the corresponding y values, the function will calculate a y value for a specified x value using linear regression. Examples of how this function can be used would be to predict future sales values based on advertising spend, or future costs based on headcount.

There are a variety of FORECAST functions available, we will just consider a **LINEAR** FORECAST.

The formula is:

=FORECAST.LINEAR(x, known_y's, known_x's)

The FORECAST.LINEAR function syntax has three arguments:

- **x**

  The new data point for which you want to predict a value.

- **Existing y values**

  The range of y data values.

- **Existing x values**

  The range of x data values.

  All arguments must be included.

In the example below, the x values are the Annual Expenses, and the y values are the Sales. We want to forecast what the Sales might be for the next year with Annual Expenses of £94,067.

	A	B	C	D	E	F	G	H	I	J
1	Year	1	2	3	4	5	6	7	8	9
2	Annual Expenses	£92,278	£89,423	£72,109	£171,989	£70,137	£94,904	£69,208	£149,205	£94,067
3	Sales	£580,703	£349,268	£295,752	£365,329	£504,413	£339,789	£235,984	£374,226	

In cell J3 we enter the formula:

=FORECAST.LINEAR (J2, B3:I3, B2:I2)

Where J2 is the known value of **Expenses**

B3:I3 are the known y values (**Sales**)

B2:I2 are the known x values (**Expenses**)

In the image below, cell J3 displays the calculated value of **Sales** based on the **Expenses** in J2.

J3 | =FORECAST.LINEAR(J2,B3:I3,B2:I2)

	A	B	C	D	E	F	G	H	I	J
1	Year	1	2	3	4	5	6	7	8	9
2	Annual Expenses	£92,278	£89,423	£72,109	£171,989	£70,137	£94,904	£69,208	£149,205	£94,067
3	Sales	£580,703	£349,268	£295,752	£365,329	£504,413	£339,789	£235,984	£374,226	£380,204

Note: all cells specified within the formula must contain numeric values.

The FORECAST.LINEAR function is equivalent to the FORECAST function available in Excel ® 2013 and previous versions.

hyperlinks

Within a worksheet, it is possible to insert a hyperlink which will provide a quick route to either another file, a website or webpage or possibly an email address.

If we wanted to insert a link to the Osborne Books website:

- select **Link** from the **Insert** menu

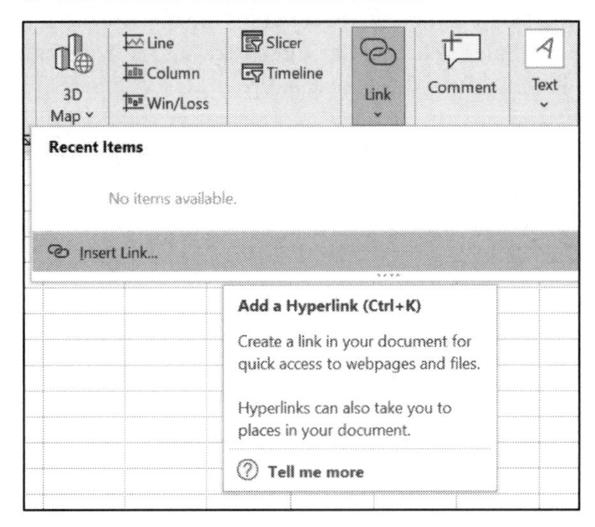

We would enter selections as follows:

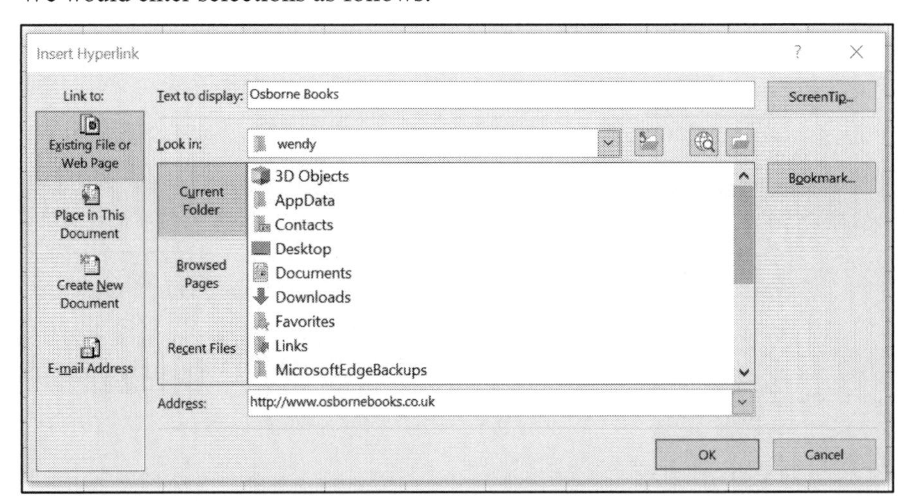

This would result in a link being added to our worksheet in the current cell, as shown below:

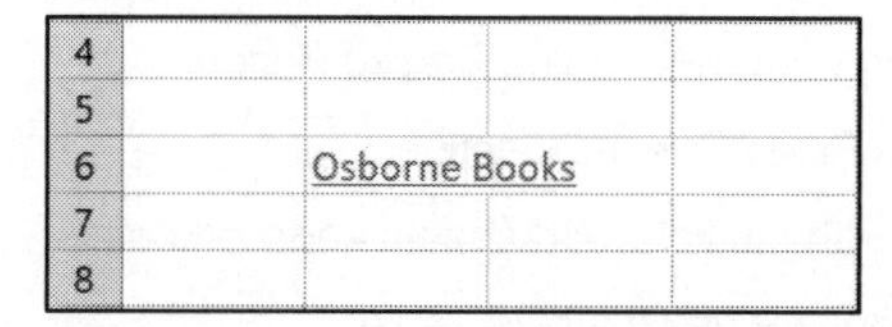

The underlining indicates it is an active hyperlink.

Similarly, we can add links to other files or documents.

An example of adding a link to an email address is shown below; notice that we can leave the subject blank:

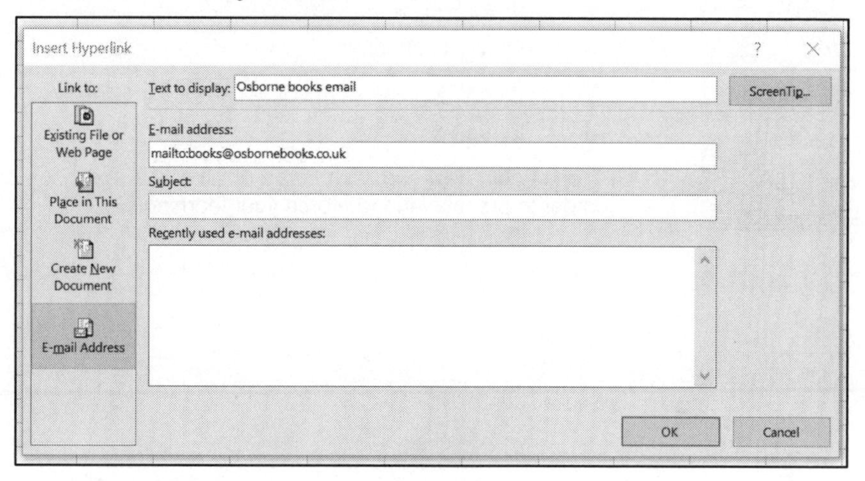

An email link will be added as shown below:

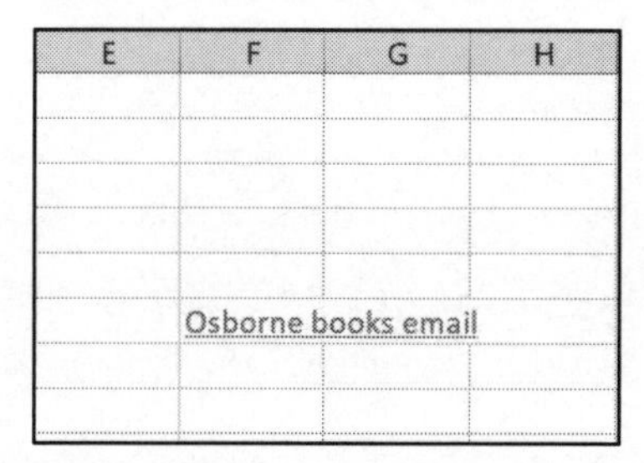

Clicking on this link will open a new email addressed to Osborne Books.

To remove a hyperlink:

- right-click on the cell containing the link
- select **Remove Link**

Chapter Summary

The text of this chapter has covered:

- managing windows – using Freeze Panes
- using the Paste Special function
- working with multiple worksheets and workbooks
- the reasons for using a pivot table
- creating a simple pivot table
- using subsets of data
- formatting pivot tables
- goal seeking
- what-if scenarios
- forecasting
- hyperlinks

You should now carry out some or all of the exercises on the next few pages in order to practise and reinforce your learning.

Activities

Here are a group of exercises to allow you to practise the topics covered in this chapter. They can be done individually, or as a sequence, working your way through them.

If you choose to work your way through them, you may not need to open the exercise workbook as suggested at the start of each exercise, as it may already be open.

The saving at the end of each exercise is also optional, although it serves as a reminder to regularly save your work. You can also save to different file names and may choose to keep using the same name to avoid having lots of files.

Exercise 1

Spreadsheet skills:

- Freeze rows and columns

1. Open workbook T8Exercises
2. Select worksheet Exercise 1
3. Select the appropriate cell, and then Freeze Panes, so that the column headings in Row 1 stay in view when you scroll down the worksheet, and the row headings in Column A stay in view when you scroll across
4. Using the normal scrolling facilities scroll the view, so that cell I14 (T F Curries, Month7 value) becomes the top left-hand cell in the viewing area

   Your worksheet should look as follows:

	A	I	J	K	L	M	N	O	P
1	Name	Month7	Month8	Month9	Month10	Month11	Month12	Month13	Month14
14	*T F Curries*	£470	£490	£244	£423	£354	£560	£309	£274
15	*Fiber Optical Services*	£0	£0	£0	£0	£0	£0	£0	£0
16	*My Provisions*	£0	£25	£0	£0	£0	£0	£0	£0
17	*Alliance services*	£0	£0	£0	£0	£0	£0	£0	£0
18	*Aluminium casts*	£72	£286	£0	£2,093	£0	£364	£1,750	£0
19	*Impala*	£0	£0	£0	£0	£0	£0	£0	£45
20	*Tool Hire*	£0	£0	£0	£0	£0	£0	£0	£20
21	*Handyfreight*	£0	£0	£0	£0	£0	£0	£327	£0
22	*Steel Traders*	£0	£0	£0	£0	£0	£0	£0	£0
23	*Fruit Supplies*	£0	£0	£65	£0	£279	£0	£0	£71
24	*Food Safe*	£0	£55	£0	£0	£0	£0	£0	£1,205
25	*Environmental Services*	£112	£0	£112	£0	£140	£0	£0	£0

Customer Sales | Sheet1

5. We now want to freeze panes so that we can visually compare the figures in Month1, and the figures in Month7

Your worksheet should look as shown below:

	A	B	C	I	J	K	L	M	N	
1	**Name**	**Total**	**Month1**	**Month7**	**Month8**	**Month9**	**Month10**	**Month11**	**Month12**	**Mo**
2	*Farmhouse Foods*	£154	£0	£0	£0	£16	£0	£0	£0	
3	*Engineering Services*	£554	£0	£0	£0	£0	£0	£0	£0	
4	*Another Food Service*	£790	£0	£0	£174	£0	£0	£0	£0	
5	*Top Quality Supplies*	£56	£0	£0	£0	£0	£0	£0	£0	
6	*Halal Foods*	£36	£0	£0	£0	£0	£0	£36	£0	
7	*Edwards Farm*	£195	£0	£65	£0	£0	£0	£0	£90	
8	*Allen and co*	£1,412	£45	£49	£0	£0	£100	£115	£77	
9	*Ahmed and son*	£340	£0	£0	£0	£0	£0	£0	£0	
10	*Green & Sons Wholesalers*	£1,827	£700	£0	£0	£363	£0	£0	£0	
11	*Higginbottom and son*	£389	£0	£300	£0	£0	£0	£89	£0	
12	*W B Meats*	£135	£0	£0	£0	£0	£0	£0	£0	
13	*The Halal Centre*	£205	£0	£0	£25	£0	£0	£0	£0	

Customer Sales | Sheet1

6. Freeze panes so that we can visually compare the figures for Allen and co (row 8), and the figures for T F Curries (row 14)

7. Save your spreadsheet with the name: Chapter8_Exercise1

   Your worksheet should look as shown below:

	A	B	C	D	E	F	G	H	I	J
1	**Name**	**Total**	**Month1**	**Month2**	**Month3**	**Month4**	**Month5**	**Month6**	**Month7**	**Month**
2	*Farmhouse Foods*	£154	£0	£112	£0	£0	£0	£26	£0	£
3	*Engineering Services*	£554	£0	£0	£0	£0	£67	£0	£0	£
4	*Another Food Service*	£790	£0	£0	£0	£58	£116	£0	£0	£1
5	*Top Quality Supplies*	£56	£0	£56	£0	£0	£0	£0	£0	£
6	*Halal Foods*	£36	£0	£0	£0	£0	£0	£0	£0	£
7	*Edwards Farm*	£195	£0	£0	£0	£0	£40	£0	£65	£
8	*Allen and co*	£1,412	£45	£68	£231	£0	£331	£37	£49	£
14	*T F Curries*	£7,245	£458	£166	£583	£225	£414	£365	£470	£4
15	*Fiber Optical Services*	£90	£0	£40	£0	£0	£0	£0	£0	£
16	*My Provisions*	£75	£0	£0	£0	£0	£0	£0	£0	£
17	*Alliance services*	£327	£0	£0	£0	£0	£0	£0	£0	£
18	*Aluminium casts*	£7,625	£72	£54	£1,856	£0	£360	£119	£72	£2

Customer Sales | Sheet1

Exercise 2

Spreadsheet skills:

- Copy and paste Special – values
- Copy and paste Special – formats

1. Open workbook T8Exercises
2. Select worksheet Exercise 2
3. Select cell B4, notice it contains the formula =SUM(C4:D4)

B4 | =SUM(C4:D4)

	A	B	C	D
1	Car sales			
2				
3		**Totals**	***Jan***	***Feb***
4	Ford	50,090	25,090	£25,000
5	Volkswagen	19,350	13,200	£6,150
6	Hyundai	2,500	1,000	£1,500
7	Skoda	4,000	1,200	£2,800
8	Kia	1,980	930	£1,050
9	Renault	39,090	7,000	£32,090
10	Vauxhall	32,500	22,000	£10,500

4. Copy the data in the Totals column (B3:B10)
5. Move to cell F3, using Paste Special, Values

F4 | 50090

	A	B	C	D	E	F
1	Car sales					
2						
3		**Totals**	***Jan***	***Feb***		Totals
4	Ford	50,090	25,090	£25,000		50090
5	Volkswagen	19,350	13,200	£6,150		19350
6	Hyundai	2,500	1,000	£1,500		2500
7	Skoda	4,000	1,200	£2,800		4000
8	Kia	1,980	930	£1,050		1980
9	Renault	39,090	7,000	£32,090		39090
10	Vauxhall	32,500	22,000	£10,500		32500

Notice, there is no formula in cell F4, or cells F5 to F10, the formatting has also been lost.

6. Copy the data in the Feb column (D3:D10)

7. Move to cell F3, using Paste Special, Formats
8. In cell F1, paste a link to cell A1

F1 =$A$1

	A	B	C	D	E	F
1	Car sales					Car sales
2						
3		**Totals**	***Jan***	***Feb***		***Totals***
4	Ford	50,090	25,090	£25,000		£50,090
5	Volkswagen	19,350	13,200	£6,150		£19,350
6	Hyundai	2,500	1,000	£1,500		£2,500
7	Skoda	4,000	1,200	£2,800		£4,000
8	Kia	1,980	930	£1,050		£1,980
9	Renault	39,090	7,000	£32,090		£39,090
10	Vauxhall	32,500	22,000	£10,500		£32,500

The cells in column F now have the same format as those in column D.

9. Save your spreadsheet with the name: Chapter8_Exercise2

Exercise 3

Spreadsheet skills:

- Link data across worksheets

1. Open workbook T8Exercises
2. On worksheet Exercise 3, enter a formula in cell C3 to link to cell C3 on worksheet Monthly Sales
3. Repeat for MIN and COUNT, linking to cells E3 and G3 respectively
4. On the Exercise 3 sheet, enter a formula in cell B8 to calculate the total sales for Ford, using the data on the Monthly Sales worksheet
5. Similarly for the other car makes, rows 9 to 14
6. Save your spreadsheet with the name: Chapter8_Exercise3

Save your workbook as T8Exercise3.

The Sales Totals worksheet should now look as shown in the image on the next page.

B8 =SUM('Monthly Sales'!B6:G6)

	A	B	C	D	E	F
1	Car sales					
2						
3		***Max***	60,000			
4		***Min***	930			
5		***Count***	42			
6						
7		**Totals**				
8	Ford	190,000				
9	Volkswagen	98,510				
10	Hyundai	9,000				
11	Skoda	15,400				
12	Kia	13,360				
13	Renault	94,820				
14	Vauxhall	166,750				

With formulas:

	A	B	C
1	Car sales		
2			
3		***Max***	='Monthly Sales'!C3
4		***Min***	='Monthly Sales'!E3
5		***Count***	='Monthly Sales'!G3
6			
7		**Totals**	
8	Ford	=SUM('Monthly Sales'!B6:G6)	
9	Volkswagen	=SUM('Monthly Sales'!B7:G7)	
10	Hyundai	=SUM('Monthly Sales'!B8:G8)	
11	Skoda	=SUM('Monthly Sales'!B9:G9)	
12	Kia	=SUM('Monthly Sales'!B10:G10)	
13	Renault	=SUM('Monthly Sales'!B11:G11)	
14	Vauxhall	=SUM('Monthly Sales'!B12:G12)	

Exercise 4

Spreadsheet skills:

- Move or copy a worksheet

1. Open workbook T8Exercises
2. Select worksheet Exercise 4
3. Copy the worksheet to a new workbook
4. Select cell C5

C5 ='[T8Exercises.xlsx]Monthly Sales'!G3

	A	B	C	D	E	F
1	Car sales					
2						
3		***Max***	60,000			
4		***Min***	930			
5		***Count***	42			
6						
7		**Totals**				
8	Ford	190,000				
9	Volkswagen	98,510				
10	Hyundai	9,000				
11	Skoda	15,400				
12	Kia	13,360				
13	Renault	94,820				
14	Vauxhall	166,750				

Exercise 4

With formulas:

	A	B	C
1	Car sales		
2			
3		***Max***	='[T8Exercises.xlsx]Monthly Sales'!C3
4		***Min***	='[T8Exercises.xlsx]Monthly Sales'!E3
5		***Count***	='[T8Exercises.xlsx]Monthly Sales'!G3
6			
7		**Totals**	
8	Ford	=SUM('[T8Exercises.xlsx]Monthly Sales'!B6:G6)	
9	Volkswagen	=SUM('[T8Exercises.xlsx]Monthly Sales'!B7:G7)	
10	Hyundai	=SUM('[T8Exercises.xlsx]Monthly Sales'!B8:G8)	
11	Skoda	=SUM('[T8Exercises.xlsx]Monthly Sales'!B9:G9)	
12	Kia	=SUM('[T8Exercises.xlsx]Monthly Sales'!B10:G10)	
13	Renault	=SUM('[T8Exercises.xlsx]Monthly Sales'!B11:G11)	
14	Vauxhall	=SUM('[T8Exercises.xlsx]Monthly Sales'!B12:G12)	

5. Save your workbook with the name: Chapter8_Exercise4
6. From workbook T8Exercises, move the worksheet Monthly Sales to workbook Chapter8_Exercise4

	A	B	C
1	Car sales		
2			
3		*Max*	60,000
4		*Min*	930
5		*Count*	42
6			
7		**Totals**	
8	Ford	190,000	
9	Volkswagen	98,510	
10	Hyundai	9,000	
11	Skoda	15,400	
12	Kia	13,360	
13	Renault	94,820	
14	Vauxhall	166,750	

Exercise 4 | Monthly Sales

7. On the Exercise 4 worksheet, edit the formulas in cells B8 to B14 to use values from the Monthly Sales worksheet within this workbook
8. Save your workbook with the name: Chapter8_Exercise4

The formulas should be as shown below:

	A	B	C
1	Car sales		
2			
3		*Max*	='[T8Exercises.xlsx]Monthly Sales'!C3
4		*Min*	='[T8Exercises.xlsx]Monthly Sales'!E3
5		*Count*	='[T8Exercises.xlsx]Monthly Sales'!G3
6			
7		**Totals**	
8	Ford	=SUM('Monthly Sales'!B6:G6)	
9	Volkswagen	=SUM('Monthly Sales'!B7:G7)	
10	Hyundai	=SUM('Monthly Sales'!B8:G8)	
11	Skoda	=SUM('Monthly Sales'!B9:G9)	
12	Kia	=SUM('Monthly Sales'!B10:G10)	
13	Renault	=SUM('Monthly Sales'!B11:G11)	
14	Vauxhall	=SUM('Monthly Sales'!B12:G12)	

Exercise 5

Spreadsheet skills:

- Pivot tables - create a pivot table

1. Open workbook T8Exercises
2. Select worksheet Exercise 5
3. Using all the data on the worksheet, including the column titles (Row 2), create a Pivot table on a new worksheet, showing sales quantities by product and month

   With Months across the top (columns), Products (rows) down the side, and detailing sales quantities

   As shown below:

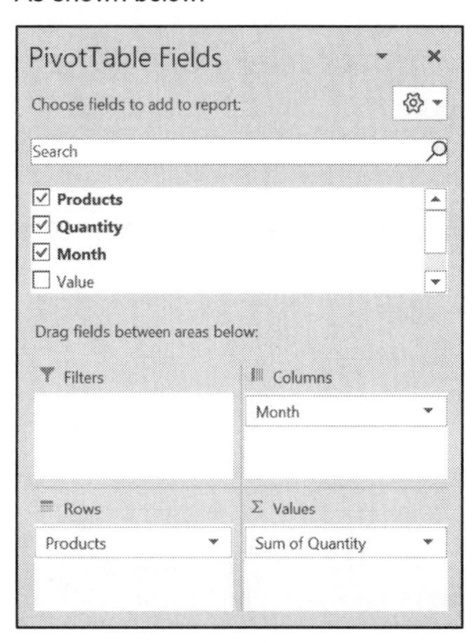

The pivot table created should look as follows (possibly with different shading/colours):

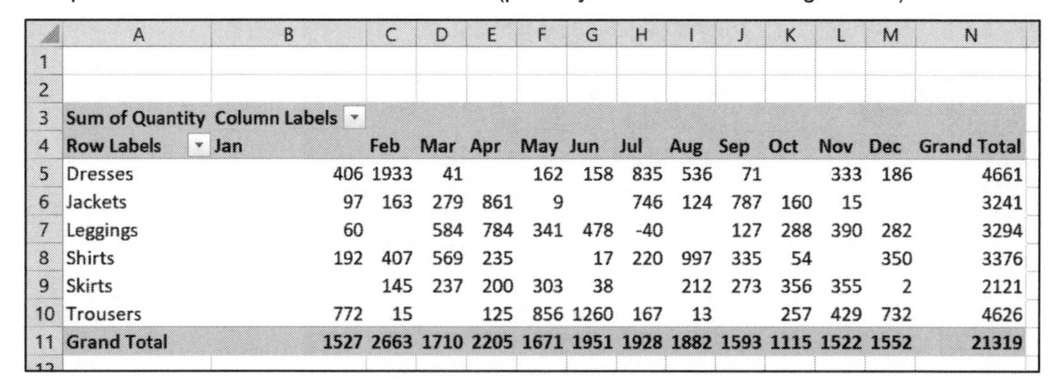

Sum of Quantity	Column Labels												
Row Labels	Jan	Feb	Mar	Apr	May	Jun	Jul	Aug	Sep	Oct	Nov	Dec	Grand Total
Dresses	406	1933	41		162	158	835	536	71		333	186	4661
Jackets	97	163	279	861	9		746	124	787	160	15		3241
Leggings	60		584	784	341	478	-40		127	288	390	282	3294
Shirts	192	407	569	235		17	220	997	335	54		350	3376
Skirts		145	237	200	303	38		212	273	356	355	2	2121
Trousers	772	15		125	856	1260	167	13		257	429	732	4626
Grand Total	**1527**	**2663**	**1710**	**2205**	**1671**	**1951**	**1928**	**1882**	**1593**	**1115**	**1522**	**1552**	**21319**

4. Filter on the column labels to only show data from Jan through to Jul

Sum of Quantity	Column Labels							
Row Labels	Jan	Feb	Mar	Apr	May	Jun	Jul	Grand Total
Dresses	406	1933	41		162	158	835	3535
Jackets	97	163	279	861	9		746	2155
Leggings	60		584	784	341	478	-40	2207
Shirts	192	407	569	235		17	220	1640
Skirts		145	237	200	303	38		923
Trousers	772	15		125	856	1260	167	3195
Grand Total	**1527**	**2663**	**1710**	**2205**	**1671**	**1951**	**1928**	**13655**

5. Drill down into the detailed sales quantity for Jackets for April (Apr)

   Your worksheet should look as shown in the image below (possibly with different shading/colours), showing the individual lines of detail which make up the total of 861 for Jackets in Apr

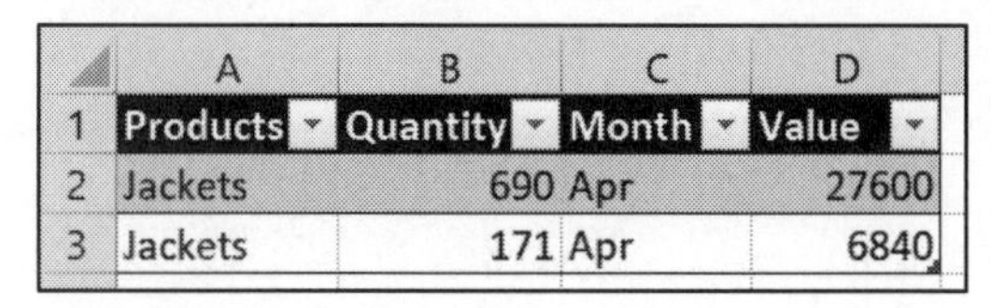

Products	Quantity	Month	Value
Jackets	690	Apr	27600
Jackets	171	Apr	6840

6. Save your spreadsheet with the name: Chapter8_Exercise5

Exercise 6

Spreadsheet skills:

- Pivot tables - create a pivot table
- Pivot tables - change format
- Pivot tables - create a pivot chart

1. Open workbook T8Exercises
2. Select worksheet Exercise 6
3. Create a second pivot table, showing product sales value by month

   As shown below:

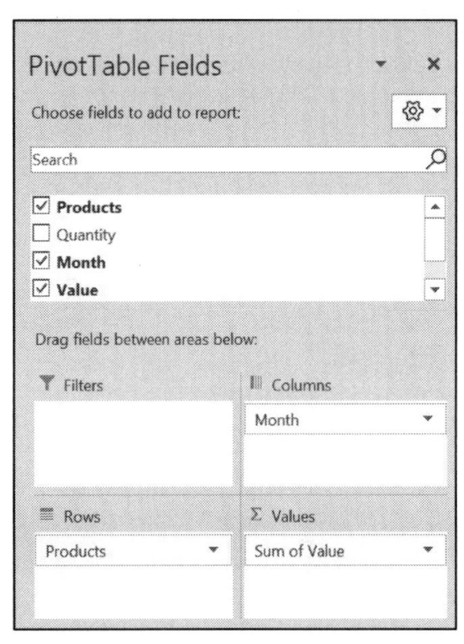

4. Change the selected design colours to be grey and white, and format the values as currency £, no decimal places

   The pivot table created should look as follows:

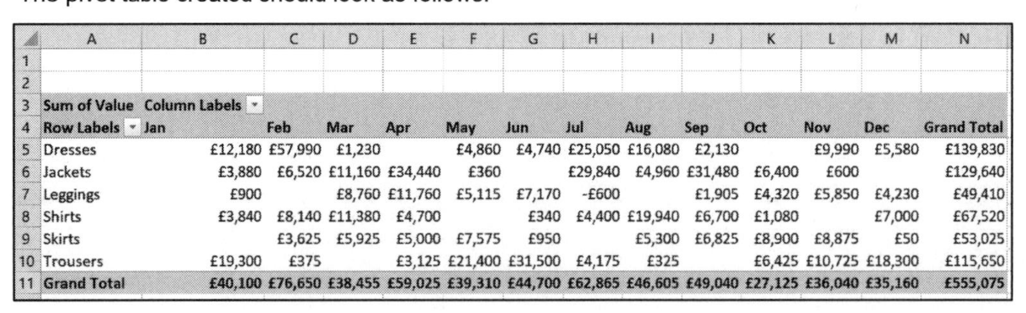

Sum of Value	Column Labels												
Row Labels	**Jan**	**Feb**	**Mar**	**Apr**	**May**	**Jun**	**Jul**	**Aug**	**Sep**	**Oct**	**Nov**	**Dec**	**Grand Total**
Dresses	£12,180	£57,990	£1,230		£4,860	£4,740	£25,050	£16,080	£2,130		£9,990	£5,580	£139,830
Jackets	£3,880	£6,520	£11,160	£34,440	£360		£29,840	£4,960	£31,480	£6,400	£600		£129,640
Leggings	£900		£8,760	£11,760	£5,115	£7,170	-£600		£1,905	£4,320	£5,850	£4,230	£49,410
Shirts	£3,840	£8,140	£11,380	£4,700		£340	£4,400	£19,940	£6,700	£1,080		£7,000	£67,520
Skirts		£3,625	£5,925	£5,000	£7,575	£950		£5,300	£6,825	£8,900	£8,875	£50	£53,025
Trousers	£19,300	£375		£3,125	£21,400	£31,500	£4,175	£325		£6,425	£10,725	£18,300	£115,650
Grand Total	**£40,100**	**£76,650**	**£38,455**	**£59,025**	**£39,310**	**£44,700**	**£62,865**	**£46,605**	**£49,040**	**£27,125**	**£36,040**	**£35,160**	**£555,075**

5. Create a pivot chart, with columns, sales values on the y axis, and products along the x axis
6. Use the filter options within the chart to show only Dresses, Leggings and Skirts

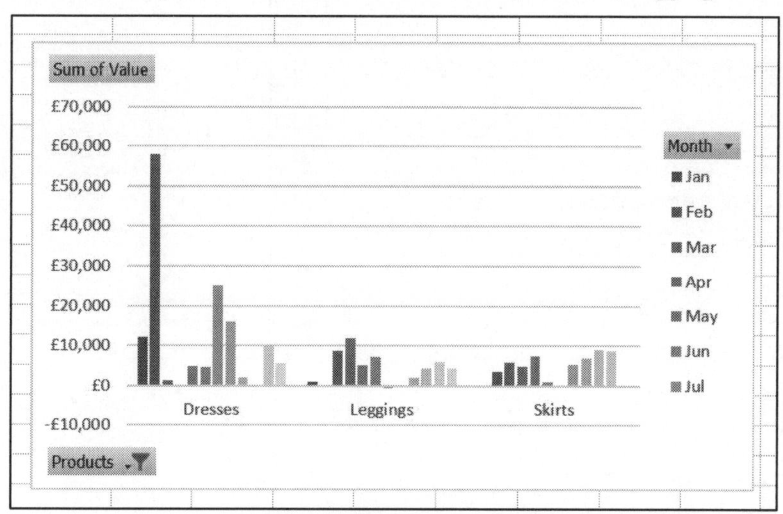

7. Save your spreadsheet with the name: Chapter8_Exercise6

Exercise 7

Spreadsheet skills:

- Statistical technique - What If Analysis

1. Open workbook T8Exercises
2. Select worksheet Exercise 7

   This worksheet shows a forecast for Sales and Operating Profit based on a number of assumptions, as follows:

   - sales will increase by 5% per qtr (cell G3)
   - cost of sales is 20% of sales value (cell G4)
   - expenses are 25% of sales value (cell G7)

   The cells for each quarter are populated with the necessary formulas to use these assumptions and calculate the quarterly values.

   We want to consider two scenarios.

   The first where we are optimistic and hope that sales will actually be higher and both the cost of sales and expenses lower than we have specified.

4. Create a scenario named Optimistic with changing cells G3,G4,G7

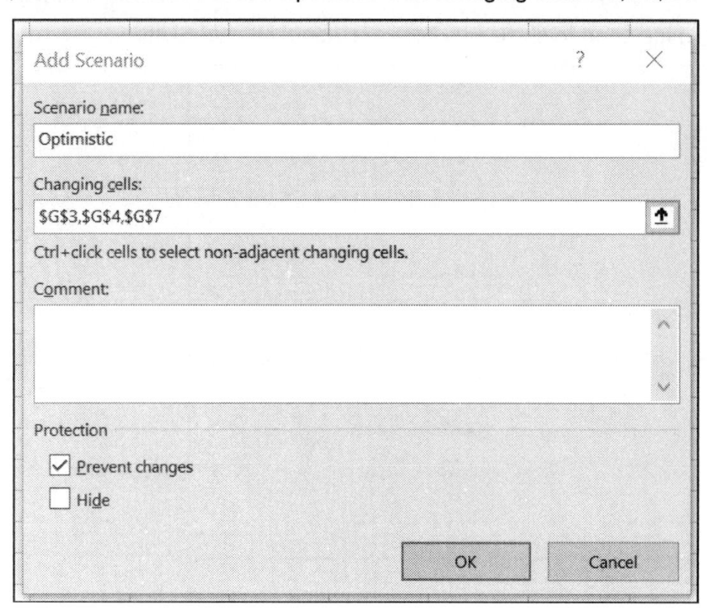

Set scenario values:

Sales growth is 10%

Cost of sales is 19%

Expenses is 22%

(**Note:** you will need to enter these values as decimals ie 0.1, 0.19, and 0.22 as shown below.)

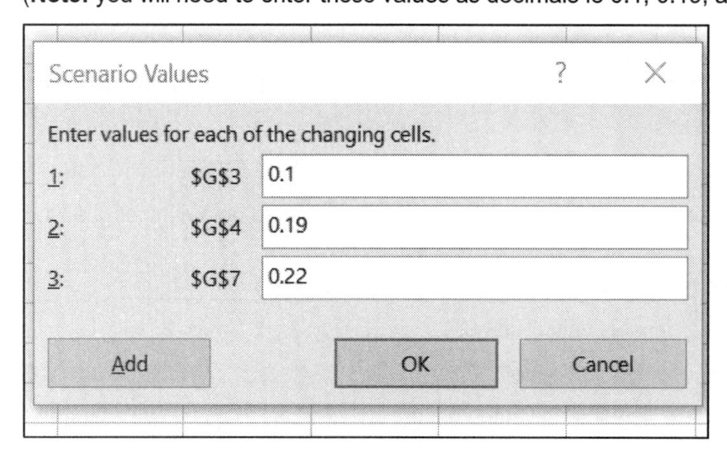

The second scenario will be Poor, with lower sales and higher costs.

5. Create a scenario named Poor

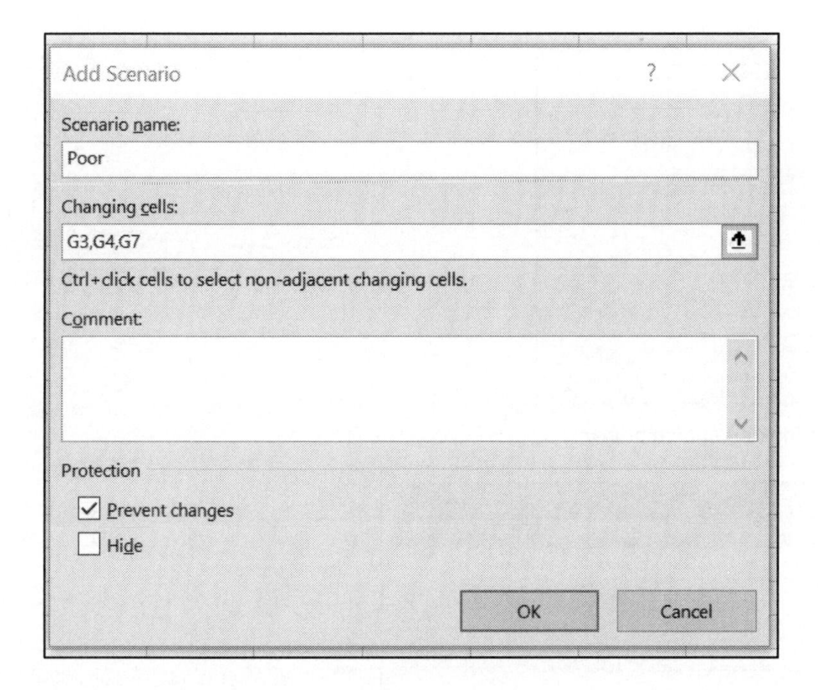

Set the scenario values as follows:

Sales growth is 2%

Cost of sales is 25%

Expenses is 30%

(Again, enter these values as decimals ie 0.02, 0.25 and 0.3 in the scenario manager.)

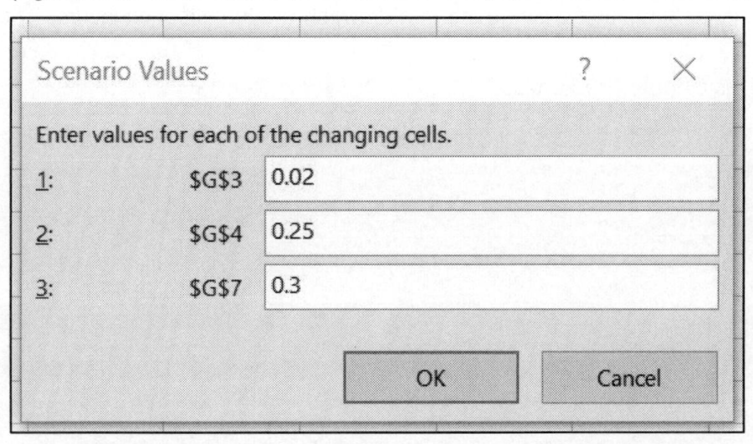

6. From the Scenario Manager, produce a summary report using these two scenarios, specify F3, F4, F5, F7 and F8 as the results cells.

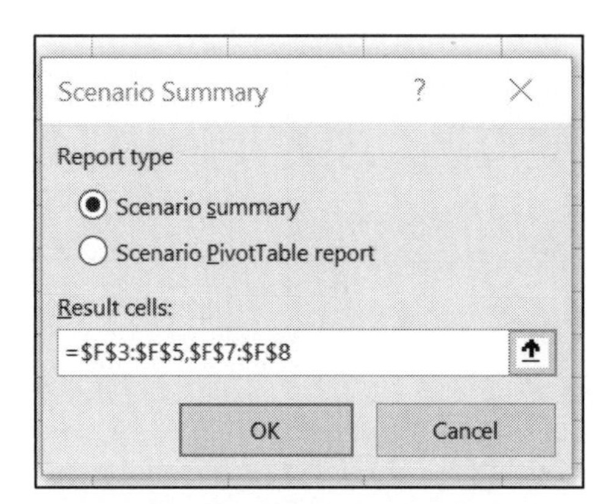

The report should look as shown below:

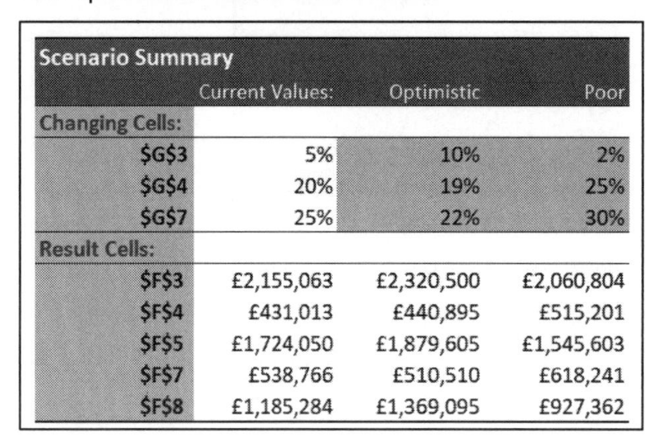

Scenario Summary			
	Current Values:	Optimistic	Poor
Changing Cells:			
$G$3	5%	10%	2%
$G$4	20%	19%	25%
$G$7	25%	22%	30%
Result Cells:			
$F$3	£2,155,063	£2,320,500	£2,060,804
$F$4	£431,013	£440,895	£515,201
$F$5	£1,724,050	£1,879,605	£1,545,603
$F$7	£538,766	£510,510	£618,241
$F$8	£1,185,284	£1,369,095	£927,362

The $F$8 row which is the total for the Operating Profit row, shows the effect on income of the two different scenarios.

7. Save your workbook as Chapter8_Exercise7

Exercise 8

> Spreadsheet skills:
>
> - Statistical technique – GOAL SEEK tool

1. Open workbook T8Exercises
2. Select worksheet Exercise 8

This contains data as shown below:

	A	B	C	D	E	F	G	H	I
1	**Forecast for year**								
2		Quarter 1	Quarter 2	Quarter 3	Quarter 4	Total	Assumptions		
3	Sales	£500,000	£525,000	£551,250	£578,813	£2,155,063	5%	(Growth per qtr)	
4	Cost of Sales	£100,000	£105,000	£110,250	£115,763	£431,013	20%	(Perc of Sales)	
5	Gross Profit	£400,000	£420,000	£441,000	£463,050	£1,724,050			
6									
7	Expenses	£125,000	£131,250	£137,813	£144,703	£538,766	25%	(Perc of sales)	
8	**Operating Profit**	**£275,000**	**£288,750**	**£303,188**	**£318,347**	£1,185,284			

We are now going to use the GOAL SEEK tool to determine the percentage value we need for Cost of Sales (cell G4 – changing cell) to allow us to generate a total Operating Profit of £1,300,000 (cell F8 – the set cell).

3. Using the GOAL SEEK tool, enter the cell reference for the set Cell, and the required value of £1,300,000
4. Specify the changing cell

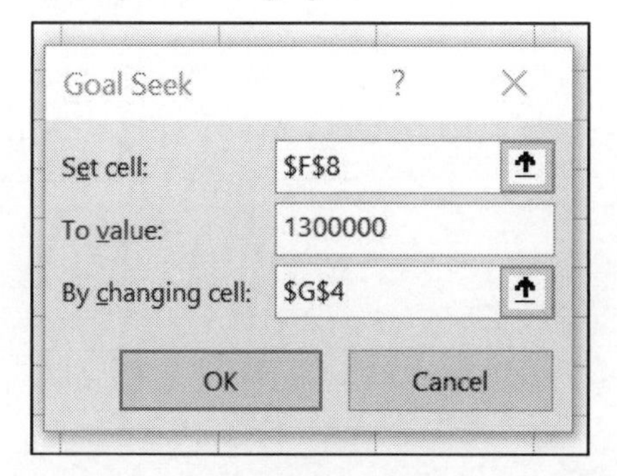

The tool will calculate a solution and display as shown on the next page.

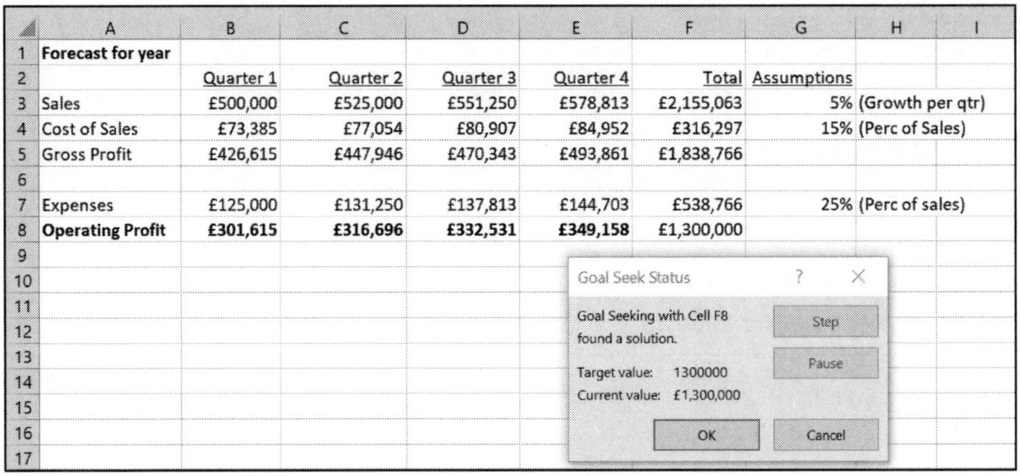

	A	B	C	D	E	F	G	H	I
1	**Forecast for year**								
2		Quarter 1	Quarter 2	Quarter 3	Quarter 4	Total	Assumptions		
3	Sales	£500,000	£525,000	£551,250	£578,813	£2,155,063	5%	(Growth per qtr)	
4	Cost of Sales	£73,385	£77,054	£80,907	£84,952	£316,297	15%	(Perc of Sales)	
5	Gross Profit	£426,615	£447,946	£470,343	£493,861	£1,838,766			
6									
7	Expenses	£125,000	£131,250	£137,813	£144,703	£538,766	25%	(Perc of sales)	
8	**Operating Profit**	**£301,615**	**£316,696**	**£332,531**	**£349,158**	£1,300,000			
9									
10									
11									
12									
13									
14									
15									
16									
17									

Goal Seek Status

Goal Seeking with Cell F8 found a solution.

Target value: 1300000

Current value: £1,300,000

Step | Pause | OK | Cancel

This shows that if the cost of sales could be reduced to 15% of sales, the total income for the year would be £1,300,000.

7. Save your workbook as Chapter8_Exercise8

Exercise 9

Spreadsheet skills:

- Statistical technique - FORECAST function

1. Open workbook T8Exercises
2. Select worksheet Exercise 9

This contains data as shown below:

	A	B	C	D	E	F	G	H	I	J	K
1											
2		Year	1	2	3	4	5	6	7	8	9
3		Headcount	50	42	45	39	41	35	52	61	*56*
4		Staff costs	£75,123	£69,346	£72,999	£70,132	£80,923	£69,166	£91,231	£93,912	

3. Enter a formula in cell K4 using the FORECAST.LINEAR or FORECAST function to calculate a value for staff costs in year 9 using the headcount specified in cell J2 and the data from the previous eight years

The result is shown below:

K4 =FORECAST.LINEAR(K3,C4:J4,C3:J3)

	A	B	C	D	E	F	G	H	I	J	K
1											
2		Year	1	2	3	4	5	6	7	8	9
3		Headcount	50	42	45	39	41	35	52	61	*56*
4		Staff costs	£75,123	£69,346	£72,999	£70,132	£80,923	£69,166	£91,231	£93,912	*£88,133*

4. Save your workbook as Chapter8_Exercise9

Exercise 10

> Spreadsheet skills:
>
> - Insert a hyperlink

1. Open workbook T8Exercises
2. Select worksheet Exercise 10
3. Cell C2 contains the web address for the Osborne Books website, convert this to a hyperlink to the website, with:

   Text to display: Osborne Books website

   Address: https://www.osbornebooks.co.uk/

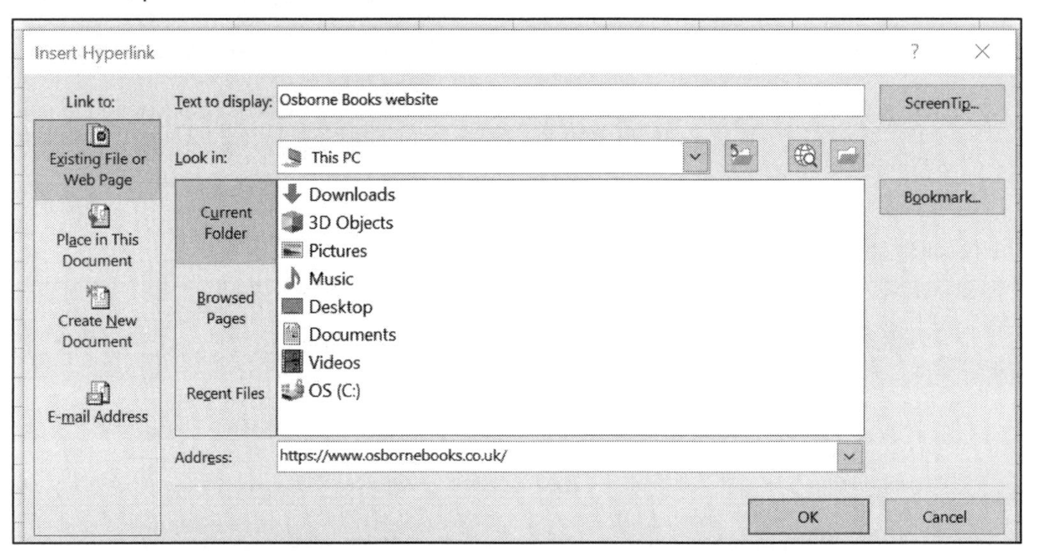

You should create a link as shown below:

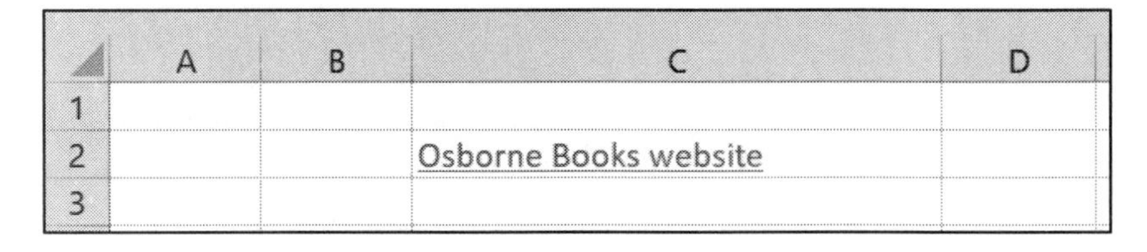

	A	B	C	D
1				
2			Osborne Books website	
3				

7. Save your workbook as Chapter8_Exercise10

Index

for your notes

for your notes

for your notes

for your notes

for your notes

for your notes

for your notes